ADVANCE PRAISE FOR

Court Licensed Abuse

"This is a stunning piece of work. It exposes the evils of the adversarial legal system in allowing defense lawyers to defeat the truth by vicious cross-examination of child victims of sexual abuse. S. Caroline Taylor's rigorous research and magisterial analysis make a compelling case for change."
—Evan Whitton, *Author of* Trial by Voodoo and the Cartel: Lawyers and Their Nine Magic Tricks

Court Licensed Abuse

Colin Lankshear, Michele Knobel,
Chris Bigum, and Michael Peters
General Editors

Vol. 11

PETER LANG
New York • Washington, D.C./Baltimore • Bern
Frankfurt am Main • Berlin • Brussels • Vienna • Oxford

S. CAROLINE TAYLOR

Court Licensed Abuse

Patriarchal Lore and the Legal Response to Intrafamilial Sexual Abuse of Children

PETER LANG
New York • Washington, D.C./Baltimore • Bern
Frankfurt am Main • Berlin • Brussels • Vienna • Oxford

Library of Congress Cataloging-in-Publication Data

Taylor, S. Caroline.
Court licensed abuse: patriarchal lore and the legal response
to intrafamilial sexual abuse of children / S. Caroline Taylor.
p. cm. — (New literacies and digital epistemologies; 11)
Includes bibliographical references and index.
1. Incest—Social aspects—Australia.
2. Feminist jurisprudence. I. Title. II. Series.
KU4182.T39   345.94'02536—dc22   2004011674
ISBN 0-8204-6171-7
ISSN 1523-9543

Bibliographic information published by **Die Deutsche Bibliothek**.
Die Deutsche Bibliothek lists this publication in the "Deutsche
Nationalbibliografie"; detailed bibliographic data is available
on the Internet at http://dnb.ddb.de/.

Cover concept by Dale Braybrook

The paper in this book meets the guidelines for permanence and durability
of the Committee on Production Guidelines for Book Longevity
of the Council of Library Resources.

© 2004 Peter Lang Publishing, Inc., New York
275 Seventh Avenue, 28th Floor, New York, NY 10001
www.peterlangusa.com

All rights reserved.
Reprint or reproduction, even partially, in all forms such as microfilm,
xerography, microfiche, microcard, and offset strictly prohibited.

Printed in the United States of America

*From the grateful adult,
to the child in me who, despite her pain and terror,
never gave up, never succumbed,
a fact I have since observed in the eyes and lives of so many other children.*

Contents

Acknowledgments ix

1 • Introduction 1
2 • Telling Legal Tales: Trials as Narratives and Theatre 17
3 • Case Study R v EF 43
4 • Case Study R v G 83
5 • Case Study R v D 135
6 • Case Study R v L 171
7 • Forced Errors 225
8 • Case Studies Analysis 253
9 • Conclusion 289

Glossary 301
Select Bibliography 305
Index 311

Acknowledgments

UNLIKE THE MOVIE *Ben Hur*, writing a book does not entail a cast of thousands, and while my commitment to and passion in the area of child sexual abuse and social justice issues underpins the energy and desire to see my Ph.D. thesis distilled into a book, such an effort would not have been possible without the dedicated assistance and support of many people. They are not thanked in order of importance, since they were all equally important to me in this endeavor.

I want to warmly acknowledge Dr. Janice Newton, Dr. Lorene Gottschalk, and Dr. Jeremy Smith, all from the University of Ballarat, who were my principal supervisor and co-supervisors, respectively. They not only gave strong support for my research proposal, but they understood and respected my commitment to this field of work, and their words of encouragement inspired me. Extra special thanks to Janice for so patiently reading though an entire draft of this book and providing her usual wisdom and advice that assisted me toward finishing the final draft in a timely fashion. Warmest thanks also to Dr. Jocelynne Scutt, currently the Tasmanian Anti-Discrimination Commissioner, for being a co-supervisor of my thesis. Her sharp legal mind and belief in me and in my work often provided succor.

I want to acknowledge Professor Catharine MacKinnon, University of Michigan Law School; Associate Professor Renate Klein, Deakin University; and Associate Professor Sheila Jeffreys, University of Melbourne. They were the examiners of my Ph.D. thesis. Their reports had a profound professional and personal impact on me since they helped me to realize not just the value of the research, but also how marginalized words can help to shatter barriers. Scholars like them have a great respect for those who understand so well the secret of why a caged bird still sings.

I am indebted to my university, which is committed to excellence and to nurturing early-career academics. To this end, I would like to acknowledge

Professor Kerry Cox, vice-chancellor (VC) of the University of Ballarat. As a postgraduate student completing my PhD research on a full scholarship Professor Cox respected and encouraged my enthusiasm and passion for my work. He so often gave generously of his time to get to know the research I was undertaking and was respectful and enthusiastic for the positive changes such work could engender. I would like also to thank Professor Wayne Robinson for providing assistance with technical support for the timely completion of this work. Not many universities can boast a VC and DVC so highly attuned to the goals and hopes of their staff.

I also wish to thank the Office of Graduate Research for granting a University of Ballarat Book Award to enable the timely completion of this work. I would also like to acknowledge other University of Ballarat staff who have been most supportive as I undertook the task of turning a Ph.D. thesis into a book: Associate Professor Helen Hayes, Professor Lawrie Angus, the late Associate Professor Kevin Livingston, Professor John Yearwood, Dr. Andrew Stranieri, Associate Professor Trevor Hastings, Faezeh Afshar, Dr. Beverly Blaskett, Adele Echter-Baltrunas, Lynne Noonan, Maryann Brown, Dr. Patricia Cartwright (Australian Catholic University), Rupert Russell, Sylvia Rooney, Jenene Bourke, and Sue Taylor (University of Ballarat Librarian extraordinaire!).

To my former post-graduate peers: it was a great privilege to do my Ph.D. with a group of people who are now lifelong friends and who hoped this work would one day become a book. Thanks to Alison Ollerenshaw, Dr. Kevin Thompson, Dr. Jan Croggon, Dr. Ron Tallent, Dr. Terence FitzSimons, and nearly Dr.'s Helen Dehn, Kate Simons, and Briony Dow. I would also like to thank Associate Professor Charles Crothers, School of Social Sciences, Auckland University of Technology, for being a great sounding board around a couple of critical arguments in this book.

It is extremely important to remember friends who have enabled me to feel I am part of a family, and who have been so unbelievably supportive throughout this book (ad)venture. Associate Professor Don Gorman and Marilyn Gorman—you inspired and nurtured a young woman to develop within and gave me abundant room in your hearts and lives. Thanks to Pam and Jim McLaren for treating me as their own daughter, for being so proud of my achievements and sharing my pain and joys; Patti Patrono, who epitomizes the concept of lifelong friendship, and who has supported my thoughts, ideas, and endeavors with the fullest energy; and Gail Harman, whose friendship and support has meant a great deal through the lonely months of writing this book. Thanks and love to Vicki Biggs—for being all that you have been in my life and being determined to show that some bonds of friendship can never be broken or forgotten.

Acknowledgments

Thanks to Kevin and Jenny Carson for unwavering support and the warmest of friendship; Fiona Dawson for a thousand kindnesses at a time when I knew so few—I know you will be proud that this book has finally come to fruition; Carole and Katherine Trusler for their abundant friendship and desire to make a difference for other children (and an additional thanks to Carol for proofreading the drafts); and Kyllie Cripps for her support and friendship. Warmest thanks to the wonderful Dr. Penny Roberts for always believing, always honoring, always encouraging. Special thanks also to Dr. Jill Ramsey for helping to give greater strength to the small light within. Also thanks to Jo and Dale Braybrook, especially Dale's patience with graphic designs for the book; Marg and Charlie Rowbotham (thank you so much Marg for seeing in me what I could not see myself at that time); and Sr. Ann Carter, dearest Ann and her ever-present support and strength. A special acknowledgment to Annette Platten and Kelly Christofferson for their unique support to this work. Special thanks to Bruce Horsburgh (Office of Public Prosecutions) and Peter Robinson (Crown Prosecutor) for being the shining examples they were and still are. And a special acknowledgment for a kindness never forgotten: His Honor Judge John Barnett.

I want to acknowledge the following people who make up my circle of friends and colleagues from my private and professional life who have each reinforced an understanding that a book dealing with this subject is both important and timely. They have also made me realize that passion is a good thing to have and that one should not be afraid of expressing it because it does make a difference. Thanks: Colin Duffy, Dr. Richard and Lauren Hall, Dr. Gordon Pryor, Ann Beasley, Marion Oke, Dr. Joan Cato, and Monique Disney. To Sharon Knight, and Shireen Gunn (who always offered to give a *Chinese burn* to those who would give me a hard time over my work and passion around child abuse!). Thanks to nearly Dr. Robyn Mason, Marg D'Arcy (CASA House Melbourne), Karen Hogan (Gatehouse Centre, Royal Children's Hospital, Melbourne), Barbara Dickson, Dr. Debbie Kirkwood, Evan Whitton, Dr. Heather Gridley, Dr. Susan Hawthorne, Dr. Doug Lloyd, Superintendent Paul Murnane (Victoria Police), Leigh Gassner (Assistant Commissioner, Victoria Police), Constable Ineke Romeyn (NSW Police Force), Sergeant Bob Larkins (Victorian Police Force), Vivian Waller (Maurice, Blackburn Cashman Lawyers), Mary Crooks (Executive Director, Victorian Women's Trust), Catherine King (Federal Member for Ballarat), Tania White, Debra Plowman, Liz Olle, Kelly O'Leary, Jane Penberthy, Kate Pepplinkhouse, Jim Fawns, Peter and Chris Hendrickson, Adriaan Bendeler (Office of Public Prosecutions librarian extraordinaire!), Annie Davies, Anne O'Brien, Jenny and Sam Neumann, Lloyd Davies, O.A.M., Joan Davies, Anne Goodfellow, Shirlene Magee, Sr. Caroline Deutscher,

Dr. David Deutscher, Sharon McDonough, Tamara Downey, Trish Sanders, Mary and Dick Hardie, Cherie Panozzo, Pat Mann, Cheryl Henry, Diana Letts, Anne Grice, Pauline Howard, Pam Dunn, Margo Rees, June and Graham Waterhouse, Nanette Fowler, Nick Rushworth, Andrew Dickson, David and Maureen Mac Phail, Father Justin Driscoll, Dr. Betty McLellan; and all the amazing women from the 2002 Townsville International Women's Conference who enriched and continue to enrich my spirit on every level. Warmest thanks and love to Monsignor Henry Nolan for unwavering support, friendship, and belief in my goals. Your support Mons has made such a difference in my life. My sincere gratitude to Rowan McIndoe, Magistrate, for insightful comments and warm friendship, and also to Helen McIndoe for her friendship and strong support for this work.

Thanks to Chris McKee who provided much help in the original research with regard to accessing trial transcripts. I want to acknowledge professional peers from the Australasian Society for Traumatic Stress Studies who have been so supportive of my work and this book: Fran McPhee-Allan, Claire Ryan, Dave Hyatt, Mary Darcy, Margot Murphy, and Dr. Gwen Roberts.

Loving thanks to Janine and Alicia Power for all that you are—and all that you continue to be—in my life. Your support for my research and work has always energized me. A special thanks to my dear friend Dr. Melanie Heenan for words of wisdom and support that enabled me to grow with confidence. I want to acknowledge Justice Lana Peto-Kujundzic and Justice Ivica (John) Kujundzic from Croatia. I was lucky enough to meet them at the 12th World Congress of Criminology in Seoul, South Korea, in 1998, and a strong friendship has developed along with shared ideas and perspectives around child abuse. I thank Lana, especially, for being generous with her wisdom.

I am grateful to Professor Marcia Neave, director of the Victorian Law Reform Commission, for including me on the Sexual Offenses Advisory Committee. This experience enabled me not only to amplify my work and ideas about child sexual abuse in a respectful and committed environment, but also to share opinions and work with the other committee members. To this end, I should like to acknowledge the other members of the Advisory Committee—working with them has been a delight, and all have shown a commitment to improve the lives of those who come into contact with the legal system as victims/survivors of sexual abuse. Thanks to Nicky Friedman, a policy research officer from the Victorian Law Reform Commission, who was just brilliant in helping me find last-minute references I had lost, at a time when I was pushed for time and patience!

Regarding the production of the book, sincerest thanks to Professor Colin Lankshear, the editor of this book series, for his editorial advice and,

Acknowledgments xiii

most of all, for believing so strongly in the value of my work. Sincere thanks also to Chris Myers and Ace Blair from Peter Lang for timely advice and sensitive support throughout the production process. Thanks to Cathie Pilbeam for working to format chapters and prepare them for production.

Thanks to my partner and soul mate, Daniel Torpy, for seeing in me what was hidden from me at that time, except in my most private dreams; for loving me holistically; for nurturing me and allowing the child in the adult me to finally come out and play as children ought to; and for reading draft after draft and pointing out all my typing and grammar errors as well as bringing his own sharp mind to the arguments I present in this book. Thanks also to my companion animals—both past and present—who have filled my life with meaning, joy, and compassion, long before I knew any of the human kind. Their unconditional love of me and joy in my company not only grounds me in my connection to the earth and all things spiritual, but also nurtured me within so that transformation within and without was possible.

And to Billy, wherever you may be—be in peace. You are free.

If I have missed anyone, my deepest apologies, but my hope is that this will be the first of many books to come.

A final acknowledgment is to all those who have experienced sexual abuse: your courage is admirable, and your sense of hope inexhaustible, despite the sufferings you have endured. It is my fervent hope that this book can be a catalyst toward legal and judicial change, as well as bring a deeper understanding of intrafamilial sexual abuse.

1 ▪ Introduction

AS A LOCUS of social control, law is sanctioned with a great deal of authority as the guardian of "truth" and provider of "justice." This book is able to demonstrate that, in essence, the law neither values nor pursues either when it comes to intrafamilial sexual abuse. Despite judicial rhetoric concerning the neutrality of law, its "objective" stance and "fact-finding" mission, and the just outcomes that result from this role, law and legal process reflect dominant social, economic, and gender inequalities. The purpose of this book is to make explicit the process by which victims of intrafamilial rape are silenced, how gaps in their evidence are created, and how these gaps and silences are filled with dominant masculinist stories and narratives about child sexual abuse. The law presents itself ostensibly as an institution dedicated to upholding legal codes of conduct and moral values. But it is in legal discourses in the courtroom that the rule of the father is replicated with frightening precision.

The trial process has the ability to reflect symbolically the same structural inequalities and abuses of power the child experiences at the hands of the perpetrator. It does so because the law replicates the same structured, male-dominated ethos found across the social stratum (including families). In essence, the child or adult complainant is attacked once more, hence the title of this book: *Court Licensed Abuse*.

A central aim of this book is to expose fundamental structures in legal process that inhibit fact-finding and neutrality, and to reveal the predilection for making trials a site where dominant masculinist stories about sexual violence are mobilized and sanctioned. Through the use of contemporary case studies of actual trials, this work reveals how legal sophistry coupled with deliberate concealment of evidence enables discriminatory narratives to parade within the courtroom as representative of the "facts" of that particular case. These "narratives" are not developed through accident or chance. There is a pattern within each narrative that exposes dominant stock-story elements that underpin all trials involving sexual allegations. The analysis provided in this book will expose the structural and thematic similarities of these defense-led narratives, as well as the role the judiciary play in delineating evidentiary boundaries that make possible the success of these narratives. These narratives are mobilized in the courtroom as prima facie evidence.

This work is intended to contribute to contemporary debates about the nature of law and its response to child sexual abuse. It provides an in-depth explication of how legal method is used to replicate dominant discourses around intrafamilial abuse, and in doing so further explicates the absorption into legal discourse of dominant psychosocial theories around child sexual abuse that negate the experiences of victim/survivors. This book offers a new kind of jurisprudence because it provides a critical reading of whole trials whereby the dominant voices of the narrators—as opposed to only the oppressed and controlled voice of the narrated—are exposed and analyzed to reveal patterns. The four trials chosen for explication were followed from their very beginning to their final outcome, including appeals. Readers are taken on a virtual walk through trials, making them privy to facts and arguments withheld from both the jury and the general public. This method allows a comprehensive understanding rarely available in legal analysis.

The manner in which the law responds to child and adult victims of intrafamilial rape and other forms of sexual violence continues to be a contentious and polemic issue around the world. The history of a socio-medical, psychosocial, and legal understanding of the rape and sexual abuse of children and women is a history of both shameful neglect and a deliberate contempt for the reality of such abuse. This book enters the debate, providing deep and much-needed analysis of a hitherto uncharted terrain around trials.[1] Bearing this in mind, this book sets out to expose a deeper truth that lies behind the euphemism of "legal justice." The expository nature of this work seeks to make clear the perfidious nature of law and legal discourse in relation to women and children and sexual violence. It is necessary to create a paradigm shift in how law is understood, in order to promote and further the kind of legal reform necessary to bring about a semblance of "justice" for children and young adults who are sexually victimized in our society.

I could write a book based on the varied comments and responses from lawyers and judges to my work. One consistent response has been to admonish me for daring to critique this work as a non-lawyer—much of the comments are simply well-crafted blocking techniques in an attempt to stifle or intimidate those who present alternative perspectives. Of particular interest has been the oft-made comment that "law" is not about seeking "truth" or "fact" but about defending a client successfully using all the legal tools, strategies, subterfuge, and sophistry available to lawyers through the justice "system." I therefore have noted with a mixture of incredulity and wry humor that these same commentators then feign outrage when I acknowledge that legal trials are less about fact or truth and more about sophistry and clever rules that conceal, modify, or transmute evidence. It appears it is one thing for the emperor to be naked, provided his admirers share in the denial, but quite another thing to actually tell the emperor and others of this fact.

Law and the Abstract Citizen

A shared theme among feminist jurisprudence is the maleness of law regarding rape and sexual assault, and the inherent bias against women and children that accompanies the application of those laws. Through a wholly male, white, middle-class conduit, law not only ignores experiences of sexual violence but also actively disqualifies them to promote a legally constructed version that accords with patriarchal views of female sexuality and the family.

Ngaire Naffine argues that law's promotion of an abstract person who is without gender, class, or race, and whom the law serves equally, is dismantled through critical examination of legal principles and legal method. Legal impartiality, neutrality, and a focus on fact-finding are putative ideals; however, they prove not to be so when analyzed and problematized. Critical readings of trials—through trial transcripts—identify the nefarious nexus between masculinist theories, stereotypes, and social myths about women and their active deployment in legal narrative, discourse, and doctrine.

The law ostensibly deplores rape and intrafamilial and extrafamilial child sexual abuse. However, an analysis and critique of law, legal process, and judicial discourse in responding to these crimes shows them to be inadequate. It becomes clear that male dominance is reflected in the absence of women's voices and experiences in legal discourse. Just as women's experiences are missing and have been subsumed in "HIStory," so too are women's and children's experiences of sexual violence conspicuously absent in legal discourse.

A Gendered Crime

A common denominator in sexual violence is the gendered structure of the crime, with the vast majority of victims being female and the overwhelming majority of offenders being male.[2] Male victims of sexual abuse are most often assaulted and raped by a male.[3] Female offenders make up an exceptionally small percentage of offenders, when compared with their male counterparts.[4] Studies drawing on professional and criminal statistics, and even retrospective reports and victim self-reports, have consistently found very few female offenders.[5] Women offenders often operate as an accomplice to a male offender[6] and evidence suggests lone female offenders appear to have been negatively influenced by extreme masculinist attitudes toward children and women, sexuality, and self-identity.[7]

In the larger study upon which this book draws, there were twelve female complainants and three male complainants. All of the accused were male and all, except two, were the biological father; the other two were stepfathers. While these figures are not statistically significant, they do reflect abundant research and statistics on intrafamilial sexual abuse which show the biological father and daughter as the most frequent constellation of offender and victim. Jocelynne Scutt has argued that the legal treatment of victims of rape and sexual assault is not necessarily linked to the fact that they are victims, but rather to their role as a woman. Scutt further postulates that whether a woman is victim or accused in a trial, her femaleness allows her to be destroyed in cross-examination.[8] Without negating their gender, allegations by male children saw them treated similarly to their female counterparts since their allegations situated them within the trial as pseudo-females with regards to their legal construction.

The Nexus Between Psychiatry and Law

A common denominator in law, medicine, and psychiatry is their male domination and masculinist imperatives, yet the disciplines have long been assumed to provide objective and incorruptible knowledge about the human race. The interlocution between the two male-dominated institutions of medicine and law has a long history.[9] The absorption into legal discourse of psychiatric theories negating sexual violence and the credibility of women and children predates Freudian psychoanalysis, but certainly the imprimatur given to Freud's work by the patriarchal enclave of psychiatry has increased legal discourse around child sexual abuse, including "incest," considerably.[10]

Women have been consistently conceived as being of an inferior gender, and thus have acquired a pathology that is intrinsic to the construction of their sexuality.[11] Theories in medicine and psychiatry have denigrated women on the basis of their "femaleness." Male-stream theories connect the biological reproductive capacities and sexuality of women with a positive correlation to physical pathology and madness. The girl-child is factored into this equation on every level—she is the *woman-infantile* in the wings, just as dangerous and just as non-credible as her adult counterpart.

Judicial utterances in sexual offense trials have long been underpinned by the view that women and children, especially girl-children, possess a seemingly natural propensity to lie about sexual abuse and to fabricate allegations. These false assertions are so well-embedded within judicial discourse and mindsets that there are often jury warnings as to the dangers of convicting on the lone evidence of a woman or girl. Indeed, the assertions have become immutable rhetoric in legal trials and immune to legal reform.[12]

Psychoanalysis, Psychiatry, and Judicial Lore

Science has long been elevated to a discipline that produces absolute truths about subjects and objects. Women have long been regarded as "objects" of inquiry, and psychiatry provided a pseudo-scientific tool for the vilification of women. The work of Freud in particular is a profound example of how theory became orthodoxy. His seduction/fantasy theory enabled the mass production of a field of knowledge that proclaimed the dishonest and pathological nature of women and children. However, the Freudian mantra encompassed binary opposites that damned children either way. On the one hand, children fantasize about sexual assault and fabricate allegations. Conversely, they are also sexual provocateurs desiring sexual contact with their parents and other adults. The allegations in this case are true, but the source of blame is the child.

From such a view, allegations of "incest" and other forms of sexual abuse could be easily dismissed as the ranting of fantasizing hysterics.[13] This double bind is embedded within child sexual-abuse discourses, enabling a legal defense promoting accusers as fabricators, while the impact of the offender's actions is diminished through discourses of mother blame, victim blame and minimal harm.

We live at a time when society and professionals are more aware of child sexual abuse than in any other period, and government-funded advertising campaigns and funds for programs and services help to promote this fact. Nevertheless, the reality in the court is that stigma and disbelief continue to be leveled at alleged victims. Proportionate to reports of sexual offenses, conviction rates for rape and other sexual offenses remains low,[14] exceedingly low in some jurisdictions.[15]

Recent studies show that the significant legal reform in Victoria a decade ago, which was designed to ameliorate some of the structural disadvantages complainants face in sexual-offense proceedings, seems to have had limited impact given that successful convictions in such cases have actually fallen further.[16] Child and adult victims still continue to face hostility toward themselves and their disclosures. And professionals and lawyers continue to argue that children and women are liars, and tend to generate excuses for successfully convicted offenders.[17]

Contemporary Analysis of Law and Storytelling

This book interrogates the law and its treatment of, and response to, intrafamilial rape and sexual abuse. It does so by walking the reader through four trials presented as case studies. The cases demonstrate law's preference for legal storytelling; for the construction of narratives that are neither representative of the facts of that particular case nor indicative of a search for facts. These narratives, however, have an internal consistency that maintain the dominant order and represent the interests of the socially dominant over the socially subordinate. Rae Kaspiew terms these narratives in sexual-offense trials as "stock-story" narratives to denote their relationship to masculinist stereotypes about sexual violence and victims of that violence.[18]

This book offers a sociological examination of the formation and dissemination of legal stories about intrafamilial sexual abuse within the courtroom. Legal methods that have been derived through a wholly male conduit, and maintained to suit the dominant patriarchal social order, are the tools used to shape legal narratives. Legal trials are a site where stock-story narratives are promulgated, often with extraordinary ease. They are often successful because they appeal to dominant social myths about such abuse. Defense-led intrafamilial sexual-abuse narratives are developed around a nexus of *motive* and *means*: *why* children make allegations of rape and sexual assault against the parent and *how* children came to have such explicit knowledge of sexual violations.

There is a growing body of contemporary Western feminist scholarship across a range of disciplines that has critically analyzed how the legal system and the judiciary treat women and female children, especially with regard to sexual violence. This rigorous and most often contentious engagement between feminist jurisprudence and judicial discourse shows a historically entrenched gender bias against women, expressed through legal dictum and judicial process. Such a philosophy underpins the analysis in this book. I hold that a feminist paradigm offers the most insightful and valuable analysis of law's development and mobilization of masculinist stock-story narratives about women and children in trials involving sexual violence. Feminist critique exposes the patriarchal underbelly of law and makes untenable its claims of impartiality and neutrality. Legal narratives favor the socially dominant dialogue while silencing the marginalized. The usurping of one voice in order to maintain the dominance of another group reflects the politics of sex and gender on a number of levels: the valuing and privileging of the male voice over the female voice; the sexual dominance of men over women and children; and the social dominance of men over women and children. This work also reveals the systemic power of law to maintain a particular framework of reference that is most often impervious to other knowledges and to external challenges.

By using legal forums as a place to tell and retell stock-story narratives, with scant regard for facts, law, as a locus of social control, exacts and replicates the dominant order of the socially and culturally powerful. Law further reaffirms gender dominance and gender stereotypes, which are, on both fronts, detrimental to women and children and discriminatory to their status as citizens of equal worth in our society.

Law as a self-regulating institution has the power to determine what it constitutes as valid knowledge, and to reject knowledge and experience that it regards as inferior. As Carol Smart asserts, a consequence of the judicial colonization of knowledge is that only the kind of knowledge and experience sanctioned by law can count as objective and factual. This powerful masculinist legal perspective produces and reaffirms narratives which are promoted as representative "truths" about social phenomena.[19] These stylized narratives most often reaffirm the views and beliefs of the powerful and dominant. These legally produced narratives become historical legal narratives, which, in turn, become precedents that the law turns to when presiding over other cases involving the same or similar crimes. Legal process is oblivious to the passing of time and the social learning of new knowledge that may well render previous narratives as not only obsolete, but unjust. In this way, the static view of women and children as fabricators of sexual offenses remains an ageless dictum. Like a nefarious Gregorian chant, judges and lawyers seem programmed to trot out ancient edicts, precedents, and warnings about the inherent dangers associated with the words of women and children. As Susan Edwards reminds us, legal precedents so often ossify legal process rather than provide a stepping-stone to legal progress.[20]

As a locus of social control sanctioned with state and public support, legal trials operate as a microcosm—albeit a powerful one—of a society where children traumatized through sexual violence are constructed in particular ways. Legal process draws on patriarchal assumptions and spurious studies of intrafamilial rape and enacts them through legal narratives. Law's colonization of knowledge allows judges to *decide* what counts as valid knowledge and to reject that deemed to be invalid knowledge. Smart noted that rather than knowledge from other disciplines diminishing the power of law as an institutional authority that proclaims "truths," law is extending its terrain of knowledge, so that it remains not only superior to other fields, but has the authority and power to validate or disqualify their claims to "truth."[21] In a related vein, sociologist and legal scholar Kim Scheppele captures this tendency to validate certain types of knowledge and disqualify or stultify others by talking about law's preference for narratives.[22] Scheppele argues that legal process concentrates on narrative and the legal construction of facts. A fact only becomes a fact when it is legally determined to be an admissible fact. As such, certain legal narratives contain certain facts that have been legally selected for inclusion. This transformation of legal stories into legal "facts" leads to alternative stories being distrusted, rejected, or not articulated at all. She further argues that the legal construction of stories tends to support those stories from white and privileged men, while discrediting and disbelieving those experiences from certain groups of people considered "outsiders"— including women. Many of the practices that disadvantage the telling of other experiences occur at subtle levels. More often it is the application of abstract legal rules and legal principles which are invoked through the rhetoric of judicial neutrality and Catharine MacKinnon's[23] notion of a legal point-of-viewlessness that work against the victim's story. Scheppele believes that one of the tasks of law and trial process is to discover the truth of what really happened, but that such a process is handicapped and distorted because of the bias which elevates the "stories" of the privileged. An Australian lawyer, interviewed on national television, admitted that truths are considered unimportant in criminal trials because they get in the way of the legal story being peddled by defense counsel.[24] He suggested that our legal system should "perhaps...be restoring truth as a central goal of a criminal trial."[25]

At this point it is important to clarify the terms "story" and "narrative" and how they are used in this book.[26] It would be unfair and unjust to suggest that women's and children's accounts of sexual violation are merely competing stories—as though their stories of their experience are somehow manufactured. The concept of "stories" and "narratives" has been used by feminist writers like Scheppele to identify how legal process sets up adversarial legal stories that privilege the dominant group over the story of lived experiences of others who are marginalized in legal process. MacKinnon has commented on the contemporary trend for lawyers and legal scholars to talk about legal trials as a process of "storytelling," arguing the need for deeper scrutiny of the place and use of storytelling.[27] MacKinnon's views on legal storytelling support the caution I urge in understanding the concept of narratives and storytelling. This book offers a detailed and critical reading of trials in order to exemplify the legal preference for silencing and modifying lived experiences into discursive legal stories that privilege men, and the authoritative positions they hold in relation to women and children.

I will use the term *truth* in the context of child sexual abuse to represent the search for facts that would prove the veracity of allegations made by a child or adult against their parent. Social constructionism and postmodern sociology are justly wary making the notion of truth objective, but extreme relativity in relation to "truths" acts to belittle the voice of marginalized groups that are just beginning to be heard.

I contend that trials involving allegations of intrafamilial sexual abuse have the very real capacity to replicate the power of the offender by recognizing and sanctioning the power of the father as accused in the trial process. The trials reflect the same power imbalance and structural inequalities the victim/survivor experienced in intrafamilial abuse. Through sexual abuse, victims are silenced by the perpetrator and told that others will not believe them, and are subjected to mechanisms that create fear, betray trust, and inhibit self-esteem through emotional and sometimes physical bludgeoning and threats. In the trial process, the victim is typically accused of being a liar, and trauma-specific behavior is most often concealed and twisted to portray them as unstable and unsavory in character. They most often face a trial that is court licensed abuse.

The inconsequential treatment of intrafamilial rape—known as "incest" in law—stems from the fact that crimes committed against one's own children are deemed less worthy of state or legal intervention. Incest has long been considered a mental health issue rather than a criminal issue. In a recent trial when a judge learned he would be presiding over an "incest" case involving allegations of incest by a biological father against his daughter, was reported to have commented, "Oh not *another* incest case; while we're stuck dealing with these *family problems* we're being kept from dealing with *real* crimes."[28]

The view that incest is a family mental health problem rather than behavior warranting a criminal sanction has been firmly entrenched in masculinist psychosocial theories around incest. Under the rubric of incest, victims are constructed theoretically in diametrically opposing ways. On one hand, abetted by tendencies in Freudian psychoanalysis, they are constructed as liars and fabricators who fantasize about having sexual contact with their fathers and raise false accusations of sexual abuse. Conversely, where incontrovertible evidence establishes their experiences of abuse, victims are constructed as being culpable—at least partially, if not entirely—for the abuse on account of their seductive behavior or supposedly passive response in the face of being raped by their own fathers. Either way, the offender is exonerated from responsibility. Moreover, such abuse is typically defined by using the term "incest," which suggests a complicit—albeit illicit—sexual "relationship" between the father and his child. Research findings consistently identify the biological father as the offender in the majority of cases. After the father, stepfathers rank second. Victims are predominantly female.

It is not inconsequential that the evolution of a masculinist discourse that negates the experiences of victims of intrafamilial rape has both permeated legal doctrine and discourse and promulgated social myths that stigmatize and denigrate victims. In a society where social and political institutions are male, and the institution of the traditional family is male, the proliferation of a mindset that disbelieves victims, ignores their experiences, and instead constructs them around dominant discriminatory stereotypes is a consequence of such a dominant hegemony.

Thus, legal jurisprudence sanctions the legal abuse of children by silencing them in the courtroom, actively concealing evidence, and regulating the evidence they and others are allowed to present. As a result, judges preside over cases in which children and young adults are treated reprehensively.

The Relevance of Australian Legal Experience to Other Countries

Many of the issues around the gendered nature of violence, and the sexist and inappropriate legal response to the same, are encountered in countries such as Canada, the US, and Britain, who have a similar adversarial system of law. As such, the substantive issues documented and analyzed in this book are applicable not only to the Australian legal system, but also those aforementioned countries founded on common-law principles. Around the world, a strong interest continues to grow in the field of child abuse, including sexual abuse. In recent years there has developed a stronger interest in the intersection of child abuse and law and legal discourse. This analysis provides an insight into the social conditioning of "justice," and ultimately enables an understanding of law's capacity for change that may benefit society by responding more fairly and more justly to children and young adult complainants in such trials.

Since the book is grounded in Australian legal process and jurisprudence, it provides an important example of how the legal system operates in Australia and the consequences for complainants in such trials.

Who This Book Will Appeal To

The contents of this book should provide both challenge and interest to a wide range of professionals as well as a lay audience interested in social and legal justice. Counselors and therapists who work with victim/survivors of sexual violence may find this book a useful tool for understanding some of the overt and complex ways in which victims of such abuse can be undermined and emotionally hurt through the trial process. This understanding can assist with post-trial interaction with the victim/survivor, as well as appreciating pre-trial anxiety. To this end, practitioners and students in the fields of psychology, psychotherapy, social work and other related fields should have exposure to this book.

Legal practitioners and scholars can benefit from this book regardless of their preferred area of legal practice as it engages the issue of fact-finding. Practitioners and scholars from related fields such as criminology and justice can also gain from the examination of concepts aligned with their discipline. For some readers, the concept of a system of "justice" (a system that invites us to regard law as a reflection of our collective values, ideal and truth-honoring) may undergo a radical shift.

The subject matter of the book is not approached through a legal lens but, rather, through a far more encompassing approach allowing a critical reading of trial transcripts. A critical feminist sociological reading of trial transcripts has, I believe, enabled certain nuances to be exposed. I also bring the details of whole trials into the open for public and professional scrutiny. Readers are privy to even more details than a jury member since jury members are not present at pre-trial hearings or legal arguments that take place during the trial, but in their absence. As such, readers are presented with information rarely provided in other mediums.

A Note on Methodology

This book is distilled from my Ph.D. thesis, "The Legal Construction of Victim/Survivors in Parent-Child Intrafamilial Sexual Abuse Trials in the Victorian County Court of Australia in 1995," completed in 2001. As such, the approach to the study and the arguments used to sustain the analysis, critique, and findings are based on rigorous research. My Ph.D. thesis received a national award,[29] and its findings have been drawn upon to support recent arguments for law reform in Victoria.[30]

The critical reading of trial transcripts offers a new approach to understanding a topical and widely debated subject. The research undertaken involved a thorough reading of the entire legal proceedings of contested trials of parent-child/stepparent-stepchild sexual abuse that came before the County Court of Victoria for the calendar year of 1995. Some trials were moved back or resulted in juries being discharged, and new trials started or retrials were held as a result of a successful appeal; thus, a number of trials were tracked into 1996 and 1997 to their completion. Trial transcripts allow us to see step-by-step how law silences children and adults in order to develop and narrate a new construction. Transcripts were read in their entirety for storyline logic; that is, to look for similarities of themes and patterns used in the construction of the defense narrative. Close to 16,000 pages of transcripts were read and analyzed using a self-developed manual coding method. Two trials during this period were directly observed, and since then I have observed a number of intrafamilial and extrafamilial child-abuse trials up until 2003.

Introducing the Chapters

This book is organized in a way that best allows the reader to understand the socio-legal placement of intrafamilial sexual abuse and victims of such abuse, and how this particular area of sexual offense is responded to legally. At a time when intrafamilial rape is coming increasingly to trial, it is crucial to examine the legal domain where such trials are conducted in order to expose the state apparatus of power that operates for the benefit of the powerful and those invested with authority and power, such as fathers.

The introductory chapter explicates succinctly the book's underlying theoretical and philosophical arguments.

The second chapter, "Telling Legal Tales," argues a perspective of trials as sites of storytelling that promote and authorize the worldview and position of the powerful and dominant, while subordinating and dismissing the experiences of the marginalized and less powerful. The chapter enables an understanding of the proclivity in law to not only adopt narratives, but to mold evidence so that it provides a "best fit" for the kinds of preferred dominant legal narratives. This chapter prepares the reader for the in-depth reading of the legal case studies around intrafamilial child sexual abuse.

Chapters 3, 4, 5, and 6 are composed of four separate legal cases that make up the heart of the book and are designed to take the reader on a virtual walk through trials. The reader is privy to everything the jury in these cases was not. These four trials were chosen to give an overview of cases involving single complainants, dual complainants, fathers, and stepfathers. However, these cases are not intended to be representative of the overall proportions of these features in the original study. In the original study, the majority of trials resulted ultimately in acquittal, and the majority of accused were biological fathers from intact families and from an Anglo-Saxon background. One consistent feature represented in these four case studies, and representative of my original research, is the nature of the offenses. Every case except one involved allegations of multiple penile penetration.

Trials are revealed as they unfolded to allow the reader to see the complex ways in which child and young adult complainants are examined and cross-examined. We see the deliberate juxtaposition of topics and the constant moving between charges and topics in the hope of confusing the witness and putting them under pressure. Detailed portions of trial transcripts are used in order to provide adequate context to the evidence of all parties and to demonstrate the patterned development and deployment of carefully scripted legal narratives. The excerpts also highlight the legal pedantry as well as the masculinist understanding of sexual violence.

Chapter 7, "Forced Errors," provides a critical reading into a specific legal stratagem involving the use of prior inconsistent statements. In sex-abuse trials, defense barristers rely heavily on creating witness confusion over minute details in order to emphasize errors in the consistency of such details to the jury as "proof" of lying. The chapter demonstrates the reliance defense barristers place on prior inconsistent statements as a legal tool to strengthen their narrative and discredit complainants.

Chapter 8, "Case Studies Analysis," explores some of the structural and thematic patterns across the case studies and, where relevant, how these correspond to other cases from the original research. The preference for stock-story narratives over an open investigation of facts is evinced through such a detailed reading of the trials. Law's transmutation of a child's experience into a legal script is demonstrated to make clear the nefarious link between masculinist theories of child sexual abuse and legal discourse.

Finally, the concluding chapter suggests strategies for legal reform to counter the current structure of sexual-offense proceedings.

A Readership Note

Elsewhere I have written about the inappropriateness of the term "incest" to describe the rape of children and young adults by their parent.[31] Throughout this book the word "incest" is very often placed in inverted commas, unless being directly referred to in its usage connected to literature or other mediums. The use of inverted commas is to denote my rejection of the terminology.

The use of the feminine pronoun when discussing child sexual abuse is generally in recognition of the fact that the vast majority of victim/survivors are female; however, this is not intended to negate the reality that males are also sexually abused. The masculine pronoun has been used in relation to discussions of offenders to reflect the reality that the overwhelming majority of offenders are male.

In the original research, every trial involved male judges, male defense counsel, and male prosecutors. Also, the appeal processes involved male judges. As the four case studies are drawn from the original study, judges and both legal counsels are male across all cases.

While the trials in this book are now eight and nine years old, it would be incorrect to dismiss them as *old* data. During the time these trials were conducted, until the present day, Victorian law has not introduced any substantive or relevant law reform that would disrupt, diminish, unsettle, or invalidate the procedural or narrative patterns found in these trials. I have continued to research trials up to 2003 and found the same defense *modus operandi* and narrative development. Concomitantly, there has been no significant shift in socio-cultural attitudes toward child sexual abuse—specifically, intrafamilial abuse—that would have a similar impact. The claims and arguments in this book are strengthened by my continued observation and research into trials post-1997, and information gathered and detailed in the recently released Victorian Law Reform Commission *Sexual Offenses Interim Report*, which continues to show the unjust treatment and unjust legal process toward those who come into contact with the legal system as victims of sexual crimes.[32] Moreover, given that stock-story narratives about women, children, and sexual violence are historically and culturally embedded in legal doctrine and law, and given the legal resistance to subverting them, the narrative patterns identified in this book should not be seen as relevant only to that time period.

None of the trials referred to in this book is identified by name, in accordance with the *Judicial Proceedings Reports Act 1958* no. 6280 that prevents publication of names in certain cases, of which "incest" is one such case.[33]

A developed understanding of a serious social problem such as child sexual abuse requires confrontation and engagement with detailed verbatim evidence that may cause distress to some readers. As an advocate, researcher, and author in this area, I have not been immune to the distressing nature of the contents of this book but have deliberately chosen not to exclude the evidence given by child and adult complainants about their alleged sexual violation. To do so would be to silence them just as they have experienced silence elsewhere. I also believe that to remove from view the lived reality of their pain, trauma, distress, and fear is to make a statement, even symbolically, that their alleged experiences are unimportant or not fit for public reading. I refuse to sanitize their pain or their experiences to create a purposely designed comfort zone for readers. When I am faced with public or professional comments that child sexual abuse is just too awful, too confronting, too indecent or offensive to talk about in public company, I remind them that, what they find offensive, I find is the lived reality of a child's life.

Notes

1. See Porter (2003). In this article, the legal commentator drew on a brief exposé of one of the trials from my original study. In commenting on the current media focus on sexual abuse, as a result of the launch of the Victorian Law Reform Commission's Sexual Offenses Interim Report (June 2002), the journalist suggested that what was really needed was a piece of work that enabled very large portions of transcripts that both contextualized the trial in question and also allowed readers to see the methodical legal approach to attacking and confusing the evidence of child and adult complainants.
2. A plethora of qualitative and statistical research supports this view globally. With regard to legal comments on this see, for example: Edwards (1996); MacKinnon (1983); and Scutt (1997). With regard to contemporary statistics in Victoria and Australia see, for example: Victorian Law Reform Commission. Sexual Offenses: Law and Procedure Discussion Paper (September 2001); Victorian Law Reform Commission, Sexual Offenses Interim Report (June 2003); Australian Bureau of Statistics, Women's Safety Survey (1996); and Criminal Justice Statistics and Research Unit, Victoria, Crime Victimisation Survey (1998).
3. Ibid.
4. Victorian Law Reform Commission, Sexual Offenses Interim Report, 87. Further, police statistics for 1996/1997 also show the overwhelming percentage of reported sex offenders were male, and less than 3 percent of accused offenders were female.
5. Edwards (1996); Victorian Law Reform Commission, Sexual Offenses; Finkelhor (1986); Saradjan & Hanks (1996); and Ashe & Cahn (1994).
6. Victorian Law Reform Commission, Sexual Offenses.
7. Saradjan & Hanks (1996).
8. Scutt (1986), 57–83.
9. For an excellent appraisal of this history, see Masson (1984), Geis (1978), Geis (1986), and Scutt (1994b).
10. See, for example: Edwards (1996); Green (1986); Masson (1984); Scutt (1994b); and Wigmore (1970).
11. Anderson & Zinsser (1988) and Brown & Bohn, eds. (1989).
12. Despite attempts at progressive legal reform regarding sexual offenses, in particular corroboration warnings and sexual-history evidence, judicial resistance to change continues to be a problem. The recent High Court Decision of Doggett v The Queen (2001), 208 CLR 343, is instructive with regard to the judicial insistence on providing jury warning even in cases where it is not required. For further discussion and analysis on this point see: Heenan (2001); Victorian Law Reform Commission, Interim Report; Davies (1999); and Scutt (1994b).
13. Edwards (1996) and Scutt (1994b) also note the influence of Freudian and other psychology in legal discourse and rhetoric of child sexual abuse.
14. Victorian Law Reform Commission, Sexual Offenses Interim Report (June 2003).
15. Examples include South Australia which reported that 1.8 percent of reported rape offenses resulted in conviction in 2002. In that same year 628 rapes were reported to police (Kelton, 2003, see also Office of Crime Statistics and Research (2002), Crime and Justice in South Australia). See also Wightman (1995) who shows that in the Australian Capital Territory in 1993/4 that of 500 reported sexual offenses only 7 proceeded to a jury trial and even then, every case resulted in acquittal.

16. Victorian Law Reform Commission, Sexual Offenses: Law and Procedure Discussion Paper 48 (2001), at 4.69.
17. See, for example: Taylor (2000); Davies & Taylor (1997); Davies (1999); Faludi (1992); Grix (1999); Hechler (1988); Heenan & McKelvie (1997); Henning (1997); Howe (1997); Kaspiew (1995); Leidholdt & Raymond, eds. (1990); Mawson (1999); Puren (1999); Wightman (1995), 251–66; Young (1998); Young (1995); and Kelly (2002). (In this last article, a forensic psychologist retained by the defense blamed a man's sexual offending against three girls on his wife's unsatisfactory sexual performance). See Taylor (2002).
18. Kaspiew (1995).
19. See the work of Carol Smart (Smart, 1989; Smart, 1995) for a very good examination of law as a powerful social apparatus that colonizes knowledge and affirms or denies that knowledge in order to privilege legal points of view.
20. Edwards (1996), 2.
21. Smart (1989), ch. 1.
22. Scheppele (1989) and Scheppele (1990).
23. MacKinnon (1983).
24. Whitton (1998). It includes the transcript of the whole interview.
25. Ibid., 38.
26. The terms "stories" and "narratives" in feminist research refer to the experiences of victim/survivor's being molded into legal "stories" for the purpose of being discredited. We need to be explicit in how these terms are to be understood in order that they are not transmuted to reflect the pejorative meaning given them by defense barristers, where the term "story" or narrative is a euphemism for lies. Also, the concept of "narrative" and "storytelling" brings with it connotations of individual agency to tell a particular story or event.
27. MacKinnon (1996), 232–7.
28. This comment was told to me by a Crown Prosecutor who was prosecuting the case in question in the Victorian County Court.
29. It was joint-winner of the Jean Martin Award, a biennial award granted by the Australian Sociological Association for the best Ph.D. thesis in the social sciences from an Australian university for the years 2000–2001.
30. Victorian Law Reform Commission, Sexual Offenses Interim Report (June 2003). I am currently a member of the Victorian Law Reform Commission Advisory Committee on Sexual Offenses.
31. Taylor (2001b), Taylor (1997).
32. Ibid.
33. See Judicial Proceedings Reports Acts 1958, no. 6280, sections 1, 1A, 1B, 1C, 2, 3, and 4.

2 ▪ Telling Legal Tales

Trials as Narratives and Theatre

> *Q. How do you make a lawyer stutter?*
> *A. Ask him: Who decided that truth is not important to justice?*
>
> E. Whitton, *The Cartel*

Introduction

IF ONE WERE to ask people to think about the word "justice" in connection with legal process, it is not unreasonable to suggest that most would regard this term as one imbued with value concepts such as equity, impartiality, honesty, integrity, and decency in the pursuit of truth so as to lead to a "just" outcome. Notions of truth-seeking and fact-finding would be highly valued given such a concept of justice. However, the actual process and conduct of law runs counter to this ideal.

The formation, dialectical process, and praxis of law have occurred and been maintained in a wholly male enclave. Legal rhetoric promotes the concept of neutral and impartial justice, with law serving the needs of persons without the bias of gender, class, or race. But, as Ngaire Naffine points out, such a claim is dismantled through a critical examination of legal principles and legal method. The judiciary's self-regulated rhetoric according to which modern law is rational and devoted to objective and neutral fact-finding is untenable given the weight of evidence exposing the patriarchal underbelly of law in its response to sexual crimes.

I have noted with increasing interest the way in which older films whose storyline centers around a courtroom drama has the lawyers and witnesses battling to bring out the whole truth, while contemporary films and television legal drama series unashamedly expose law and the courtroom as a vehicle and forum for pushing stories and not truth.[1] The facts—however crucial and central to any trial—are simply not relevant. Indeed, the disinterest in truth and fact-finding among lawyers and the judiciary can be a shocking discovery. As one Australian QC (Queen's Counsel) is reported to have said, "You really feel you've done something when you get the guilty off."[2]

As a system of justice, law and legal process has come under increasing scrutiny from a broad cross-section of disciplines and professions outside of the law. A particular trend has emerged in which law is understood as a place that both procures and delivers stories and narratives. Scholars and critics are less likely to be mesmerized by judicial wordsmithing, or chided into silence by lawyers and judges who would have us believe that only the initiated could hope to make intelligent or "objective" comment on law and legal practice. Simply saying that the law tells stories and narratives about matters under investigation is not so new, or so startling, but theorizing and explicating law as a system that deals exclusively in dominant storytelling is emerging as a strong field of inquiry.

Situating trials as a place in which the "stories" of the dominant are given precedence over subordinate "stories" allows for a more in-depth analysis; but, more particularly, it allows an examination of how an adherence to traditional legal method and ancient precedents leads to development, maintenance, and replication of "stock stories." Just as legal scholars claim that legal process privileges the interest of a dominant, more powerful group, so too scholarship around legal storytelling examines how dominant interests are disseminated in trials at the expense of subordinate and marginalized groups and individuals. Stock stories preserve the interests of dominant groups. They have an internal consistency that is recognized and interpreted as though it were representative of a socially determined truth or reality.

Trials involving sexual violence mobilize stock-story narratives about women, in particular, and children based on strong stereotypes and social myths that are deeply embedded with professional, legal, and social discourses. In such trials, stories by the dominant social and gender group are given precedence to the stories told by the subordinate and less powerful group. As a male-dominated institution—one predicated on patriarchy and the privileging of the white, middle-class male—legal discourse and dominant legal stories represent the experiences and beliefs of white, middle-class men and subjugate the experiences of others, especially women.[3] The gendered nature of law and its treatment of women and other socially marginalized groups has been well documented, and a 1998 report of the New South Wales Law Reform Commission acknowledged judicial proceedings around sexual-offense matters had involved "sexist assumptions" by the judiciary, allowing sexist claims concerning alleged victims to become relevant to trials.[4] A reading of legal dictum and discourse around sexual offenses reveals the inherent and entrenched prejudices against both alleged and *proven* victims of sexual crimes and reveals how trials have become a site for mobilized bias to reign supreme.

The public discourse and rhetoric of the courts is that of an objective and neutral forum whose purpose is to seek truth and provide justice. However, Evan Whitton provides compelling evidence that the law may be understood as a legal cartel deliberately designed to promote a male elite class system of power and dominance.[5] The system of law was made complex and extremely technical, with an emphasis on concealing evidence. The centralization of law influenced a self-referential system of power impenetrable to outside scrutiny and proper regulation. He argues further that the judicial opposition to legal reform represents the self-interest and esoteric nature of law, and that legal education eschewed a liberal approach to law and legal knowledge, opting instead for a narrow focus on procedure and technical elements of the tools of law.[6] Whitton's work reveals an institution based on adversarial principles, sharply aware of its flaws and disturbing ethical shortcomings yet unable or unwilling to meaningfully engage with critiques generated both from within and outside its profession. Far from being a vanguard of equitable treatment of those seeking justice, law is another avenue for competing discourses and narratives to be embedded and mobilized to varying degrees.

This chapter will discuss this burgeoning field of jurisprudence, both to clarify some of the arguments and to draw out those arguments that parallel my own arguments. It is also a good opportunity to highlight tensions and points of difference entailed by the theoretical, contextual, and philosophical position I take in this work. The notion of a trial as a form of theatre is complementary to legal storytelling and legal narratives. I have, elsewhere, written a good deal about this point and will draw upon it here in order to advance my contention that courtrooms are also places that promote a trial as theatre.

Since it is the state that brings prosecutions, one might expect that the dominant "lead" with regard to evidence and dialogue within the courtroom is the prosecutor. I argue and present evidence to show that this is not so. Though judges preside over cases, various devices of our Anglo-Saxon "adversarial" system of law allow defense barristers to establish and assert hegemony over the trial as a whole. Judicial discretion, the ability for judges to apply individual *discretion* when determining the admissibility or inadmissibility of evidence and legal precedents, very often favors the defense case, thus delineating the centrality of judicial discretion as an enabling factor in the construction and mobilization of legal narratives. As this book will show, evidentiary rulings delineate the boundaries of the prosecution case. Some evidentiary rulings may crush the prosecution case as crucial evidence is eroded or completely excluded. Established historic precedence about the supposed character of those who have alleged rape and sexual assault provides another layer of discourse operating as a legal device to undermine prosecution cases.

The common assumption is that the master narrative is led by the prosecutor since it is the state that has brought the criminal charge; however, as has been demonstrated before (and will be made explicit in later chapters), the prosecutor is often *forced* to follow and *accommodate* a legal narrative defined by the presiding judge, often at the behest of the defense counsel. Consequently, while legal trials purport a master narrative led by the prosecutor, one that the defense barrister must argue against or overcome with competing evidence, the opposite is often the case. Moreover, patterns in defense narratives across trials and patterns in judicial rulings indicate that a kind of legal template is applied to sexual-offense proceedings to enable deeply held stereotypes and social myths about women, children, and sexual offenses to be mobilized.

Defense counsel are given access to all prosecution evidence prior to the trial and must be made fully aware of any and all evidence the prosecution wishes to present (hence, they know every word and question the prosecution wishes to lead) whereas the prosecution knows very little of the defense case.

Thus, in a trial, the judicial discourse and its historical bias against child and adult rape complainants plays a role in establishing evidentiary boundaries. The legal narratives of both legal counsels are in competition, and the protagonists are limited in ways not known to the jury, yet are portrayed as the "lead" bodies in the court. Likewise, the complainants are viewed as witnesses who are able to present their story—their evidence—within the courtroom, when in fact they are silenced and subverted by both the judge and legal counsel in a variety of ways. Other professional discourses will be presented in court through various expert witnesses retained by both sides. All of these dialogues, voices, and legally constructed narratives interact over a period of days or even weeks prior to the defense counsel and the prosecutor summating their arguments and positions into a legal package upon which the jury adjudicate.

Storytelling as an Ideological Tool

The telling of legal stories occurs within a social and political discourse. Stories create bonds and shared meanings, and build consensus. Richard

Delgado talks of legal stories using the terms "outgroups" and "ingroups."[7] Ingroups represent the dominant in society and occupy a superior position, which they use to justify the construction of marginalized and subordinate outgroups and the world as they see it. He argues that it is important that the powerful stories, narratives, and parables from the subordinate outgroup, which Delgado refers to as "counter-storytelling," are used to defeat dominant ingroup stories and mindsets. In a telling example, Delgado shows that racial discrimination is not a problem to be remedied with beneficial laws, since discrimination—and, hence, subordination—of people of color can be the result of prevailing mindsets that law alone cannot remedy.

American sociologist Kim Lane Scheppele's research in the area of legal narratives provides an instructive insight into the role of narrative in law.[8] She proposes that the legal process concentrates on narrative and the legal construction of facts. The transformation of legal stories into legal "facts" allows for alternative stories to be distrusted or rejected, or not articulated at all. Drawing on the work of other scholars on legal narratives, Scheppele argues that the legal construction of stories tends to support those stories from white and privileged men while discrediting those experiences from certain groups of people considered "outsiders" (this group includes women).

Scheppele further notes that legal storytelling is similar to folktales in that both have deep structures. She makes the valid point that legal storytelling may be even more structured because of its legitimization through the institutional framework of law. The stories of these "outsiders" are omitted from legal discourse, and their exclusion can be directly related to overt forms of racism and sexism. Yet Scheppele argues that many of the practices that disadvantage the telling of other experiences occur at a much more subtle level.[9] This latter point is supported in the work of lawyer Gilbert Geis who, while clearly articulating the misogyny underpinning the legal response to rape and sexual-assault complainants, makes the valid point that misogyny is not always expressed crudely or overtly, but may be deployed and maintained in other more subtle ways to conceal its presence.[10]

It is this subtlety that is harder to see and more difficult to correct. Exclusion via rejection of the experiences of those considered "outsiders" certainly occurs, but more often it is the application of abstract rules and legal principles—invoked through the rhetoric of judicial neutrality and MacKinnon's notion of a legal point-of-viewlessness—that work against the complainant's story. Since legal method distorts the pursuit of fact-finding, and has the ability to impede and repress certain voices, the "stories" of the privileged—who are usually white and male—are elevated within the courtroom. More importantly, those stories given prominence as legal narratives have the power to create facts.[11] These "facts" have prominence mainly because they have been authenticated in legal discourse and enshrined in legal doctrine enabling them to be reused and mobilized and in later trials so that a preferred narrative becomes a historical legal artifact to be reused and applied across trials.[12]

Sociologists Patricia Ewick and Susan Silbey are interested in the production of what they term "hegemonic narratives"—stories that reproduce existing relations of power and inequality, and compete with subversive narratives.[13] Such stories are also hegemonic in their ability to colonize consciousness. This is achieved through their coherent and believable plots and scenarios, as well as by preempting alternative narratives with their underlying dominant themes. Importantly, the authors point out that hegemonic narratives are able to obscure any recognition of the social organization that produces and maintains them. Their dominant repetition affords them credibility, and the assumptions and claims that underpin them are not scrutinized or challenged. Moreover, they are a potent form of social control and homogenization, making powerful and persuasive "truth claims" about what constitutes normal or appropriate conduct and values. Such "truth claims" are of course shielded from debate or any verification as to their accuracy.[14]

Narratives should not be understood as simplistic stories that capture an uninformed audience. While narratives may appear to have a simple storyline—by that I mean a story that is coherent and fairly straightforward—the stories are generated through powerful conduits. Narratives are marked by a reliance on implicit assumptions rather than explicit evidence. Ewick and Silbey report that the use of discriminatory images and stereotypes, along with other performative features of the narrative—such as the coherence of the narrative "plot," repetition, and use of characteristics of certain individuals—contribute to the generation of an emotional identification and commitment to the narrative, making epistemological challenges more difficult.[15]

Some social theorists suggest witnesses in trials can be viewed as legal actors who possess individual power to impact legal narratives and the narrative construction of identity.[16] For some witnesses this concept may well be accurate; however, in general it presupposes degrees of power and agency that many witnesses, such as children, lack—both in the social sphere as well as the legal sphere. Moreover, I am wary of reducing individuals and social problems to abstract theoretical constructs. This leads to a kind of theoretical nihilism in which the individual's voice, experience, and the social situation are transmuted into academic paradigms that make the person invisible, or at the very least, far less tangible to the problem under investigation.

Much of the dominant literature on child sexual abuse reflects the hegemonic, ideological narratives that construct social phenomena, and thus negates the experiences of children and affords their stories little credibility. Stereotypes portraying children as fantasizers and liars about sexual abuse—

and as blameworthy in proven abuse—continue to be accepted in professional and public discourse. Likewise, stereotypes of their familial background and the scenario in which *real* sexual abuse occurs continue to have currency in professional and public discourse. Lawyers are only too aware of these maintained stereotypes and prejudices, and seek to mold legal narratives that appeal to public and legal prejudice rather than to reason or fact.

The Unimportance of Truth to the Provision of Justice

Judges and lawyers are not averse to admitting that the adversarial concept of law promotes a central objective above all else: winning the case, regardless of the factual basis of a client's story and regardless of the evidence.[17]

While the concept of legal ethics seems an oxymoron, lawyers are apt to talk of professional ethics as though to do so promulgates the sincerity of law as a locus of social control and procurer of proper justice. A legal ethicist from an Australian law school admitted that lawyers "frequently lie to opposing counsel and/or the court [and] do things for their clients that they would find immoral if they acted similarly for themselves or non-clients."[18] Likewise, legal ethicist David Luban has suggested that lawyers often "check in their morals at the courtroom door" prior to a trial, and that our current system of law actively promotes conduct among lawyers and the judiciary that negates moral standards.[19] He is critical of the method of humiliating and attacking the credibility of witnesses whom lawyers know are telling the truth but unjustly attack in order to advantage their client. Although legal technicalities enable such a process, Luban maintains such conduct is "unconscionable." In a different context this approach would be regarded as immoral; however, within the adversarial system, it is considered good legal skill.

Luban's point is a telling one, particularly as it broadly reflects the contention of feminist jurisprudence that legal justice is unjust and causes harm to marginalized and disempowered groups. What we would consider a moral deficiency—the distortion of facts and fabrication of stories to discredit and emotionally harm others—is considered a virtuous and valued skill in legal trials. One of the rules of the New South Wales Bar Association advises that if a client confesses guilt to his or her barrister but wishes to maintain a plea of not guilty, the barrister may use whatever legal rules and stratagems necessary to argue his client's innocence. Whitton notes that, on occasion, lawyers have been known to provide their client with a better lie than the one the client instructed the barrister to run with at court.[20]

When commenting specifically on sexual offenses, one Victorian lawyer noted the defense lawyers' job, regardless of an admission of guilt by their client, is to maximize a positive outcome for the client.[21] He argued that lawyers are in the habit of telling their client not to give them any "account" of what is alleged to have occurred, since they will want to wait and see what material the prosecution presents to prove their case, before deciding on a course of action.[22] In other words, the defense narrative depends on the prosecution material, and then, what can be excluded—and the gaps filled in with an alternative account. This approach can be identified when one closely examines a trial from its inception to its conclusion. The committal hearing, also referred to as a preliminary hearing in other international jurisdictions, is a fishing expedition, with no clear defense narrative, the purpose being one to glean information that might be useful to develop a narrative for the trial. A Canadian lawyer is reported to have advised defense lawyers in sexual offense proceedings to "whack" the complainant with everything they have at the preliminary hearing, in the hope the complainant will be too fearful to return to the court for a trial.[23]

Promoting trials as a place for storytelling—in which one or more narratives being mobilized within a trial may well be understood by all legal parties as non-factual—occurs predominantly because an adversarial legal system allows for such a process to flourish. An important part of law is its operation around a set of ancient rules that are not grounded in concepts of truth-seeking or the logic of fact-finding. Rather, law's rules are derived from the English adversarial system, with its central edict that judges were not responsible for the investigation of truth. They were merely a kind of umpire who would preside over the legal rules governing the combatants, i.e., the lawyers from either side.[24] In several trials I researched, I heard judges refer to themselves as being merely an "umpire" whose job it was to preside over the trial to ensure the "playing rules," as one judge called them, were adhered to. Whitton believes the Anglo-Saxon judicial system of an adversarial contest, with judge as umpire presiding, opened the way for lawyers to "invent a series of truth-defeating devices" that make fact-finding excruciatingly difficult in a legal setting.[25]

Whitton describes the "classic defense" process used in trials as one in which the defense barrister argues to have as much relevant evidence as possible concealed from the jury. The next step is to hector and deliberately confuse witnesses. Both are easily accomplished, especially given the reality that no one gives their evidence at a trial in exactly the same way as they gave it in their police statement and at other hearings such as the committal and even previous trials. As such, lawyers seize slight alterations in evidence to browbeat, confuse, and cajole witnesses in front of the jury.[26] Whitton's encapsulation of the classic defense is telling, and as the reader proceeds to the case studies, this defense strategy will be apparent in specific detail and pattern.

Judicial Mistrust of Legal Process

The notion that legal process is about winning at any cost, and at the expense of any truth, is certainly well understood among lawyers and the judiciary.[27] After presiding over a 1994 case involving sexual offenses, a Sydney judge commented that the truth "is being hidden from juries, at times in circumstances which are productive of injustice and unfairness."[28] The former chief justice of the Victorian County Court, Judge Glenn Waldron, described the cross-examination of many victims of crime as "trial by ambush."[29]

A survey of lawyers and the judiciary in Victoria conducted a few years ago provided a telling indictment of the inability of the legal system to respond fairly and appropriately to alleged victims of sexual violence.[30] In response to a hypothetical question about the advice they would give to a relative or friend who disclosed that he or she had been raped or sexually assaulted, the majority of participants had reservations about encouraging their relative or friend to report the incident and proceed to trial, while 14 percent of lawyers stated that they would definitely advise a relative or friend *not* to report the rape/sexual assault. Their reservations and emphatic resistance to reporting such a crime, let alone going to trial, stemmed from their beliefs that the trial process is damaging and that the complainant would be treated in ways considered to be as bad, if not worse, than the actual rape or sexual assault itself.[31] Obviously lawyers and the judiciary were aware of the legal narratives employed to castigate complainants and the legal principles that eschew fact-finding.

To be fair, there are, no doubt, judges and lawyers who aspire to make the courtroom a forum that honors truth and upholds the dignity of all who come before it. Of this I am sure, because I have had the pleasure of meeting and working with some of them. But acknowledging such a fact does not diminish the reality that the process of law enacted in trials is predominantly about storytelling.

This storytelling is intended to influence jurors. In particular, to stimulate discriminatory stock-story narratives about women, children, and sexual abuse that continue to inform contemporary attitudes about sexual violence.[32] In 2000, a retiring Supreme Court Judge from Tasmania declared a need to reconsider the usefulness of a jury system in criminal trials, saying he believed that they returned what he described as the "wrong verdict" in approximately a quarter of all cases. The reasons for these *wrong verdicts*, he argued, were particularly prevalent in cases involving serious sexual offenses. While others from the legal profession dismissed such a view on the basis that trial by jury was necessary to democratic society, the views expressed by this judge would resonate as having great credibility among many others both within and outside the legal profession.[33] As this book will demonstrate, *wrong* jury verdict should not be regarded as the problem of legally untrained peers adjudicating on their fellow citizen, but rather has much to do with the decidedly unjust operation of our adversarial system.

Legal Storytelling and Legal Narratives: A Critical Appraisal

As a basis for this book, I have derived the most useful and powerful arguments advancing storytelling and stock-story narratives in law from a multitude of feminist and non-feminist theories of these practices. Over the past decade, a number of feminist scholars have engaged in a rigorous and iconoclastic analysis of rape trials by examining masculinist storytelling and narratives about rape and sexual assault. These scholars strengthen our understanding of the role of dominant discourses in sustaining or regulating rather than prohibiting or proscribing sexual violence.

Regina Graycar has made the point that despite feminist activism, which has brought out into the open the reality of physical and sexual violence in the lives of women and children, this reality is "rarely (and barely) acknowledged in legal discourse [parentheses in original]."[34] Feminist scholarship, she argues, has responded to this by researching and producing literature that is a powerful indictment of the law and the systematic disadvantaging of women and children who come before the law as complainants in sexual-abuse trials.[35] Specifically, feminist analyses have developed into what has been described as a focus on "legal storytelling" or "feminist narrative scholarship." Graycar considers this a logical progression, since one of the central tenets of feminist scholarship has been to recover the subjugated and repressed stories from women about their experiences.

Graycar's work provides a lucid appraisal of legal storytelling and its presence and persistence across a broad range of legal settings, not just criminal trials. She argues that the power vested in the judiciary to make pronouncements about what they consider to be the "facts" (which are transformed into legal "realities" and "truths") provides a powerful apparatus for judicially constructed storytelling about women's and children's lives and experiences. Moreover, these stories are considered sacrosanct and exempt from outside criticism or challenge. An example is the maintenance of the corroboration warning, which is underpinned by the narrative of women and children as colluders and fabricators of sexual violence committed against them.[36] Graycar is not alone in advancing the argument that through such a regime the law perpetuates an indifference to, and indeed a tacit complicity in maintaining, a particular discriminative narrative about violence against women. Jocelynne Scutt's work also provides a rigorous critique and mapping of the legal response to adult and child sexual violence, including intrafamilial abuse, in Australian courts.[37] Challenging legal stock stories about women's lives requires the dismantling of the legal framework that allows, and provides for, the gendered nature of law to reproduce itself in legal narratives.

The development of particular legal tools and defense stratagems has obviously facilitated the deployment of legal narratives. Doreen McBarnet maintains that since legal method and legal principles actually work against fact-finding in legal trials, the resultant manipulation and editing of raw evidence leads to the production of narratives in which one narrative dominates the other.[38] Through such a process, McBarnet argues, law's "truth" and "reality" become problematic. Legal discourse decides who can speak, who cannot speak, and what can be said within the legal narrative that takes the form of a trial. She is not alone in articulating the role of legal method and principles in subverting the voice of others and, at the very least, diminishing the fact-finding process. A good deal of legal scholarship around legal narratives also exposes how legal method operates to produce and mobilize such narratives.[39] Law, according to Scheppele, is concerned with creating "insider" and "outsider" stories. Broadly, "insider" stories are those that conform to a dominant view, while "outsider" stories are those experiences and stories of marginalized and oppressed groups that are silenced through legal process.[40] This silencing is achieved through the process of legal selectivity with regards to evidence, as judges and lawyers decide who will be heard, what can they say, and, of course, what credibility will be afforded certain witnesses.

Rae Kaspiew argues that examining the treatment of complainants in legal trials involving allegations of rape and sexual assault allows for a greater understanding about the extent to which the articulation of complainants' stories is denied them in a legal forum, and how such denial allows masculinist accounts of rape to remain unchallenged in law. Many of the legal stories told are what Kaspiew calls "stock stories," also known as rape myths.[41]

British feminist legal scholar Sheila Duncan proposes that legal discourse operates in a way that provides sustenance for dominant discourses, which operate not to proscribe sexual violence, but rather to sustain it.[42] According to Duncan, women's experiences of sexual violence are constructed through a male conduit that is external to women's experiences. The rationale underpinning rape laws is constructed through the power of the *male* speaking subject. Such a view concurs with MacKinnon's expositional writing on the maleness of the state and of law. She argues that rape laws reflect men's definitions of women's experiences and, so, through such a regime, rape laws are almost unenforceable; and rather than rape being prohibited, it is regulated. This regulation occurs both as a result of the application of legal method and the positioning of "rape" within a wholly male discourse.[43] Legal stock-story narratives of rape and sexual assault are promulgated in literature—both creative and theoretical—as well as the media, resulting in social myths about sexual violence. Legal trials, therefore, present narratives that continue to be accepted in society: women and children lie about rape and assault, fantasize about it, exact revenge through false stories, consent to sex and then claim rape, and are complicit in their own protracted abuse and thus culpable for the crimes committed upon them.

The romanticization of rape in popular literature and films spills over into public and legal discourse about women and children complainants in rape cases. Law even enacts complex narratives about the vaginal hymen. The hymen has been constructed through masculinist theories of medicine and law as an invincible site of proof, not only of virginity, but also of whether rape occurred. The hymen represents an important narrative tool: how it came to be broken or, more importantly, remain intact despite claims of penetration.[44]

Those interested in legal narrative and storytelling examine legislation and legal texts to bring out such narratives and identify the power(s) driving them. The general view of the courtroom as a place of biased storytelling provides food for thought with regard to entrenched legal discrimination based on race, class, religion, and sex and gender. As MacKinnon reminds us, storytelling emerged out of the civil rights and women's liberation movements, with their speak-outs and consciousness-raising, which produced a deeper analysis of dominance and abuse, both racial and sexual. The value of storytelling also emerged from indigenous cultures where stories provided a sense of belonging, collective identity, history, and purpose.

Storytelling provides individuals with a socially produced blueprint of their position and identification with their group. Thus, one's social class, race, gender, and religion are made up of stratified layers of storytelling. Some socially produced stories are designed to affect the experience of an individual regardless of his or her religion, race, or class. Sexual violence is one such area affected by dominant socially produced stories, which work to subjugate and inhibit the telling of the experience and the belief in the experience.

The privileging of the dominant story over the subordinate "story" (read "story" as "experience") allows legal process to create what Scheppele and other legal narrative theorists have termed a "legally sanctioned reality."[45] This brings us to the role of legal storytelling with regard to sexual violence within the family unit.

"Incest" Narratives

Intrafamilial rape allegations bring the greatest punishment from male enclaves such as law and psychiatry probably because the allegations attack the most powerful figure in male dominance: the father, and, where the mother supports the child, the husband. Few things expose the underlying patriarchy of law and psychiatry as do allegations of "incest." Such allegations challenge the rule of the father, the literal meaning of patriarchy. Historically, the role of men, especially in the role of father and/or husband, has been socially and institutionally sanctioned with enormous power. Despite social progress—much of it achieved as a result of feminist agitation—women and children, especially girls, continue to face trial by ordeal, within both professional and legal discourse and praxis, when they allege intrafamilial rape and sexual assault.

British sociologist Charlotte Mitra analyzed sixty-three appeal decisions in cases involving father-daughter "incest" during 1970–80.[46] Previous studies have alerted us to the discriminatory practices in procedural and evidentiary law and entrenched judicial bias against "incest" victims. Reading appeal decisions to identify commonalities in judicial reasoning, Mitra found judges minimizing harm to victims of abuse while rationalizing the father's conduct. This was most often achieved by imputing elements of blame to the victim and her mother, and was a deeply entrenched practice. Mitra considers that "incest" cases contain three important aspects of "patriarchal power": "the law, the family and male sexuality."[47] According to Mitra, dominant masculinist theories of intrafamilial child sexual abuse, including family dysfunction theory, are those that inform and maintain the kind of appalling judicial bias meted out to victim/survivors of such abuse.

Duncan's work on sexuality and legal narrative, almost a decade after Mitra's, demonstrated the legal tendency to transmute victims' experiences of rape and sexual abuse through a male conduit that subverts the female speaking voice. Regarding intrafamilial sexual abuse, Duncan, like Mitra, notes the rhetoric of minimization and victim culpability inherent in judicial discourse around this crime.[48]

A more recent critique of the use of legal narratives in "incest" cases is made by American lawyer Leslie Feiner.[49] Feiner demonstrates how evidentiary exclusions severely disadvantage child witnesses of long-term abuse because they stultify the child's experience and allow a defense narrative to be created that fits commonly held discriminatory stereotypes about such abuse. Another layer in this process is the distilling of long-term abuse into a small number of charges. She notes how evidentiary rulings and the distilling of long-term abuse into only a handful of charges creates "gaps" in the child's evidence. The defense counsel seizes upon these "gaps in the storyline" to discredit the complainant by superimposing an internally consistent and coherent alternative story. Feiner notes that the storyline for the side of the accused is most often simple, as opposed to the storyline of the complainant, which has been deliberately fragmented and disjointed as a result of legal editing. Evidentiary rulings that advantage the accused make evidence of rebuttal much easier, and constraints on prosecution cross-examination of the accused allow for a storyline that can avoid the kinds of silences and gaps imposed on the evidence of the complainant as a result of evidentiary exclusions. Feiner believes it is crucial that the complainant in long-term intrafamilial abuse be able to tell a jury as much as possible about her experience of such abuse in order that a jury (and judge) can understand the unique dynamics found in this kind of abuse. However, most often, the story of the child is truncated in a way that allows defense counsel to consistently render her story as improbable or bizarre.

Feiner's points are specifically relevant to many of the case studies presented in this book. Evidentiary rulings result in the fragmenting of evidence, and gaps and silences are subsequently imposed on the complainant. In turn, complainants' evidence very often seems out of context, as opposed to the stock-story narrative of the defense, whose narrative is underpinned by an internal consistency, albeit usually a false one.

Precedent and Its Role in Legal Narratives

Rape myths and child-abuse myths are a good example of dominant narratives about how a "real" rape victim would act, and the personal and social characteristics of a "real" rape victim. As is well documented, the idea that women and children are possessed of a seemingly natural propensity to lie about rape and sexual assault—and, therefore, that such allegations should be viewed with suspicion and extreme caution—has been canonized in legal doctrine.[50] Jocelynne Scutt and other legal scholars have argued that the centuries-old legal principles underpinning the corroboration warning have had an extraordinary impact on determining contemporary rape laws and legal process in the Anglo-Saxon system.[51] Essentially the warning is given by judges to jurors in sex offense proceedings advising them to exercise *caution* (sometimes *extreme caution*) when considering the evidence of alleged victims. The eagerness with which the judiciary continues to utter the need for juries to exercise caution when considering the evidence of rape and sexual assault complainants continues to be a mainstay in twenty-first century Australian law. This belief, which is firmly grounded in the misogynistic legal writings of British jurist Lord Hale, has played a significant role in the legal development of stories about women and children as liars and colluders, fantasizers and fabricators. John Henry Wigmore's legal tome—published in the 1930s, and which continues to inform legal procedure in contemporary sexual-offense proceedings—exemplifies the de facto relationship between law and psychiatry in establishing legal edicts about the lying and conniving nature of women and children regarding allegations of rape and sexual assault.[52]

Susan Edwards describes legal precedents as a "universalized particular, applied over and over again to future particulars," regardless of relevance.[53] Edwards observes how the doctrine of precedent is capable of ossifying law, rather than allowing for a "stepping-stone" to social change and improved understanding of different phenomena.[54] Like well-preserved time-travelers, the same-old patterns of legal thought and stories are applied as a blanket provision in sexual-offense proceedings.

Like powerful superstitions that lead people to hang garlic outside their door or spin three times while saying certain words—all to ward off evil intentions—legal precedents such as the corroboration warning are hung over the words of women and children to protect the accused from a jury falling under the spell of the "credible" woman.

The power of legal precedents ensures that regardless of time, place, and context, judicial rhetoric around certain issues remains largely static with the judiciary all singing from the one hymn sheet. Of course, dissenting opinions do occur and may even lead to change. However, in sexual-offense proceedings, dissenting opinions are often "corrected" by judges at a higher court, thus reaffirming the precedent and making it even more powerful and immutable. As Melanie Heenan's work demonstrates, hybrid narratives in legal reasoning do occur and the corroboration warning in Australia has undergone various shifts that enable hybridized warnings in accordance with judicial discretion.[55] Even though the warnings are open to challenge by higher courts, they still reflect the principles of an ancient precedent: complainants' words in sex-offense proceedings need more scrutiny than the evidence of other witnesses. This reveals the stock-story power of precedents.

The intersection of historic precedent and centuries-old legal doctrine continue to prevail within Australian courts, and while there have been some progressive changes, the patriarchal philosophy underpinning law means that the judicial response to sexual violence is more often than not regressive.[56]

Legal precedents can enable the promotion of a dominant narrative that negates women's and children's experiences of sexual violence. Based on precedents like the corroboration warning, judges comment on the inherent dangers of accepting evidence by women and children, even to the point of retelling age-old legal stories uttered in trials more than a century before.

The practice evinces the legal preference for embedding traditional and discriminatory thinking into contemporary legal settings. Ancient legal precedents, such as the corroboration warning, are a lynchpin in legal trials. Given at the completion of all evidence, immediately prior to jury deliberation, the warning is both an explicit and symbolic representation of the entire legal process and, moreover, a representation of social discourses about sexual violence.

Mind Your Language in the Presence of Patriarchs

> *Q. When is rape not rape?*
>
> *A. When it is your father or stepfather.*

At all levels of a trial, including sentencing and the appeal process, complainants (and those who could later be classified legally as "victims") are saturated within a sexualized judicial discourse. My original research is replete with examples of how complainants and victims are positioned within a lascivious legal narrative. At times this also involves enforcing linguistic silences and boundaries upon complainants when speaking about their experience. Take, for example, the language of "incest" and "rape."

A feature of linguistic boundary setting concerns the use of the word "rape." In my research, I found many examples of judges and lawyers giving mini-homilies about "incest" not being "rape" because "incest" could be "consensual." It was not uncommon for a judge to agree that the word "rape" be removed from evidence on a similar understanding. At other times, the defense counsel was concerned about the word "rape" being used to describe "incest," even when it was used by the alleged victim. In one case, the defense counsel had the complainant threatened with contempt of court if she continued to refer to her father as having "raped" her. The judge agreed the complainant in this case should not be allowed to use her own language to describe her long-term sexual abuse, and even suggested perhaps her reference to "rape" was part of a performance.[57] The defense counsel in this case was concerned the word "rape" may suggest force and violation whereas "incest" carries with it a deep-seated social stigma.

The pejorative values attached to the word "incest" are well recognized by lawyers, and judicial discourses continue to situate "incest" as a lesser crime—and one that clearly involves victim culpability. Not surprisingly, notions of victim culpability to varying degrees were found alongside judicial discourse in "incest" trials.[58] One trial judge complained bitterly about having to preside over "another incest case," claiming it was a "mental health issue" and not a legal one. The judge further complained that while the court was forced to deal with "incest" cases, it was prevented from dealing with trials involving "real" crime.[59]

With regard to intrafamilial rape, Duncan identifies the entrenched legal rhetoric that "incest" is not rape, with victim/survivors being considered culpable agents to their own sexual violation, and Mitra's research strengthens this finding considerably.[60] She indicates that judicial narratives minimize "incest"—both in terms of the consequence to the child victim and the seriousness of the crime—as well as promote a kind of seductiveness around victims. Mitra found that the discriminatory ideology of female sexuality that pervades the law and judicial thinking is "most marked in cases of intrafamilial" sexual abuse.[61]

The linguistic positioning of victims of "incest" in legal discourse and narratives reflects the similar positioning of victims in a good deal of masculinist psychosocial literature on "incest," especially family dysfunction theory. The use of legal language when referring to victim/survivors will be noted throughout this book.

Prior Inconsistent Statements: The Legal Storyteller's Sculpturing Tool

In legal trials, prior inconsistent statements made by the witness (particularly the complainant) are often used against her. These are inconsistencies in evidence given by a witness, and can also occur when witnesses agree to defense questions that are shown to be inconsistent with either her police statement or evidence given at previous hearings. This particular legal strategy will be discussed in detail in chapter 7, "Forced Errors." Suffice to say that prior inconsistent statements greatly enhance barristers' stock-storytelling.

The Stock-Story Narrative Cloak

In legal discourse, complainants of "incest" allegations have an established identity awaiting them upon entering the witness box. This identity is no accident of labeling. It is the result of careful examination of all those theories and legal dictums that have consistently disqualified women's and children's experiences of sexual abuse, and which have enabled defense barristers to construct a dominant alternative narrative. Judges and other barristers easily recognize these narratives because of their dominant and stereotypical structure. The narratives work so well because they complement procedural law with its emphasis on weighting the evidence of sex-abuse complainants with warnings about their credibility.

Because of the degree of fit these narratives have, law has created a kind of designer-label cloak. Cut from the finest patriarchal cloth, and sewn together using the strongest legal dictums, the "one size fits all" cloak is created by the judiciary for the express use of defense barristers and judges in the legal storytelling they adopt in trials. This cloak envelops any person, usually female, who dares to allege sexual assault and rape against a male—especially where such allegations concern father-daughter rape. Sewn with the strongest misogynistic thread, this cloak is marked "in-credible witness"[62]—denoting the complete absence of credibility that is afforded such a witness even before she has spoken.

The cloak—trimmed with labels such as liar, slut, whore, addict, immoral, simpleton, lunatic, mad-girl/woman, bad-girl/woman, troublemaker—will be placed upon her by defense barristers who will portray her as the mad, bad daughter. The alleged victim of sexual crime(s) is constructed with contempt as epitomizing, in the extreme, all that is regarded as bad, mad, and inferior in the female. This construction relies heavily on disqualifying and fragmenting the victim's evidence through rulings so that a stock-story narrative can be mobilized.

In authoritatively deciding a child's reality, law commissions the construction and deployment of narratives about those who allege sexual violence by their parent or other adult. Moreover, narratives that have dominion over the less powerful, the oppressed, and the marginalized have a certain permanency since challenges to their reality are all the more difficult given the pervasive nature of legal doctrine. The "cloak" that shrouds the child victim in the court is difficult to shed since the authority that commissioned it is the same one that maintains it.

Trial as Theatre

Many trials promote the event as a form of theatre, with witnesses acting in a drama put on especially for the jury. Inviting jurors to view a trial as a form of theatre, to judge witness performance and give consideration to their body language, is quite common. Since law decided that the truth, however interesting, was irrelevant to the "justice" system, trials could be viewed as a form of theatre, a place where social actors told stories that could be assessed by a jury as they might assess the acting ability of those in a theatre performance. A critical reading of many trials revealed that judges were in the habit of emphasizing to juries that part of their role was to summate and appraise the visual images or performances of witnesses in the trial, especially the witnesses' body language and demeanor. Trials were very often situated as a dramatic performance. Take, for example, the following judicial comment to a jury in a case of child sexual abuse:

> Your assessment of the witness...is a matter of commonsense. You can now see why it is important to have the witness box over there opposite you. You are in the box seat, just as you might be at some theatrical performance or concert, always very nice to have the seat that enables you, not only to hear what they are saying, but to observe the way in which they are saying it. We call that the demeanor of the witness and it is obvious to all of us that you have concentrated on that task and have not only watched the witness giving evidence and taken account not only of what was said but the way in which the witness said it. You are asked to bear in mind the demeanor of the witness.[63]

This judge went on to tell the jury of the deceiving "demeanor of a clever" person who comes across as very "plausible," so the jurors must be "on guard" to detect such a suspect witness.[64] In another case of child sexual abuse, the trial judge provided some handy tips on things the jury ought to consider when deciding the case:

> You are entitled to take into account the *body language* of a witness. Some witnesses exude body language when cross-examined in particular, or when placed under pressure. Other witnesses are more confident and can cope. Those are the sort of matters which are entirely within your domain. You have to make judgement....There are other matters which you take into account. Is this particular witness *dramatizing* the event, or is this particular witness understating the event? [emphasis added][65]

On the one hand, jurors are instructed to make a decision based on the *evidence* presented to them while, on the other, being explicitly invited to subjectively assess witnesses as though they were actors in a performance and take account of body language. The thought of going to court often causes apprehension and nervousness in many people—especially a victim of a crime or one accused of committing a crime. Others may be quite confident, especially those who have frequently given evidence in a courtroom, perhaps as part of their occupation. Inviting a jury to assess body language and demeanor as a yardstick of witness credibility is fraught with problems.

Nevertheless, reference to trials as a form of entertainment or theatre is common. Examples include referring to the imminent start of an "incest" trial as "getting the show on the road," describing witnesses as "actors," telling the jury a trial is a "pantomime," and referring to legal counsel as possessing "theatrical license" to color their arguments.[66] One barrister complained the presence of a legal observer in the courtroom was unfair and disruptive because it "enter[ed] into the theatre of the trial,"[67] as if the person's presence was an ill-timed cameo appearance that removed some of the spotlight from the central actors in the narrative. A critical reading of trial transcripts shows a dialogue and commentary that makes the trial a forum of entertainment and dramaturgy. The extract below is from a trial involving allegations of long-term sexual abuse, and, from the moment the trial began until its closure, defense counsel displayed an obsessive and repugnant interest in portraying the trial as a comical piece of theatre. This is part of his opening address:

> Ladies and gentlemen, *congratulations.* You have got a really interesting trial. Many juries aren't nearly so lucky. Indeed, lawyers are born and lawyers die, without having trials like this. The allegations are of course *outrageous.* The defense is quite simple: [names victim] evidence is all lies....You can judge the demeanor of the witness...and you'd be asking yourself is she giving the appearance of a witness who is telling the truth or is she *laying it on with a trowel, feigning modesty, breaking into tears.* Is this natural or is [names victim] breaking into tears in order to get time to think, and then answer. No *pantomime* is complete without props, and here in this case we'll see a screen that will be placed next to the dock. What you are about to see is an *elaborate performance for her own self-interest, for this, money* [transcript records in brackets that defense demonstrates this point with hand gestures], *but not just money, not just money. It's never as simple as that. You'll see a performance, and it is an interesting one. So, sit back, relax and enjoy it.* [emphasis added][68]

Apparently blissfully happy to denigrate the evidence the complainant was yet to give, the judge seemed to get into the spirit of the trial as a form of theatre by the end of the first day's evidence. He suggested the defense barrister was "no doubt...looking forward" to tackling the complainant in cross-examination, adding that the barrister had a "very pleasant night ahead" as he planned his forthcoming cross-examination.[69] During the trial this same judge advised the barrister he could take advantage of evidentiary restrictions and the complainant's frequent distress, to portray her as presenting nothing more than a "theatrical and exaggerated performance" and an "academy award performance" before the jury.[70]

Motive and Means:
A Legal Narrative Construction in Sexual Offenses

While legal scholars and sociologists have focused more intently on law as a process of legal storytelling, my original research (upon which this book is based) examined the legal construction of intrafamilial rape complainants via dominant stock-story narratives developed and mobilized both within legal discourse and the courtroom. Extensive and closely detailed analyses of trial transcripts revealed dominant and recurring structural and thematic patterns in the defense case across trials. Indeed, as each case was documented, it was not unusual to find different defense barristers in different trials putting almost identical questions to complainants, as well as set patterns in the way a particular defense barrister approached trials involving intrafamilial sexual abuse. Likewise, it was not uncommon to find judges who had approached intrafamilial abuse cases in a certain way. Most importantly, judges often recognized the defense narratives being developed and were aware of how their evidentiary rulings allowed a particular narrative to be mobilized.

In my research I developed a model in which narrative patterns and themes were based on two main tiers: "motive" and "means." These two dominant structures in legal storytelling are each composed of sub-groups, and become articulated throughout the trial process and the wider legal discourse. Evidentiary rulings are crucial in the development of legal narratives since the obliteration, modification, or inclusion of certain evidence can advantage a particular narrative. Evidentiary rulings most often make the complainant's evidence amenable to an alternative legal construction; and since all legal parties must adhere to these evidentiary boundaries, the alternative storyline is legitimated through such a "game plan."

As part of the defense portrayal, motive establishes *why* complainants have made such allegations and, where applicable, the role of mothers who support their child/children's allegations. Means concerns the development of a narrative to provide alternative explanations as to *how* children and young adult complainants came to have knowledge with such explicit detail of the alleged sexual activities.

Narrative stratagems that focus on *why* and *how* enable defense lawyers to present a story that exhibits internal coherence and cohesion. The prosecution narrative has various pitfalls, not simply because of evidentiary constraints, but because of the added factor of not being able to suggest a "motive" to explain the behavior of the accused. In most other criminal trials, the prosecution at least attributes a motive for a murder, robbery, or bodily assault, but the rape and sexual assault of one's own children is devoid of a narrative of motive. Ironically, a motive is usually provided by the defense counsel if the accused is convicted and the motive most often conveniently locates external factors as the cause, especially marital discord.

The defense construction of motive to explain why the allegations were made is based on certain dominant themes: the child of the accused being "bad" or "mad"—and, in some cases, a mixture of both. In cross-examination of analyzed trials, motive was the first identifying feature. The "bad" narrative positioned the complainant as being motivated by some form of revenge against the father. In every case where a mother supported the allegations of her child/children, revenge was portrayed as an act of mother/child collusion. Thus, revenge was portrayed as either direct—that is, instigated solely by the child—or mediated by the mother, making it collusion. The other side of the "bad" daughter narrative was a motive of "greed." The complainant, and in some cases, their mother, was in need of money and fabricated false allegations in order to receive Crimes Compensation, which was then available under the Victorian State Government. The "mad" narrative positioned the complainant as being motivated to make false allegations against the father because of individual mental instability.

Crucial to a narrative of motive is a narrative of means to explain the "how" factor in explicit descriptions of sexual violence. An important element in developing stock-story narratives about complainants' alleged experiences of sexual violence is to design alternative narratives concerning the means by which complainants sought to create their "story" of sexual abuse. Like narratives of motive, the structural and thematic patterns in defense constructions of means were apparent throughout the trials. According to defense barristers, the means by which child and adult complainants could provide such convincing evidence of oral, vaginal, anal, and digital rape, and accompanying threats, were gained through contact with knowledgeable sources.

That many of the narrative tactics and stratagems based on "motive" and "means" were recognizable, even in embryonic form, to some trial judges indicates that these patterns of narrative construction are entrenched and well practiced within the courts. When the trial process is mapped and dissected, the pervasiveness of masculine hegemonies is clearly evident.

While cross-examination to establish motive and means was sometimes crude, and often harsh and offensive, the narrative was developed in a sophisticated, systematic way. The family tensions, broken relationships, and opposing camps that so often occur after disclosures of sexual abuse further enhance legal narratives. They often provide an excellent battleground for the defense to reveal family secrets, draw on historical bitterness between family members, and present evidence from family members unsupportive of the complainant of her real or alleged behaviors within the family unit for the purpose of discrediting her.

Much of the ammunition is obviously provided by the accused, given the sensitive information used against children and ex-wives. The accused was safe in the knowledge that his character could not be impugned with real or suggested past conduct, and two of the accused in the original study had prior convictions relating to sexual offenses. They, too, were safe knowing that such information could not be used at the trial.

Conclusion

Portraying intrafamilial rape complainants under the two rubrics of motive and means is common in legal narratives. It is vexing that, despite this reality, law occupies a strong ideological position as a place where the truth of a matter is tested to the limit, and that law is associated with "justice." One expects the courtroom to be a place where proper, honest, and full investigation is conducted. Those who maintain this view are probably in for a rough ride if they read any further. Those who believe that, to some degree, the law can be an "ass" but that, generally, judges are "impartial" agents in the quest for truth and fact-finding, may well raise eyebrows. For those who believe that law is really a site where stories are told and truths and facts regarded as inconvenient are excluded, or otherwise neutralized and modified to varying degrees, the following case studies may disturb, but not really surprise. In any case, most readers may well experience feelings of distress, anger, and even outrage as facts become casualties to the legal game of sophistry, where storytelling is embraced as an artform and legally sanctioned lying is a virtue of good forensic skill.

As the following case studies and chapters will demonstrate, evidentiary rulings provide enormous strength and power to legal narratives based on motive and means. Judicial discretion and attitudes toward sexual violence complement the development, maintenance, and mobilization of stock-story narratives within the courtroom.

The legal system operates to facilitate the development and deployment of legal narratives through examination and cross-examination of a witness.[71] A trial can be produced as a narrative because truth-defeating stratagems that involve the application of precedents, discretion, and the kind of bullying cross-examination common to these trials are not simply allowed, but encouraged and rewarded. Even jurors in a trial are managed in a way that removes them from the trial in progress, so that legal discussions can occur. In this way, the narrative can still be woven as a seamless garment, to be presented to the jury, while minor difficulties or inconsistencies in the preferred narrative are sorted out in private.

As the trials unfold in the next section of this book, the legal process is unmasked as a series of legally sanctioned maneuvers that enable the development and deployment of dominant stock-story narratives and stereotypes about women and children. Such narratives all lead to the blanket warning about the dangers in accepting the stories of women and children. This convoluted legal discourse is a product of the entire legal process, which maintains stock-story narratives and damaging stereotypes about sexual-abuse victims.

A reading of the trial transcripts bears out the centrality of storytelling and the sacrifice of fact-finding in the legal arena. The use of the language and metaphor of theatre aids the defense construction of coherent dominating stories of motive and means. Legal precedent, warnings, and evidentiary practices act to create a non-credible witness and a less-coherent experiential narrative for the complainant.

Metaphorically, legal process can be described as producing, in many cases, the palimpsest, where the words and evidence of the complainant are rubbed away—not completely, but enough to fragment and disjoint their evidence, enabling defense counsel to fill the gaps with stock-story narratives. In this way, law can be understood as a regime of "truths" (i.e., stock-story narratives) as opposed to the individual truths that reflect the experiential life-story of the complainant.

Notes

1. For example, films such as *A Civil Action* and *Philadelphia*, and US drama series such as "The Practice."
2. Cited in E. Whitton (1998), 10.
3. Naffine (1990); Graycar & Morgan (1990); Heath & Naffine (1994); MacKinnon (1989); Mossman (1986); Scutt (1990a); Scutt (1990b); Scutt (1994b); J. Scutt (1997); Seddon (1993); Smart (1995); and Edwards (1996).
4. This point is noted in the Victorian Law Reform Commission, Sexual Offenses Interim Report, June 2003, 188, at 5.42.
5. Whitton (1998).
6. Ibid.
7. Delgado (1989).
8. Scheppele (1989).
9. Ibid.
10. Geis (1978) and Geis (1986).
11. Ibid.
12. Weisberg (1996)
13. Ewick & Silbey (1995), 197.
14. Ibid., 211–5.
15. Ibid., 214.
16. Mertz (1994).
17. Whitton (1998). See especially chs. 1 and 16.
18. Ibid., 100.
19. Luban, quoted in Fife-Yeomans (1997), 4.
20. Whitton (1998), 101.
21. Silverii (2003).
22. Ibid.

23. Schmitz (1988) and Blanchfield (1996).
24. Whitton (1998), 25–7. As Whitton points out, most judges and lawyers are completely ignorant of the foundation and history of the development of our adversarial system.
25. Ibid., 26.
26. Ibid., 101.
27. Whitton's (1998) *The Cartel* provides abundant fascinating and disturbing anecdotes and evidence of the judicial mistrust of the system of justice they uphold.
28. Ibid., 125.
29. Waldron (1995), 27.
30. Heenan & McKelvie (1997), 355–9.
31. Ibid.
32. Neame & Heenan (2003), 1–15.
33. Henning (2000–2001)
34. Graycar (1996).
35. Ibid.
36. For a good comment about the maintenance of the corroboration warning and the mindset underpinning such a view, see Davies (1999) and Scutt (1994b), 139–60.
37. See, for example: Scutt (1990a); Scutt (1990b); Scutt (1990c); Scutt (1994a); and Scutt (1994b).
38. McBarnet, cited in Kaspiew (1995), 350–82.
39. For particular discussions around the concept of "legal method" see, for example: Scheppele (1989); Beaman-Hall (1996), 125–39; and Mossman (1986).
40. Scheppele (1989).
41. Kaspiew (1995).
42. Duncan (1994).
43. MacKinnon (1983).
44. For a fascinating account of the role of the media and literature in promoting rape narratives and their mobilization in rape trials, see Benedict (1992). See also Puren (1995). Puren's work provides an interesting insight into the policing of women's bodies by constructing rape narratives around the presence or absence of the vaginal hymen.
45. Scheppele (1989); Graycar (1996); and Kaspiew (1995).
46. Mitra (1987).
47. Ibid., 121.
48. Duncan (1994), 20–1.
49. Feiner (1997).
50. Geis (1986); Davies (1999); Scutt (1990a); Scutt (1994b); Scutt (1991); Jackson (1988); Graycar & Morgan (1990); Edwards (1981); and Edwards (1996).
51. Scutt (1994b); Geis (1978); Geis (1986); Jackson (1988); and Davies (1999).
52. Wigmore (1970). This work was first published in 1934 and drew heavily on Freudian psychoanalysis to support claims that allegations of rape and sexual assault by women and girls were dangerous given their propensity to lie. Wigmore provided advice on how to impeach the credibility of such witnesses.
53. Edwards (1996), 2.
54. Ibid.
55. Heenan (2001).
56. See, for example: Mawson (1999); Grix (1999), 93–4; and Davies (1999).
57. R v J (Victorian County Court, retrial, Campton, J. 1995), at 205 (31/8/95).

58. See Taylor (2001b), 211–28. See also Taylor (2001a).
59. Personal communication from a Crown Prosecutor, May 1997.
60. Mitra (1987).
61. Ibid., 133.
62. Scutt (1992). Scutt uses the term "the in-credible witness" to demonstrate the historical and patriarchal construction of women in legal discourse.
63. R v C (Victorian County Court, Spence, J. 1995), at 378.
64. Ibid.
65. R v L (Victorian County Court, retrial, Lewis, J. 1996), at 805.
66. See "Acting in Court Dramas," in Taylor (2001a)
67. R v J (Victorian County Court, retrial, Campton, J. 1995), at 485.
68. Ibid., 38–9.
69. Ibid., at 61. Note elsewhere in the trial transcript where the prosecutor made submissions objected to the facial grimaces which included laughing and other body language exhibited by the defense barrister and his instructing solicitor. See, for example, 256–8 and 322.
70. Ibid., 90 & 259.
71. Ewick & Silbey (1995), 209–11.

3 • Case Study R v EF

Background to the Case

THIS CASE INVOLVED allegations from two sisters of vaginal and anal penetration perpetrated against them by their biological father. At the time of the alleged offenses, the girls were age seven and ten, respectively. In accordance with legal precedent, the presentment was severed and two separate trials ordered so that the complaints would be heard separately. Neither child was able to give evidence in support of the other's allegations of similar sexual abuse. The family was from a non-English-speaking background and, although the two girls spoke fluent English, their parents did not. The family comprised two parents and five children, three female and two male. The eldest female child was fifteen at the time of the trial and her two younger siblings, who were the alleged victims in the case, were nine and twelve at the time of the trial. One of the brothers was a teenager and the other brother was very young, but neither was involved in giving any evidence. From a reading of the transcript, the eldest sibling appeared to be the strongest member of the family emotionally, and was protective and very supportive of her two younger sisters and her mother. She allegedly confronted her father about his alleged sexual abuse of her two younger sisters.

The mother had sought a traditional Muslim divorce from her husband prior to her children's disclosures, and at the committal hearing the defense counsel used this information to accuse the mother of concocting false allegations of child abuse to improve her chances of a divorce. This claim was strenuously denied by the mother. At the trial, this claim was less explicit in cross-examination but most likely made explicit in the closing address by the defense counsel. Corroboration of the children's allegations came via several sources. The mother and eldest sibling made a police statement detailing alleged admissions to them by the husband/father with regard to his sexual abuse of his two youngest daughters and his reasons for doing so. This claim was also corroborated by independent evidence alleging the same thing: that the accused made explicit admissions regarding his sexual abuse of his two young daughters, including his reasons for doing so.

After police were notified of the children's allegations, the husband was removed from the family home but continued to make unwanted and allegedly threatening contact with his wife and children. He was served with a court order preventing him from approaching or contacting his wife and children, and it was alleged that he breached this order a number of times and made threats to kill his wife and children. At the time of this trial, the accused was facing separate charges involving threats to kill his wife and children, which would be addressed at a later trial.

The accused was on an invalid pension, but no mention was ever made of his previous occupation, or the reason for his being on a pension. The mother worked at a bakery belonging to her cousin. Prior to the commencement of the trial, the defense counsel argued that the accused was not fit to stand trial because of his psychiatric ill health. Independent psychiatric assessments were conducted, and a jury empanelled expressly for the purpose of adjudicating on the psychiatric evidence found the accused fit to stand trial.

The first case heard related to the allegations of the twelve-year-old daughter. After deciding the evidentiary rulings, the judge in this case became ill, necessitating a new trial to begin with a new judge. A second judge was appointed making the evidentiary boundaries once again open to legal debate. This second judge presided over both cases and the same defense and prosecution counsel appeared in both cases, which no doubt provided continuity for all parties concerned, and allowed the judge to have a grasp of the legal arguments for both sides. This resulted in a more expedient trial involving the second child. Since the same judge, defense counsel, and prosecutor were involved in both trials, and since the evidentiary rulings, defense approach and narrative, and prosecution style were almost identical in both cases, I have decided to discuss the two trials under the one case study. For ease of reading and digestibility, the allegations of the two children are discussed separately but consecutively, and transcript excerpts from cross-examination in the two cases will be used to demonstrate similarities as well as differences in narrative structure and theme.

The Prosecution Evidence

Regarding the twelve-year-old child, the accused was charged with nine counts of "incest," including both vaginal and anal "intercourse" and one count of indecent assault, which the judge later directed the jury to acquit due to insufficient evidence. I shall refer to this girl and the trial as child/case E. The younger child, aged nine, gave evidence relating to two counts of "incest." I shall refer to her and the trial as child/case F.

Aside from the evidence of the complainants, the prosecution was relying on what they considered to be compelling evidence of alleged admissions by the accused to both his wife, his eldest daughter, and to a social worker in the presence of an interpreter. The prosecution case also involved evidence from a forensic medical practitioner who examined the children.

Evidentiary Rulings

Major evidentiary rulings discussed in this section relate almost entirely to the transcript involving case E, since this was the first trial heard and since the same rulings applied to case F which followed. Cases E and F were heard consecutively.

Four witnesses provided evidence alleging explicit admissions by the accused with regard to his sexual abuse of his two daughters. Defense counsel vehemently opposed any introduction of such evidence, beginning with the evidence of the social worker from the Child Protection Unit appointed to the children after the incidents were (was) reported. So let us begin with an appraisal of the social worker's evidence given in case E, and the legal response to that evidence.

After making several complaints to the social worker that her husband was continuing to breach a court order preventing him from attending the family home or contacting them in any way, the mother requested that the social worker speak with her husband to advise him that he was breaching the court order. In response to this request, the social worker arranged a meeting with the accused (to take place at her office), in order that she could explain to him that, in accordance with the court order, he must not continue to contact his family. The mother also reported to the police that her husband had threatened to kill her if she did not have the charges dropped and allow him back into the family home.

Since English was the second language of the accused, the social worker arranged for an interpreter to facilitate communication at the meeting. The interpreter failed to attend the meeting, so an interpreter from the Legal and Telephone Interpreting Service was provided as a communicator between both parties in a telephone link-up.

In a pre-trial *voir dire*[1] hearing, the social worker's evidence was that, during the course of the meeting in which she advised the accused that a court order against him meant that he could not contact his wife or children, the accused suddenly made voluntary admissions about having sexually abused his children. In her statement and in *voir dire* evidence, the social worker explained that the accused admitted to sexually abusing the two daughters who were alleging abuse against him. The social worker said that she clarified with the accused that he was now admitting that he had sexually abused his two daughters, to which the accused agreed. The social worker also said that the accused told her that he had wanted to stop his wife from working outside the home because it required her to work with other males. The accused allegedly told the social worker that he believed that his behavior toward his daughters would pressure his wife into leaving her job and remaining at home. He said he wanted to tell the social worker about the abuse so the matter could be over and done with.[2]

In her *voir dire* evidence, the social worker said that she had never sought to question the accused about the sexual allegations and that the accused had volunteered such information. She said she questioned him about his admissions only to clarify his admissions. The social worker checked with the telephone interpreter to verify that she was not misunderstanding in any way the admissions made by the accused, who spoke at times with a little English mixed with his own native language. Immediately after this conversation, the social worker contacted the police and made a formal statement. The professional interpreter also made a police statement that corroborated the evidence of the social worker.

The defense counsel subjected the social worker to lengthy cross-examination, most of which revolved around the mechanics of how she took down her notes and how the interpreter communicated between the two parties. Since it appears the accused interspersed his conversation with English and his native language during the meeting, the barrister was keen to highlight that the social worker only had the word of the interpreter regarding the alleged admission by the accused.[3] The interpreter was also subjected to strong *voir dire* cross-examination—the bulk of which related to whether she could specifically recall interpreting every detail of the conversation, which, by the time of this trial, had occurred more than six months previously.[4]

The barrister presented a two-pronged argument for the exclusion of the evidence of alleged admission by the accused. Firstly, he argued that the evidence of the social worker and interpreter was unreliable because it was not taped, and, therefore, a court should not be "forced to accept" such evidence because it was "grossly unfair" to the accused.[5] In the second strand of argument, the defense sought to invoke Section 464 of the *Crimes Act* (which relates specifically to investigating officers), after claiming that the social worker had acted as an investigating officer by questioning the accused about his alleged admission.[6] The first line of argument (that the conversation was not mechanically recorded, and was therefore unreliable) raises questions about the admissibility and reliability of *any* evidence that is not tape-recorded. The defense's argument that the way in which the evidence was obtained by the social worker was "unfair" to the accused is a familiar line trotted out by many barristers in sex-offense cases where credible evidence is considered damaging to their client. The argument that an admission that is not mechanically taped is not reliable as evidence is simply fallacious, since taped evidence of various kinds of admissions by accused in other sexual-offense proceedings were sometimes routinely removed from the police record-of-interview under the shibboleth of *fairness to the accused*—so evidence of an admission appears to be legally damned either way.[7]

The absurdity of the latter argument seems obvious. The *Crimes Act, Victoria 1958* applies very specific criteria to the evidence gathered by an investigating officer.[8] By arguing that the social worker's questioning of the accused placed her in the realm of an investigating officer, rather than that of an independent witness, the barrister hoped to have her evidence excluded. This argument was made despite the social worker's claims, reiterated by the prosecutor in counterargument, that any *questions* put to the accused were solely for the purpose of making abundantly clear that he was admitting to the sexual abuse of his two daughters for which he had been charged and was awaiting trial. With regard to the professional interpreter, the prosecutor argued that the job of an interpreter is simply to interpret what they hear and are told. As they are not personally involved in discussions, but are there on a professional basis to interpret what is said, it is not incumbent upon them to specifically recollect the context and detail of every word of every conversation that they have interpreted.[9]

Asserting his right to "exercise (his) discretion," the judge supported the defense's claim that the social worker had adopted an investigational role by asking questions of the accused about his alleged admission, and promptly excluded that evidence. In part, the judge stated that the social worker "began to question the accused in order to determine his involvement in the offenses rather than for the objects of the meeting itself."[10] The word "discretion" was thus invoked to exclude evidence of a very powerful nature that corroborated the evidence of the children. Rather than looking for evidence that supports "truth-seeking," the judiciary often creates evidentiary rulings and practices that are "truth-defeating."[11] The judge further believed that the interpreter's need to view the notes kept by the social worker to refresh their memory of the specific conversation, and the fact that they did not keep their own notes, diminished the prosecution's argument.[12] As the prosecutor emphasized, the interpreter translates many and varied conversations every day as part of his or her job and is not required to document the details of conversations—only to interpret them. There is no legal requirement for them to keep notes of conversations they have interpreted. Besides, if they had kept notes, they would probably be accused of acting as an investigator, and, therefore, having their evidence summarily dismissed.

Pushing the boundaries of common sense even further, the judge claimed the use of an interpreter made any admissions hearsay evidence, because the alleged admissions were relayed to the social worker. Let us follow this line of argument to its logical conclusion. Interpreters were used in case study R v EF for both the accused and his wife. Interpreters were also used in two other sexual-offense trials I researched, and have been used in a myriad of other trials, including murder trials. Applying the rationale underpinning the judge's claim (that an interpreter's evidence is only hearsay), should it not automatically follow that the entire evidence in the case he presided over was invalid because it was relayed to the court by interpreters? The ramifications of this reasoning would mean that any dialogue facilitated by language interpreters invalidates the speaker and reduces the credibility of his or her spoken word. If this is the case, only those fully conversant with the English language could give acceptable evidence in our Anglo-Saxon courts.

With the social worker's evidence safely out of the way, the barrister got to work on having the specific evidence of the eldest daughter removed from the case. Her evidence, that her father admitted to her in a phone conversation that he sexually abused her two younger sisters to force the mother to give up her employment and remain in the home, mirrored the alleged admission the accused made to the social worker. The barrister argued that the daughter's evidence was unreliable since the conversation could not be linked to a particular date, and that the admission was generalized since it could not be related to a specific charge or charges on the presentment. This line of argument was not successful as the judge ruled the eldest daughter's evidence admissible.[13] Soon after establishing these evidentiary boundaries, the judge was unable to continue with the case, leading to its adjournment so that a new judge could be appointed.

A new judge was appointed and a new jury empanelled; thus, the case began all over again. The new trial judge was informed by the prosecutor that he would not be seeking "another bite of the cherry" regarding the previous judge's ruling that excluded the evidence of the social worker, and the previous ruling was left to stand, delivering an easy win to the defense case. In contrast, the defense barrister wasted no time in re-ventilating the argument before the new judge to have the eldest sibling's evidence excluded. Perhaps fearing his former line of argument might again fail, he now had a new line of argument concerning the inadmissibility of the sibling's evidence. His new argument involved two tiers. The first strand of argument concerned specific terminology in the sibling's statement, especially her use of the word "touched" when describing what her father said he had done to her two younger sisters.[14] He argued at length that the word "touched" could mean many things not connected with sexual abuse. In seeking to rebut this reasoning, the prosecutor countered that, from the context of the conversation between the girl and her father, it was quite clear the word "touched" was understood by both parties to refer to sexual abuse of the two girls. However, the barrister's wordsmithing approach to the term "touched" garnered the support of the judge, who said the word "touched" was "ambiguous" in meaning and was certainly good grounds to reject the sibling's evidence.[15] The second tier of the new argument was that the entire statement of the sibling was legally out of bounds: since the trials had been severed, the sibling's statement contained "overwhelming prejudice" to the accused since it related to an alleged admission of sexual abuse of two children—not one. Thus, how could her evidence be admitted in a trial that covered only one child?

The prosecutor thought he could solve this by suggesting that the sibling could give the evidence about the admission without making it "plural," that is, without referring to the fact that more than one child was involved. In fact, the prosecutor went on to suggest that questions could be "framed" and "formulated" in such a way that the eldest sibling could give answers without stating that two sisters were involved. He also relied on case law precedents to argue that although the sibling's evidence did not relate to specific charged incidents, it did deal with a general admission by the accused.[16] The judge was not convinced. He remained concerned that the sibling's evidence was prejudicial because it "suggests that there may have been illicit conduct with a child other than this one."[17]

The prosecutor maintained his argument that there were ways of modifying her evidence so as not to arouse any "suspicion" in the jurors' minds that her evidence of her father's alleged admission involved more than one child. Such a view held no sway with the judge, who went on to accuse the prosecutor of trying to make admissible evidence that would, in effect, be "tying" the defense barrister's "hands behind his back."[18] This point seems somewhat jaundiced given the evidentiary rulings up to this point. The prosecutor was being asked to try a case in which compelling collateral evidence had been eroded and with further evidence now also being eroded.

Demonstrating some of the tenacious argumentation most often displayed by defense barristers in evidentiary hearings, the prosecutor maintained his argument, informing the judge that the sibling had been told explicitly that should she be able to give evidence of her father's admission to her, she was not to give any evidence—or any indication in her evidence—that there was more than one complainant. Perhaps in order to soften judicial resistance to his argument, he articulated a number of ways defense counsel could quite easily attack the credibility of the sibling's evidence of her father's alleged admission, so cries of foul play were not deserved. Equally staunch in his resistance, the judge remonstrated with the prosecutor, saying he was forcing the barrister to "play" by the prosecutor's rules and, furthermore, that the barrister had an "uninhibited right to conduct his case as he sees fit."[19] It seems this "uninhibited right" occludes the investigation of facts damaging to the accused and supports manufactured defense narratives. Rather than the barrister being forced to "play by the rules," it was clear that the prosecutor, as in most other cases, was being forced to organize his case around evidentiary boundaries that advantaged the defense case.

As with so many other documented cases of sexual abuse, information that disrupts or discredits a stock-story legal performance is simply obliterated from consideration. The truth—however crucial, however central—to establishing fact, is simply irrelevant. The prosecutor vainly fought to have the evidence of the sibling included, based on the legal promise that the child's evidence could be molded and stymied to ensure it was confined to an alleged admission about one child only and not children plural. This promise, though, was not enough to assuage the concerns of judge and defense barrister. The judge revised the first judge's ruling to now exclude the alleged admission by the accused to his eldest daughter. She could still give evidence, but it would be restricted to matters not connected with the alleged admission. As though to ensure her evidence was suitably constrained to the designed legal script, the judge informed legal counsel that he too would remind the sibling that her revised evidence must always be in reference to just one sister, not "sisters."[20] In his ruling, the judge also excluded the mother's evidence about the alleged admissions made by the accused.

With the preferred legal script in place, the trial was almost ready to commence. The issue of the prosecutor leading evidence from a sibling that related to *uncharged acts*[21] needed to be clarified for all parties concerned. Here the prosecutor was not so much relying on alleged incidents of sexual abuse, but rather the father's conduct toward one of the children, which was observed by the older sister. The judge allowed this evidence provided that it could be confined as evidence of propensity—that is, conduct by an accused said to be in keeping with his conduct toward the alleged victim.[22] As is frequently the case in legal discourse, this sexualized conduct was referred to as conduct that may indicate "guilty passion" or, as the judge described it, "lusting for a particular" child.[23] Either way, the linguistic frame again saturates child rape within a sensuous (albeit illicit) dialect.

Just when it seemed all was ready the prosecutor signaled his intention to call an additional forensic medical practitioner should defense counsel lead an argument that the inconclusive medical results from the examination of the genitalia of child E were indicative of no offense having taken place. Since trials are largely pre-scripted, and surprises in evidence not generally well received (especially when the surprise is against the defense case), another *voir dire* was arranged so that the defense barrister could be satisfied with what this other forensic expert was to say (should he be allowed to give evidence).[24] Preemptive action by the prosecutor on this point showed good insight. Defense barristers in child sexual-offense cases have a penchant for framing questions that limit forensic medical evidence while isolating and highlighting the proverbial phrase "inconclusive" findings, in order to later reinforce the defense storyline of false allegations.

In *voir dire* evidence, the senior forensic practitioner reported that she was present at the examination of one of the children but not the other. Her evidence in this case, case E, was given as an expert witness, one that could give opinion evidence concerning the medical examination results for the child she did not attend. In giving evidence, she explained why an absence, or inconclusive findings, of any clinical signs of vaginal or anal penetration neither confirm nor preclude the possibility of sexual abuse. She provided the various reasons why normal medical findings in an examination do not necessarily negate allegations of sexual abuse, and reminded the court that it was only in a very small proportion of cases that actual physical evidence of penetration is found. A central reason for this lack of physical evidence has to do with the natural elasticity of human tissue of this part of the anatomy and, also, the frequency of assaults. Another central factor was the covert nature of sexual crimes. As the forensic practitioner stated, such crimes are "designed to be carried out in [a] private, undetected" environment, and creating little obvious pain or discomfort is important for an offender in order to minimize the risk of exposure.[25] In addition, penetration of the female vagina may extend past the labia but not penetrate the hymen. This latter point is important since a good deal of masculinist arguments for rape not taking place are based on the assumption that an intact hymen is proof of false allegations.[26] Furthermore, the frequency of penetration contributed to the difficulty of finding physical evidence.[27]

Of more interest was her opinion that while physical evidence of sexual trauma is found only in a very small number of cases, one is less likely to find such evidence in cases involving parent/child sexual abuse. She reasoned that a child abused by her parent is more carefully *prepared* by the offender prior to the actual penetration, thereby reducing physical detection through an examination. In her opinion, significant physical change is more likely to show up in a case where the offender is a stranger to the child because the child is less well prepared for this kind of crime.[28]

In later *voir dire* cross-examination, the forensic practitioner told the court that long-term sexual offense usually involves delayed disclosure, whereas acute cases, especially involving a person not known to the child, often result in an almost immediate disclosure and hence, medical examination. These latter cases are often the types of scenarios where those small number of physical changes in the genitalia are found.[29]

As *voir dire* cross-examination of the forensic practitioner continued, the barrister maintained a focus on the technical aspects of penetration, suggesting that children may say they were penetrated when in fact "something less than penetration" occurred. In an excellent response, the witness explained that while penetration is codified in law, a child does not understand such a technical concept. A child, she said, has "no idea where the hymen stops and the vagina starts, or even where her labia exactly are. All the child knows is: 'Something went between my legs from the front,' or 'Something went between my legs from behind,' and to the child that is penetration."[30]

I would also suggest that many adolescents and even adult women would not be familiar with the anatomical placement of their hymen, or the extent to which their labia suddenly becomes their vagina, and so on. It might well be that, given the history of the legal fraternity vilifying women and child rape complainants, barristers and judges are the experts on the female vagina, hymen, and labia, since they have spent such a good deal of time procuring legal questions about penetration, depth of penetration, duration of penetration, and whether it was "real" penetration or not.

His technical bent about *real* vaginal penetration provoked, the barrister suggested that the reason so few children are presented with any detectable changes in their genitalia despite disclosures of sexual abuse was "because many, many of the others may have thought it had happened, but it hadn't?"[31]

The witness agreed that might be one explanation, but went on to explain the various forms of penetration that would not result in any anatomical change, and reiterated her point about the difficulties presented by adults' and children's differing conceptions of penetration. If significant anatomical change was not found, it was not uncommon, she said, that "we" begin to say that "children make it up, or children fantasize, or whatever."[32]

The "we" in this final comment is the adult world's mind-forged manacle of denial when it comes to accepting the words of children. The scientific admission that physical evidence of sexual penetration is not easily or necessarily found is often cited in court as evidence against the allegations of the child.

The judge hearing these two cases closed the court to the public and both children then gave their evidence to the court via Closed Circuit Television (CCTV).[33]

Evidence-in-Chief of Complainants

Prior to giving her evidence, child E was subjected to the usual legal formalities, which included informing her that she may be "exempt" from giving evidence against her father if she wished, on the grounds that it can be "damaging to the relationship" between child and father. While the child agreed to give evidence, she appeared at first confused by the rules of "exemption." Certainly the technical language of the court is frequently used against children, with little regard for their linguistic and conceptual development. When children are required to give legal evidence, they are first subjected by the judge to a competency assessment—the style and content of which is arbitrary but involves questions designed to ensure the child understands the nature of swearing an oath. In this case, the child was asked about the importance of telling the "truth," and the difference between telling the "truth" and telling "lies." The child was also asked about her religious beliefs and whether she attended religious services. After checking that the child understood sufficiently the seriousness of swearing an oath on the Koran, the judge considered the child to be competent to give sworn evidence before a jury.[34]

The first alleged incident occurred on Easter Saturday, 1993, when the child was ten years old. Her mother was at work and her father called her to the parents' bedroom, where the blinds had been drawn and the father locked the door behind her. She stated that her father removed her trousers and panties before proceeding to penetrate her:

CHILD E: He moved over and then he put his penis into my vagina and anus.

PROSECUTOR: How long was his penis in your vagina for?

CHILD E: I'm not sure.

PROSECUTOR: Was it a long time or a short time?

CHILD E: A short time.

PROSECUTOR: *Do you know how far in his penis went into your vagina?*

CHILD E: No.

PROSECUTOR: *Did you want him to do that?*

CHILD E: No.

PROSECUTOR: How did you feel when he was doing that to you?

CHILD E: I don't know. I didn't—I didn't know what he was doing then.

PROSECUTOR: Well, after he put his penis in your vagina, did he do anything else to you?

CHILD E: Oh, and then he put his penis into my anus.

PROSECUTOR: How did he do that; where was your body and where was his body?

CHILD E: He was sitting, like—he was over here and I was over here, and then he turned; he came over onto my side where I was sleeping.

PROSECUTOR: At the time this happened, were you on something or were you standing up; what was the situation?

CHILD E: I was on the mattress.

PROSECUTOR: Was the mattress on the floor or was it on the base or something?

CHILD E: It was on the bed.

PROSECUTOR: So after he had put his penis in your vagina, what did he do?

CHILD E: Oh, he came on to my side, onto the side of the mattress, and then he put his penis into my anus.

PROSECUTOR: How did it feel when he did that?

CHILD E: It hurt a bit.

PROSECUTOR: And again, are you able to say how long he had his penis in your anus for or not?

CHILD E: It was a very short time.

PROSECUTOR: What happened then; after that?

CHILD E: Oh, and then—I don't know. Then I put my undies and pants back on and he left. And he told me not to say anything to my mum. [emphasis added][35]

Note the legal obsession with how deeply penetrated the child was. The focus on technical details of penetration reveals not just the masculinist understanding of rape, but how easily sexual violence is reduced to a focus on technical, anatomical details that are almost impossible to give and, therefore, provide enormous latitude for discrediting, humiliating, and destroying the evidence of children in sexual-offense proceedings. Asking complainants whether they "wanted" the sexual abuse inflicted upon them is another question consistently put to child and adult complainants alike as prosecutors must prove "non-consent." This stock question is deeply flawed and reveals the internal contradictions in law around "incest." Although "incest" laws claim that consent is not a defense to the crime, lawyers and judges frequently argue that "incest" can never be regarded as "rape" on the basis of the culpability of the two parties and the consent that may be involved.[36]

The next incident is alleged to have occurred near the birthday of one of the child's siblings and involved her father coming to her bedroom during the night and taking her to the toilet. After going to the toilet, the child said her father took her to a spare room nearby where there was a towel laid out on the floor and two handkerchiefs nearby. There he instructed her to lie down and upon doing so he removed her pajama bottoms as well as his own shorts and then proceeded to "put his penis into my vagina…and moved it up and down."[37] After this, she alleges he made her roll over and he penetrated her anus. She thinks it was in the very early hours of the morning, just after her mother had left for work at the bakery. Again, the prosecutor asked her how far inside her vagina her father's penis went in and, again, the child had no idea how far she was penetrated. Afterwards she was told to wipe herself with the handkerchief and, when asked if she noticed anything after she wiped herself, she said that there were "yellow marks" on the handkerchief.[38]

Child E shared her bedroom with her two female siblings, whom she described as heavy sleepers. The child also had two male siblings who slept in another bedroom and then, her parents who shared the master bedroom of the house. In her evidence she alleged the third incident occurred close to Easter the following year, and involved her father coming to her room at night, waking her up and removing her pajama bottoms and again penetrating her vagina and anus. Her evidence was that her two sisters were in the room asleep at the time, and the bedroom light remained off during this incident. Again, she believes her mother had not long left for work when her father entered her bedroom. When asked if she yelled out to her sisters to wake up while this was occurring, the child said she did not and when the prosecutor asked her why she did not, the child said she did not know why.[39] On the assumption that defense questions will no doubt focus on the child's lack of immediate outcry—as is par for the course in these types of trials—the prosecutor's questions are designed to give the child an opportunity to explain, if possible, their lack of immediate outcry or disclosure. As I have stated elsewhere, while a plethora of literature identifies delayed disclosure as a kind of fear response from the child, especially in situations of parental abuse, the preferred legal parlance is to highlight the apparent failure of the child to make a hue and cry, and then denounce her publicly for it. In his *Child Sexual Abuse Accommodation Syndrome*, Roland Summit notes that defense barristers continually attack child complainants for a failure to protest immediately (despite research countering such a belief), revealing the entrenchment of this stock-story narrative, played out in front of juries.[40]

Next, the child recounted an incident alleged to have occurred a few months later, which, again, took place in the parents' bedroom while the mother was at work and all the siblings of the child had left for school. She was waiting to be collected by the person who took her to school, and she alleges that her father then told her to come into the house where he forced her onto the parents' bed and began to kiss her. In the final charged incident, the girl gave evidence that she was home from school on this particular day because she was not well. Her mother was in bed asleep, having come home from her work at the bakery. The child recalled that there were people in the front yard of their house working on something, but she cannot recall who they were. Her father took her to a two-room building outside of the house, located in the backyard, which was used as a sewing room and storeroom. She stated that her father removed her lower clothing and made her lean against a chair while he stood behind her and put his penis into her vagina and anus. When asked by the prosecutor how she felt, the child replied:

CHILD E: When—when he did that, it hurt and I was upset

PROSECUTOR: When he did what, what thing hurt you?

CHILD E: When he put his penis into my anus.

PROSECUTOR: You say that you were upset?

CHILD E: Yes.

PROSECUTOR: On that day, did he do anything else to you?

CHILD E: Yes. Then I went back inside, and then he saw my mum was still sleeping, so we went to the—there's a sewing room, the one near the tool room, and—and then the clothes that I was wearing when I was in the other room, I put them in the wash. And then I went and put a dress on. And then, we went to the sewing room…and my dad took—I was wearing a top and then—it's a dress, but I'm wearing a top over it, because there's a button broken on it. And I wore—he took the top off, and then, there was a pin on the button that was broken; he undid the pin and he moved my top over to the side. And then he started kissing me on my breast and sucking my breast.

PROSECUTOR: How long did that go on for?

CHILD E: About twenty minutes.

PROSECUTOR: How did you feel when he was doing that to your breasts?

CHILD E: It hurt.[41]

The child went on to recount the approximate time of day these things are alleged to have happened, and what kind of work the people in the front yard were doing. The evidence then quickly moved to the girl identifying two photographs taken of her breast area, which show severe bruising that the child states was caused by her father "sucking" her breast. The child said the photographs were taken approximately two days after the incident. The defense counsel objected to the photos being shown to the jury on the basis that the child could not provide the exact date they were taken, only that they

Case Study R v EF 57

were taken after what her father allegedly did to her. The judge allowed the photos to be tendered to the court and presented to the jury as prosecution exhibits.[42]

Regarding the last incident that led to the bruising on her breast, she was asked by the prosecutor if she told anyone about this. The child said she told some of her girlfriends at school about what her father was doing to her, and then told her mother. The child said that she had disclosed the sexual abuse to her mother prior to this, and her mother took her to a medical practitioner but nothing more was done about it. After the incident involving vaginal and anal penetration and the bruising on her breast, the girl told her teacher and the school principal, and they contacted the police.[43]

The child also recounted how, on one occasion, when her father had locked her in his bedroom and was sexually abusing her, her older sister knocked on the door and asked her father where child E was. The father told her that she had gone to the local shop.[44] In finishing her evidence-in-chief, the child was asked to view and describe in great detail a number of photographs taken of the various rooms in the family home, including the front and rear yard.[45] This is standard procedure as it supports the prosecution case about the physical environment described by the child where the alleged incidents occurred, while defense barristers routinely use the same evidence to challenge the child's evidence and extract minute details about the size, shape, or décor of the room(s).

Just before commencing a lunch break during the child's evidence-in-chief, the judge had cause to speak to the defense barrister about what the judge described as the "gratuitous comments" made on a number of occasions by the accused from the dock, and directed toward the judge, prior to the jury entering the courtroom. The comments appeared to indicate that the judge in some way approved of the actions of the accused, and the judge wanted to make it very clear that this was far from the case, and that if the accused continued to make such gratuitous comments, the judge would not hesitate to reprove his conduct in the presence of the jury.[46] The defense counsel assured the judge that he would make this clear to the accused. Since the conduct did not occur again, it seems appropriate to infer that the accused understood this request. If so, it challenges somewhat the defense claim that the accused was not mentally competent to stand trial.

For ease of readership, I shall move on to the evidence-in-chief of child F, before discussing the cross-examination of both children, and then the remaining evidence from other witnesses. To reiterate my earlier point, the trials were held separately, but consecutively, with the same judge, prosecutor, and defense counsel presiding in both. A similar defense narrative and style was mobilized in both cases, albeit in more detail in the case E, since there were far more allegations and witnesses in the case, and their evidence was largely the same across both trials.

Child E was nine years old at the time of the trial and gave evidence of two counts of "incest," relating to one incident, which occurred when she was seven years old. In her statement and committal evidence, she alleged a good deal more of sexual abuse by her father, which included other alleged incidents of oral, vaginal, and anal penetration. The prosecution sought to lead some of this evidence to establish propensity of conduct by the accused. While the defense barrister strongly opposed the introduction of uncharged acts to show propensity on behalf of the accused, the judge viewed otherwise. The judge felt that, in his discretion, such evidence was important to remove the artificial context of the girl's evidence of one single isolated incident, and stated that he would be careful to advise the jury as to the limitations of using evidence of uncharged acts in their deliberations.[47] The judge felt this was the only fair way to conduct the trial, and his view did recognize the importance of contextualizing the child's evidence. Still, the judge excluded evidence that was even more powerful and corroborated by several witnesses. Here I am referring to the evidence presented by the social worker, the wife of the accused, and the eldest daughter relating to alleged admissions by the accused.

The two counts of "incest" refer to an incident that allegedly occurred on a day when the girl stayed home from school because she was not well. Her father, she alleges, took her to the parents' bedroom and, after removing her lower clothing, "he put his penis in my vagina and bum," she stated.[48] While courts expect children to adhere to a technical application of language, clearly they are unable to deal with a child's attempts to explain human anatomy. Thus, to ensure that "bum" meant "anus," the prosecutor patiently led the child's evidence toward the kind of technical details that satisfy courts:

PROSECUTOR: When you say "bum," can you tell us a bit more about that? Whereabouts do you say he put his penis exactly?

CHILD F: Well, he put it in my bum and vagina.

PROSECUTOR: Do you know the cheeks of your bum, when you sit down?

CHILD F: Yes.

PROSECUTOR: Where did he put his penis in relation to the cheeks of your bum?

CHILD F: I don't know what you call it, that hole thing, I don't know what to call...

PROSECUTOR: You know when you go to the toilet?

CHILD F: Yes.

PROSECUTOR: In relation to your bum, you're talking about, as you call it, the hole thing; is that right? The hole?

CHILD F: Yes.

PROSECUTOR: Did he put it into that?

CHILD F: Yes.[49]

The child said that it "hurt" when her father put his penis in her "vagina" and "bum" and said that she told him to "stop" but he would not and told her that she would "get used to it."[50] Moving on to introduce limited evidence of uncharged acts, the child was asked about other incidents of sexual abuse, and told the court that she was "often" abused in similar ways to that described in the charged incidents. She said her father sometimes came to her room to wake her prior to assaulting her, and would kiss her face or stomach to wake her. She recalled that on one occasion her two sisters awoke to find their father kissing her stomach, and the two sisters later told her mother and then she herself told her mother, also. When asked about not disclosing the abuse immediately to her mother, the child said that her father told her that if she told her mother she would be hit; and so, fearing this physical punishment, she did not disclose her abuse until her older sister intervened.[51]

When asked about any other things the father had allegedly done to her, the child said she had been made to "suck [her father's] dick." The prosecutor proceeded to ascertain whether the child consented, or enjoyed it, or why she even allowed such a thing to happen:

PROSECUTOR: You say he made you suck his dick?

CHILD F: Yes.

PROSECUTOR: What's another work for a "dick"?

CHILD F: Penis.

PROSECUTOR: Did you want to do that? Did you like doing that?

CHILD F: No.

PROSECUTOR: Why did you suck his penis?

CHILD F: Well, he just told me to.[52]

The third question by the prosecutor is really two entirely different questions rolled into one, but this point aside, the last question about why the child even sucked on her father's penis seems gratuitous to me. While the child may not have viewed it as gratuitous, there are plenty of examples in a number of trials of children and adult complainants being asked why they took part in an act of obvious sexual violation of themselves. The question assumes the victim has a degree of autonomy and agency that she ought to have used to avoid being sexually victimized. With young children, the authority figure of the parent is often enough to counter any resistance and, as the abuse becomes ongoing and chronic, other mechanisms have long been established to ensure the compliance by a child or adolescent, such as the kinds of emotional bludgeoning discussed elsewhere in this book.

Note also that the prosecutor wanted the child to adopt an alternative phrase for describing her father's genitals. Legal counsel is often obliged to use the sometimes-explicit vernacular used by young children when giving evidence. Perhaps the prosecutor's own discomfort with using the term "dick" when clarifying the evidence of the child led him to have the child adopt the term "penis," thereby enabling him to phrase his next question with what he may well consider to be a more sanitized phrase. I noted, in the committal proceedings, that the defense barrister, who was not the same one who then proceeded with both trials of R v EF, also got one of the children during cross-examination to adopt a more sanitized description of anal rape. In this instance, child E was asked about her father putting his penis to her "back passage" and a reading of the transcript suggests the child did not know what this meant, as she gave no reply when asked if she knew what the term meant. She was told that it meant her "anus area," and, from then on, defense counsel at the committal proceedings referred to the alleged abuse as penetration of her "back passage."[53]

It may well be that legal counsel on both sides adopted this method to deal with their own discomfort, or it might be (either deliberately or unconsciously) an attempt to somehow sanitize such confronting and explicit allegations by a child. This aside, there is the added dilemma about the strong penchant for defense barristers to focus on a child's description of anatomical details. On occasion, children are accused of using sophisticated language, which leads to accusations of false allegations and of adult coaching in terminology. But as examples in this case reveal, at a subtle level, children's vernacular is often replaced with sanitizing phrases, which may well leave them open later to accusations of coaching and/or falsity of allegations because of the language they use.

To complete her evidence-in-chief, child F was asked about the mother taking her and her siblings from the family home. The child gave evidence that at first the children were all separated from each other before being reunited a few days later with their mother at a women's refuge. Since then, the family has moved back into the family home; however, the father continues to live apart from them.

Cross-examination of the Complainants

As stated earlier, the defense barrister showed a keen interest in the *voir dire* evidence of the forensic medical practitioner, especially around technical questions on penetration. When cross-examining child F, he highlighted the fact that she was unable to say just how "far" her father's penis allegedly penetrated her; and, further, that since she never actually saw how her father supposedly penetrated her—because of the physical position of her body in relation to his—then she could not even be sure that her father even did any such thing to her.

The child protested this logic by saying that her father told her he had put his penis in her "vagina" and "bum," but this was not enough to counter the barrister's argument. After all, he asserted, "just because he said so [that he penetrated her] doesn't mean that he did, does it?" The child agreed.[54] This closely follows the argument he made against the forensic medical practitioner. Not surprisingly, a similar type of question (but not as explicit in the logic) was put to child E—that is, that she could not be sure that her father actually put his penis in her "vagina" or "anus."[55]

Both children faced technical questions regarding penetration and the physical layout of the home environment where the incidents were alleged to have occurred. These questions were far more detailed and lengthy for child E, given the number of charges and the fact that she gave evidence of telling several school friends, a teacher, and the school principal. Questions became more complex and prolix as child E was asked to recount exact details of what she told her friends, what they were alleged to have said to her, and who was present when that was said to the teacher, and so on. The obvious intention was to confuse the child, but a reading of the transcript suggests that, far from confusing her, such questions seemed to strengthen her evidence, as she remained confident in who and what she told. At one stage she told the court that one of her friends had been sexually abused so she knew all about what child E was talking about! In other trials, the defense counsel uses the child's knowledge of—or contact with—other children who have been allegedly sexually abused to infer false allegations made by the child.[56] Such a narrative link was not highlighted in cross-examination, and it is not known if it was used in the closing address since such addresses are not transcribed; however, the defense barrister did highlight the counseling the child received, which, he suggested, enabled the child to make false allegations:

DEFENSE: You have seen a counselor, have you not?

CHILD E: Yeah.

DEFENSE: That counselor, that is someone you speak to talk about all these things you say happened to you?

CHILD E: Yeah.

DEFENSE: How many times have you seen that counselor?

CHILD E: I don't know.

DEFENSE: You were talking about these things that had happened to you. When you see them, do you have to tell them each time what had happened to you?

CHILD E: No.

DEFENSE: When they talk to you about it, they try and talk you through it to see whether you have got any problems from it, do they not?

CHILD E: Yeah.

DEFENSE: Each time you see the counselor, they say, well, how are you getting on [names child], after all these terrible things have happened?

CHILD E: Yeah.

DEFENSE: Each time you do that, you have got to remember what had happened, do you not, because they jog your memory?

CHILD E: Yeah.

DEFENSE: Remember earlier, when you spoke to my learned friend here [prosecutor], you talked about the sexual abuse that your father had committed on you, do you remember that?

CHILD E: Yeah.

DEFENSE: *Sexual abuse, those words, they are something you have learned from those counselors, is it not?*

CHILD E: Yeah.

DEFENSE: Because that is the way they talk, and when they say to you, well, sexual abuse means all these different things...It can mean something like a penis into your vagina or your anus, it can mean touching your breasts, it can mean kissing, sometimes, can it not?

CHILD E: Yes.

DEFENSE: You have had to speak to social workers as well? They wanted to know what you had to say about this too, didn't they?

CHILD E: Yes.

DEFENSE: It's true, isn't it, every time you told someone about what you say happened here, they said "well, this is sexual abuse, isn't' it"?

CHILD E: Yes.

DEFENSE: So what's happened over a long period of time here is that...you believe that what has happened here, actually happened? Because it didn't actually happen?

CHILD E: It did happen.

DEFENSE: What I put to you [names child], is that because you have had to speak to all these people so many times, that you believe it's happened when it didn't?

CHILD E: It did. [emphasis added][57]

Reminiscent of my earlier point about the language of sexual abuse used by children, the barrister in this example clearly infers a form of coaching in which the child has not only adopted a false belief but also the language with which to support this *belief.* While he did not go into the same detail or depth, the barrister broached a similar theme with child F as that above.[58] Furthermore, the barrister focused on the language used by child F in her police statement. He highlighted that she used the words "arse" and "bum," and that she thought "arse" meant "vagina." He highlighted that she was now aware that "vagina" was the "proper" word to describe that part of her anatomy and immediately linked this information with her access to social workers and sexual-assault counselors.[59]

In both cases the defense barrister canvassed evidence from the children relating to marital disharmony between their parents.[60] Child F was cross-examined about arguments between her parents, how they "did not get along well," and how the father was not happy with the mother's working arrangements. Possibly building on the theme of collusion, the barrister highlighted the fact that the child's oldest sister had been in trouble at school and did not like the father.[61] These hearsay assertions are presented to a young child, and her innocent adoption of them allows them to become fuel for the defense narrative of revenge and parent/children collusion. Also, a sympathetic profile of the father began to emerge through cross-examination of child F regarding the father's heart condition, an accident some years previously, and his inability to work.[62]

While judges and barristers are particularly mindful and ever on alert for "hearsay" evidence and "speculation," it seems that the defense's asking children to speculate or agree to questioning about the supposed quality of their parents' marital relationship are par for the course; and the younger the child, the more complex the questions.

A particular focus in defense cross-examination of child E was the degree of physical "hurt" felt as a result of the alleged multiple incidents of penetration. In a series of questions, she was asked if the second incident of alleged anal penetration hurt just as much as the first incident, and whether the second incident of vaginal penetration hurt as much as the first incident. Each time, the child said the "hurt" was "the same" as the time before. What was the barrister expecting: a total recall of the degrees of pain felt by a nine-

or ten-year-old child regarding past incidents of rape? Questions of measuring and comparing pains—as if by using a slide-rule indicator of pain—continued. The barrister wanted to know if child E felt "a little bit" of hurt, "or a lot of hurt?" Did it hurt "like having a cut finger, small cut on the finger with a knife...or more than a cut on the finger?"[63] A short time later, the barrister again revisited the concept of physical hurt, this time asking the child if it hurt as much "as if you had hit your finger with a hammer or something like that?"[64] Just exactly how this absurd and pedantic line of questioning advanced the defense narrative remains unknown; but, in later cross-examination of the forensic medical practitioner, the barrister was keen to know whether children reported much pain when being vaginally or anally penetrated. Neither prosecutor nor judge objected to these questions to the child. A child's language abilities depend on various things, including developmental stages, and it is not surprising that many young children do not have the language skills to articulate concepts such as pain, other than by saying it "hurt" a bit, a lot, etc. In a legal setting the child is pushed to give greater accounts of her "hurt," and again, this reflects a masculinist focus. Asking a child to assess her hurt at being anally and vaginally raped in comparison to a finger being cut or bashed with a hammer reveals the inappropriate focus on specious accuracy as opposed to the content of the child's evidence about the actual incident.

Technical questions about her exact state of undress prior to and during alleged anal and vagina rape were also put to the child: Were her "undies" down around her knees or her ankles? Were other items of clothing completely or partially off, and exactly who took them off—her or her father? Were her clothes fully or partially removed across different incidents?[65] Demands for details like this are frequently made of child and adult complainants, and a failure to recall, or the slightest discrepancy in recollection, is lauded as proof of fabrication and lying.

Recall the prosecutor's examination-in-chief of child E, when he asked briefly about her delay in disclosing the alleged abuse, which included her not calling out to her nearby sleeping siblings during an alleged incident of sexual abuse in the child's bedroom. I noted that this was an attempt to allow the child to give some explanation for her behavior, which—while a common feature of child abuse—is promoted in masculinist narratives as negating the reality of the child's allegations. In cross-examination, these masculinist assumptions about delayed disclosure and failure to cry out for help during rape and sexual assault consistently come to the fore. Right on cue, the barrister trotted out the well-worn series of questions about delayed disclosure (after all, she admitted she had a good relationship with her mother, so there is no good reason for not telling her straight away). He stressed the failure by the child to "scream for help" (after all, her siblings were so close); and, of course, the fact that she did not like what was allegedly done to her (so why did she not take affirmative action and demand her father stop it?):

> DEFENSE: ...of course, you could have yelled out to your sisters, because they were right next to you, couldn't you?
>
> CHILD E: Yes.
>
> DEFENSE: You could have called out for them...because they were in the room. You could have stopped it right then?
>
> CHILD E: Yes.
>
> DEFENSE: And you could have yelled loudly enough for [older sister] to wake up...but you didn't try?
>
> CHILD E: No.
>
> [A short time later in cross-examination on a different incident but the same theme:]
>
> DEFENSE: Your mum was sound asleep in the house, yet you did not cry out at all then, did you?
>
> CHILD E: No.
>
> DEFENSE: Did not make a sound at all, and afterwards, after it had happened...you knew this sort of thing should not go on, did you not?
>
> CHILD E: Yeah.
>
> DEFENSE: But you did not go and see your mum straight after this happened?
>
> CHILD E: No, I went back and finished my work, my homework.[66]

The child did disclose to her mother and was taken by her to see the family medical practitioner, where her mother spoke in private to the practitioner. The practitioner examined the child and apparently told the child "nothing was wrong" with her, and no further action was taken.[67] Since no evidence was given or called from this practitioner, it is speculation to consider the implications of this evidence. However, it is possible that having been told "nothing was wrong" the child was wary of repeating her disclosure to her mother. This suggestion is amplified somewhat by the fact that her next disclosures were to a teacher. Note, in this above excerpt, the focus is clearly on a failure of the child to stop the father, and reinforced with the point that the child *knew* that such conduct was wrong, but still failed to stop it or to make prompt complaint. Emphasizing that child and adult complainants knew it was wrong for their father to abuse them as such, yet *allowed* it to happen, and further suggesting they had played a passive role in engaging in sexual activity with their father or stepfather, are frequent self-serving lines of cross-examination found in such trials. Publicly reminding a child or adult complainant that the rape or sexual assault of their bodies was wrong, with its implicit suggestion that a *real* victim would never have allowed such conduct without yelling and screaming for help or making immediate disclosure, is a favorite defense tactic—one that some barristers (through trial observation and through my reading of transcripts) appear to take great pleasure in canvassing.

The cross-examination of child F was intense but quite short, as opposed to the cross-examination of child E. Like many other cases, the latter faced a good deal of cross-examination around minute details regarding the layout of rooms where she was allegedly abused; the exact timeframe in which things occurred; exactly what side of the bed was she on and which direction was she facing when she was being anally raped by her father; how far down her legs did her father remove her underwear—to her knees or her ankles; and so on.[68] Invariably, both children were subjected to cross-examination based on previous evidence they had given at the committal hearing and selected pieces from their police statement (which the jury are not allowed to read), in order to assess answers to questions demanding recollection of minute and pedantic details. Like token offerings to be presented to the jury as representing entire truth, these "prior inconsistent statements" were collated, as they are in other trials, as exhibits for the jury to ponder over when they deliberated. As though building a crescendo on prior inconsistent statements for his finale, the defense counsel finished his cross-examination of child E by highlighting inconsistencies around minute details.

No reexamination by the prosecutor of child F occurred, but the prosecutor did re-examine child E, especially on the issue of her seeing a counselor, and to clarify a comment made in her statement which the defense barrister suggested may not have been in her statement. Not unexpectedly, the barrister, as happens in many other trials when the prosecutor attempts to highlight a point the defense successfully obscured in cross-examination, objected to the clarification of a comment that was actually in the child's statement, but his objection was dismissed by the judge.

Recall that the defense barrister suggested that the child's access to counseling was the cause of her adopting a story that she had been vaginally and anally penetrated by her father. In reexamination, the prosecutor sought to clarify an important piece of information regarding the timeframe of the child's access to a counselor. Immediately the barrister was on his feet objecting to the revisiting of this evidence. The child and jury were asked to leave the court while this legal debate was settled. The prosecutor informed the judge that it was important that he address the suggestion by the barrister that the child's access to counseling with a social worker had led to her adopting a narrative of sexual abuse. The prosecutor noted the child only had access to counseling some three months after making her police statement about the allegations. One might consider this a reasonable request under the circumstances. Not so, according to the defense barrister. He vehemently opposed any such clarification, suggesting that to do so was unfair to the accused. The judge rejected this point, saying that the barrister was clearly "suggest[ing] concoction," and on that basis ruled that that the prosecutor was entitled to clarify the sequence of events regarding the child's police statement and her seeing a counselor.[69]

From a reading of the transcript it is obvious the judge was cognizant, implicitly, of how the defense barrister's obscuring of the sequence of events would be used to promote a narrative, in a closing address, of fabrication. Realizing that an important element in his narrative was being thwarted, the barrister continued to oppose the prosecutor's clarifying the sequence of police statement and later access to counseling; however, the judge remained steadfast in his resolve. In fact, as the debate heated up, the judge cautioned the barrister with the advice "you will be wise enough to bear in mind that I speak last to the jury and I say that advisedly."[70]

This settled, the prosecutor continued with his reexamination of child E, and clarified with her that she made her police statement prior to having any access to counseling, thus hopefully rebutting the defense's suggestion of recent invention. While the judge's intervention clearly disrupted an element of the defense's narrative of concoction, the exclusion of compelling evidence from other prosecution witnesses still served to advantage the promotion of a defense narrative of false allegations.

When cross-examining child F, the defense barrister regurgitated (albeit with more caution following his judicial rapping over the knuckles) a similar theme: that access to a counselor contributed to child F making her allegations against her father.[71] Judicial intervention on this point was not taken lightly, though, and the friction it created culminated in a submission by the defense barrister the following day, to have the trial aborted on the grounds the judge had evinced bias against the defense.

The barrister further claimed the judge had intervened in his cross-examination of child E on several occasions, interrupting the "flow" of cross-examination and possibly giving the jury the impression that the barrister was being unfair in his cross-examination.[72] The judge rejected both grounds stating that the decision to allow the prosecution to reaffirm the child's access to counselor post her police statement was for clarification, and his intervention in defense cross-examination was done to ensure the child fairly understood certain questions being asked of her; an example of one of those questions in which the judge intervened being the following:

DEFENSE: Do you remember being asked—this is at page eighty-nine of the committal depositions, Your Honor—at the top of the page, you were asked, "You told that person on Tuesday 26 April, your father had taken you into the back garden, where there are a couple of rooms; do you remember saying that to that person?" And do you remember answering, "Yes" to that?

CHILD E: To what?

JUDGE: Mr. [barrister], I think it might be fair if you identify the person to whom this question refers...[73]

This clarified, the judge promptly dismissed the barrister's application to discharge the jury and begin a fresh trial.[74] It is interesting though that the judge's rightful intervention to ensure the child understood complex questions put to her by defense counsel culminated in the barrister crying foul and demanding a new trial. In many trials I have observed and examined children have clearly been confused by questions, sometimes being unable to respond verbally, yet there was no intervention by the judge or prosecutor. In this particular case, the judge was alert to ensure some degree of fairness to the child by ensuring she understood sophisticated and complex questions and statements put to her. Defense counsel's reaction suggests that notions of *fairness* is not a concept that ought to be extended to children.

The above question is relatively short compared with some of the long and complex questions put to children, especially where long slabs of previous evidence are read to them (examples of which are given in other case studies in this book such as R v D and R v G). Case study R v EF provides a good example of a judge ensuring that child witnesses understood questions put to them. This was seldom the case for children in other cases, as will be highlighted elsewhere in the book. From an analysis of transcripts it was clear that some child witnesses did not understand questions put to them and that on occasion they were confused by questions and terminology. On occasions children indicated they did not understand a question yet no one intervened on their behalf; on other occasions they gave no response or a response indicating confusion; and on other occasions it is clear that children agreed to long and convoluted statements without comprehending their meaning. On occasion, adult complainants and witnesses also expressed confusion or requested clarification of a question and sometimes this was ignored.

Before finishing the reexamination, the prosecutor asked child E about being penetrated by her father, asking her if "for instance, did you feel proud about it?" (vaginal and anal penetration). While the question was asked to elicit evidence from the child about her feelings toward the abuse, it is framed insensitively. The defense counsel objected to the way the question was delivered, though did not express why it concerned him.

My feeling is that his concern was less to do with its insensitive nature and more with the prosecutor's attempt to highlight the gross actions of the accused. The prosecutor rephrased the question, asking the child instead of her "feel[ings]" about father "putting his penis into your anus and so on," leading her to respond she felt both "angry" and "scared." She was scared of her mother finding out and did not know how to tell this kind of "stuff" to her sisters.[75]

Prosecution Witnesses

THE SIBLING

The eldest sister gave evidence-in-chief in both trials. At the time of the trial she was approximately fifteen years old. Her evidence was subjected to much modification: her evidence of alleged admissions by her father in a telephone conversation was excluded, and she was required to ensure that her evidence remained singular and never indicated alleged abuse of both of her younger sisters. Regarding case E, her evidence concerned the bruises she saw on the breast of child E, and the eldest sister identified a police forensic medical photo of her sister's bruised breast as the same incident. She also noted the time she went looking for child E and found that the child had been locked in her parents' bedroom with her father, who had earlier told the eldest sister that he had no idea of the whereabouts of the child.[76] This evidence corroborated the evidence of child E.

The sister's evidence in case F was much shorter and consisted only of her observation of her father coming into their bedroom (where all three girls slept), kneeling at the bed of child F and lifting her pajama top before kissing her stomach. When the eldest sister asked the father what he was doing, he told her he was trying to wake the child to take her to the toilet, before telling her to go back to sleep.[77] This evidence did not relate to any specific charge but was admitted as part of the context of the prosecution case or, as the judge said earlier, to indicate "guilty passion" or "lusting" for the child. Certainly this evidence supported child F's evidence that sometimes her father would come into the bedroom that she shared with her sisters and kiss her in all different places, including the stomach, to wake her up on the pretext of taking her to the toilet.

Cross-examination of the eldest sister in both cases was brief, centering in part on questions designed to suggest collusion: she was asked about her dislike for her father, of marital disharmony between her parents, and her positive support for her mother and sisters. In case F these questions built up toward the narrative of collusion and revenge, as they attempted to defuse any sexual connotation around the sister's observation of her father's behavior toward her youngest sister in the bedroom, and stressed the issue of parental discord:

> DEFENSE: ...the reality is that when you saw that [father kissing child F's stomach] you put a really bad connotation on it; do you know what I mean by that?
>
> SISTER: No.
>
> DEFENSE: Assumed the worst.
>
> SISTER: What's he doing kissing her on the stomach anyway?
>
> DEFENSE: You thought it was bad?
>
> SISTER: Yeah it is bad.
>
> DEFENSE: It may have been innocent?
>
> SISTER: No.
>
> DEFENSE: But that's what you thought isn't it?
>
> SISTER: That's what I know; he shouldn't be kissing her on the stomach.
>
> DEFENSE: You don't think that's got anything to do with the fact that you don't get on with your father?
>
> SISTER: No.
>
> DEFENSE: Or that he doesn't get on with your mother?
>
> SISTER: No.[78]

Now, a reader might take the line that defense barristers have every right to try to suggest ulterior motives to evidence, since that is what a good adversary does. And, after all, the legal system is adversarial and promotes good stories rather than factual ones. But the fact remains that scenarios of children seeking revenge, concoction, and mother/child collusion work not just because they are a dominant storyline in child sexual-abuse narratives, but because our legal system is complicit in their development and deployment. Imagine if the evidence of the social worker had been admitted, as well as the evidence of this sister and her mother with regard to alleged admissions in a telephone conversation: how difficult would it be to maintain a stock-story narrative of vengeful and colluding children and their mothers?

THE FORENSIC MEDICAL OFFICER

The forensic medical practitioner who examined both children gave evidence in both the cases. The forensic examiner's evidence was brief. With regard to child E, he found no evidence of bruising on her breast; however, it was pointed out that he examined the child nine days after the photo of the bruising was taken, and he held that it is not unusual for a bruise to disappear in that time. He confirmed that the medical examination did not reveal any physical evidence of penetration, with the child's genitalia and anus being "normal" in appearance. Asked by the prosecutor if such findings confirmed or denied the allegations, the practitioner stated that an absence of physical findings does not exclude the possibility of sexual abuse since it is possible that no physical signs are detected after sexual abuse. His evidence in case F was almost identical: the child's genitalia and anus appeared normal. Cross-examination in both cases was brief. The defense counsel highlighted, in case E, the fact that there was no sign of injury or penetration of the respective children. In case F, defense counsel suggested in cross-examination that if a child had been anally or vaginally penetrated only nine days before an examination it is possible that evidence of such penetration would have been found. The examiner agreed that it may be possible, but reiterated that it would depend on the degree of penetration, how the penetration occurred, and the healing capacity of the particular child's body.[79]

In case E, the forensic medical practitioner (considered an "expert" witness, who gave *voir dire* evidence) was called by the prosecution basically to establish an expert opinion that a lack of physical evidence in a child's genitalia or anus does not necessarily negate allegations of sexual abuse. Her evidence was in keeping with that she gave in the *voir dire*.[80]

THE MOTHER

The mother of the two girls was called to give evidence only in case E, and in accordance with legal rulings confined her evidence only to the allegations concerning child E. Like her children, the mother was given the option of being excused from giving evidence against her husband since she was his wife and by giving evidence it was likely that she may "damage" her "relationship" with him.[81] In order to give her evidence, the mother required the assistance of an interpreter, who was duly appointed and sworn as an interpreter. In evidence-in-chief, the mother confirmed the prosecutor's statement that her daughter, child E, had complained to her that her father had "done" things to her. When asked if she remembered the time she approached her husband about her daughter's complaint, the mother indicated that she had spoken to her husband on more than one occasion about disclosures from her daughter. Asked about any physical marks on her daughter, the mother recounted the bruising she saw on her daughter's breast around the nipple area, and said that when she confronted her husband about this he said, "Don't believe her; she's lying." He later told the mother, "I am testing her to see whether she let anyone touch (her) or not."[82] She said that two days after this conversation she took her children and left the family home. The mother also confirmed that one of her husband's relatives came to perform some work in the front yard of their house. This evidence supported child E's allegation about the final incident of penetration and having her breast "sucked" by her father. Finally, the mother was asked about any other occasion that she confronted her husband about her daughter's disclosures, and she responded that her husband admitted sexually abusing the child because:

> MOTHER: He said, "I am frightening you, because I want you to leave work."
>
> PROSECUTOR: Did he say why he wanted you to leave work?
>
> MOTHER: No.[83]

At the committal proceedings, the mother had stated that her husband had admitted abusing the two girls in order to "scare" her into "staying at home."[84] This evidence directly supported the excluded evidence of the social worker (who stated that the accused admitted to her that he had sexually abused both of his daughters in order to scare his wife so she would leave her job and stay at home) as well as the excluded evidence of the oldest daughter. In the absence of the jury, the judge expressed concern that this final piece of evidence came "perilously close" to the evidence which he had excluded, that is, the evidence of the husband's alleged admissions in two phone calls. The judge was concerned with the loose phrasing of the question that led to this evidence being given, but noted the defense barrister did not object—probably, the judge thought, because he realized the "delicateness" of the situation and how his objection might be interpreted by the jury. The prosecutor conceded this point but added that the excluded evidence related to alleged admissions after the family had separated, whereas the mother's evidence related to things the husband had said to her prior to her leaving him.

As though fearful that the mother's evidence may well be the undoing of the prosecution case, the prosecutor informed the judge that he and his instructing solicitor made it "clear" prior to the mother entering the witness box that she must not talk about the conversations with her husband after their separation. The tension around this piece of evidence was further relieved when the prosecutor was able to identify the passage in the mother's police statement that *prior* to leaving her husband, he had allegedly told her that he had sexually assaulted his daughters to scare her into leaving work and remaining in the family home. It is ironic that the truth in this instance saved the day—not because it was heard in front of the jury, but precisely because it showed that what was hidden from the jury, had not been breached![85]

Cross-examination of the mother began with an appraisal of the mother-daughter relationship being a positive one, and that child E was a "frank" child able to express herself—a description the mother agreed with. The obvious purpose of these questions was to present an independent, confident child that one would not expect to delay disclosure.

Immediately following these questions, the barrister highlighted part of the mother's own evidence that when she confronted her husband on one occasion he told her not to believe child E because she was lying.[86] The mother became hesitant to adopt this specific piece of evidence she gave at the committal proceedings; perhaps because it was isolated and fragmented from context, she was unsure of adopting it as a stand-alone statement. Her hesitancy prompted the barrister to remind the mother that the committal hearing was only ten months ago, as though her reluctance were a case of deliberate amnesia rather than a possible difficulty with affirming an isolated comment, devoid of context and meaning. Her reluctance to adopt the statement led her to try to provide content to her statement:

> DEFENSE: Are you saying that, really, you don't have a very god [sic] recollection of what your husband said at all?
>
> MOTHER: I remember very well that he said, "I'm testing my daughter, to see if anybody touches her—how she'd react if somebody touches her," and I remember very well that he said, "I am frightening you so that you leave work." That's all I remember.
>
> DEFENSE: Are you saying all this happened at the same time now?
>
> MOTHER: There were always arguments at home about this matter.
>
> DEFENSE: There were always arguments at home, but it's true, is it not, that your husband always denied doing anything with your daughter?
>
> MOTHER: No, he did not deny this. He said, "I did it."[87]

This exchange brought out evidence by the mother that certainly damaged her husband's plea of "not guilty" to all charges (and was, no doubt, exactly the kind of information the barrister did not want); and so, in response, he read aloud lengthy excerpts from the mother's evidence at the committal hearing in which she repeatedly agreed that her husband denied the allegations. An admission by the mother that she herself found it "impossible" to believe that a father could do such a thing to his own daughter was read aloud, as though such a comment was a self-evident statement of fact.[88] Many women whose husbands have raped and abused their own children would certainly want to believe that men are not capable of doing such a thing, but wishing it were not so does not equate with negating such a reality.

In all the excitement of regurgitating aloud a seemingly endless number of questions and answers from the mother's evidence at the committal proceedings, the barrister almost fell on his own sword when he began to read an excerpt that related alleged abuse of children *plural* and not child *singular*. Fortunately for him, he performed a rather brilliant verbal hand-brake stop midway through the evidence in question to substitute the word "a daughter" instead of daughters.[89] I am sure the jury was none the wiser.

It was also put to the mother that her daughter was a "happy" child at home who had no problems with her schooling, and had a normal appetite and no problems sleeping. The mother responded that she could not comment on whether her daughter slept well because she did not see her in her room at night. She added that her daughter often seemed "sad" and often wanted to be by herself at home, away from her siblings.

To rebut her evidence, the barrister again drew on excerpts of the mother's evidence at the committal proceedings in which the mother had agreed with defense assertion that the child was "cooperative" and "happy" at home.[90] The mother's own evidence was used against her to show a supposedly happy and cooperative child.

The concept of social desirability, especially with regards to the management and presentation of our social self, is something we learn to cultivate and project both consciously and unconsciously, and tends to be something we consciously manage. Through socialization we come to learn that society strongly expects that we present a reasonably manicured and controlled image of ourselves. It is also culturally ingrained in us that our private problems should be kept relatively private.

A mother may well want to believe, consciously or unconsciously, that she has helped to provide an environment that is happy and secure for her children. As canvassed in other areas of this book, abused and neglected children can, and do, consciously and unconsciously try to create a sense of stability or outward "normalcy" to family members and others. This does not mean that others do not observe a sense of sadness, distress, or social problems with a child, but whether we act on these observations, or immediately assume child abuse, is another thing. Certainly, abuse can lead to a sense of distress and emotional pain that begins to fracture the everyday demeanor and social well-being of the child; and not detecting this condition (perhaps because a child hides it easily) can enable a discourse of children as liars and fantasizers. It can also lead to a discourse of minimal harm as a result of the abuse, as adults impose their own biased or ignorant interpretations on the child or young adult.

As cross-examination of the mother drew to a close, it was revealed that on the day police became involved following child E's disclosure to her teacher and school principal, she and her mother (and possibly the other child) were taken to the police station at 5:30 p.m. and remained there, being questioned, until 2:30 a.m. the next morning.[91] Similarly, in case study R v G the teenage complainant was detained and questioned by police for more than ten hours; and, in case study EF, children as young as seven and ten endured in excess of eight hours straight of police intervention. It is somewhat disturbing that children are subjected to such lengthy police involvement in circumstances that would be distressing and confusing for children.

In reexamination, the prosecutor indicated, in the absence of the jury, his desire to clarify with the mother that in her police statement she had mentioned one particular alleged admission made by her husband *prior* to the family separating. It was not a dissimilar vein to his earlier argument concerning the sequence of events in which child E accessed a counselor *after* making a police statement.

Here, the prosecutor sought to clarify the mother's evidence to rebut the defense's assertion that she was concocting her evidence in the witness box. The defense counsel did not embrace this idea, and neither did the judge. The defense counsel trotted out the argument that he did not so much suggest recent invention as show that the alleged admission by the accused did not relate to the timeframe indicated by the mother.[92] This is an extremely technical point, but then the truth—no matter how crucial to fact-finding—is simply irrelevant in an adversarial legal system. And, so, no such reexamination was allowed and the mother's evidence was thus finished. No reason could be found for not calling the mother in case F, but since the child in that case did not disclose directly to her mother first, it is possible that her evidence would not advance the prosecution or defense case and so she was not called to give evidence.

The final evidence led by the prosecution was the police record-of-interview, which was edited prior to the jury hearing it. The accused exercised his legal right to give no evidence, and no evidence was called on his behalf. The legal counsel gave their closing addresses to the jury, of which no transcript was available, nor was the judge's charge to the jury available on transcript.

Trial Outcome

The jury in the first case returned a verdict of guilty on all of the remaining seven counts. The jury in the second trial returned a verdict of guilt on both charges. Child E faced 384 prosecution questions, 402 defense questions, and thirty-eight questions from the judge—totaling 824. Child F faced ninety-eight prosecution questions and sixty-two defense questions—totaling 160. The accused gave no evidence in either trial, therefore facing no questions.

Sentence Plea and Sentence

Sentencing plea and sentencing for both trials were combined with the defense barrister submitting psychiatric reports stating that while the offender was not suffering any identifiable mental illness, he was considered unfit to provide legal instructions for his sentencing plea. Thus, the barrister argued, the offender should be committed to a psychiatric hospital rather than prison. Although expert witnesses retained by the defense could not agree on a diagnosis, two reports suggested that the offender could have been "faking" his condition to avoid the consequences of his actions. One of the expert witnesses told the court that sex offenders, in particular, were apt to go into extreme denial to avoid acknowledging their offense.[93] This does not surprise, given that denial of the reality of child sexual abuse is given so much expert support (in theory and praxis), and finds its way into contemporary trials.[94]

The prosecution's reply to the defense claims was that the offender be classified and sentenced under the category of a "serious sex offender" because of what he described as the aggravated nature of some of the charges, including the biting and bruising of the nipple area of one of the children, of which photographic evidence was submitted.[95] The barrister countered that the incidents were not serious enough to meet the requirements of a serious sex offender. This barrister's stance is reminiscent of an example in a British study of father-daughter rape appeal outcomes by the sociologist Charlotte Mitra. In the example, a defense barrister had explained a father's biting of his young daughter's nipple in the course of sexually abusing her as a case of "misplaced ardour."[96]

The judge accepted mental illness as a mitigating factor for the offender, but rejected the idea that such illness played a role in causing the offenses. He further acknowledged the need to denounce the conduct of the offender by imposing a just punishment, and saying the crimes were "serious" and "disturbing" since each act involved penetration of either the vagina or anus of the two young girls. Factors of mitigation favoring the accused included his current health problems, his age, and an absence of prior convictions, and that the offender was to be considered a "person of previous good character."[97] As the offender never indicated any remorse for his criminal conduct against his two daughters and the impact it has had on the rest of the family, the positive character judgment seems irrelevant.

Victim Impact Statements[98] were tendered to the court by the children and their mother; and, while no specific mention about them was made at sentencing, the judge commented that he found their statements "reasonable and credible."[99] One wonders what the judiciary regards as "reasonable" with regard to individual trauma caused by father-daughter rape. On a positive note, the statements were not wholly rejected or dissected, leading to portions being legally accepted and the rest dismissed, as occurred in a number of other trials; case study R v L is one such example.

In sentencing the offender, the judge classified him as a serious sex offender and sentenced him to nine years in jail, with six years to be served before he could be eligible for parole. He was yet to face trial regarding threats to kill his wife after she reported her children's disclosures to police.

Appeal and Outcome

Despite the claim that he was so mentally incapacitated he could not give instructions to his barrister at the sentencing plea, the offender was somehow able to instruct the barrister to lodge an appeal against sentence on his behalf.

At the time of the appeal, the offender was still awaiting trial on a charge of threatening to kill his wife and daughters—a point known and articulated by the Court of Appeal. The legal counsel for the offender argued the judge's sentence was "manifestly excessive," even though if we divide the sentence up, the man received less than twelve months jail on each conviction of "incest," which carries a maximum sentence of twenty years for each offense.[100]

While the Court of Appeal acknowledged the offenses were "odious" and "destructive to the family structure and *potentially* damaging" to the child victims, they considered the sentence "unreasonably excessive for a man of the [offender's] health, age, and previous good character [emphasis added]."[101] His sentence was reduced to seven years with a non-parole period of five years. Once again the arbitrary claim of "good character" is recited like a verse whose meaning is never examined or scrutinized but simply articulated as one of the standard exculpatory homilies used to diminish sexual offending. Taking the analysis a bit closer, the claim that the offenses are *potentially* damaging to the child victims promotes a personal legal opinion rather than the evidence provided by the actual victims.

The Court of Appeal also suggested that the "community" had to be protected from such offenses. There was no mention of the protection of the children from a predatory father. By contrast, the judges were concerned that such abuse is destructive to the concept of "family," and the welfare of the "community" is noted as the principal purpose of sentencing. The harm to the children becomes invisible as the concepts of "family" and "community" become paramount to the principles of sentencing. There was no claim that such offending can be *potentially* harmful to a community or family, as was said of the suffering of the children—the judges were obviously quite certain of the degree of damage such offenses cause the family and community.

With regards to the actual sentence imposed on the offender by the trial judge, his brethren judges on the Court of Appeal believed he had "erred" in sentencing the offender because he had failed to give due weight to a mitigating factor they considered positive for the offender. What was this other mysterious mitigating factor not taken into account? The Court of Appeal argued that since the offender's wife had "taken the children away from the sphere of *influence* of the [offender]," it negated the prosecution's argument that the offender was likely to re-offend; hence, he was not a serious offender [emphasis added].[102]

The term "influence" carries with it connotations of a degree of complicity by the children. It is as though the offender was able to "influence" his children in partaking in their own vaginal and anal rapes. Again, the terminology is, at the very least, ambiguous but certainly the language is proactive and invokes mutuality. Any concept of violence, coercion, or paternal violation of a most heinous kind is missing from this sentencing appeal decision, and certainly was missing from most appeal decisions examined in this research.

But probably the most crucial point to be made is that the mother's revulsion at her husband's brutal sexual abuse of her children, and fear of her husband as a result of his threats to kill them, led to a situation in which the mother moved to a secret location. Effectively, she and her children were in hiding. The mother had made the decision to remove herself and her children from the community and friends they knew in an attempt to ensure their safety and security and, no doubt, sought to provide an opportunity for her children to heal. Yet these actions are considered a factor that goes directly to the credit of the offender!

Almost identical logic was applied at the sentencing of another case from my original research. In that case, the complainant had no contact with her father, and this was used to justify a mitigated view of non-re-offending of the father since the daughter had severed all ties with him.[103] In case study R v EF, the forced lifestyle-upheaval foisted on the children and their mother actually served his interests at sentencing.

This court and others are in effect saying that because the offender destroys his relationship with his wife and children (often forcing them to make drastic lifestyle changes), a more favorable view of the offender should be taken, since he will not have the opportunity to repeat the same crimes.[104]

Comment

Mother-children collusion formed an undercurrent of the defense narrative. Marital discord was highlighted through cross-examination of the children, while the mother was constructed via these questions to her children. Even the eldest sibling was constructed, via questions to her younger siblings, as a girl in conflict with her father, therefore heightening a narrative of mother-children collusion. It is my contention that the mother may well have been perceived by the jury as someone with strong credibility on the basis that, in this particular case, the stereotypes of Muslim women worked in favor of the mother. By that, I mean that a jury may have been more convinced by a mother from a cultural and religious background strongly identified with traditional patriarchy and conservatism giving evidence against a husband, which would no doubt be viewed as a very serious matter in her culture.

In this case, the narrative of *motive* was an inferred collusion between a mother and her children on the basis of marital discord, and the narrative of *means* was that the children's access to counseling provided them with linguistic and knowledge skills to fabricate their allegations. Notably, the evidence given by forensic medical experts in front of the jury was more detailed than that given in some other cases studied, one of which will be discussed in this book. The prosecutor was alert to rebut any defense claims that may seek to extract evidence, suggesting that a lack of clear evidence somehow weakened claims of penetration. The forensic witnesses appeared confident in the delivery of their evidence, as they were clear, succinct, and devoid of hesitation when answering questions. In this case, despite the evidentiary rulings, the stock-story narrative was not able to convince the jury.

Notes

1. See Glossary for an explanation of this legal procedure.
2. R v E (Victorian County Court, Wodak, J. 1995), at 14–5.
3. Ibid., at 15–28.
4. Ibid., at 35–48.
5. Ibid., at 7–8.
6. Ibid., at 4.
7. In almost every case from my original research, the police-taped record of interview with the accused was edited at the trial to remove responses considered prejudicial to the accused, prior to the jury hearing the tape played in court. For example, in R v K (Victorian County Court, Lewis, J. 1994) an admission by the accused about an incident of sexualized behavior toward his young son was removed from the record of

interview. In R v J (Victorian County Court, retrial, Campton, J. 1995) a taped conversation between the accused and a police inspector that revealed highly damaging evidence against the accused was excluded after defense counsel successfully argued that the law protected his client from having his own admissions used against him at trial (R v J, retrial, 1995, at 198). In another case not covered in my original research, a teenage girl who alleged repeated sexual abuse by her stepfather taped him coming to her bedroom and sexually abusing her. In pre-trial arguments the defense counsel in that case cried foul, accusing the girl of "entrapment," that is, that she deliberately planted a hidden tape for the purpose of getting evidence against her stepfather. (Information about this particular case was provided confidentially by the police informant involved.)

8. Information taken from the Victoria Police Criminal Legislation 2002 (Butterworths: New South Wales). Section 464 is very extensive and very technical and makes clear that any person acting as an "investigating officer" has specific obligations to meet with regard to interviewing a person suspected of criminal conduct.
9. R v E, first trial, at 55–8.
10. R v E, first trial, ruling, at 76.
11. Young (1992), 17. Young discusses the propensity of legal practice and process as one which does not allow for "truth seeking" but instead allows for a practice of "truth-defeating" through laws of evidence.
12. R v E, ruling, at 76.
13. Ibid., at 77–8.
14. R v E, new trial, at 175–203.
15. Ibid., revised ruling, at 229.
16. Ibid., at 204.
17. Ibid., at 206–7.
18. Ibid., at 206–8.
19. Ibid., at 206–9.
20. Ibid., at 210.
21. See Glossary for an explanation of this legal procedure.
22. See Glossary for fuller explanation of this term.
23. R v E, at 241.
24. Ibid., at 246.
25. Ibid., at 261.
26. For a good discussion around this, see Puren (1995).
27. R v E, at 261.
28. Ibid., at 261–2.
29. Ibid., at 272.
30. Ibid., at 275–6.
31. Ibid., at 276.
32. Ibid., at 276–7.
33. See Glossary for an explanation of this legal procedure.
34. R v E, at 300–1.
35. Ibid., at 308–9.
36. See the chapter on literature around intrafamilial abuse for further comment.
37. R v E, at 311.
38. Ibid., at 312.
39. Ibid., at 312–3.

40. Summit (1983).
41. R v E, at 315–6.
42. Ibid., at 317–20.
43. Ibid., at 328–9.
44. Ibid.
45. Ibid., at 330–7.
46. Ibid., at 324.
47. R v F (Victorian County Court, Wodak, J. 1995), judge's ruling, at 50–9.
48. Ibid., at 60.
49. Ibid., at 61.
50. Ibid., at 62.
51. Ibid., at 62–4.
52. Ibid., at 64.
53. R v E, at 368–9. This is the trial transcript and the defense counsel draw questions put to child F by the barrister at the committal proceedings, for the purpose of tendering prior inconsistent statements.
54. R v F, at 73–4.
55. R v E, at 346.
56. Examples of this from my research alone can be found in cases R v A (Victorian County Court, Davey, J. 1995); R v G (Victorian County Court, O'Shea, J. 1996); R v J; R v K; R v L (Victorian County Court, Kelly, J. 1993); R v N (Victorian County Court, Stott, J. 1995).
57. R v E, at 361–2.
58. R v F, at 72–3.
59. Ibid.
60. R v E, at 365–7; R v F, at 71–2.
61. R v F, at 71–2.
62. Ibid., at 70–1.
63. R v E, at 339–40.
64. Ibid., at 344.
65. Ibid., at 347–9.
66. Ibid., at 348–9.
67. Ibid., at 346.
68. Ibid., at 338–47.
69. Ibid., at 377.
70. Ibid.
71. R v F, at 23–4.
72. R v E, ruling, at 439–43.
73. R v E, at 355–6.
74. Ibid., ruling, at 439–43.
75. Ibid., at 383–4.
76. Ibid., at 448–50.
77. R v F, at 78–80.
78. Ibid., at 81–2.
79. R v E, at 496–500; R v F, at 82–4.
80. R v E, at 501–5.
81. Ibid., at 457.
82. Ibid., at 459.

83. Ibid., at 460.
84. Ibid., at 464. This comment is taken from the trial transcript where there was a discussion about the mother's previous evidence in the absence of the jury.
85. R v E, at 466–7.
86. Ibid., at 476–9.
87. Ibid., at 479.
88. Ibid., at 480–2.
89. Ibid., at 480.
90. Ibid., at 486–7.
91. Ibid., at 488.
92. Ibid., at 488–91.
93. R v E and R v F (R v EF), combined sentence plea, at 5–30.
94. A similar line was run in R v J. At trial, the defense case was a complete denial of all charges, which was very handy as much of the corroborating evidence was excluded. With the exclusion of what the appeal court later described as extremely damaging evidence against the offender, at the trial level the defense barrister conducted the case along the narrative of a "good" father in control of all his faculties as opposed to a daughter constructed as both "bad" and "mad," motivated by greed, revenge, and mental instability. However, when convicted, the defense narrative underwent a back flip as the barrister argued that the offender was mentally unstable around the times of the majority of offenses, which greatly mitigated the culpability and seriousness of the offenses. R v J (retrial, 1995), sentencing plea.
95. R v EF, combined sentencing transcript, at 62–6.
96. Mitra (1987).
97. R v EF, combined sentencing transcript, at 110–4.
98. See Glossary for an explanation of this legislation.
99. R v EF, at 103.
100. R v EF, appeal judgment, at 2–9.
101. Ibid., at 9–12.
102. Ibid., at 10.
103. The case in question is R v M (Victorian County Court, Dixon, J. 1995) and is discussed in detail in my Ph.D. thesis.
104. Lifestyle changes include the victim/survivor legally changing their name for safety, and other reasons. There are several examples of this in the trials I examined for the original research. It also includes moving to a new suburb or town and even a new state. It has also involved victim/survivors and supporting mothers changing schools and even leaving their employment as a consequence of the offender's crimes.

4 ▪ Case Study R v G

The Allegations and Complainant Background

THE COMPLAINANT, a teenage girl, made an allegation of rape and sexual assault against her biological father. At the time of the alleged offenses, the girl had just turned fifteen years old and had been estranged from her father since her parents divorced when she was an infant. She had lived with her mother and stepfather over various periods of time, as well as living with various foster parents and in special youth accommodations. Approximately eight months prior to the allegations, the girl established contact with her biological father and began to see him on a fairly regular basis. The father was re-married, lived in Victoria, and was a self-employed truck driver. The girl lived in another state and had traveled to Victoria to visit her father, and he had traveled interstate to visit her.

In her police statement, the girl alleges that her father invited her to go on an interstate truck-drive and she agreed since she was hoping to reestablish a bond with him. She alleges she was indecently assaulted in the cabin of the truck while traveling between states, and was raped at a motel room the following night. She claims that after her father briefly penetrated her in the motel room she fled to the motel's main office to seek help.

In a police statement, the manager of the hotel confirmed that the girl came to his office in a distressed and disheveled state and told him that her father had just sexually abused her. Another worker at the motel made a statement supporting the evidence as detailed by the hotel manager. They immediately contacted police who attended the motel and proceeded to investigate the girl's allegations. The girl was taken to a specialist clinic to undergo a medical forensic examination in which semen samples were taken from the girl and from the bed sheets at the motel where the incident is alleged to have occurred. Following this examination, she was required to complete a police statement, which she did not finish until just after 6:30 a.m. the following morning. This means that following the alleged incident, the girl was deprived of rest or sleep for almost the next twelve hours and had been awake for at least twelve hours prior to the alleged incident.

Welfare documents and other files subpoenaed by the defense counsel indicate a girl whose childhood and early adolescent years were marked with both alleged and proven sexual abuse by family members and at least two non-family members, and a very difficult family life. For example, the girl's older brother pleaded guilty to—and was convicted of—sexually abusing her and another sibling. Several other incidents of sexual abuse against the girl were supported by independent evidence and, not unusually, some relatives had rejected the girl as a result of her previous disclosures of sexual victimization. The brother convicted of sexually abusing her as a young child was hostile toward her and supported his father, the accused, in this case. Just prior to the trial commencing the brother was jailed for contempt of court after confronting her and her mother and verbally threatening them as to the consequences they faced if they gave evidence against the defendant.

Information from case documents reveal a girl who remained reasonably close to her mother, although the mother experienced periods of deep emotional distress and depression, which had led to her being hospitalized in a psychiatric institution for treatment for short periods of time over several years. These difficulties resulted in the girl being made a ward of the state on occasion and living with several foster families. A maternal aunt had custody of her for a short time, and in her own evidence the girl said that she found life with her aunt difficult because her aunt would constantly denigrate her mother, which she found hurtful. The girl had minimal contact with her maternal grandmother since her own mother was somewhat estranged from her parents. The girl's mother was a trained nurse, and following an incident of sexual abuse against her daughter, the mother joined a support group for parents whose children had experienced sexual abuse. The mother had previously supported her daughter's disclosures of sexual abuse, which court and other files show to have been proven or strongly supported. In this case, the mother continued to support her daughter and thus was prepared to give evidence for her at this trial.

The Prosecution Evidence

Aside from the complainant's evidence, the prosecution witness list comprised the girl's mother, who would give evidence in support of her daughter; the motel manager and motel waitress; and a forensic pathologist recognized as an expert in his field. The latter witness formed a crucial part of the prosecution evidence since the pathologist had conducted tests on semen samples taken from the clothing of the girl and the motel sheets. The semen samples were subjected to DNA (deoxyribonucleic acid, herein referred to as DNA) testing, with the results concluding with 96 percent accuracy that the donor of the semen could not be excluded as having paternity of the complainant.[1] In other words, the biological father was considered with 96 percent accuracy to be the donor of the semen sample taken from his daughter.

The Evidentiary Rulings

Four judges were appointed to this trial before it was heard to completion, resulting in a multitude of transcripts and repeated legal arguments. This case study refers to only three judges since it appears that one judge was only very briefly appointed to the case for the purpose of officially aborting the trial and setting a new date. As such, only three of the judges were actively involved in evidentiary rulings, and the transcripts only indicate rulings made by three judges.

The first judge appointed to the trial became ill prior to any evidence being given before a jury. However, he did make two crucial evidentiary decisions prior to the trial being aborted. The first dealt with DNA semen evidence. Both legal sides presented expert testimony, in a *voir dire*[2] hearing, about the DNA evidence. The prosecution argued for its inclusion as an integral part of their case, while the defense counsel claimed the evidence was not conclusive enough and thus prejudicial to the accused and so ought to be excluded from jury consideration. The judge sided with defense arguments, suggesting a "non-expert" jury of laypeople would find the DNA evidence difficult to follow, adding that the evidence was "confusing" and "scientific speculation."[3] The fact that disputed DNA evidence is used in other criminal cases and paternity disputes begs questions about the prerogative of a judge to exclude evidence because he finds it "confusing." DNA evidence is especially important when it is the *only* evidence, such as in paternity disputes, whereas in this case its inclusion was as collateral, albeit powerful evidence to support the rest of the prosecution case. Why is this judge's "confusion" elevated to become the self-referential view through which evidence is disqualified? Almost 350 pages of transcript were devoted entirely to arguing over the DNA evidence, with most of the argument coming from the defense barrister who keenly sought to have the evidence excluded. The judge's "confusion" may well have stemmed from the imbroglio style of defense attack—as DNA experts were cross-examined about chi squares, methods of deduction, databases, and population samples. Those in the courtroom would have needed a dictionary and science degree to follow the well-primed speeches of the defense barrister, which appeared deliberately designed to confuse the evidence rather than enhance it. This smoke-and-mirrors tactic is all the more deceptive since the defense barrister would later draw extremely selectively on one part of the semen sample evidence to support the defense narrative of the "bad" and "mad" daughter.

The second crucial evidentiary ruling concerned the defense barrister's submission for leave to cross-examine the complainant on her previous sexual history. The barrister had subpoenaed all known counseling and medical files pertaining to the complainant and sought to cross-examine the girl about previous instances of abuse as well as any consensual sexual activities. He had also subpoenaed all medical and counseling files pertaining to the mother of the complainant, including her files from a psychiatric hospital. This presiding judge firmly dismissed the defense's request for leave to cross-examine the complainant about her previous sexual history, saying in part that the legislation was "clearly designed" to prevent the kind of "hurtful and demeaning cross-examination" that would cause "distress" and "trauma" to the girl. The judge further commented that he felt it would be improper use of judicial discretion to allow the defense to "abrogate s.37a."[4] This evidentiary ruling is positive for demonstrating the intended efficacy of the legislation, and a judicial awareness that such evidence, aside from having no relevance to the charges under investigation, may well cause very real and unnecessary hurt to the complainant. Adding weight to his ruling were the judge's comments that, after reading the counseling and medical files of the complainant, he found them to contain evidence supporting her previous disclosures of sexual abuse against other males. Since the defense barrister's plan was to use cross-examination around previous sexual history to infer the complainant's mental instability and history of making *false* allegations of abuse, the judge's findings and subsequent ruling may well have inhibited an integral part of the defense narrative. This remains a moot point though, since the appointment of a new judge brings with it the prospect of new evidentiary rulings, providing the opportunity for the defense counsel's legal argument to succeed where it had elsewhere failed. The same applies to the prosecutor, who could once again argue for the opportunity to present the DNA evidence.

A new trial did not begin for almost twelve months, and while judges tend to make themselves familiar with the evidentiary rulings and structure of the previously aborted trial, they are open to hear new submissions and legal arguments. In front of the new judge, the prosecutor sought to re-argue the DNA evidence on the grounds that the semen samples had been subjected to new more highly developed techniques advancing DNA testing. This included blood samples from the mother and daughter to enhance the DNA profile testing. The accused did not submit a DNA sample to the prosecution, as it is his legal right to refuse. Furthermore, it was argued, new databases and other tests, which the defense relied on to successfully argue the exclusion of the evidence, were now in place and the prosecutor had availed the DNA testing to these new advances. Despite these arguments, the second trial judge upheld the original ruling that the DNA evidence would remain excluded. In law, facts are there to be challenged. Facts do not have to be regarded as "real" since they will become "real" only if and when a judge makes them "real" by admitting them as evidence.

The defense barrister had better luck. He sought to re-argue the first judge's ruling, which blocked him from being able to cross-examine the complainant about her previous sexual history—in particular, her previous sexual victimization by other males. What is obvious from a reading of these transcript is that the strategy developed by the defense barrister was one comprised almost entirely of aggressively attacking the credibility of the complainant and her mother, based on historical incidents from their lives, along with a good deal of innuendo and rumor. To accomplish this, he desperately needed the judge's approval to use the private counseling and medical files of not just the complainant but her mother as well, despite the mother being a witness only and not someone who had made any allegations against the accused. In essence, the defense barrister wanted to have a trial within a trial; he wanted to put the character of the mother and daughter on trial to draw attention away from the substance of the charges. He was no doubt confident that their counseling and medical files could be used to promote narrow and pernicious stereotypes and social myths about the complainant and her mother that may well arouse the kinds of prejudices commonly held by society and reflected in a jury.

Building on his original argument, the defense counsel acquainted the newly appointed judge with the complainant's private counseling files as well as the private counseling files of her mother. Raising the obvious interest of the judge, the barrister began to unfold a hypothesis of Herculean proportions, claiming that the mother of the complainant was suffering a rare mental illness that was also manifested in her daughter, and which led to them colluding to make false allegations of sexual abuse. The barrister argued his right to "paint a picture"[5] for the court about this *illness* and had found an "expert" witness in the form of a forensic psychologist who, while never having met the complainant or her mother, was prepared to give evidence of a possible diagnosis of a specific form of mental illness causing this type of collusion.

The second step in advancing his quest to be able to cross-examine the complainant about her previous sexual history, as well as introduce a narrative of specific mental illness, was *voir dire* evidence from the forensic psychologist. The psychologist began by explaining the specific illness he was referring to, with regards to the complainant and her mother, was termed Contemporary Munchausen's Syndrome by Proxy (CMSP), adding that the word "contemporary" was applied because it referred to "sexual abuse" allegations, hence the label of supposed modernity.[6] Munchausen's Syndrome (MS) is a kind of illness that causes a person to invent fictitious stories. It is considered a rare condition and one found predominantly in males.[7] In some contemporary psychological literature, Munchausen's Syndrome by "proxy" (MSP) has come to be associated as mental disorder almost exclusively among women, more specifically mothers, with the "proxy" indicating that they are instigators of fictitious allegations of physical or sexual abuse made by their children. A mother with this disorder fabricates stories on behalf of her child and induces the child to believe these fictitious stories, thus leading to false stories and allegations. As child sexual abuse is beginning to emerge as a serious social issue, some psychological literature claims that clinicians need to be vigilant in assessing children's claims of sexual abuse on the basis that MSP may be present. While diagnostic literature considers the syndrome rare, its promotion as a "factitious disorder" in child sex-abuse cases is vigorously promoted in some quarters and is signified by a heavy reliance on extreme subjectivity as opposed to any empirical evidence.[8]

Despite scouring the subpoenaed file of both mother and daughter, including evaluations and diagnosis of the mother by a treating psychiatrist, the barrister was forced to admit he found no evidence whatsoever to indicate or suggest the presence of such a mental disorder. Nevertheless, the development and mobilization of a patriarchal narrative about mentally unstable females did not necessarily have to rely on a factual basis.[9] Pressing ahead with his narrative of a shared mental illness, the defense counsel proceeded to lead evidence from the "expert" witness.

The psychologist explained CMSP as a diagnosis applied to cases where "parents and children share beliefs about the child having been a victim of sexual abuse...the child has been, if you like, somewhat persuaded and brainwashed by the parent that the child has been a victim of sexual abuse."[10]

The psychologist went on to claim that the "disorder" was "used by the mother for instilling the syndrome in a child as a payback or revenge against a husband or parent surrogate."[11] Here, the dominant stereotype of the colluding mother and daughter seeking a deluded form of revenge underpins this *contemporary* mental "disorder" the defense were hoping to lay as a foundation for their legal narrative.

Asked for "indicators" that might lead a professional to suspect the presence of CMSP, the psychologist obliged with a list of factors, such as a parent making the accusation on behalf of the child, and where the adult also "describes herself as having been a victim of sexual abuse though evaluation of other family members leads to some doubt about that."[12] The psychologist's opinion that these factors should arouse suspicion, given the reality of the extent of sexual victimization of children, appears to have more to do with personal prejudice than fact. Even more worrying on this point is the expert's opinion that should other family members *not* support the disclosure of an adult victim/survivor, then that in itself suffices as reason to doubt not only the disclosure, but the mental stability of the person. The psychologist's view also ignores the fact that many who have experienced sexual violence, particularly within the family unit, face rejection and family division when they disclose the abuse. They also face family members deliberately closing ranks to protect the offender while scapegoating the victim, leading to their expulsion from the family.[13] These facts were conceded by some of the judiciary.[14]

Like a top-ten list of pop psychology hits, the expert witness noted "danger signs" associated with a diagnosis of CMSP. According to the expert, the mother's private counseling records revealed a disclosure to her counselor that she too was sexually abused in childhood. Alleging her father as the offender was, the expert said, a "sign of considerable concern pointing towards the possibility of this syndrome."[15] This was a strong claim, given that the psychologist had never met or talked to the mother and only had her counseling and other files, which he later admitted under cross-examination to have not even fully read. As noted above, claims of childhood sexual abuse across time by a mother and, later on, her child, is treated as tantamount to possessing a mental illness, and colluding to frame innocent men. "Danger sign number eight," according to the expert, is "when allegations become bizarre or highly improbable, you know, four relatives having abused the same child."[16] So, it is doubtful enough that a child could have been sexually abused by the father, but now the "expert" would have the court believe that evidence of victimization by more than one offender puts the child in the "bizarre" category.

The assumption here is that sexual abuse only ever entails one perpetrator, and any allegation of more than one is again an indicator of psychological disturbance in the child. This opinion ignores literature dealing with the sexual victimization of children by multiple perpetrators.[17] Continuing the enumeration of so-called "danger signs," the "expert" considered the mother's training as a nurse to be another indicator of CMSP because it provided her with the necessary "skills" to deceive others into believing that her child had been the victim of sexual abuse. The psychologist considered those with a background in psychology, social work, or counseling might well be afflicted with this modern mental illness—an interesting proposal. Taken on face value, this evidence suggests that any persons (or any *women?)* who study in one of these areas might be in danger of developing a psychiatric illness—moreover, a specific one in which they believe they or someone close to them was sexually violated. The mother's association with a community support group for child victims of abuse was also considered a factor that added "weight" to the possibility to this "syndrome."[18]

The evidence given by this witness shows the means by which some professionals are able to mobilize familiar yet superficially complex and elaborate narratives in order to challenge the veracity of women's and children's experiences of sexual violence. That these patriarchal narratives of good (professional men and falsely accused fathers) and bad (females who contrive false stories and pass them on to their children) are accepted with little if any deep scrutiny seems extraordinary. If we juxtaposed the evidence of the "expert" alongside the DNA evidence, the older brother's plea of guilt to sexually abusing the girl, and the original judge's finding that the files actually contained evidence to support the girl's disclosures of multiple offenders, then the evidence of the "expert" seems misguided at best, and jaundiced at worst.

The intent of the defense barrister was to secure the judge's support for the mental illness as explicit evidence, or at least to have a confluence of mental instability and previous sexual history introduced at the trial. It appears to have been successful. After listening to the "expert" witness, the new presiding judge began to talk about the girl as someone who had an element of the "boy who cried wolf," despite being made fully aware by the prosecutor that the previous judge had found evidence negating such a stance. In an unusual move, it was the *judge* who canvassed the application of s.37a, saving the defense barrister the worry of having to formulate his own argument. The judge said:

> Gentlemen, I address both of you—give some thought as to whether or not the matters raised by Munchausen or cross-examination of the prosecutrix [complainant] or her mother in relation to it, does come within s.37a.... It would seem to me that *imagined or feigned* sexual activities would not come within the section [referring to s.37a].... I don't imagine the section is there to deal with cases where *the boy cried wolf, if you will remember your fables.* It may be permissible and proper to put to the witness "you've made a lot of false claims for insurance in the past." To give another illustration: if someone has made a *number of false allegations against other persons which have been found to be untrue,* I don't imagine that would be covered by s.37a. [emphasis added][19]

The judge arrived at his opinion that the girl in this case had a history of making false accusations of sexual abuse, despite there being no tangible evidence of such; however, there was tangible evidence demonstrating the opposite. In a display of overt personal bias, the judge rejected the prosecution's arguments that the defense counsel not be granted leave outside of s.37a, saying, "I don't think the law has reached the stage where the person charged with a sexual offense has to conduct his case with one hand tied behind his back." He added that s.37a was not designed to deal with persons who "had, on previous occasions, made a series of false allegations."[20] This sardonic expression of sympathy for those accused of sexual abuse provides some insight into what might be considered a jaundiced view of sexual violence.

The analogy of one hand tied behind the back ought to be applied to the prosecution case, since strong collateral evidence in the form of a DNA sample was excluded from the trial, and it was certainly shaping up to be a case in which previous proven sexual assaults against the girl were going to be used in a truly deceptive, humiliating, and destructive manner in order that the trial focus on her and not the charges facing the accused. More disturbing was the judge's comment that since the counseling files provided "*clear evidence* [of] *false allegations*...then the accused is entitled to attack her credibility [emphasis added]."[21] In response, the prosecutor appropriately argued that the judge "has with respect, stepped, as it were to the threshold question and *assumed* that there is a false allegation [emphasis added]."[22] In reply, the judge relied on an unusual form of logic, suggesting he was not concerned with her sexual activity but her "lack" of sexual activity, since her allegations of sexual abuse were, according to him, based on "false" accusations.

The power to interpret or avoid applying protective legislation to suit a judge's personal identification with a particular storyline mobilized in a trial underscores the degree of discretionary power that judges possess. Moreover, recent law-reform literature has been concerned with this judicial resistance to applying legislation to protect complainants questioned about their sexual history.[23] That this grossly subjective interpretation served as the basis for not applying s.37a should be cause for serious concerns about the discretionary liberties that the judiciary regards as sacrosanct.

Two judges, so far, and two diametrically opposed rulings with regard to interpreting and applying s.37a. Incredibly, the second judge was also not able to hear the trial to completion and so, once again, it was aborted, but not before the complainant and her mother had presented their evidence in front of the jury. As will be discussed in detail later in chapter 7, "Forced Errors," the defense case was advantaged since the barrister now had another transcript, alongside the committal hearing transcript, to draw upon as a means of confusing and discrediting the complainant and her mother should there be the slightest variation in the evidence they would give at the new trial.

A third presiding judge was appointed and this trial was heard to completion. This case had the same defense barrister for the whole duration. A new prosecutor was appointed for the third trial and so the evidentiary boundaries were again open for legal argument.

In pre-trial arguments, the new prosecutor suggested he was still finding his way around the case and stated that he would not be seeking to re-ventilate legal arguments regarding the previous rulings that excluded the DNA evidence. However, he did seek to re-argue the ruling by the second trial judge, which allowed cross-examination of the girl outside of s.37a, arguing it was not appropriate for the complainant to be cross-examined on previous allegations of sexual abuse. However, he did not oppose defense counsel having some leave to cross-examine the girl about previous allegations and whether such allegations were true.[24] It was as though the prosecutor was ambivalent when it came to s.37a—he was prepared to allow "some" leave, as though it was only right to let the defense barrister get what one prosecutor described as their "rightful pound of flesh" when cross-examining complainants in sexual-offense proceedings.[25] Considering prosecutors are supposed to protect complainants from unwarranted attacks on their character, his ambivalent attitude toward the defense having "some" leave to see if previous allegations were "true" identifies some of the problems articulated by alleged victims who have confronted the legal system and find prosecutors claiming that they prosecute on behalf of the Queen, with the alleged victim as a mere Crown witness.[26]

And so, the defense barrister wasted no time in familiarizing the third presiding judge with his submission about the mental illness of the mother and daughter, and how imperative it was that he be granted leave to cross-examine the girl outside of s.37a.

Early in the defense argument, the judge provided support in principle for the defense submission, saying that the counseling files had some "relevance" to the current trial since her previous disclosures of sexual abuse may or may not be true, and because:

> she's now claiming that the same sort of thing happened with someone else, and it might be thought, well, why would a young girl be saying that if she'd had no prior sexual experience and she's giving all these descriptions of what took place when she does have sexual experience...in a case such as this, where it's her father, and it seems to cry out for some explanation as to why she would do this, make this allegation against him, because they were getting on well, and it's very important to know if she did have prior sexual experience and it's very important to know of she had made false allegations before.[27]

Again, the judge's exercise in discretion is replete with sexist assumptions. He claimed that a female's having prior sexual knowledge is a cause for suspicion, in that the knowledge gives her the "know how" to fabricate false allegations. The fact that it is her *father* appears to create further incredulity, as though the very thought of accusing one's father is so outrageous it is difficult to comprehend, a point elsewhere observed in psychiatric literature on "incest."[28] This latter point reminds me of an observation by a psychiatrist in early "incest" literature who said that the "enormity" of a young woman's claim of rape by her father "destroyed" its "probability."[29]

Of greater importance, though, is the selective amnesia of the judge as he pondered the question why the girl would make such an allegation, forgetting of course that formidable piece of DNA evidence removed by a legal sleight of hand.

The defense narrative of mother-daughter collusion under the auspice of a supposed mental disorder not only swayed the third judge; he was ready to drive the narrative bandwagon himself, when he added his view to these well-heeled narratives:

DEFENSE (to judge): As part of this syndrome [CMSP], often mother and daughter work together.

JUDGE: That often happens. I mean in all sorts of things.

DEFENSE (to judge): The mother uses the daughter to—really for her own devices—and often the deficiencies in the mother are found in the daughter as part of the syndrome, and the mother herself has been an inmate in a psychiatric institution [and] she herself was a victim of incest.[30]

The defense barrister's plan to have the "expert" psychologist apprise the jury of the mental disorder of the mother and daughter unraveled a little during the trial, as the "expert" was unable to attend court and so a replacement "expert" came along. The barrister reiterated that the complainant was suffering a mental illness which resulted in her "tell[ing] lies when making complaints of a sexual nature."[31] His replacement "expert" proved to be not as malleable when it came to adopting a diagnosis of CMSP (or even Munchausen's without the "contemporary" bit). The "expert" said instead that such a mental illness was incredibly "rare," and that he would not be willing to provide any diagnosis based on what he considered the scant evidence presented before him, adding that he would find it inappropriate and unethical to do so.[32] While this replacement "expert" approached the subject matter very differently to expert number one, he explained that he did engage in some discussions outside the court in the hallway with a cousin of the complainant, who was supporting the accused. The cousin told him of her observations of the complainant from some years ago—these "observations" about her supposed bizarre behavior consisted of cruel assertions, but they also indicated the complainant's feelings of depression and distress. While the replacement "expert" would not make a diagnosis based on this alone, he pointed out to the court that the cousin's observations indicated the "mental" disturbance of the girl.[33]

Failure to have the replacement expert adopt CMSP did not subvert the narrative of mental illness. Though the barrister conceded to the judge that he had no evidence to prove the existence of a specific mental disorder,[34] he had, at the previous trial, cross-examined the complainant and her mother to detect any "danger signs" of CMSP—as outlined by the first "expert"—so he had lost very little ground. At this final trial, he would still be able to accomplish a narrative of "madness" and "badness" despite an absence of any factual evidence of mental illness.

Perhaps to heighten the narrative of the "mad" daughter, or simply to inject drama into the legal narrative being orchestrated, the defense barrister had previously requested that the director of the Office of Public Prosecutions[35] (OPP) order that the girl be psychologically examined before the trial.[36] The OPP ignored this request. (A focus on unproven assumptions about the mental stability of complainants in sex offense trials appears a favorite of this barrister since he sought to have a judge in another intrafamilial sexual abuse case "warn" the jury that the female complainant was not mentally fit to give credible evidence.[37])

While the DNA evidence was wholly excluded, the prosecution was permitted to introduce evidence of semen stains found on bed sheets from the motel room and in the girl's underwear. It seems a superfluous exercise in legal discretion to allow the prosecutor to introduce a selective piece of evidence but exclude the compelling and pivotal piece of evidence pointing to the likely donor of the semen. It is like giving the jury a jigsaw to assemble but deliberately withholding vital pieces of it. Perhaps the prosecutor thought that at least alerting the jury to the presence of semen might strengthen the evidence of the girl. However, the defense barrister, as we shall see, had a ready-made narrative for this also.

Evidence-in-Chief

At the beginning of her evidence, the complainant gave her occupation as a "dancer, stripper, barmaid," and agreed that she had lived at a number of places, including homeless shelters.[38] I assume this was done to get such information out as early as possible, knowing that defense counsel draws on some of this evidence in cross-examination. The prosecutor led evidence from the complainant of her family constellation and how her aunt organized for her to meet her biological father when she was fourteen, after not seeing him since she was an infant. She gave further evidence that her father came and visited her a few times and that they maintained contact by phone but that there was a sudden break in contact for several months before she initiated contact by phone. She said that her father invited her to accompany him on an interstate truck trip between her home city and Melbourne, Victoria, so that they could get to know each other better. She agreed to go on this three- or four-day trip. After being asked by the prosecutor to describe the truck model and its interior, the complainant was asked specific questions about the first alleged incident of indecent assault. She said that she wanted to stay awake until they crossed the state border because she had never traveled interstate before and wanted to experience driving across the state border:

PROSECUTOR: After you had crossed the border, what then happened?

COMPLAINANT: I got sleepy and got in the back.

PROSECUTOR: Did you have any covers in the back?

COMPLAINANT: I still had, like, everything on and I had a blanket over me, I think.

PROSECUTOR: What were you wearing?

COMPLAINANT: A white like dress with, like, blue polka dots and a red jacket and stockings and shoes.

PROSECUTOR: Did you take anything off when you went into the back bed?

COMPLAINANT: No.

PROSECUTOR: So when you got in there did it just consist of the bench and a blanket?

COMPLAINANT: M'mm.

PROSECUTOR: When you got into that position, which way did you lay, was your head towards the passenger door or towards the driver?

COMPLAINANT: Towards the passenger door.

PROSECUTOR: Did you go to sleep?

COMPLAINANT: Yeah.

PROSECUTOR: After you had been asleep for some time did something occur? Did you wake up?

COMPLAINANT: Yeah, I was like half asleep, half dosing, half awake, and I felt [father's name] lean over to the back and, um, I felt him, like, his hand went under the blanket and touched my leg.

PROSECUTOR: Where else did he touch you?

COMPLAINANT: I remember him...I remember him, um, reaching up, putting his hand on my breast and then I remember him putting his hand, like, back under the blanket and putting his hand underneath my stockings, in my panties and touching me on my vagina.

PROSECUTOR: How long did his hand remain in that position, are you able to say?

COMPLAINANT: Probably only for a second or two.

PROSECUTOR: Did you say anything or do anything while you were in that position?

COMPLAINANT: No.

PROSECUTOR: What did you feel at that time?

JUDGE: How did you feel, is that what you mean?

PROSECUTOR: Yes.

COMPLAINANT: I didn't know what to feel. I sat up and got in the front.[39]

Asked by the prosecutor about the remainder of the trip to reach their destination in Melbourne, the complainant said she fell asleep again, and when she next woke up they were in the city of Melbourne, but she did not know whereabouts. The prosecutor asked her whether she discussed this incident with anyone, including her father:

PROSECUTOR: Did you refer to the incident, say anything about it to your father at that point?

COMPLAINANT: No.

PROSECUTOR: Was there any reason for that?

COMPLAINANT: What do you say when you are in a strange place and you don't know anyone, you know.

PROSECUTOR: I meant to your father, did you say anything to your father?

COMPLAINANT: Yeah. No, I didn't.

PROSECUTOR: You didn't say anything to anyone else?

COMPLAINANT: No.[40]

The above exchange is typical of prosecutor questions to complainants, and its purpose appears to be to anticipate the tenor of cross-examination questions complainants face from defense barristers. The barristers often feign incredulity that the complainant did not behave according to a masculinist view of rape and sexual assault, which would have them fight off any assault, create an immediate hue and cry, and immediately complain to someone. During the day that followed, the complainant's evidence was that the father drove across many parts of the state collecting and making deliveries, and that evening drove to a motel outside of Melbourne. The prosecutor must lead a complainant carefully through her evidence and avoid any questions that may be considered leading or prompting the memory of the complainant. As such, the questions are ordered chronologically, and may even seem excessively basic in structure and sequence, but are certainly not as complex, lengthy, and drawn-out as cross-examination. As discussed in the introduction, much of the transcript quotation is necessarily lengthy. Having said this, the following excerpt from the complainant's evidence relating to the second alleged incident involving penetration is edited for ease of readership only, not to remove context or content, as are other transcript excerpts.

PROSECUTOR: When you got to the motel, did your father check in?

COMPLAINANT: Yeah, he told me to wait in the car—in the truck and he would go and organize a room.

PROSECUTOR: Then what happened?

COMPLAINANT: He come out and got me and we grabbed our things and went into this room.

PROSECUTOR: Do you recall what number the room was?

COMPLAINANT: I think it was number twenty-nine but I am not sure.

PROSECUTOR: I want you to just now to tell the jury what took place, really, from the time that you went into the room with your belongings; all right? So you went in the room, your father had checked in?

COMPLAINANT: M'mm.

PROSECUTOR: And then what happened?

COMPLAINANT: We had something to eat and, um, we were watching tele. I don't know what we were watching or anything. And after dad ate, he went and had a shower and then he come out, and then after I finished eating and this show that I had watched finished, I think, I went and had a shower, and I remember that the door didn't lock on the bathroom, and I tried to make it lock but it wouldn't lock, and he said, "What are you trying to do? You don't worry about that?" And then I had my shower and I got dressed, changed into tracksuit pants and a jumper and—

PROSECUTOR: Did you have anything under the tracksuit pants and the jumper?

COMPLAINANT: Yeah, my bikini bottoms and a bra.

PROSECUTOR: And so you have your shower, you have dressed, and then what took place?

COMPLAINANT: I think I offered to sleep on the—like, there was a sofa in the lounge room where you can fold it out to a bed, and he told me to sleep in the bed in the bedroom because I would be warmer.

PROSECUTOR: What type of bed was that, the bed in the bedroom?

COMPLAINANT: It was a double bed.

PROSECUTOR: After you had had your shower, was that after you had watched the television?

COMPLAINANT: Yes.

PROSECUTOR: And did you stay up any longer after your shower with your father before you went to bed?

COMPLAINANT: Um, I remember having a cup of Milo, which tasted funny and—that's all I remember.

PROSECUTOR: Well, after having the Milo, how did you feel?

COMPLAINANT: I was pretty tired.

PROSECUTOR: Did you take off any of your clothes before you went into bed?

COMPLAINANT: No.

PROSECUTOR: Do you recall what happened after you had gone to bed in the double bed?

COMPLAINANT: Um, I must have gone to sleep, like, pretty much straight away. I remember waking up and I was just sweating from head to toe, because I was just so hot.

PROSECUTOR: Yes. Was anyone present with you when you woke up and you were sweating?

COMPLAINANT: I must have called out or something because dad come into the room and I must have told him, like, you know, I was hot or something, and he took off my tracksuit pants and then, um, I remember lifting up my arms and he pulled off my jumper. And then...

PROSECUTOR: What were you wearing at that point?

COMPLAINANT: Just my bikini bottoms and my bra.

PROSECUTOR: Then what took place?

COMPLAINANT: I remember him walking round the other side of the bed and I remember hearing him take his clothes off and then getting into the bed next to me. I remember him, like, moving over. He was on my right side and he moved over close to me and pulled down my bikini bottoms down past my knees.

PROSECUTOR: And what about your top?

COMPLAINANT: And he just like, um—I think I remember him pushing my bra out of the way; I don't think he actually took it off.

PROSECUTOR: And did he do anything with his hands?

COMPLAINANT: Um, I remember him touching my breast and moving his hand down to my vagina. I remember him putting his finger inside me, and it was probably there for a second or two, and then I remember him rolling over on top of me and I remember him putting his penis inside me.

PROSECUTOR: Are you able to say how long he was inside you for?

COMPLAINANT: Um, maybe for a minute or two. Not very long.

PROSECUTOR: And then what took place? Did he move around, or did you move around?

COMPLAINANT: Um, I remember squirming, as if to say—to let him know I was waking up.

PROSECUTOR: Did you say "screaming" or "squirming"?

COMPLAINANT: Squirming. He must have realized that I was waking up and he got off [witness distressed] and he got out of the bed and he picked up his clothes and he walked out.

PROSECUTOR: What did you then do?

COMPLAINANT: I got out of bed straight away, put my clothes back on, grabbed a cigarette and said I was going out to get some fresh air.

PROSECUTOR: And you left the motel room and where did you then go?

COMPLAINANT: Into the restaurant. You go in through a door and there is, like, a foyer and through another door and there is, like a restaurant.

PROSECUTOR: How were you feeling at that point?...

COMPLAINANT: Pretty [inaudible], pretty upset, pretty hurt. Lots of things. [parentheses in original][41]

The complainant continued her evidence, saying there was no one in the foyer so she continued into the motel restaurant, approached a waitress and told her that her father had just "tried to sleep with her."[42] She said that the waitress got the manager, who asked her what happened, and she told him the same thing. He then got his wife and she again asked the girl what had happened and again, she says, she told the manager's wife that her father had just tried to sleep with her. The manager's wife then drove the girl to the local police station. Although delayed disclosure is a common feature of sexual abuse, the girl's prompt disclosure following the second incident may have been due to a lack of parental bonding between her and her father, since contact between them had only recently been established.

In her evidence, the complainant told of being taken to a police station and speaking with a male police officer before being sent to another police station to undergo a medical examination. After the examination, she was required to make a statement. When asked details about the length of time this took, the complainant said that she was unsure, adding that she felt "out of it...very vague, very, very, very tired, like I hadn't slept in a month."[43] Her evidence about having a hot drink of Milo that tasted funny, and then feeling extremely tired, indicates the possibility that she ingested some kind of sedative. The use of medication by long-haul truck drivers assisting them to control their sleep and waking patterns is common knowledge, and it is surprising that no one thought to conduct tests to see if the complainant had been given intentionally, or unintentionally, sedatives of some kind.

It is of deep concern that this girl was made to stay awake the entire night so she could complete a statement, when she was obviously in no fit state to do so. She finished her statement a little after 6:30 a.m. the following morning, and in later evidence said that she kept falling asleep while trying to make her statement, causing the police officer to tell her to "stay awake" so that she could continue.[44] Furthermore, the girl said she was frightened, confused, and anxious. She was in a different state, where she knew no one, and was not even aware of the location of the police station where she was making her statement. After making her statement, the police drove her to a shelter for women, where she later made her own way back interstate.

Cross-examination

With her brief evidence-in-chief concluded, cross-examination began. Like much cross-examination, the opening questions focus on the character of the complainant or on an issue not connected to the charges she has just given evidence about. And it was in this case too.

The narrative of the "mad" daughter was mobilized in this trial to an exacting standard and the first question faced by the complainant was not about the charges against the accused, but about the sexual assault she endured from her brother, which of course was put to her as one of her "false allegations":

> DEFENSE: You have made an accusation previously, haven't you, against your brother?
>
> COMPLAINANT: Yes. It was an allegation [that was] correct.
>
> DEFENSE: Well, you said, didn't you, that your brother committed incest on you?
>
> COMPLAINANT: Yes, and he did.
>
> DEFENSE: Did he? On how many occasions?
>
> COMPLAINANT: Several.

DEFENSE: Are you quite sure about that?

COMPLAINANT: Yes.

DEFENSE: What occurred on those occasions...did he have fellatio with you?

COMPLAINANT: I don't understand that word.

DEFENSE: Did he have oral sex with you?[45]

Cross-examination about her brother continued and reflected the same tone and questions put to her at the previous trial that did not go to completion. I want to add a particular line of cross-examination questions put to the complainant at the previous trial to highlight not only the badgering of complainants on the same issue over and over, but also to highlight the offensive style so easily adopted, and so infrequently objected to, by the prosecution counsel and judges. The transcripts of both trials record instances where the complainant became very distressed and was unable to continue until she had time to compose herself. The following excerpt is taken from the previous trial that was aborted prior to a jury verdict. After being repeatedly asked to provide "exact" details about her brother's "alleged" abuse of her when she was approximately eleven years old, she stated:

COMPLAINANT: From trying to have sex with me to making me give him a head job.

DEFENSE: How many occasions did this happen?

COMPLAINANT: Several.

DEFENSE: Did you make a complaint about each occasion?

COMPLAINANT: I don't remember it was too long ago.

DEFENSE: *You don't remember the number of times you gave your brother a head job; is that your evidence, that you can't remember the number of times you gave your brother a head job?*

COMPLAINANT: No.

DEFENSE: The complaint against your brother was lies. [emphasis added][46]

The grossly offensive paraphrasing by the defense barrister seemed designed to demean the girl, and neither the judge nor prosecutor objected to his acerbity of speech. Clearly, the complainant's previous sexual abuse by her older brother, which occurred when she was approximately eleven years old, had nothing to do with the current charges under consideration in this trial. The defense barrister made them central to the trial on the basis that the evidence was vital in demonstrating a narrative of a girl with a history of false allegations. From the outset she was accused of lying, an accusation that would escalate in frequency as cross-examination continued.

More importantly, the complainant's brother pleaded guilty and was convicted and jailed as a result of the sexual abuse he perpetrated on her. At no stage did the defense barrister or prosecutor inform the jury that the offenses against the complainant by her brother were proven. The defense barrister was free to accuse her of being a liar about this abuse without incurring any challenge. The gravity of this deliberate, misleading information is all the more disturbing since it was made central to a trial convened on unrelated charges. This issue was repeatedly re-canvassed throughout the trial and linked with other previous allegations taken from her files, no doubt to have a cumulative impact on the jury, as the narrative of falsity was built upon. The absence of any information to disrupt this deceptive narrative demonstrates the propensity for defense narratives to be almost invincible to a rebuttal by factual evidence. These questions were then directly linked with information obtained by the defense barrister from the private counseling files of the girl relating to her sexual victimization by her older brother:

> DEFENSE: Did you speak to [counselor] about the allegations that you made against [names brother] your brother?
>
> COMPLAINANT: I spoke to her about a lot of things; I don't remember if I mentioned that.
>
> DEFENSE: Did you say to her that [brother] had never really touched you and that you had been *frolicking* as kids but nothing had happened; did you say that to her?
>
> COMPLAINANT: I don't remember.
>
> DEFENSE: That is something you wouldn't forget about, would you?
>
> COMPLAINANT: I don't know. [emphasis added][47]

This counselor would later give evidence for the defense in this trial based on her notes, in which she claims the complainant, then a child, minimized her abuse and claimed the abuse had been part of playing a game. The term "frolicking" seems an odd word for a child to use, and as it was revealed that the counselor's notes were quite rough and ready and had been added to contemporaneously; one wonders just whose terminology is being used here. Much has been written about children recanting factual disclosures of sexual abuse for a variety of reasons, and minimizing notions of harm that was suffered as a result is not uncommon among victim/survivors. There is credible research evidence to suggest that children may recant or minimize allegations of sexual abuse as a defense mechanism against their own traumatic feelings, because of adult disbelief, or fear of possible reprisals.[48] The comment that it was part of "playing" games does not negate the fact that abuse occurred. Many child victims tell of offenders sexually abusing them under the pretext of it being part of a "game" or of "playing." The girl, however, does not recant the abuse—although this is what the barrister would later accuse her of. She minimizes the assault and suggests it was part of playing. Hardly the grounds to suggest evidence of false accusations, especially given the guilty plea of the brother. However, in this trial, the narrative was that the girl had a history of false allegations of sexual abuse and the counselor's notes have obviously been perceived as a bonus card for the defense case. A major concern about the use of these counseling files is also the difference between a child's exploration of their abuse in a therapeutic setting as opposed to their explanation of abuse in a legal setting. A child's dialogue will be very different in a therapeutic setting as opposed to a legal setting and may lead to the a re-abuse of the victim as lawyers extract and isolate comments made by children in a therapeutic setting.[49]

Very quickly the narrative seeds of mother/daughter collusion were introduced by the barrister. Inferring collusion around the motive of revenge provided a launching platform for the defense to build upon the narrative of mother and daughter working as co-agents against other family members. The defense began by highlighting that her mother had been charged with striking her older brother, and suggested this occurred at the same time she made her "allegations" against her brother. The complainant said he had no idea of the timeframe involving the incident between her mother and older brother, but the defense quickly moved on to allegations the complainant had made against her former stepfather. The topic then moved to her previous allegations against her stepfather, and again the defense barrister asked her if she made her allegations against her stepfather around the same time her mother was in the "middle of an access row" with him.[50] Not surprisingly, she was then made to give a full account of the allegations of indecent assault she made about her stepfather. So far this cross-examination was designed, as signaled by the defense, to portray a girl who tells lies about sexual abuse, thus inferring a "motive" to tell further lies against her father, and later on a "motive" of revenge was clearly articulated. The questions also raised the narrative concept of the "bad" daughter plotting against her father. This narrative of the "bad," sexually promiscuous daughter explained her means of fabricating allegations of sexual assault, i.e., having sexual knowledge. It was put to the complainant that she began having sexual intercourse at the age of fourteen and that she frequently engaged in sex "around three times a week" with a former boyfriend.[51] The complainant remained noncommittal to the barrister's numerical suggestions as to how frequently she engaged in sexual intercourse with her former boyfriend on a weekly basis. When accused of having unprotected sexual intercourse with her former boyfriend "immediately" prior to her trip with her father that led to the current allegations, she denied this, saying she had no sexual relations with her former boyfriend for several months prior to the alleged incident with her father.[52]

Now I want to flag for the reader that at the committal hearing the former boyfriend agreed with the prosecutor that he had broken off his relationship with the complainant several months before she left to go on the interstate trip with her father and, therefore, had not engaged in any sexual activity with her for several months prior to the alleged incident. However, now at the trial, the narrative was very different because the defense were claiming the boyfriend had unprotected sex with her and—with good reason, as you shall see—it fitted in exceptionally well with the modified evidence concerning the semen samples.

Cross-examination then moved on to specific details of the incident alleged to have occurred in the cabin of the father's truck. The obligatory question about whether she had reread her statement to refresh her memory was asked, and the complainant agreed that she had, but didn't say when this was. When asked if her father had penetrated her vagina with his finger, she said she could not remember. Now the barrister, having her statement and other transcript evidence in front of him, knows that she did claim his finger had penetrated her vagina. He proceeded to read excerpts from the committal hearing and 1995 trial transcript, where she gave evidence that her father had penetrated her vagina with his finger, with evidence about what she was wearing, the sequence and order of her father's alleged actions, and the exact position of her body while this was occurring. After reading this lengthy excerpt, the barrister asked the complainant:

> DEFENSE: Is it the situation that you have forgotten what happened since giving evidence on the 1st August 1994?
>
> COMPLAINANT: Yes, I have forgotten.
>
> DEFENSE: *You forgot that your own father had his finger in your vagina?*
>
> COMPLAINANT: I don't remember things like that—all right.
>
> DEFENSE: Don't you?
>
> COMPLAINANT: You don't really want to—hey.
>
> DEFENSE: All right. Did you know that to be inappropriate behavior?
>
> COMPLAINANT: What?
>
> DEFENSE: Your father putting his finger in your vagina?
>
> COMPLAINANT: Yes, I know that is inappropriate.

DEFENSE: Did you know what to do about it?

COMPLAINANT: Not really, no.

DEFENSE: Your mother had been a member of a sexual-assault support group for quite some period of time, hadn't she?

COMPLAINANT: I think so.

DEFENSE: And you were a member of, as it were, a group of young people—weren't you, under the auspices of that group?

COMPLAINANT: I guess you could call it that. [emphasis added][53]

The purpose of highlighting this evidence is to suggest that a difficulty to remember every fact at hand is seen as evidence of fabrication. The gratuitous comment by the barrister regarding her father's digital penetration of her vagina was never challenged.

Asking whether she realized her father's conduct was inappropriate is designed to demean the witness, by suggesting their lack of "appropriate" response diminishes the truthfulness of their claim. It is a style of questioning frequently posed in sexual-assault cases. Child and adult witnesses alike are asked questions about how wrong they should have known the conduct to be, and *yet* they failed to do anything to stop it. These assertions ignore the literature on delayed disclosure and traumatic responses by victim/survivors, choosing instead the simplistic but effective berating of child and adult complainants for behaving or responding in a seemingly bizarre manner to incidents, especially repeated incidents, of sexual assault inflicted on them.

Questions about her contact with a support group for non-offending parents and sexually victimized children were used to bolster the defense claim that the girl had access to support and knowledge that surely meant that if she was ever in a situation of abuse she would know what to do to stop it. Continuing to revisit her previous allegations prompted the complainant to say that she "didn't like to remember [her] childhood."[54]

Technical cross-examination highlighting a difference in her evidence about the exact placement of her father's hands on her vagina area in relation to the first charge prompted the prosecutor to object that the questions were unclear. At this point the complainant became distressed and required a break in proceedings.[55] How viable is the therapeutic encouragement to work through trauma and move on when a legal forum convening some years after the event, and possibly dragging on over a couple of years as happened in this case, demands every minute detail be recalled? While some individuals can recall amazing details (for a variety of reasons based on their own memory recall and/or things about the event that make certain facts stand out from the rest in memory), an inability to recall every detail is often used to portray complainants as liars. It was obvious from the evidence in her transcript that she has not forgotten what she alleges her father did to her. That she could not recall in these circumstances her exact evidence from the committal put to her in lengthy excerpts two years later is not surprising.

When court resumed immediately, the defense barrister moved on to a different topic that seemed unrelated to anything, this time about allegations of rape the girl was supposed to have made when she was barely thirteen years old. In rapid-fire action, the barrister put times and dates to the complainant about an allegation she made against two males who assaulted her, to which the girl replied that she did not know what incident the barrister was talking about. Ignoring this comment, he continued to ask questions of an absurd kind, such as asking her to confirm the address of a place she lived at some seven years ago, and even asking her to confirm the telephone number at that particular address.[56] Without any warning, the barrister asked the complainant whether she received any injuries, prompting the judge to ask the barrister to identify the incident he was talking about. The structure of the questions appeared a deliberate tactic, as though somehow demonstrating the absurdity of the girl's evidence as well as trying to confuse her and the jury as to what timeframe and event was being asked about. The barrister then put to her that she had no reason to dislike her father, and had in fact been getting on well with him, and she agreed with both statements. It was then put to her that she had told her grandmother and aunt that she intended getting her father "back" for leaving her and her mother. The complainant denied ever making such a statement.[57]

The questions then moved back to her statement about injuries related to the allegations against her father concerning the incident in the motel room:

> DEFENSE: Did you say to the police that you didn't get any injuries? In relation to this episode with your father, did you say this to the police: that you didn't get any injuries "From what dad did and I am not sore anywhere"—did you say that to the police?
>
> COMPLAINANT: Yes, I did, but it is not true.
>
> DEFENSE: You made that statement at 6:38 a.m. on the 19th May 1991…isn't that right?
>
> COMPLAINANT: Yes.
>
> DEFENSE: You acknowledged that that statement was true and correct and you made it in the belief that a person making a false statement in the circumstances is liable to penalties of perjury; you made that acknowledgement, didn't you?
>
> COMPLAINANT: Yes.

DEFENSE: Firstly, did you say to the police: "I didn't get any injuries from what dad did and I am not sore anywhere"; did you say that to the police?

COMPLAINANT: I don't remember saying it but I must have because it is in my statement.

DEFENSE: And you said something that was untrue to the police?

COMPLAINANT: Yeah, I guess.

DEFENSE: You said to the police too, didn't you, "That his dick was hard and I felt it go inside my vagina. This hurt a little bit and I could feel dad sort of moving around a lot while he was on top of me"; did you say that to the police?

COMPLAINANT: Yes.

DEFENSE: Was that true?

COMPLAINANT: Yes.

DEFENSE: It hurt a little bit, did it?

COMPLAINANT: Yes.

DEFENSE: Did you say this: "I felt my dad sort of move up and down a couple of times and I think his dick went inside my vagina for about an inch, [and] he kept his dick inside my vagina for five or so minutes"; did you say that?

COMPLAINANT: Yes, I did.

DEFENSE: Was that true?

COMPLAINANT: It wasn't five minutes, it was only a minute or two, but you have no—what is the word—when you are upset, you don't realize what time is.

DEFENSE: Was it five seconds that he spent inside you?

COMPLAINANT: About that.

DEFENSE: What—five seconds?

COMPLAINANT: Well, if you are going one and two and three and four and a five, yeah, about that.

DEFENSE: Five seconds. Do you know the difference between five seconds and five minutes?

COMPLAINANT: Yeah, I do now but...

DEFENSE: You didn't when you were fifteen?

COMPLAINANT: When something bad is happening five seconds can feel like five minutes.[58]

The focus in this sequence is on the duration of penetration, and it was quickly followed up with questions about a common "genital infection" present in the girl. While it is common for nearly all women to suffer minor genital bacteria, not all girls or women would necessarily be aware of its presence. The defense barrister asked the complainant about this "infection," which she said she had no knowledge of, and followed it with a ridiculous and offensive question as to whether she had "scratched" her vagina on that particular day (five years previously) and whether she had a "whitish" discharge coming from her vagina on that day. This question had a purpose since the forensic pathologist who examined the girl had said that the small recent tears in her vagina may have been caused by "rough intercourse" or digital trauma such as scratching the vagina.[59] The barrister wanted to suggest the latter and the evidence of a minor common vaginal infection obviously enhanced such a scenario.

These questions were soon followed up by questions about the degree of penetration, and while the excerpt is long, it is necessary in order to demonstrate the kind of details demanded from complainants:

DEFENSE: On the occasion that your father is alleged to have put his penis inside your vagina, have you previously said that it had gone in about halfway?

COMPLAINANT: I don't think at that time I knew distances, if you understand what I mean.

DEFENSE: So you wouldn't be able to say whether it had gone in one inch, two inches, or three inches?

COMPLAINANT: Not at the time, no.

DEFENSE: And if you couldn't say that at the time, then you couldn't say it subsequently, could you?

COMPLAINANT: I don't know.

DEFENSE: What, you wouldn't say something that wasn't true now, would you?

COMPLAINANT: No.

DEFENSE: Page sixty-four, Your Honor. On the 1st August 1994 before the magistrate were you asked these questions and did you give these answers: "How far did it go inside your vagina?" "Only about halfway." Were you asked that question, did you give that answer?

COMPLAINANT: I don't remember.

DEFENSE: Were you asked these questions and did you give these answers: "When you say he put it in halfway, how far were you talking about?" Answer: "I don't know, probably about two inches." Were you asked that question, did you give that answer?

COMPLAINANT: I don't know.

DEFENSE: Were you asked this question: "Pardon?" And did you then say: "Probably about two inches or three inches?"

COMPLAINANT: I don't remember.

DEFENSE: Were you asked this next question: "It went in quite a distance?" Answer: "Yes?" Were you asked this question, did you give that answer?

COMPLAINANT: I don't remember.

DEFENSE: "Two or three inches?" Were you asked that question, did you answer "Yes"?

COMPLAINANT: I don't remember.

DEFENSE: "It was in your vagina for how long?" Were you asked that question and did you answer, "Only about five seconds?"

COMPLAINANT: I don't remember.

DEFENSE: Is it the situation that you never knew how much of—firstly, how long you were penetrated for by your father with his penis? You don't know, is that the situation?

COMPLAINANT: No.

DEFENSE: You don't know?

COMPLAINANT: I know what it felt like; I don't know how to tell you in measurements, all right, hey.

DEFENSE: Five minutes or five seconds, you can't say which one is right and which one is wrong?

COMPLAINANT: Oh, how long. Like I said yesterday, when something bad happens to you, it can feel like it takes forever if it only takes five seconds.

DEFENSE: You never had the capacity to say how much of his penis went inside you?

COMPLAINANT: I don't know what you mean?

DEFENSE: You never saw it; right?

COMPLAINANT: Yeah, but I know what I feel, hey.

DEFENSE: Could you tell half of it?

COMPLAINANT: No.

DEFENSE: Why did you say half of it?

COMPLAINANT: I didn't say half of it.

DEFENSE: So when you were asked this question—page sixty-five Your Honor—"How far did it go inside your vagina?" "Only about halfway?"

COMPLAINANT: Maybe I mean halfway of me.

DEFENSE: Oh, is that right?

COMPLAINANT: Yeah.

DEFENSE: When you were asked this question: "When you said he put it in halfway, how far are you talking about?" "I don't know, probably about two inches," you were talking about you too, were you?

COMPLAINANT: Yes.

DEFENSE: Because you could make an estimation as to the distance at that time, could you?

COMPLAINANT: No, but you know what you feel.

DEFENSE: You are telling lies, aren't you?

COMPLAINANT: No I am not.[60]

The above excerpt exemplifies the means by which cross-examination on alleged incidents focuses, particularly, on inconsistencies in minute details, which are then magnified and reinforced through exaggerated questioning in front of a jury; sometimes, as in this case, the errors are used in a humiliating manner against the complainant. In the above cross-examination, the defense barrister continually led the complainant's evidence into an area where he already had evidence of inconsistency. Throughout the sequence of questions, the defense barrister continually pushed the complainant to provide an answer that could be further juxtaposed to previous evidence, no matter how minute. This was a common occurrence in the majority of trials analyzed in this research. The defense barrister in this case knew he could show evidence of inconsistency between the committal and trial, and strung the questions out to re-ventilate what he considered to be minor inconsistencies.

However, this supposed inconsistency was nothing more than two generalized comments from a young girl's police statement, which she gave in a distressed and exhausted state. The girl maintained that her comment about the length of time she believed her father penetrated her was a figure of speech. She consistently stated that her comment about how far she was penetrated was connected more to how far she *felt* penetrated. *Sine qua non* to these two areas is the whole maleness of the evidence required in rape and sexual assault cases: a victim of rape is put in a position where her statement is supposed to reflect technical details like depth and duration of penetration, since this reflects a patriarchal understanding of "real" rape. The cross-examination reads more like a pornographic vignette than an investigation to identify factual evidence. Would this evidence have meant so much if the results of the DNA testing were admitted? The specifics of depth and duration of penetration would be difficult for anyone to provide in a description of consensual sex, let alone non-consensual sex.

The complainant was reminded that in her committal evidence, when asked if she was physically injured, she replied that she was not. At this trial, when asked if she suffered any physical injury, she said she did, because "it hurt" and also "how can I say it—from emotional and psychological injuries [more] than physical injuries?"[61] The barrister reminded her that in her police statement she said that she experienced a small amount of blood from her vagina after the incident but failed to mention this at the trial. Prior to a trial, every complainant is advised to provide the briefest possible answers to questions and to give only that evidence that corresponds to the question. In numerous trials researched, I found examples of prosecutors, and even judges, reminding complainants, especially children, of what evidence is not allowed to be given (because it is excluded), and to provide brief answers giving only evidence asked for in the question and avoid elaborating unless specifically asked. So it is not surprising that she did not give the evidence of a small amount of blood shortly after the alleged incident. Of course the defense counsel made much of this oversight. The failure of the girl to make an immediate outcry after the first alleged incident was canvassed by the barrister, and the almost-poignant response from the complainant—"I was scared; I was by myself in a city. I didn't know anyone. I was a child. What do you want me to do?"[62]—was met with a series of harsh questions from the defense barrister:

DEFENSE: A child. You have never been in that situation before?

COMPLAINANT: Not when I am in a strange city where I don't know anyone or anything, no.

DEFENSE: You had lived on the streets for quite some period of time, hadn't you?

COMPLAINANT: In [names home city], yes.

DEFENSE: Lived on your wits, wouldn't that be right?

COMPLAINANT: In (names home city), yes, it is different when you are in another city.

DEFENSE: There was no one you could have gone to, is that what you say?

COMPLAINANT: Yes, that is what I felt like.[63]

Highlighting the periods of homelessness experienced by the complainant as a child was a deliberate strategy to make her a non-person, to create prejudice toward her by attaching the stigma of a "homeless" "street-kid." But it was also to suggest a kind of toughness about her, in order to discredit her evidence of feeling frightened and alone. Immediately after this, the barrister re-canvassed the topic of her contact with an organization that provided support for child victims of sexual abuse and their non-offending parent(s), and suggested that this organization would have provided the complainant both with contact with other children who had been sexually abused as well as protective education around sexual assault:

> DEFENSE: You had been at—what is it—PACSA; what does it stand for?
>
> COMPLAINANT: People against child sexual abuse.
>
> DEFENSE: You were a member of that for how long?
>
> COMPLAINANT: My mother was a member of that.
>
> DEFENSE: You were at the youth group, were you?
>
> COMPLAINANT: All us kids used to get together while the adults used to do their bit. We never had an actual organization or club or nothing.
>
> DEFENSE: Still, you had extensive counseling there, didn't you?
>
> COMPLAINANT: No, I didn't have counseling there.
>
> DEFENSE: Speak to anyone at the youth group, did you?
>
> COMPLAINANT: Yeah, I probably did.
>
> DEFENSE: *And did they teach you to go into motel rooms, did they, with people who have just penetrated your vagina with their fingers, especially if they are your father, is that the kind of thing they had taught you?*
>
> COMPLAINANT: No. [emphasis added][64]

The regularity of gratuitous comments continued, and never prompted intervention by the prosecutor or judge. To reinforce the narrative of a knowledgeable streetwise kid, the barrister made the complainant read an old newspaper article written by a journalist, quoting her as a survivor of sexual abuse who wanted to advise other children they should "tell someone even if you feel scared."[65] The girl was only eleven years old at the time of article and said her contact with the journalist arose from her mother's contact with the above-mentioned organization. Undeterred, the barrister behaved as though the complainant had set herself up as an expert on child abuse, saying to her, "You had gone into print, hadn't you, on what children ought to and ought not to do in a situation like that?"[66] The complainant again reiterated that she did not write the article but simply told the journalist, from a child's perspective, that children should tell others about their abuse, even if afraid. In a demeaning sequence of questions, the barrister asked the complainant to tell the jury which parts of the article were not accurate with regards to comments about herself. How can the complainant answer for a journalist, especially one who asked her a couple of questions as a young child and then used them in an article more broadly based on child abuse? The questions seemed more to be an exercise in self-serving hectoring of a complainant.

The legal narrative of "means" was also developed through this line of questioning, especially the girl's access to sexual knowledge, and proximity to other children who had experienced sexual abuse, through contact with this support organization. She was also questioned about alleged discussions with her mother about sexual abuse. These questions were interwoven around questions about her sexual activity with other males and her homelessness and frequent changes in residential locations, and seemed deliberately designed to create an image of a savvy, but unsavory, sexually promiscuous, streetwise kid who had lived rough and knew how to take care of herself.

The topic then moved more specifically to questions about her mental stability. She was asked a burst of short and sharp questions about whether she ever intentionally injured herself, deliberately cut herself, referred to herself by different names, or written herself Christmas cards and signed them as coming from others. She denied ever doing any of these things, and *after* the questions were asked and denied by the complainant, the prosecutor got to his feet to object. Too late, the judge said, the questions had been asked and answered, and he felt the questions went to the credit of the complainant.[67] The questions were designed to support the narrative of mental disturbance, and the apparent green light by the judge about the questions led to further defense questions as to whether the girl used different names, each with a different personality. These were assertions denied by the complainant. Then questions were introduced about her mother questioning her repeatedly about sexual abuse, which the complainant also denied.[68] The question sequence promoted a narrative of shared mental illness between mother and daughter, as well as preparing the evidence the complainant's cousin would give—the one who apprised the replacement expert in the courtroom hallway—about the supposed bizarre behavior of the complainant.

As the cross-examination unfolded, the narrative of the "mad" daughter was combined with questions designed to also further the "bad" daughter narrative. First, previous allegations of sexual abuse, unrelated to the charges faced by the accused, were canvassed in great detail, followed by questions around minute details to highlight errors in recall, which are used to suggest fabrication. Questions about her boyfriend suggested promiscuity by a young teenager, and her homelessness and being made a ward of the state suggested something negative about her character and her home life. Accusations, without any foundation being established, about her use of different names each with a different character pushed the notion of mental instability, and were juxtaposed with information on her mother's conduct to suggest collusion and mental instability between mother and daughter. To saturate the jury's mind with these themes, the barrister again revisited her "allegations" against her brother, as well as a previous accusation against her stepfather.

Here the barrister conducted a series of trials within a trial—examining the complainant about prior *proven* and alleged abuse that were not contended at this trial. The prosecutor objected to the re-canvassing of these issues; however, the judge disagreed, claiming they were "permissible" topics for cross-examination. So, with another green light, the barrister launched into a no-holds-barred reading aloud of the entire police statement made by the complainant against her stepfather when she was ten years old. She was then cross-examined at length about these allegations, and it was noted that they were withdrawn but no reason for their withdrawal was given.[69] The issue is left wide open, and a new topic relating to another previous incident of sexual abuse was canvassed at length.

An almost obsessive focus on duration of penile penetration by the father was also introduced into cross-examination about the *alleged* sexual abuse of the complainant by her brother. Revisiting this topic *ad nauseam*, the defense counsel asked the complainant about the duration of penile penetration by her brother and whether he ejaculated inside her vagina. He then highlighted the most technical differences in her evidence on this issue as compared to her evidence at the previous trial—as though this trial were all about her brother's abuse of her and not the father. He then linked this evidence to her application for crimes compensation—most likely to enhance the narrative of false allegations for fiscal gain.[70]

Her sexual character was again revisited, especially to suggest sexual promiscuity. The barrister accused her of being "expelled" from a boarding house as a young teenager after being caught having sex with someone—an accusation the complainant denied.[71] She was negatively portrayed against those family members supporting the accused and others. The aunt with whom the girl went to live when she was made a ward of the state was described as a woman who was in a "wheelchair" *but* who still took the girl in because her mother was in a *"mental hospital."* The complainant was very young at this stage, and said she did not know the whereabouts of her mother at that stage. She was also accused on a number of occasions of telling relatives (those who were supporting her father) that she was going to revenge her father for divorcing her mother, a claim she denied.[72] Here the narrative is of the promiscuous and ungrateful child unable to be controlled by the "good" family members and others.

As though to cement the link of an unstable and promiscuous child, the defense counsel accused the complainant of sexually harassing her father, saying "It was you who joined your father in the double bed" (in the motel). Her denial to this simply prompted the defense barrister to accuse her of lying.[73] And to ensure the jury did not forget the bulk of defense claims, the barrister promptly rattled off, in quick succession, eight statements about the

Case Study R v G

falsity of all her evidence, punctuating the end of each statement with the accusation that it was all lies. In fact, she was accused of being a liar eight times in a row. A few questions later she was again accused of lying.[74] The degree of penile penetration in inches was again revisited, with the barrister reminding her that she had not been able to tell the jury whether her father's penis entered her "one inch, two inches or three inches."[75] Her previous agreement with a random figure of "two or three inches," and her admission now that she could not be sure exactly how many "inches" allegedly penetrated her, prompted the barrister to remark: "What, you wouldn't say something that wasn't true now would you?"[76] The cross-examination ended with the proverbial comment that her entire evidence was lies.[77]

Complainant Reexamination by the Prosecution

In reexamination by the prosecutor, she was asked whether she retracted the allegations against her stepfather, and she agreed that she did. When asked why she did so, her response was moving in its honesty:

PROSECUTOR: Why did you retract it?

COMPLAINANT: Because...because I was abused so much as a child, well, I was pretty mixed up, you know, pretty confused, didn't really understand about sex or the way it goes or anything. When that happened to me, I didn't think it was that bad and I did tell my mum and my mum did say that it was wrong and that it was rude. Since then me and my stepfather have made up on mutual terms and he said to me he didn't mean it in that way and I will accept it.

PROSECUTOR: Did you go back on it in terms of that incident didn't happen, or was it your attitude to it that changed?

COMPLAINANT: Yes, it was my attitude to it, it did happen.[78]

Her accusation against her stepfather was that he inappropriately touched her bottom, and her reason for retraction is honest (and very likely, given her history). The prosecutor sought to clarify the complainant's emotional state and the context in which she gave her police statement, and the complainant reiterated she was required to remain awake all night, despite being upset and exhausted, and that the policewoman kept telling her to stay awake to complete her statement, which she finished at 6:30 a.m. the following morning.[79]

When asked by the prosecutor to provide information as to whom she had been previously sexually abused by, she included her brother and biological father and two other males (evidence of the latter two males was found in medical, legal, and welfare files subpoenaed by the defense). When asked if she had ever made false allegations of sexual abuse against anyone, she said she had not. This evidence caused the defense counsel to object to what he claimed was "rebuild[ing]" of the complainant's "veracity" through reexamination. He argued it was "unfair" on the grounds that he ought to be able to subject her once again to cross-examination on the males she named as having abused her previously.[80] The judge agreed with the objection and allowed the barrister to re-cross-examine the complainant on previous allegations. The defense counsel presented documents to show that previous charges of sexual abuse against a family member (alleged by the complainant) were "pulled" (meaning for some reason they did not proceed)—as though the complainant and jury would understand this vernacular. The complainant was then questioned about other allegations with the familiar defense claim that they too were made around the time her mother was allegedly involved in disputes with family members of the alleged perpetrators. Re-cross-examination finished on this note and there was no further reexamination by the prosecutor.

Evidence-in-Chief and Cross-examination of the Mother

Prosecution-led evidence from the mother was very brief and consisted mainly of establishing that the complainant was her daughter, and that she had commenced contact with her biological father a short time before the allegations of sexual abuse were made by her daughter. Cross-examination of the mother in both trials was as harsh and almost as lengthy as that faced by the complainant. Her private counseling and psychiatric files were used against her in a most demeaning way. Some transcripts excerpts included here are taken from the 1995 trial as they are very similar to the 1996 trial.[81] The mother's past psychiatric treatment; her later disclosure in adult life that her own father had sexually abused her and her sister, resulting in limited contact with her family; and her childhood and failed marriages were all canvassed in cross-examination. One of the earliest topics canvassed related to her previous psychiatric treatment:

> DEFENSE: You have been under a number of psychiatrists haven't you?
>
> MOTHER: Yes.
>
> DEFENSE: You were suffering delusions weren't you?
>
> MOTHER: Yes, I was.
>
> DEFENSE: When you went into the hospital, you thought you were sitting in a nest of vipers, didn't you?

MOTHER: Yes.

DEFENSE: And you were hearing hissing?

MOTHER: Yes.

DEFENSE: You were diagnosed, weren't you, in 1993 as suffering manic depression?

MOTHER: Yes.[82]

Following the above topic were questions about her childhood health:

DEFENSE: You had asthma as a child?

MOTHER: Yes.

DEFENSE: How old were you when you developed asthma?

MOTHER: I think I was about two years old; that's what I was told how old I was when I was diagnosed with asthma.

DEFENSE: Sometimes if you didn't want to go to school, would you say that you were sick?

MOTHER: No, not that I remember. I may have done. All children try that one.

DEFENSE: Would you pretend that you had an asthma attack?

MOTHER: No.

DEFENSE: You never pretended that you had an asthma attack?

MOTHER: No, I don't believe I did.

DEFENSE: Well you said before that all children try that one. Were you one of those children?

MOTHER: No, not pretending asthma.

DEFENSE: You remember that do you?

MOTHER: I remember having [asthma attacks] very clearly; it's not something you forget.

DEFENSE: If your mother said that you would bring on an asthma attack to avoid doing domestic chores as a child, that would be quite wrong?

MOTHER: From my point of view, I don't believe I ever did.[83]

Her childhood health was made an issue even to the point of bringing her mother, with whom she has a difficult relationship, into a trial that is supposed to be about a father's sexual abuse of his daughter. The tactic here was to portray mental instability and deceitful conduct by the mother as a child to create a narrative link to adult instability and deceitful conduct by way of mother-daughter collusion. Directly following this line of questioning, the barrister asked the mother questions about her own childhood and relationship with her parents, who were supporting the accused in this case:

DEFENSE: Did you ever inflict bruises upon yourself?

MOTHER: Yes I did.

DEFENSE: When did you first inflict bruises on yourself?

MOTHER: When I was a young teenager.

DEFENSE: Whereabouts would you inflict bruises on yourself?

MOTHER: Mostly on my arms.

DEFENSE: Would you do this after you had an argument with your parents?

MOTHER: No.

DEFENSE: Why did you bruise yourself?

MOTHER: Because I had very low self esteem and I saw myself as not a very good person.[84]

Questions about her private disclosure to a counselor about alleged childhood sexual abuse by her father were, of course, made public knowledge through the trial. At one point, the mother commented she had endured "an awful lot of sadness in my life," and that she did not want to remember many things.[85] This statement only resulted in the defense barrister making continual reference to her status as an "inmate" in a psychiatric institution and more humiliating details about her behavior while under care, for example:

DEFENSE: There have been occasions you couldn't hear people talking because of the hissing of vipers in your skull; that would be right, wouldn't it?

MOTHER: Yes.

DEFENSE: When speaking to admitting doctors you would say to them "I am Yaweh, you are Satan"; you would say that to them?

MOTHER: Yes.

DEFENSE: You have also been a counselor, haven't you, and you would counsel people who have been the victims of sexual abuse?

MOTHER: No. I worked as a volunteer coordinator.

DEFENSE: Not as a counselor?

MOTHER: No.

DEFENSE: You have had some experience with satanic abuse, haven't you?

MOTHER: I have had no experience with it personally.

DEFENSE: What is satanic abuse?

MOTHER: It's usually called ritual abuse.

DEFENSE: Tell us what ritual abuse is.

MOTHER: I guess where people believe—worship Satan.

DEFENSE: What's it got to do with abuse?

MOTHER: The children are abused in a ritual fashion.[86]

In this excerpt, the barrister directly linked her medically diagnosed delusions with her volunteer work in the field of child sexual abuse. The questions then addressed her contact with people whose children had been sexually abused, the purpose of which was to mobilize the narrative of "means" to gather knowledge about sexual abuse. In a similar style to the questioning of the complainant, the mother was asked about previous allegations her daughter made against others, and (incredibly) was asked to provide specific details, such as the number of incidents alleged by her daughter against a person more than nine years previously. Her inability to recall such specifics, including the "chronological" order of incidents occurring a decade previously, was treated with disdain. Without any apparent opposition from the prosecutor, the defense counsel roamed at large, asking the mother questions about the abuse of her daughter and other children that were not the subject of any counts in this particular trial.[87]

In finishing his cross-examination, the defense counsel reiterated that the mother "feigned" asthma attacks to get out of chores and linked this to her daughter as someone who told "lies."[88] It may well be that the juxtaposition of these two concepts is a coincidence, but it might also be deliberate to position both mother and daughter as liars—especially since the defense counsel told the mother her own mother's evidence would support both of the above claims. Finally, he reminded the mother that, at the previous trial, her own mother and other relatives gave evidence to the court that she and her daughter were not the type of people who should be believed "under oath." Perhaps to emphasize this point, the defense counsel claimed that the mother's knowledge of this evidence triggered her to avoid attending court on that occasion on the basis that she was not well.[89]

The unrestricted cross-examination of the mother consisted almost entirely on revisiting her previous psychiatric treatment and counseling as though her previous medical history was relevant to the allegations made by her daughter. It enabled defense counsel to draw out past life experiences of the mother reflected in her private medical and counseling records, and use them in a contemporary setting in a case that was convened to examine allegations of father-daughter rape. Using counseling and other medical records against complainants in sexual offenses is the staple diet of many defense lawyers[90] and this case highlights the application of this tactic to supporting mothers.

Reexamination was brief, and consisted mainly of the mother acknowledging that she had been diagnosed with a bipolar disorder and had taken prescribed medication. Her periods of psychiatric hospitalization were brief and occurred on a couple of occasions prior to the disorder being diagnosed. She also clarified that her involvement with families alleging ritual abuse was only as a volunteer, and her role involved helping supervise children attending counseling. She had never conducted any counseling of child-abuse victims.[91]

The Accused: Evidence-in-Chief and Cross-examination

Defense-led evidence-in-chief from the accused was succinct and very brief, consisting basically of a complete denial of all allegations. Such a course of action was all the easier since evidence that might otherwise have challenged this denial was safely removed from jury scrutiny. The focus of prosecution cross-examination was the events leading up to the two charges, with the accused often relying on a stock answer that he could not remember details surrounding the events.

The accused described the accusations as a "nightmare" he had been forced to live with for five years, although when it came to details about the events surrounding the "nightmare," the accused often said that he simply could not remember.[92] For example, when asked about the sequence of events when they arrived at the motel, the accused replied that he could not remember—after all, he said, it was "five years ago." That is reasonable. But of course this sense of reasonableness was never afforded the complainant, not just about specifics from the incident, but other incidents going back eight and nine years. The same went for her mother; they were called liars for not being able to remember particulars even more miniscule than those being asked of the father. But, for the accused, the inability to remember is taken as a credible comment. The issue of the daughter being the one to invite herself into the father's bed was canvassed. The father alleged his daughter got into his bed and that he immediately left the bed to go and sleep elsewhere in the room.[93]

As cross-examination unfolded, the accused was able to freely express a good deal of information about things he had "heard" about his daughter prior to the allegations, and in giving this information he also promoted himself around the "good father narrative." The following excerpt is a good example of the latitude afforded the accused to damage the character of his daughter by introducing hearsay evidence while promoting his own alleged good intentions. He told the court his wife had warned him not to "trust" the complainant, after he expressed a wish to bring his daughter to live with him in Victoria because he was concerned about her lifestyle. He also added that she was living in a "women's shelter," despite being only fourteen years old:

> she was fooling around with boys...when she was in the women's shelter, she was not sticking to the curfew time and I spoke with the lady in charge, she was out on the beach with boys until three, four o'clock in the morning...she was going out with [his son's] best friend, [name's son] being my son, and his best friend [name's friend], and they were sleeping together to my knowledge, and I had convinced my wife it would be a good thing to get her off the street and out of the shelter and live in a family environment, go to school, and maybe it would turn her life around.[94]

This "hearsay" evidence about what someone told the father is the kind of character assassination that the accused engaged in during a number of trials researched. Fathers told of "hearing" about something, or being told something "bad" about their child by someone who never comes to court to give such evidence. The son, mentioned by the accused, is the same son who pleaded guilty and was convicted of sexual abusing the complainant. Moreover, prior to this trial he was convicted and sentenced to jail for contempt of court when he threatened the life of his sister and his mother should they give evidence against the accused.[95] The former boyfriend of the girl (as also mentioned by the accused in the above excerpt) also happens to be the best friend of the brother and was also supporting the accused, and gave evidence for the defense at this trial.

Prosecution questions continued to center on details leading up to alleged incidents, and continued to result in claims by the accused that he could not recall specifics. This constant lack of recall was a common feature in the evidence of accused fathers across trials, and also one which largely went without any adverse challenge, as was the case in this trial. It was also discomforting that the prosecutor in this case was not more alert to how the framing of his questions to the accused actually served to provide him with opportunities to enhance himself as the "good father," while condemning his daughter's character. An example of this is the aforementioned excerpt in which the father introduced all manner of hearsay evidence about his daughter's alleged conduct prior to reestablishing contact with him.

The accused's evidence concluded with the judge allowing the defense barrister to lead further evidence from the accused: his daughter's allegations had caused him to go "bankrupt" because he sold his truck to allegedly fund part of the trial, and the trial had severely disrupted his business.[96] This information was most likely deployed to elicit sympathy from the jury, and again reveals the degree of wide-ranging information that can be used by the defense counsel, as opposed to the limited factual evidence that can be led by the prosecution. After all, the complainant was not permitted to relate to the jury any adverse effects she had suffered, or was currently experiencing as a result of the allegations and the protracted legal proceedings that followed.

The Penis and the Beer Glass: Expert Opinion

An extraordinary piece of evidence immediately followed the evidence of the accused, when the defense counsel called "expert" testimony from a pathologist who measured the length and circumference of the father's penis. The *penis measurer* described to the court how he examined the penis of the accused in the semi-erect position, and told the court that, at this level of erection, the penis measured "eighteen centimeters in length, or approximately seven inches" with a "circumference of fifteen centimeters, or approximately six inches."[97] The defense counsel asked the "expert" if he could in any way compare the thickness of the man's penis to an "ordinary everyday object." The witness obliged with a very macho locker-room analogy, saying that the penis of the accused could be compared to a "seven-ounce beer glass."[98] Finally, the barrister wanted the witness to tell the court if the penis fell within the "normal" range of penis size. The "expert" suggested that the penis was "larger" than the accepted norm.[99] This last piece of extracted evidence appeared to have more to do with parading a masculine obsession with size, than anything else. Perhaps it was thought the jury might be impressed with this bit of information. After all, the relevant facts were obliterated, so why not entertain the jury with statistics about the male appendage? Not surprisingly, the prosecutor had no cross-examination for the penis measurer.

The exact purpose of this bizarre evidence was not articulated, although it is reasonable to suggest that the defense would use this evidence in their closing address (which is not transcribed) in relation to the complainant's evidence under cross-examination regarding the degree of penile penetration. Inconsistencies in the girl's evidence regarding the size of her father's penis, and how many inches she was allegedly penetrated, identify the male understanding of rape that is central to legal narratives of rape. The assertion is that, for such an allegation to be true, the girl should be able to give a description of the penis as to its exact size (length and circumference!), and how far in inches or centimeters it penetrated her.

Other Prosecution Witnesses

Evidence was given by the motel manager who contacted the police after the girl sought assistance from his staff. He told the court that after the police came and collected the complainant he kept a close watch on the motel room, since he knew the accused remained there. His evidence was that after the police left the motel the accused "ran off to his truck and drove away" and since he did not leave through the front door of the motel room, the manager believed he must have left the motel room via the back window.[100] His evidence of the emotional demeanor of the complainant also supported the evidence of the motel waitress, who had said that the complainant appeared to be in shock when she entered the restaurant and asked for help, saying that her father had just "raped" her.[101] When the motel manager was asked about his observation of the complainant when he first saw her in the motel foyer with the waitress, he said:

> I saw a little girl, quite young, shaking. I have never seen anybody shake like that in my life...she was quite hysterical...she couldn't really talk, she was sobbing. Every time she tried to talk, the tears sort of overwhelmed her and she couldn't get any words out...[I] tried to figure out what was going on and she told me her father had tried to get into bed with her.[102]

Despite attempts by the defense counsel to confuse the manager about his evidence it was evident from the transcript that the manager was confident and firm in his recollection. This obviously irritated the barrister, whose questions became increasingly annoying and almost bizarre. For instance, when the manager maintained that he had kept the motel room under constant observation until the police arrived, the barrister demanded to know how the manager came to be standing at the window. This led to the manager giving evidence of the physical machinations of how he walked through the foyer door, turned around, and looked through the glass. Seemingly still not convinced that the motel manager could remember watching the motel room from the foyer window, the defense counsel queried that the manager could actually "recollect...five years after the event, turning around [to look through the windows]." As the manager said, he would have to turn around in order to look outside.[103]

The mother of the complainant was also chastised for being able to "recall" certain things, but harangued for not being able to recall other things. Inconsistencies due to the complainant's inability to recall details were met with incredulity and accusations of lying. The accused, however, was never challenged for a lack of recall or ability to recall details.

The police informant gave very brief evidence, and quickly attracted the ire of the defense barrister after he claimed that he believed the accused had "some knowledge" of his daughter's accusations to the police.[104] The judge asked the prosecutor to ensure the policeman kept only to what was said, and not his observed impressions. This request is reasonable; however, one cannot help but juxtapose this comment to the abundant defense evidence given by the accused and other witnesses about what they *heard* and what they *thought* about the complainant. It appears that the latitude afforded defense witnesses is rarely if ever afforded prosecution witnesses.

The male forensic pathologist who examined the girl gave evidence that her vagina was "non-virginal" and had a vaginal discharge, which he described as "smelly," "thick," and "white." He described recent small "tears" to the vagina that were consistent with either "rough intercourse," an unlubricated vagina, or digital trauma such as that caused by scratching.[105] In cross-examination the defense counsel highlighted the latter point by suggesting to the pathologist that scratching one's vagina with the hand might cause the kind of small tears in the vagina that he found, and the pathologist agreed. Securing such an agreement would assist the defense counsel to explain the presence of vaginal trauma as self-inflicted by the girl scratching herself. Recall that in cross-examination of the complainant prior to the pathologist's evidence, the defense counsel asked the complainant if she "scratched" her vagina at some time during the day of the alleged incident (an incident that occurred almost five years ago now).

Despite the actual DNA results being excluded from the trial, the prosecutor led evidence from the pathologist who conducted the tests and isolated, at least, the fact that there were seminal stains found in the girl, in her underwear, and on the double-bed motel bed sheets. With the DNA safely out of the picture, the defense barrister was free to actually turn the limited pathology evidence to his advantage. In cross-examination, the pathologist admitted he was unable to "age" the spermatozoa taken from the girl and other items, leading the defense to claim that "spermatozoa are pretty tough things" before articulating medical literature which suggested that spermatozoa could live for up to seven days.[106] The pathologist agreed. The barrister went on to ask a number of highly scientific questions based on literature on semen testing, which did little to enhance any understanding for the jury. It appears to have been a deliberate strategy to make the original evidence of semen found in the girl seem complicated and open to wide conjecture as to how it got there. And this is precisely the direction in which the defense narrative would develop.

The former boyfriend of the complainant gave evidence that he had engaged in unprotected sexual intercourse with her the night before she left to go on the interstate truck trip with her father. The girl had denied such an accusation when mentioned to her in cross-examination, and it appears that such a story may not have been in the mind of the boyfriend to begin with. At the committal hearing, he had agreed that their relationship had broken up some months before she accompanied her father on the interstate trip and, therefore, they had not had any sexual contact for those months. Between the committal hearing and the trial, the boyfriend's evidence had undergone a complete change, and he explained this gross inconsistency by suggesting he was not good with dates and, further, that whenever the alleged offense was said to have occurred, he had had intercourse with the complainant the day before. The convenient nature of this evidence is, of course, easily complemented by the defense narrative of the possible longevity of spermatozoa, the self-inflicted vaginal trauma caused by scratching, and the character assassination of the girl as a fabricator of previous false allegations. With the DNA profiling of the semen removed from the jury, the advancement of the narrative of casual sex with a former boyfriend the night before her father allegedly raped her comes to the fore free from any evidence of rebuttal.

Other Witnesses for the Defense

The defense counsel called the counselor, whom the complainant was accused of telling that her brother had not really abused her, to give evidence against the complainant. The way this counselor interpreted the girl's exploration of her pain in private counseling sessions, and recorded them in writing, was used to bolster the defense narrative of a girl with a history of false allegations and mental instability. Although the counselor indicated that she made those notes as a result of her therapeutic contact with the girl, the issue of counseling notes of any kind is deeply disturbing—in this case, for two reasons. Counseling records used against the girl were from previous—and, in one case, *legally proven*—abuse that had no connection to the charges under consideration. The girl's private exploration of her pain, with a counselor she obviously trusted, was not just made available for public scrutiny, but was stripped of therapeutic context and isolated from any deeper analysis, making the comments malleable to a defense claim of falsity and recantation.

As documented in mine and others' research, the use of counseling files against complainants is a common legal tool, one that has caused considerable concern and debate.[107] The defense counsel routinely subpoena such files in order to go on what is often described in trials as a "fishing expedition" to try and find any evidence they might use to discredit the allegations and character of the complainant. As stated earlier in this chapter, in a therapeutic environment many victim/survivors of rape and sexual abuse—both child and adult—explore their pain in ways that frequently involve paraphrasing social myths that hold victims accountable for being raped and sexually assaulted. Minimizing harm to oneself is often a defense mechanism used by hurting children and adults in an effort to assure themselves that they are alright. This is a common response to trauma, and it is to be hoped that counselors and therapists trained in understanding the impacts of sexual crimes would always explore these issues with a client. It is my view that as long as the courts continue to allow defense lawyers to seize on these private pains, counselors and therapists ought to note the literature around these common defense mechanisms in order to introduce this counterintuitive evidence within the courtroom.

To complete the character assassination of mother and daughter, the defense counsel were able to lead evidence from various relatives (who had been estranged from them for some time, and were supporting the accused) that the character of the mother and daughter was such that they were not credible people under "oath." The complainant's maternal grandmother was allowed to give evidence about her daughter's (the complainant's mother's) childhood to reinforce the defense narrative of the "mad" mother. She told the court that her daughter had colluded with her granddaughter as a "payback" against her former husband and her own father. The grandmother went on to say that her daughter falsely accused her own father of "incest" because he had given her a belting when she was a child. She further told the court that she believed her granddaughter, the complainant, had fabricated allegations of sexual abuse against the accused as a form of revenge, a "payback" for divorcing her mother when she was only an infant.[108] This evidence fulfilled the narrative prophesy already established by the defense in the form of their "expert" witness, who said one of the "danger signs" was when other family members dismissed an alleged victim's claims of sexual abuse. In this courtroom, the judge allowed a double condemning of mother and daughter based on evidence that lacked substance and had no relevance to the charges under consideration.

Outcome

The jury acquitted the accused on the charge of sexual intercourse with his daughter. They remained unable to reach a verdict on the lesser charge relating to the indecent assault in the truck. The OPP decided against proceeding with the undecided charge and a *nolle prosequi,* was recorded, meaning that any further trial to hear the charge was permanently discontinued.

Case Study R v G

As the entire transcript from the 1995 trial was not available, it is not possible to give an exact breakdown of the questions faced by the complainant and accused; therefore, the following breakdown is incomplete. At the 1996 trial, the complainant faced a total of 830 questions: 624 of them from the defense barrister, 197 from the prosecutor, and nine from the trial judge. At the 1996 trial, the accused faced 416 questions: 328 from the prosecutor, seventy-nine from his defense barrister, and nine from the trial judge. Including the committal, 1995 trial (partial transcript) and 1996 trial which went to completion, the complainant faced 441 questions from the prosecutor, 2,162 questions from the defense barrister, and nine questions from the trial judges. By comparison, the accused, who is supposed to be the person on trial, faced seventy-nine questions from his defense barrister, 328 questions from the prosecutor, and nine questions from the trial judge.

Comment

The defense narrative mobilized in this case was that of the "mad" and "bad" daughter who was supposedly motivated by revenge against her father, and this—coupled with her supposed mental instability—led to a false accusation, not just against him, but others as well. Judicial discretion plays a pivotal role in deciding the evidentiary boundaries and tenor of a trial. Indeed, the mobilization of competing discourses and stock-story narratives is dependent largely upon judicial decisions delineating evidentiary boundaries.

The defense narrative developed and mobilized in this trial was clearly advantaged by judicial decisions that diluted the strength of prosecution evidence while allowing the introduction of evidence about the complainant's previous sexual history, including previous alleged and proven sexual abuse, though the proven abuse was not made explicit to the jury. Two vital evidentiary rulings and an almost unfettered right to impugn the character of a girl and her mother, with barely any evidence to sustain such assertions, enabled a very powerful and pernicious narrative to take center stage. Complementing this strategy was defense cross-examination, which moved frequently and quickly between topics and timeframes. This is a common stratagem designed to confuse the complainant, put her under pressure, and force her to make errors in her evidence.

The evidence of the accused was very simple compared to the complex storyline deployed against the complainant. While complex, it was also virtually seamless in that evidence of rebuttal about her character and sexual history was conspicuously absent. The evidence of the motel manager was strong, but perhaps the damage to the complainant's character had been so well executed that evidence supporting her disclosure and emotional state at the time could not compete with the master narrative. It is appalling that the jury were never given information about her brother's conviction for sexually abusing her. He gave no evidence at the trial and quite possibly this was a tactic to ensure that his previous convictions, including the conviction for contempt of court in threatening his sister and mother, were never revealed to the jury. One wonders how the legal narrative might have fared if the original judicial ruling excluding all prior sexual-history evidence had stood.

The selective use of pathology evidence based on the semen sample highlights the propensity for judicial rulings to aid and abet defense narratives. It is my view that when the defense barrister introduced the narrative of the boyfriend being the donor of the semen sample, the prosecutor should have been able to rebut this evidence—if not by alerting the jury to the DNA results, then at the very least by being able to inform the jury that DNA tests did not support the defense claim.

The prosecution case was, in many ways, completely ineffective in trying to establish a discourse that strengthened the basic facts of the case. The prosecutor faced an extremely difficult task in trying to present an alternative discourse and alternative facts. In some ways, it was almost impossible for the prosecution to present effectively when crucial forensic evidence was removed from jury consideration, and the supposed sexual and psychological character of the girl and her mother were allowed to become the sole focus of the trial.

I contend that on a number of occasions, defense cross-examination contravened sections 39 and 40 of the *Evidence Act*, which prohibit a witness from cross-examination that humiliates, harasses, annoys, or may be considered insulting or offensive.[109] Recent research on sexual-offense proceedings, including cases involving very young children, has identified levels of aggressive and derogatory cross-examination.[110] Research also revealed that judges and prosecutors failed to intervene to protect complainants when cross-examination breached these standards.[111] In response to one of these studies, it was counter-argued that provisions in the *Evidence Act*, namely sections 39 and 40, protect complainants from any cross-examination that humiliates, harasses, annoys or may be considered offensive or insulting.[112] It has further been suggested that Victorian barristers would not conduct cross-examination in such a style because it would contravene these sections.[113] Clearly, research negates such a claim.

In this trial, the complainant was the brunt of crude humor between the judge and legal counsel on several occasions. One judge described his experience of reading the complainant's counseling and other files was like reading a "file so thickened [with] sexual misbehavior, it is like meeting a combination of *God's Little Acre* and *A Streetcar Named Desire* without the literary panache [emphasis added]."[114] The current incumbent judge in the 1995 trial said he recalled reading that comment and found it provided him with the "only bit of levity" he had on that particular day.[115] The prosecutor in that trial also found it amusing, describing it as a "classic," and said he intended having it included in the *Bar News* (a legal journal for lawyers).[116]

The judge in the 1995 trial also commented that the girl's history of sexual violence had achieved "Rabelaisian proportions."[117] In the same trial, the defense barrister claimed that the number of allegations of "incest" detailed in the complainant's counseling files placed her evidence outside the boundaries of "normality." This line of argument prompted the judge to draw an analogy between her history of sexual abuse and the conduct of a prostitute, leading the defense barrister to retort that "even a prostitute would not have sex with so many members of her own family."[118] The analogy aside, the notion that it is the girl child who engages in sexual intercourse, rather than the one who is violated by adult males, remains one of the many proactive ways in which "incest" is identified and discussed in legal discourse. It also suggests that the number of allegations of intrafamilial rape can indicate normality or abnormality, which in turn affects their believability.

Such offensive persiflage on the part of the judge and defense barrister suggests the girl has become a legal parody—so much for the objective treatment and dignity of all persons who come before the law.

Finally, as with a number of other sexual-offense proceedings, the time delay between the complainant's police report and the eventual legal proceedings is of concern. The delayed trial makes it difficult for victim/survivors to heal as best they can from their trauma and move forward, and allows the legal emphasis on the recollection of peripheral and minute details to disadvantage them.

Notes

1. R v G (Victorian County Court, Campton, J. 1995), at 96. Note that evidence regarding the semen evidence was actually given at the first trial of R v G (Victorian County Court, Villenue-Smith, 1994), but the transcript of this trial was not intact, and the pathology results were found in the transcript of the 1995 trial where they were commented on by legal counsel.
2. See Glossary for an explanation of this legal procedure.
3. R v G (1994), at 348.
4. Ibid., judge's ruling, at 72–5. See Glossary for an explanation of this legislation.

5. R v G (1995), at 248.
6. R v G (1995), at 198.
7. Diagnostic and Statistical Manual of Mental Disorders, 3rd ed., revised (Washington, DC: American Psychiatric Association, 1987).
8. See, for example: Rand (1989); Rand (1990); and (1993).
9. I am thinking in particular of the work of early 20th century North American jurist John Henry Wigmore, who wrote odiously of women and girl children who made allegations of sexual abuse and even the most cursory reading of his writing reveals the entrenched misogyny. He promoted a view of alleged victims as prone to mental illness and fantasy based on Freud's work as well as personal letters he received from psychiatrists prepared to proclaim the lying and unstable nature of women and girls. See Wigmore (1970). Examples can be found in contemporary literature and discourses linking mental instability to allegations of sexual abuse. The false memory syndrome is one example of syndromizing the frequency of sexual abuse disclosures.
10. R v G (1995), at 171.
11. Ibid.
12. Ibid., at 172.
13. My research has found numerous examples of this occurrence, and it is discussed in my Ph.D. thesis and other work. See Taylor (2001a) and Taylor (1997).
14. See, for example, the appeal decisions in R v J (1998), no. 2, 3 VR 602; and R v Ware (1997), 1 VR 647. The Appellate Court in Ware's case noted the "alarming" frequency in which victims were rejected by family members who chose to rally to the support of the offender.
15. R v G (1995), at 176.
16. Ibid., at 173.
17. See, for example: D'Arcy (1999); Armstrong (1994); Finkelhor (1986); and Russell (1983), 133.
18. R v G (1995), at 175.
19. Ibid., at 202–7.
20. Ibid., at 208.
21. Ibid., at 209.
22. Ibid.
23. Sexual Offenses Interim Report. Victorian Law Reform Commission (June 2003). See also the work of Professor Jennifer Temkin, a British laywer who has written extensively on this area: Temkin (1984), Temkin (1993), Temkin (2002), and Temkin (2003).
24. R v G (Victorian County Court, O'Shea, J. 1996), at 24–33
25. Private communication between author and a prosecutor, 1997.
26. Gewirtz (1996) discusses the way trials have evolved to become a government function and victims of crime as simply a witness for the state.
27. R v G (1996), at 10.
28. See, for example, Masson (1984), 49, which provides a specific example. Freud is another who falsified his early case studies where fathers were accused of perpetrating sexual abuse against daughters. To accommodate his own discomfort with this reality, he identified "uncles" instead of "fathers" as frequent perpetrators, and only admitted to this cover-up many years later. Further, Henry Wigmore's legal tome contains examples of psychiatrists expressing outrage that girls would accuse their fathers, and in contemporary legal trials and psycho-legal discourses, the social status or character of

an accused father is often lauded as evidence of the falsity in cases of intrafamilial and extrafamilial sexual abuse, as though such evidence were axiomatic with regard to the innocence of the accused.

29. Masson (1984), 49.
30. R v G (1996), at 11.
31. Ibid., at 249.
32. Ibid., at 255–64.
33. Ibid.
34. Ibid., at 258–60.
35. See Glossary under "OPP" for explanation.
36. R v G (1996), at 248. This tactic is reminiscent of Wigmore's writing on sexual abuse complainants in which he argued that any girl alleging sexual abuse against her father must first be examined by a psychiatrist to assess her mental stability. See Wigmore (1970).
37. R v J (Victorian County Court, retrial, Campton, J. 1995).
38. R v G (1996), at 47.
39. Ibid., at 51–2.
40. Ibid., at 52.
41. Ibid., at 54–6.
42. Ibid., at 56.
43. Ibid., at 57.
44. Ibid., at 118–9.
45. R v G (1996), at 58–9. Note the same type of questions put to the complainant at the 1995 trial, at 408.
46. R v G (1995), at 408.
47. Ibid., at 59.
48. See, for example: Australian Law Reform Commission and Human Rights and Equal Opportunity Commission, in Seen and Heard: Priority for Children in the Legal Process, Report No. 84 (1997); McConaghy (1995); Grunseit (1991), 143–50; Summit (1983).
49. For comment about the potential for harm when the therapeutic voice of the child is drawn into legal arena via the use of expert testimony by counselors and psychiatrists, see King & Piper (1995).
50. R v G (1996), at 60–1.
51. Ibid., at 63.
52. Ibid.
53. Ibid., at 64–5.
54. Ibid., at 73.
55. Ibid., at 66–8.
56. See, for example: R v G (1995), at 410; and R v G (1996), at 73.
57. R v G (1996), at 70–1.
58. Ibid., at 74–5.
59. Ibid., at 148–51.
60. Ibid., at 110–1.
61. Ibid., at 90.
62. Ibid., at 81.
63. Ibid.
64. Ibid., at 82.

65. Ibid., at 82–3.
66. Ibid.
67. Ibid., at 93.
68. Ibid.
69. Ibid., at 95–100.
70. Ibid., at 100–1.
71. Ibid., at 104.
72. Ibid., at 103–4.
73. Ibid., at 104.
74. Ibid., at 105–6.
75. Ibid., at 110, 112.
76. Ibid., at 110.
77. Ibid., at 113.
78. Ibid., at 116.
79. Ibid., at 118.
80. Ibid., at 118–9.
81. Extensive notes were taken from the 1996 trial, and it was noted that they almost mirrored the questions put to the mother at the 1995 trial, which did not go to completion. I later encountered difficulty accessing the complete 1996 trial, despite having extensive notes. I did have the entire 1995 transcript, so for ease of readership and clarity of question design and structure, a number of excerpts are from the 1995 trial, as I did not always have full quotations from the 1996 trial regarding the mother's cross-examination.
82. R v G (1995), at 335. See R v G (1996), trial transcript, at 187–90, for similar cross-examination examples.
83. Ibid., at 346. See also R v G (1996), trial transcript, at 190–6, for similar cross-examination examples.
84. Ibid.
85. Ibid., at 333–4.
86. R v G (1996), at 190.
87. Ibid., at 190–3. See also R v G (1995), trial transcript, at 364–73.
88. Ibid., at 196.
89. Ibid., at 198.
90. Cossins & Pilkington (1996).
91. Ibid., at 201–3.
92. Ibid., at 219.
93. Ibid., at 213.
94. Ibid., at 225.
95. Ibid., at 213. Note the son was jailed in 1994 for this incident and it is mentioned in both transcripts.
96. Ibid., at 227.
97. Ibid., at 245.
98. Ibid., at 246.
99. Ibid.
100. Ibid., at 130–7.
101. Ibid., at 125.
102. Ibid., at 129.
103. Ibid., at 137.

104. Ibid., at 151–2.
105. Ibid., at 148.
106. Ibid., at 155–62.
107. See Taylor (2001a); Bronitt & McSherry (1997); and Victorian Law Reform Commission, Sexual Offenses Interim Report.
108. R v G (1996), at 277–83.
109. Evidence Act 1958, Section 39, states: "Indecent or scandalous questions. The court shall forbid any questions or inquiries which it regards as indecent or scandalous, although such questions or inquiries may have some bearing on the questions before the court, unless they relate to facts in issue or to matters necessary to be known in order to determine whether or not the facts in issued existed." Section 40 states: "Questions intended to insult or annoy. The court shall forbid or disallow any question which appears to it to be intended to insult or annoy, or which though proper in itself appear to the court needlessly offensive in form."
110. Puren (1999) and Heenan & McKelvie (1997).
111. Heenan & McKelvie (1997). Note the authors of this report suggest a failure of judicial intervention to protect complainants in cases that, in their opinion, contravened Sections 39 and 40.
112. Curtain (1999).
113. Ibid.
114. R v G (1995), at 150. Note: This comment is recorded in this particular trial transcript but does not make it clear which judge made the comment, as four different judges were appointed to this case before it proceeded to completion in 1996.
115. Ibid.
116. Ibid.
117. Ibid., at 277.
118. Ibid., at 247.

5 ▪ Case Study R v D

Background to the Case

A MALE CHILD, who turned eleven at the time of the trial, made a police statement, at the age of eight, that his stepfather had sexually abused him when he was between the ages of seven and eight. The boy alleged several incidents of abuse involving anal penetration by his stepfather, who was of Chinese origin. Aside from the sexual penetration, the boy told police his father had threatened serious consequences if he ever disclosed the abuse, which included being threatened with weapons, including a firearm. The accused was charged with three counts of penetration of a child under ten years of age, two counts of indecent assault, and one count of a threat to kill. The accused was a self-employed tradesman and the family lived in an outer Melbourne suburb.

In his statement, the boy identified two specific incidents in which he describes anal penetration by his stepfather. The boy was able to provide contextual evidence to these alleged episodes, saying that the first occurred on a visit to a worksite with his stepfather, which was in fact a house construction. The boy linked the second alleged incident to a particular day he recalls, a day on which he was not able to go on a school excursion to a dinosaur park. The boy's evidence-in-chief at the trial was consistent with his police statement, which is a credit to the child, considering the time gap of three-and-half years between making his police statement and the matter going to court.

As with all complainants of rape and sexual assault, whether child or adult, police often require they provide details such as the clothing worn by the alleged victim and offender at the time of the incident(s), and activities and communication leading up to and after the incident(s), and this child was no different. In addition, complainants are required to provide dates and times of alleged incidents or other information that might help to identify approximate dates and times. All witnesses are required to certify that their statement is truthful. At the bottom of this child's statement is the declaration: "I know that it is wrong to tell lies and everything that I have told [names police officer] in this statement is the truth."

The child's family constellation included a full sibling and two half-siblings, all younger than himself. At the time of the alleged abuse they lived with their mother and stepfather in an inner Melbourne suburb. Throughout the trial, the child had the full support of this mother. The accused migrated to Australia from China as a child. At the time of the trial the accused was serving a jail term for the abduction and rape of a young woman and also had a number of other previous convictions.

While on bail for the aggravated rape, he left the country with the assistance of his wife. She was supportive of him at that time, despite his history of police involvement, which caused the family hardships that appear to have negatively impacted the children. For example, on one occasion a school social worker contacted the mother to express concern about drawings done by the boy depicting his father using certain objects to beat him and his younger siblings. The boy was also described as showing emotional difficulties and acts of aggression against other children.[1] Two other children in the family reported a fearfulness of the accused because of what they described as violent acts against them and their mother. It was also reported that the family had been forced to relocate on previous occasions to avoid problems associated with the criminal activities of the accused. On occasion, the mother had also taken the children to court during the period that the accused was applying for bail pending the charges on aggravated rape, for which he was later convicted and jailed.

After securing bail in relation to the rape charges, the accused left the country with the knowledge and probable assistance of his wife. She consequently endured financial hardship as she struggled to care for her children. The circumstances around her husband's absence and secret whereabouts made it difficult for her to claim welfare support, and at some point her parents became involved in caring for the welfare of the children. It was during the stepfather's absence that the boy, after seeing something on television about child sexual abuse and hearing his mother talk about the topic with a friend visiting the home, disclosed to his mother that he had been sexually abused by his stepfather. The mother subsequently contacted the police.

At this juncture, I want to make a comment about the mother since she gave evidence at the committal hearing but was not called as a witness at the trial. At the committal hearing the mother was called to give evidence. She spoke of her husband going overseas while on bail and told the court that he wanted her and the children to meet him overseas on the promise of starting a new life together. She made covert arrangements for herself and her children to travel to the country where he was in hiding, but he failed to appear at an agreed destination, leaving her destitute in a foreign country. She says she was forced to contact her parents in Australia, who provided help and the financial resources to bring them back to Australia. Her evidence at the committal was that some time after arriving back in Australia, her son disclosed to her his alleged sexual abuse by the accused, leading her to contact police immediately so her son could make a complaint. She told the court that after her son disclosed the abuse and made his police statement, she received an international phone call from the accused requesting her to help him reenter Australia as he was experiencing difficulties where he was. She said that she told him that she did not wish to see him again and that the marriage was over. She also said that she never told him of her son's disclosure.

The mother faced harsh cross-examination at the committal hearing as the barrister suggested mother/child collusion to exact revenge against her husband for their supposed failed marriage. The mother denied this claim. As stated earlier, the mother was not called to give any evidence at the trial, and at the time of the trial the child was living with his maternal grandparents, who were very supportive of him. The child's mother also remained supportive of him but invisible at the trial. No reason could be found for the mother's absence from the trial; however, at the committal hearing the mother was accused by the defense barrister of being involved in financial deception. The mother was in a desperate financial situation with four children and no direct means of income, and it may well be that the defense intended to use this situation as damaging evidence against the mother. The mother was forced to sell their furniture and other major possessions in order to survive financially, and later on her parents became involved with the welfare and care of the children with the boy going to live with his grandparents interstate.

Before detailing the trial, I also want to comment on the committal hearing. At the time of the committal, the boy had just turned ten and expressed extreme fear and distress about traveling to Melbourne to give evidence, but was reluctant to speak about his fears. He had developed a trusting rapport with the policewoman who took his statement, and she traveled interstate to talk to the boy about his fears. Despite assuring the child that he could give evidence via Closed Circuit Television[2] (CCTV)—and, therefore, would not see his stepfather and would not have to be in the same room with him—it did little to alleviate the terror expressed by the child about giving evidence against his stepfather. The reason for the boy's terror was soon revealed. In a statement, the policewoman detailed her visit to the boy and reported that he told her his stepfather had threatened him in other ways regarding disclosure of the abuse. Aside from telling him that he would kill him and his mother, the child is reported to have told the policewoman:

> that the respondent [accused] had held a gun to his head on a camping trip in Sale, threatening to kill the complainant if he ever told anyone what had happened to him. He expressed that he did not want to come to Melbourne to give evidence as he was convinced the respondent would kill him...I believe that his fear is genuine since the threats were made when he was eight and nine years old respectively and this fear has been maintained up until the present day, the complainant is now ten years of age.[3]

A complainant in another trial I researched also reported being threatened with a firearm, and threats to harm the child and/or their mother have been reported by other complainants in child sex-abuse cases.[4] In his police statement, the boy also said that his stepfather had threatened him with a martial arts weapon, which had also frightened him. As a result of his fear, the child was allowed to give evidence via CCTV from another state at the committal hearing. The defense barrister objected, unsuccessfully, to such an arrangement on the grounds the accused had a right to face his accuser.[5]

The common judicial practice of a competency assessment to ensure the child is able to give sworn evidence occurs at all levels of legal proceedings, and I include the following exchange between the child and the magistrate as it is representative of the kind of questions that are put to children, and the child's response in this case is poignant in its clarity and honesty. The magistrate asked the child if he understood what "telling the truth means":

> CHILD: Yes...um, telling everyone around me what really happened and not telling a lie.
>
> MAGISTRATE: Okay. If I asked you to hold on to the Bible and promise to tell the truth—you told me you understand what the truth is?
>
> CHILD: Yes.
>
> MAGISTRATE: So if I ask you to hold on to the Bible and promise to tell the truth, what do you think would happen to you if you didn't, if you didn't tell the truth?
>
> CHILD: Well, I would be unrevrand [sic], I think is the word.[6]

The Prosecution Evidence

The child's evidence was without independent corroboration, and the fact that his mother would not be giving evidence made the prosecution's list of witnesses very short. The forensic medical practitioner who examined the boy was called to give evidence. In essence, the boy's evidence of each allegation was given in isolation from the context of his family environment, which of course would be an advantage for the accused.

The Evidence

With no collateral evidence, aside from the boy's testimony, arguments about evidentiary boundaries were virtually nonexistent. Though not an evidentiary ruling, it is due process that the previous convictions of the accused cannot be mentioned in court. Since the accused currently resided at Her Majesty's Prison, he was never asked to provide details of his current address; instead, his previous address was used. The boy traveled to Melbourne for the trial and was granted permission to give evidence via CCTV from a room near the courtroom and was allowed to have his maternal grandfather sit with him. As is usual, the child was examined by the judge prior to giving evidence, to ensure he understood sufficiently the giving of evidence on a sworn oath.

Complainant's Evidence-in-Chief

After providing the usual background evidence about his age, where he lived, how many siblings he had and their ages, and identifying that the accused was his stepfather, the boy gave evidence of the first charged incident. The incident is alleged to have occurred at a building site for a house, and on a weekend because the boy recalls he had no school that particular day.

Asked about the activities leading up to the incident, the boy explained that he and his cousin played in the backyard of the house where his father was working and the boy and his cousin built a cubby house with broken plaster sheets and that they had a pie for lunch that day. The boy's step-grandfather was also working at the site, helping his son. The boy also gave evidence of plaster sheeting falling off the wall, and that he and his young cousin helped the men fix new plaster to the wall. The alleged incident occurred at the end of the day. While the boy's cousin and step-grandfather were packing tools and equipment in the stepfather's vehicle, the boy went looking for his stepfather:

> CHILD: I'd been called into the house, and I was looking for [stepfather].
>
> PROSECUTOR: Did you find him?
>
> CHILD: Yes.
>
> PROSECUTOR: How did you find him?
>
> CHILD: Followed his voice.

PROSECUTOR: You followed his voice?

CHILD: Yes.

PROSECUTOR: Was he calling out or saying something…?

CHILD: Yes, he said, "[child's name], come here"…

PROSECUTOR: So he said, "[child's name], come here," and you followed his voice, and where did you find him?

CHILD: In the toilet.

PROSECUTOR: What was he doing?

CHILD: He was sitting down on the toilet.

PROSECUTOR: Did you notice anything about him at that stage?

CHILD: Yes, his pants were down.

PROSECUTOR: When you say his pants are down, how do you mean?

CHILD: Well, around his ankles.

PROSECUTOR: So his pants were round his ankles; did he say anything, or do anything at that stage?

CHILD: Yes, he said, "Come here."

PROSECUTOR: What did you do?

CHILD: I went to him.

PROSECUTOR: What happened then?

CHILD: And he said, "Sit on my penis," and I said "Do I have to?" and he said, "Yes," and so I turned around and he picked me up like that [demonstrating], and put me down, and he was trying to force his penis into my bottom, and it went in, but it didn't go very far, and then he took me back off, and then he spat on his fingers and he started rubbing it on my bottom, and then he told me to get back on, and then it went in just a bit further, and I started crying, and then—'cos it hurt, and then screamed out a little bit, and he hit me on the back and said, "Sshh," and—gees…

PROSECUTOR: What happened then?

CHILD: Then he took me off and just got up and pulled his pants up.

PROSECUTOR: When he said "Sshh," what did you do—you said you screamed a little bit, I think is what you said, and then he said, "Sshh." Did you say anything after that?

CHILD: I can't remember.

PROSECUTOR: Do you remember anything about his penis, do you remember how it was?

CHILD: It was pretty hard.

PROSECUTOR: What happened after that—you've hopped off?

Case Study R v D

CHILD: Yes, and...

PROSECUTOR: How did you get off, do you remember?

CHILD: I just stood up, and he said to me, "If you tell your mum, I'll kill you and your mum."

PROSECUTOR: How did you feel when he said that?

CHILD: I got scared.

PROSECUTOR: After he'd said that, what happened?

CHILD: He patted me on the head, and then we went out to the car.

PROSECUTOR: I think you said before that you cried a bit?

CHILD: Yes.

PROSECUTOR: Had you stopped crying, or what, when you went out to the car?

CHILD: Yes, I wiped all the tears away and stuff, yes.

PROSECUTOR: When you went out to the car, do you remember where [paternal grandfather] and [cousin] were?

CHILD: Yes, they were sitting in the car waiting.

PROSECUTOR: Do you remember where you got into the car?

CHILD: Well, as we were walking to the car, he was holding my hand, and he got in the front, and I got into the backseat where I was in the morning.

PROSECUTOR: When you got into the car, where did the car go?

CHILD: Back home.

PROSECUTOR: Was there any talking in the car on the way home?

CHILD: Yes, I was talking to [cousin], and [stepfather] was talking to his [father] in Chinese, and...

PROSECUTOR: His [step-grandfather] is Chinese?

CHILD: Yes.

PROSECUTOR: Could you understand Chinese?

CHILD: No, and every now and then he'd turn around and frown at me, and then smile, and then keep looking where he was looking before.

PROSECUTOR: Eventually you got home?

CHILD: Yes.

PROSECUTOR: Do you remember what happened when you got home to Lewisham Road?

CHILD: Yes, we went inside and then I went to the toilet, and nothing come out.

PROSECUTOR: When you say you went to the toilet, what did you want to do?

CHILD: Business.

PROSECUTOR: What do you mean by that when you say "business"?

CHILD:...it's really...

PROSECUTOR: Just tell us, it doesn't matter...?

HIS HONOR: Do not worry about it.

CHILD: I had to do a poo.

PROSECUTOR: And it wouldn't come out?

CHILD: No.

PROSECUTOR: So what happened then? Do you remember what happened then?

CHILD: I didn't tell my mum.[7]

I have chosen to provide this very lengthy excerpt to demonstrate the kind of detail that is required to be given by child and adult witnesses in such cases and to show that such evidence is given according to direct and specific questions that control the flow of communication. Also, the technicality of questions is used not just to establish specifics but is designed to allow only a specific concept or activity to be identified. The evidence of the child is not given as a detailed explanation that flows from the child but, rather, through a lengthy series of carefully worded questions.

The technicality of questions is also evident. This evidence is consistent with the child's police statement and, I think, indicates not just the recall of such a traumatic event but also the fact that the child has had to somehow keep this information alive in his mind for the purposes of retrieving it for a trial more than three years later. In his police statement the child used the word "bum" when referring to the incidents but at the trial uses the word "bottom." It is possible that as he is now three years older this is a natural progression in his language, or it might be (as discussed in case study R v EF) that he has been influenced to change this term of reference. Note also the fact that the child, still only eleven years of age, is embarrassed about his inability to use his bowels and refers to it as going to the toilet to do his "business." I noted in his statement that he used the same terminology of "business" to describe how he felt unable to open his bowels. However, in the trial process the emphasis on exactness in words requires the boy to be more specific and his obvious embarrassment is routinely dismissed by the prosecutor and the judge.

Evidence-in-chief immediately moved on to the second charge. For ease of reading, the evidence is edited, but still lengthy, so that technical questions not crucial to the presentation of the case study are minimized.

PROSECUTOR: If I can take you to the second incident. Do you remember when that happened?

CHILD: Well, it was at the end of the year except it wasn't quite at the end of the year. I think it was in October.

PROSECUTOR: Now, do you remember anything about the day that the second incident happened on?

CHILD: I know it was a weekday.

PROSECUTOR: How do you know that?

CHILD: Because that day—or like the class went on an excursion to this dinosaur park and I didn't go and I had to go to another class, and that night mum was yelling at me because I wasn't watching [younger sibling], and [stepfather] couldn't stand the yelling so he grabbed me by the shoulders and took me out and we got in the car and I got in the passenger seat and he started driving. I said, "Where are we going?" and he says, "To the park," and well, I thought, yes, okay, we're going down to the park to play.

They establish that the child had been to that park before, that on this occasion it was between six and eight in the evening but that it was not too dark, and that the child played on the swings and slide.

PROSECUTOR: So after playing on the swings and slide for about ten minutes, what happened then?

CHILD: He said to go to the car, so...went—went to the car and got in.

PROSECUTOR: Where did you get in the car?

CHILD: To the passenger seat again.

PROSECUTOR: Yes?

CHILD: And then he—he said to me, "Do you remember what I done here at work?" and I said, "Yes" and he said, "Well, I'm going to do it again now" and I says, "Do I have to?" and he says—no, I said, "I don't want to"—and he says, "If you don't, I'll kill you and your mum and your sisters and your brother" and so I got scared so I just thought I'd better do it. So—and then he hopped over into my seat.

PROSECUTOR: How did he do that?

CHILD: Well, just got up and walked over.

PROSECUTOR: So he got over into your seat, and what happened then?

CHILD: Well, he pulled his pants down and told me to take my pants down and then he wiped the spit on my bottom again and then...

At this point the defense barrister asks if the "witness" would slow down as he is taking notes. The judge tells the child he is doing well but would he slow down a bit in giving his evidence.

PROSECUTOR: So he wiped spit on your bottom?

CHILD: Yes.

PROSECUTOR: How did he do that?

CHILD: Spat on his fingers and wiped it on.

PROSECUTOR: What happened then, [names child]?

CHILD: And then he told me to sit on his penis again. And he done that and he kept telling me to get off and get on again. That happened about four times.

PROSECUTOR: Do you remember anything about his penis?

CHILD: Yes, it was hard again.

PROSECUTOR: You said it happened about four times, did you say?

CHILD: Around about that, yes.

PROSECUTOR: Was anything said?

CHILD: *Hold on, I've just got to remember now. I can't remember.*

PROSECUTOR: Do you remember whether you cried or not?

CHILD: Yes. *Hold on, yes, something was said.* I said [indistinct], "Stop for a minute."

PROSECUTOR: You said, "Stop for a minute"?

CHILD: Yes.

PROSECUTOR: Why did you say that?

CHILD: Because it hurt.

PROSECUTOR: When you said that, what happened?

CHILD: He said, "Okay" or—well, he—I don't know if he did say okay or not but he did get up—get—get up and pull his pants up. I pulled up mine.

PROSECUTOR: So you pulled your pants up and he pulled his pants up; what happened then?

CHILD: Then we drove home and on the way home he showed me a pair of numchucks he had in the thing—glove-box.

PROSECUTOR: Tell us what numchucks are?

CHILD: Well, these—piece of metal about that long [indicating]. There's a chain on it about that long [indicating] and another piece of metal about this long [indicating].

PROSECUTOR: So he showed you that?

CHILD: Yes, and that had sticky tape round—wrapped around—or that gray sticky tape stuff wrapped around the handles.

PROSECUTOR: Have you seen them before?

CHILD: Yes. I caught a glimpse of them once, I didn't know what they were.

PROSECUTOR: He showed you them...?

CHILD: Yes.

PROSECUTOR: And did he say anything when he showed you them?

CHILD: Yes, he said, "Have a look at these."

PROSECUTOR: You saw them, and what happened then?

CHILD: That scared me, that really scared me. [emphasis added][8]

The child said that they drove home without further incident and, upon arriving home, his mother had, in his words, "calmed" down and he ate his dinner, which he remembers was spaghetti Bolognese, and then went to bed.[9] On a couple of occasions the child stopped in his evidence and made comments suggesting he was putting a lot of effort into trying to remember things, as is highlighted in the above excerpt. These moments indicate a child trying to will himself to recall as many details as he possibly can about an event that occurred more than three years ago, which is a considerable period of time between experiencing alleged traumatic events and then being required to recall them for the purpose of a legal inquiry. In cross-examination, the child would again make clear he was trying very hard to bring every detail he could back into focus—details that he would have been encouraged to forget as part of his healing.

Numchucks—or "nunchakus" as they were also spelled in the transcript—are a martial arts weapon. The detail given by the child is very clear, and when he told the prosecutor to "hold on" because "I've just got to remember now" indicates how hard the child was trying to recall as much detail as possible. The prosecutor raised the ire of defense counsel when he then tried to establish evidence from the child regarding his stepfather's sudden departure overseas:

PROSECUTOR: [names child] at some stage after all this did [stepfather] leave?

CHILD: Yes.

PROSECUTOR: He left the home?

CHILD: Yes, he went to [names country].

PROSECUTOR: Do you remember when it was that [stepfather] went to [overseas country]? It was some time ago, wasn't it?

CHILD: Yes.

DEFENSE: With respect, Your Honor, there's a matter that I wish to debate in the absence of the jury, Your Honor.[10]

Not surprisingly, the defense barrister was "apprehensive" that such information might lead to a suggestion or inference that the accused "fled" the country to avoid possible disclosure by the child. Secondly, he believed such evidence was simply not relevant.[11] While the accused "fled" the country to avoid prosecution for rape, the management of this information was crucial for the defense since they were keen to use the vanishing act of the accused as part of their narrative of mother/child collusion. Notwithstanding this point, I would have thought it important for the prosecutor to clarify this piece of information—albeit in the clandestine manner befitting legal trials—because the stepfather's absence, indeed his global distance, more than likely provided the degree of comfort necessary for the child to feel able to disclose the alleged abuse to his mother.[12] The boy's evidence, clearly, is that he was extremely fearful of his stepfather, which would help to explain a delay in disclosure and, likewise, his absence from the country could provide a jury with some context as to the child's ability to disclose.

As the trial proceeds, it will become obvious that what is deemed not relevant for the prosecution to pursue does not negate its relevance for the defense to pursue (for their own means). The defense argument was successful, and any further examination of the boy on this issue was discontinued and his evidence-in-chief finished here.

Cross-examination

The defense case was approached around two central tactics in cross-examination. The first involved a heavy reliance on revealing minor discrepancies in the child's evidence. This was a lengthy and tedious process, designed to unsettle and confuse the child, and to discredit him on minor changes between his police statement and committal hearing evidence. Such a process enabled the defense barrister to continually confront the child with accusations that he was telling lies, which from a reading of the transcript obviously upset the child. The second part of cross-examination focused on attributing motive to the child, and involved constructing an unflattering image of the mother through the child. The child's own honesty in acknowledging arguments between his mother and stepfather was used to suggest motive for revenge for mother and child, and strengthen the defense narrative of mother/child collusion.

Cross-examination commenced on an aggressive note with the boy being asked where he lived at the time of the first alleged incident. On giving his response, the defense barrister confronted the child with a *Melways* map of Melbourne and the greater city, and pointed out that the child had, in fact, given the wrong suburb when providing his original address. While the correct suburb for his address was not far away from the wrong suburb, the child was only eight years old when he lived at the address and only nine years old when he gave this information in his police statement. He had also lived at approximately three other addresses in a reasonably short period of time, so some confusion about the suburb was not unusual in a child that young. After all, most young children "rote learn" their address anyway. It is highly unlikely that a child of this age would have experience reading detailed road maps, but this barrister wasted no time copying specific parts of the map and tendering them to the court as evidence for the defense case.[13]

The barrister remained fixated on errors in the boy's statement regarding previous places of residence and gave particular attention to the location of the first incident, which the child said he thought occurred at a suburb called Coburg. The *Melways* map got another workout by the barrister as he again sought to highlight mistakes in the child's geographical skills. On the latter issue, the barrister appeared almost contemptuous of the child's inability to pinpoint the exact inner-city suburb. While lawyers are apt to claim the moral high ground on demanding facts and not assuming when it comes to detail, the barrister blustered that "we all know Coburg because that's where the gaol[14] is, on Sydney Road."[15] This axiomatic statement was followed up with questions as to why the child thought the construction site was in Coburg. Quite reasonably, the child responded he had seen a sign saying "Coburg that way"[16] and since the car went that way he assumed they were in Coburg, adding that, if they did pass the jail, he did not see it. Fixated now on suburban topography, the barrister said to the child, "You drove past the city, didn't you?"[17] as though such a comment is a surefire indicator that the child must have known whether he was in a particular suburb or not. Again, the assumptions in this statement were enormous and were clearly designed to hector and unsettle the child at the earliest stage of his cross-examination. The boy had never made a steadfast claim that the construction site where the first alleged incident occurred was Coburg, only that he *thought* it was Coburg, and this point was highlighted by the prosecutor.[18]

On the topic of the first alleged incident, the child was asked to tell the court what time he got up that particular morning before being asked to give details of the layout of the house in which the incident of anal penetration was alleged to have occurred. Building on the child's claim that he believed the incident occurred in Coburg, the barrister mentioned the names of two other suburbs to the child, suggesting these were the only two worksites the boy had accompanied his father to. When asked if he recalled these suburbs, the boy said he could not.[19] These questions assume a working knowledge of a very large capital city and, I dare say, that even an experienced taxi driver would be challenged by some of the questions that are put to this child about the geography and topography of Melbourne suburbs.

In a drawn out series of questions, the child was asked about the time he left with his stepfather on that particular morning, what time they picked up his step-grandfather, and to describe the layout of the house at the construction site, including whether it had cupboards, sink, windows, doors, and other fittings. The boy only knew that they picked the step-grandfather up early and that the house had a toilet inside. He could not remember details of fittings inside the house.[20]

Defense cross-examination focused heavily on highlighting inconsistencies in the child's evidence and, after demonstrating suitable outrage at the child's lack of inner-city geographical knowledge at age eight and nine, the barrister moved on to dissect the child's evidence of the first incident of penetration in the toilet at the construction site:

DEFENSE: [Accused] just calls you in, does he?

CHILD: Yes.

DEFENSE: And says, "Come here"?

CHILD: Yes.

DEFENSE: You say his pants were down to his ankles, right?

CHILD: Yes.

DEFENSE: That he just said that to you, "Sit on my penis"?

CHILD: Yes.

DEFENSE: Is that what he said, was it?

CHILD: Yes, as far as I can remember.

DEFENSE: He just said, "Sit on my penis"?

CHILD: Yes.

DEFENSE: I want you to be accurate about this. Is that what he said?

CHILD: I don't know. As far as I can remember he said that or something to the same line.

DEFENSE: You said, "Do I have to"?

CHILD: Yes.

DEFENSE: You're sure about that, aren't you? That you said, "Do I have to"?

CHILD: Yes.

DEFENSE: You're also sure that he spat on his fingers.

CHILD: Yes.

DEFENSE: You see, do you remember being asked some questions about this matter a couple of months ago in September of this year; *only a couple* of months ago?

CHILD: Yes.

DEFENSE: You remember me asking you some questions about this matter, don't you?

CHILD: Yes.

DEFENSE: One of the questions I asked you was—twenty-six, line twenty-nine—"Did you say anything like 'Why do I have to sit on your lap?' or 'I don't want to do this' or anything like that?" and your answer was "No."

CHILD: Well, when I read may [sic] statement things started to materialize and I can remember a bit more now.

DEFENSE: So what you say now is that you said, "Do I have to"?

CHILD: Yes.

DEFENSE: But previously in September when you were asked, "Did you say anything like 'Why do I have to sit on your lap?' or 'I don't want to do this' or anything like that" you had answered that question "No," is that right?

CHILD: Yes.

DEFENSE: That was wrong, wasn't it?

CHILD: Yes.

DEFENSE: You were giving evidence in a court?

CHILD: Yes.

DEFENSE: And you were sworn to tell the truth, weren't you?

CHILD: Yes.

DEFENSE: What you told the court on that occasion was wrong, was it?

CHILD: Yes. [emphasis added][21]

The barrister begins to use statements and questions like "You're sure about that?" or "I want you to be accurate," which begin to create anxiety and doubt in the child, since they suggest that the child is wrong. Thus he responds to one question, "I don't know...as far as I can remember." In an all-too typical scenario, the barrister had begun his campaign early to unsettle the child by highlighting errors in the child's evidence with accompanying comments such as "wrong about that, were you?" and so on. On one occasion, this prompted the child to assert that it was the defense barrister who was getting it wrong, not the child, indicating that the references were having their desired effect in upsetting the child.[22]

Unsettling a witness by heightening their nervousness and diminishing any small confidence they may possess is a common strategy and, most often, has devastating consequences on children. In the next series of questions the boy was quizzed about his evidence concerning what the accused was doing with his hands at the time the child was allegedly being anally raped:

DEFENSE: You were also on that occasion [committal hearing] asked some questions about whether anything happened with his hands; remember that?

CHILD: Yes.

DEFENSE: On that occasion you said nothing about him spitting on his hands; is that right?

CHILD: Yes.

DEFENSE: You remember that, don't you?

CHILD: Yes.

DEFENSE: You remember saying nothing about that matter only *three* months ago?

CHILD: Yes.

DEFENSE: You were asked questions about that particular matter both by myself and [prosecutor] weren't you?

CHILD: Yes.

DEFENSE: You didn't say anything at all about spitting, did you?

CHILD: No.

DEFENSE: The reason why you didn't say anything about it [names child] was this, because it didn't happen, did it?

CHILD: It did so.

DEFENSE: You're just giving evidence, I suggest to you, from having read your statement, aren't you; only recently having read your statement?

CHILD: Yes, and stuff started materializing. I can remember stuff that I didn't remember before. [emphasis added][23]

The child's comment that he began to recall more and more details when he reread his statement was a reasonable and honest comment. Witnesses are allowed to read their statements prior to giving their evidence, and defense barristers always make much of this in trials, regardless of the fact that many witnesses provide a statement months (or perhaps years, as in this case) before a case goes to trial. In nearly all cases, expert witnesses such as medical practitioners, psychologists, pathologists, and others are able to refer to their notes as they give evidence without attracting claims of fabrication, which is what often results when complainants admit that they refreshed their memory by reading their statement.

Concerning the boy's evidence about the first alleged incident, he told the court that on the way home his stepfather, who was seated in the front passenger seat, frequently made eye contact with him, alternating between smiling and frowning at the child. This obviously had an effect on the boy since he mentioned it in his police statement and again at the trial. No doubt the child recalls this because of its connection to an alleged traumatic incident and also because these furtive glances would have appeared strange. The boy was probably recognizing, unconsciously, non-verbal cues—a kind of signaling often employed by child abusers. The child begins to recognize and associate this conduct as a type of surveillance, reinforcing that the person who has power over the child is monitoring him or her. That these cues can be used in the presence of others without them being aware of anything untoward, and yet recognized by the child, often produce a very deep fear in abuse victims, as has been reported elsewhere.[24] At the committal hearing, the child did not include this information about his stepfather's furtive glances at him in the car, and he was castigated by the barrister for mentioning this evidence at the trial and not at the committal hearing. In fact, the child was accused three times of lying about this information and each time the boy insisted he was telling the truth, prompting the barrister to again come out with the phrase that the boy was "wrong again" in his evidence.[25]

The barrister was not concerned that the information may indicate any kind of non-verbal cues. He indicated that when asked at the committal whether anything "happened" in the car on the way home, the child did not mention these strange glances. The omission probably had more to do with the fact that the child did not link a question about further "happenings" in the car (following the alleged abuse) with his comment in his police statement about his stepfather's alleged strange glances toward him.

And while constantly reminding the child of his mistakes in evidence, the barrister appeared to forget his own multiple mistakes on important dates upon which the child gave evidence. On one occasion he accused the child of forgetting evidence he gave only a *couple* of months ago and, a short time later, suggested the committal was *three* months prior to the trial before reverting to the claim that the committal hearing was only *two* months prior to the trial. In the space of a couple of minutes, he appeared to have great difficulty with his own recollection of dates, despite the details being under his nose, while admonishing the child's memory with regard to the minute details given more than three years ago.[26]

As cross-examination unfurled, a familiar defense stratagem was used: putting complex and multiple questions to the child about one particular area of evidence and then, without warning, changing the topic and timeframe before coming back to the original topic. This tactic creates witness confusion, puts witnesses under enormous pressure as they are forced to think about events across many times and places, and produces minor inconsistencies that can be seized upon. In this case, comparing minor inconsistencies in the child's evidence was a mainstay of cross-examination. One of these inconsistencies had to do with the child's evidence concerning his stepfather's alleged threats to ensure the child's silence:

> DEFENSE: Had he mentioned anything about the little secret in the previous three or four months?
>
> CHILD: Um, he had asked me now and then if I told anyone but I said no and he said, "Good, you're smart."
>
> DEFENSE: He had said that three or four times, had he?
>
> CHILD: Yeah.
>
> DEFENSE: Where about was he when he had said those things to you?
>
> CHILD: I don't know.
>
> DEFENSE: Well, where were you?
>
> CHILD: With him.
>
> DEFENSE: But you don't know where you were?
>
> CHILD: They were all in different places?
>
> DEFENSE: That is why I am asking you, where were you when he had said those things?
>
> CHILD: I don't know.
>
> DEFENSE: You simply don't know, is that right?
>
> CHILD: Yes.
>
> DEFENSE: They might have been at home?
>
> CHILD: Yes.
>
> DEFENSE: Might have been in the park.
>
> CHILD: No, no, never at the park.
>
> DEFENSE: Or it might never have happened at all. Did he say those things to you at *night or during the day?*
>
> CHILD: I don't know.
>
> DEFENSE: Did he say it to you when your brothers and sisters were around?
>
> CHILD: No.

DEFENSE: Did he say it to you *when your mother was at home?*

CHILD: No.

DEFENSE: Are you saying 'No,' or do you mean you just don't know?

CHILD: No, I am saying 'No' he didn't say it when anyone was around. [emphasis added][27]

One gets the impression the sequence of questions was designed to promote a satirical exposé of the child's evidence of living in fear of the alleged threatened consequences of telling about the alleged abuse. Child-abuse literature is replete with examples of children reporting threats by an offender, but it is turned into a legal parody here as the barrister demands to know a list of times and places, and the proximity and presence of others. Recanvassing parts of this issue a short time later, the barrister once again castigated the child for not being able to recall whether he was threatened by his father on the way home from the park, resulting in further accusations that the boy is lying.[28]

The defense's questions move on to the second alleged incident of anal rape and, again, questions focused on discrepancies in the child's details concerning the date of the incident. In his police statement, the boy said his family frequently visited the park during the daytime but, on the occasion of the alleged incident, he was taken to the park in the evening. However, the barrister focused on two errors in the boy's previous evidence. He highlighted that, at the committal hearing, the child could not recall the specific date he went to the park when this alleged incident occurred, but in his police statement, made three years prior to the committal hearing, he said he believed the incident occurred on the day he missed going on the school excursion to a dinosaur park. The second "error" related to playing on the swings. Again referring to the evidence the child gave at the committal hearing, he mentioned to the child that he had agreed with the defense barrister that he in fact did not get out of the car to play on the swings, and after highlighting this point again accused the child of lying. The child rejected the assertion that he was lying.[29] Considering the child's frequent visits to the park, it may well be that his memory of playing on swings and slides is confused with another time or simply that a child's association of a park with playing may lead him to assume that a visit to a park naturally involves playing on the playground equipment.

Similar to a number of other cases, the family vehicle was allegedly used as a site to sexually abuse children.[30] In this case, the child alleged the second incident of penetration occurred in the family car. So, not unlike other cases, the child was asked for specific details of the family car before the barrister cited large slabs of committal transcript for the purpose of highlighting inconsistencies. From a reading of the transcript, it is obvious the child was baffled by some questions and unable to answer them. When asked by the barrister if the car his stepfather drove was a "sedan," the child responded by asking, "What's a sedan?"[31] The barrister simply ignored the child's inability to understand the question and neither the prosecutor nor judge intervened to clarify the terminology. On the same topic of the car, the barrister asked the child this highly stylized question: "The clear impression from the evidence was that you were contending that [stepfather] got out of the car."[32] The child's non-responsive answer most likely indicates the difficulties he was having in trying to understand deliberately complex questions, and, again, there was no intervention to ensure the child understood the questions.[33]

As the defense barrister reeled off one minor inconsistency after another, there appeared a gratuitous exchange on a couple of occasions as the barrister reminded the child of mistakes in his evidence. For example, the barrister reminded the child that his committal evidence was given under "oath before a court only a couple of months ago" (obviously still having trouble with whether it was two months ago or three months ago) and suggested that the boy was lying:

CHILD: It wasn't a lie.

DEFENSE: It was a mistake, was it?

CHILD: Yes, I don't lie.

DEFENSE: We'll come to whether you lie in a moment...[34]

Soon after, the barrister was intrigued by the exact sequence of events leading to the child being allegedly anally penetrated by his stepfather, prompting a series of questions designed I believe to produce a parody more than anything else:

DEFENSE: Is it the case, is it, that you can't remember what you did after that?

CHILD: Well, I know somehow I don't know if he told me to sit down on his penis or not, but I know I got there somehow.

DEFENSE: *Somehow just happened?*

CHILD: No.

DEFENSE: *Tell us how it happened.*

CHILD: I don't know.

DEFENSE: Because it didn't happen at all, did it?

CHILD. Yes.

DEFENSE: You tell us what happened.

CHILD: Well he put his penis into my bottom.

DEFENSE: How did he do that? Did he touch your bottom?

CHILD: No.

DEFENSE: You see I thought you told us earlier that he had touched your bottom with his fingers?

CHILD: Yes.

DEFENSE: You've just told me a moment ago that he didn't touch your bottom?

CHILD: Yes, he didn't touch my bottom while he was putting his penis in.

DEFENSE: *Can you tell us how it is that you came to sit on it?*

CHILD: No.

DEFENSE: Can you tell us now how many times it was that you say his penis touched (penetrated) your bottom?

CHILD: I can't remember.

DEFENSE: But you do say that you remember crying?

CHILD: Yes.

DEFENSE: Although you told the court in September that you didn't cry?

CHILD: Well, in September I hadn't read my statement.

DEFENSE: Yes, but you'd remember crying, wouldn't you?

CHILD: Not really, sometimes you forget. [emphasis added][35]

The technical point about "touching" the child's bottom, the number of times the child was supposedly penetrated by his stepfather's penis, and just exactly how he came to be sitting on it obscure the boy's evidence overall. Under the guise of cross-examination, details of an almost offensive type are demanded of the child and seem to be more part of a practice of humiliation than anything else. In this exchange, the word "touched" is used without clarifying whether the child and the defense counsel are using it in the same way. It is apparent that the boy did not associate penile penetration with being touched and, so, the barrister's emphasis on this word clearly advantages the point of view he wishes to ascribe to the boy's evidence while creating confusion for the child. A little earlier, the barrister had canvassed this same issue: the child had said his stepfather had not "touched" his body at the time of anal penetration, and the barrister had then said to the child that he did not attempt to "stop" his stepfather from these actions before again accusing the child repeatedly of being a liar.[36]

Concomitantly, the child was accused of lying on the basis that his evidence at the trial, where he mentioned numchakus, differed from his evidence at the committal hearing. In cross-examination, the defense counsel stressed that at the committal hearing the child did not mention the alleged incident involving him being shown numchakus at the car park, whereas he mentioned that incident in his evidence-in-chief. It is important to highlight, though, just how the question was put. Inferring a recent invention on the part of the child, the defense counsel suggested the child's omission of this evidence at the committal was another example in which the child "had just forgotten about the alleged threatening behavior on the way home." This prompted the child to ask, "What threatening behavior?"[37] Only when the barrister mentioned the numchakus did the boy associate being shown the numchakus with legal questions around further incidents of "threatening behavior." Clearly the child did not associate his being shown numchakus with stylized legal questions about further incidents of alleged threatening behavior, and this misunderstanding of concepts is always detrimental to the child since their confusion is often ignored and, therefore, as in this case, used to promote a narrative of lying and recent invention.

In relation to the alleged incident in the car park at the local park, the defense counsel highlighted that there was a police station not far from the park, as though such a comment was evidence of the falsity of the boy's evidence.[38] A little further into the cross-examination, the barrister re-canvassed the issue, producing recent photos of the car park for the boy to see. The prosecutor objected on the grounds that the environment may well have changed in the four years since the child's alleged abuse in that particular spot; however, the judge dismissed the objection, saying he would rather wait and hear the child's response to the evidence. Again, the defense counsel's highly stylized language was at the fore as he asked the child if he could "recollect" such and such "in the foreground," and how it "depicted" such and such. The transcript reveals a hesitation by the child in response to the questions, with a series of "yes," "maybe," and "I'm not sure" answers.[39] I feel confident in suggesting that this hesitation had more to do with the child possibly being overwhelmed or confused by the language use rather than him being unsure of the evidence per se.

What followed next was an interesting exchange between the defense counsel and child when counsel mentioned to the child that there was a:

DEFENSE: ...police station opposite where you used to park when you visited the park with you [sic] brother and sisters; isn't that right?

CHILD: Yes, but the parking spaces stretched for a while.

DEFENSE: The what?

CHILD: Those white lines went way past the police station.

DEFENSE: What white lines are we speaking of?

CHILD: The white lines where you park your cars.

DEFENSE: Have you spoken about this matter over lunch with anyone?

CHILD: No.

DEFENSE: Have you spoken to anyone over lunch about the area where the [names suburb] police station is?

CHILD: No.[40]

The child's response put the defense barrister on his back foot—he wanted to establish that a police station was right in front of where the family car would have been parked on any visits to the park, but the boy pointed out extensive parking bays which stretched far beyond the police station. The prosecutor for a number of reasons objected to the photos used in evidence. The angle used when taking a photo of the park included the police station, which is, in fact, a new police station that was not there when the alleged incidents occurred. The original police station at the time of the alleged incidents was located in another street near the park. Also, the boy stated that his stepfather had parked under a "massive tree," which, based on the photos, is no longer there. Both of these things, argued the prosecutor, altered the original context and environment as described by the child in his statement.

It is a well-known code in legal practice that one only asks a question for which one already knows the answer. Statements by witnesses are examined so that when they are asked questions in court the lawyer already knows the kind of evidence they will give in response. The defense counsel does not like surprises in evidence—especially from child witnesses. In this case, the child has disrupted the defense narrative by identifying a flaw in their narrative construction, and this inevitably leads to bullying or accusations of coaching by adults (as documented in other cases as well) to promote a narrative of confabulation or recent invention.[41]

Until now, much of the cross-examination focused almost solely on inconsistencies in the child's evidence so that the jury heard repetitive dialogue of defense-led errors in the child's testimony. This is designed to have a cumulative effect on the jury, so that they are immersed in a court dialogue revealing what the defense promotes as a litany of errors in the testimony of the child.

Cross-examination then shifted into the second tier of the defense narrative, which focused on attributing a narrative of motive to the child. The mobilization of a narrative of revenge commenced with questions linking the absence of the accused from the family, indeed the country, to an alleged phone call to the child's mother that clearly suggested marital discord and revenge:

DEFENSE: ...you knew of a telephone call from [accused] to your mother, didn't you?

CHILD: Yes.

DEFENSE: You knew that [accused] was in [overseas country] didn't you?

CHILD: Yes.

DEFENSE: You knew that your mother was very angry as a result of that telephone call, wasn't she?

CHILD: Yes.

DEFENSE: That as a result of that call, you learnt that [accused] and your mother were splitting up?

CHILD: Yes.

DEFENSE: That you would no longer have a father?

CHILD: Yes.

DEFENSE: That you learnt, as a result of that phone call, that [accused] had said to your mother that it was all over between them didn't you?

CHILD: Yes.

DEFENSE: *Your mother said if that's what you're going to do, you'll pay for it. You had learnt that she said that to [accused], hadn't you?*

CHILD: Yes.

DEFENSE: You learned those matters the day after the telephone call, didn't you?

CHILD: Yes, in the morning.

DEFENSE: It was a very tense phone call wasn't it?

CHILD: Yes.

DEFENSE: Your mother was very angry as a result of it, wasn't she?

CHILD: Yes.

DEFENSE: She was very angry that [accused] was saying their relationship was over?

CHILD: Yes.

DEFENSE: What you were upset about was that you would no longer have a father?

CHILD: Yes.

Case Study R v D

DEFENSE: [Accused] had been your father?

CHILD: Yes.

DEFENSE: You have been close to him?

CHILD: Yes.

DEFENSE: You had liked him.

CHILD: Yes.

DEFENSE: You had wanted to be like him indeed, hadn't you?

CHILD: Yes.

DEFENSE: That fact that your parents were splitting up was a matter that greatly upset you, wasn't it?

CHILD: Yes.

DEFENSE: You thought [accused] was being unfair didn't you?

CHILD: Yes.

DEFENSE: Your mother in fact said to you that you wouldn't have a father any longer?

CHILD: Yes.

DEFENSE: That she would have to bring you up?

CHILD: Yes, but one thing she did tell me was that I'd have something that was near a father and would be my...

DEFENSE: Grandfather?

CHILD: Yes.

DEFENSE: Your grandparents never really liked [accused] did they?

CHILD: No.

DEFENSE: You came to hate [accused] didn't you?

CHILD: No.

DEFENSE: Over the last couple of years, haven't you?

CHILD: Not really, I just don't see why he done [*sic*] what he did to me and that's something I'm going to have to live with.

DEFENSE: Let's just concentrate upon the phone call and what was happening around August 1992 and the time just before you were examined by the doctor...you were very upset, as a result of learning that you wouldn't have a father any longer, weren't you?

CHILD: Yes.

DEFENSE: You were very upset about your parents splitting up, weren't you?

CHILD: Yes.

DEFENSE: You thought that [accused] had been unfair to your mother; is that right?

CHILD: Yes. [emphasis added][42]

In this lengthy excerpt, the reader can see how the child's monosyllabic agreements, juxtaposed with a long series of statements, are leading to a narrative cul-de-sac; and much of this is being produced by the child's passive agreement with supposed comments attributed to his mother. The cross-examination links supposed marital discord, and indeed a marriage breakup by phone, with a child's support for his mother and anger at his stepfather. The cross-examination further connects these events to a child's desire to revenge the stepfather. Clearly the inference is that the mother's supposed threat to avenge her husband is the precursor for the child's allegations against his stepfather.

Immediately before questions about the phone call from the accused, the defense counsel got the child to agree that he was examined by a medical doctor on a particular date.[43] In evidence-in-chief, the child could not recall when he visited this doctor for an examination, and that is understandable since it was three years prior to this trial. However, the defense barrister sought the same information but went about it differently; he instead told the child the exact date the child saw the doctor three years ago and obtained agreement by the child. It is more likely that the child did not know the date and simply agreed with it, since he knew the barrister had that information in front of him—a phenomenon I have encountered consistently in trials. Having the child agree to this date prior to cross-examining him on the phone call was necessary in order to establish the defense narrative that the child was medically examined *after* his stepfather had contacted the child's mother by phone. In contrast, the mother's police statement indicated that the child had disclosed to her *prior* to husband's overseas phone call and as such he was medically examined *prior* to the phone call. The prosecutor did have telephone records supporting the mother's evidence but, as stated earlier, for reasons unknown, she did not give evidence at the trial.

Cross-examination then centered on the family going to the overseas country in question to meet the accused, who never turned up, leading to the mother and children returning home alone. Agreement with these questions led back to the mother's supposed feelings about this, and, quite extraordinarily, the defense counsel stated to the child that he had knowledge that his stepfather was having "affairs" with other women.[44] No doubt the point of this was to suggest information-sharing between the child and his mother, promoting the defense narrative of a child and mother intent on avenging the accused. The child said he knew nothing about any such affairs, prompting the following questions:

> DEFENSE: You came to hate [accused] didn't you?
>
> CHILD: Sort of.
>
> DEFENSE: And I suggest to you that it's a result of your hatred of [accused] over the matters that I put to you, his not turning up and meeting the family in Christmas of 1991, and the splitting up of the family and the related phone call in August of 1992 that have motivated you to tell these untruths against [accused]?
>
> CHILD: No, they're true.
>
> DEFENSE: Because they never happened these two incidents, did they?
>
> CHILD: Oh yes, they did too.
>
> DEFENSE: ...you are making these allegations out of a background of hatred of [accused]?
>
> CHILD: No, I'm just telling the plain straight-out truth.
>
> DEFENSE: And that is because you are so upset and angry with him that you are making these allegations?
>
> CHILD: I ain't angry with him so more [sic]. That was in the past. He done what he done [sic].[45]

Again, the idea of the child's hatred of his stepfather came to the fore. While the child's honesty in admitting his feelings would provide fertile ground for the barrister to build on the narrative of revenge, the child remained steadfast in his evidence against his stepfather. The motive factor was continually enhanced through questions about the mother's supposed feelings of anger, and even hatred—feelings which are then attributed to the boy—leading to false allegations of abuse as a form of revenge. Questions of extra-marital affairs are put to the child in an attempt to attribute a vengeful mindset to mother and child. The mother is constructed by proxy through the passive agreements of the child. Even the child's agreement that his grandparents—whom he was now living with—did not like the accused, fitted neatly into the motive narrative.

The malleability of the child's evidence is indicated by his passive and monotonous series of agreements with clearly constructed defense questions. It is reasonable for a child to agree that his mother was upset at this time but, of course, the entire context is missing. The mother and her children were living in impoverished conditions, making it exceptionally difficult for the mother to cope. It is also reasonable for a mother to explain to her children—especially her eldest—that the father/stepfather would not be returning to the family. However, the family was split up as a direct consequence of the accused skipping bail on serious rape and abduction charges involving a young woman.

The age of the child makes him extremely malleable and vulnerable to questions that imply he did not like the accused. Each question highlights that the child was upset and that he was close to his maternal grandparents, who also supposedly did not like the accused. When pushed about his feelings toward the accused, the child's open and descriptive reply has great credibility in the context of the complex world of emotional distress experienced by child-abuse victims, especially their feelings of entrapment.[46]

Given the relatively young age of the child in this case, it is not surprising that he so readily and honestly admitted to feeling upset that his stepfather had suddenly left the family home, despite him giving evidence that his stepfather had sexually abused him. The barrister sought to highlight apparent contradictions in the child's evidence; that is, the child agreed with the defense's suggestions that he admired his stepfather and had wanted to be like him, yet almost suggested hatred of the stepfather for leaving the family. It is not uncommon for a sexually abused child to feel confused or ambivalent about their feelings toward the abusive parent. A child may have genuine feelings of affection for a parent who, while abusive of them, may also display positive parenting elements.

Child victims also face the difficult task of consciously identifying the abusive conduct of a parent with the dominant socio-cultural and socio-religious view of parents as caregivers and nurturers that children should idolize. It can be extraordinarily difficult for a child to reconcile complex emotions caused by abuse within the family unit when their tormentor is also their parent or stepparent.

As though wanting to finish by reminding the jury of the seemingly endless list of (minor) inaccuracies in the child's evidence, the barrister re-canvassed the whole issue of the child not having a fundamental understanding of the geography of Melbourne City. This time, the barrister focused on the child's claim that it took about fifteen minutes to travel from his home to Coburg and, once again with the help of *Melways*, made a hue and cry of the fact that it would have taken much longer than fifteen minutes. The concept of time differs remarkably between a child and an adult. To an eight-year-old child, fifteen minutes in a car might seem like an eternity, or his discussion with his cousin might make the trip seem very short. The fact that the child has no idea of the other two suburbs he is accused of going to indicates his total incomprehension of the layout of Melbourne. As stated previously, the defense barrister suggested the child never went to Coburg with his stepfather, but had gone to two other suburbs with him, nowhere near Coburg:

DEFENSE: And I put to you that the only residential properties that you've ever been with [accused] at were in Wantirna and Endeavour Hills.

CHILD: Where the hell are they?[47]

In keeping with the tenor of the trial, there was no judicial or prosecution intervention to advance the claim that such a question may well have been confusing to the child.

Reexamination

The prosecutor's reexamination of the child was very brief and consisted mainly of questions to clarify issues around the overseas trip, and the boy's memory that the second incident occurred on the same day as his missed school excursion to the dinosaur park. His last question to the boy noted that the defense was accusing him of lying, to which the boy replied, "I'm not lying, I don't even tell lies."[48] The prosecutor was allowed to submit to the jury that the school records show that the boy did in fact miss the school excursion to the dinosaur park.

The prosecutor sought to submit part of the boy's statement as an exhibit for the jury in order to counter the defense cross-examination, which he argued had strongly suggested "recent invention" by highlighting inconsistencies in the boy's evidence. Naturally the defense barrister was affronted by the possibility of the jury being given access to the child's police statement, and countered with two interesting points. First, he argued that his constant accusations that the boy was a liar were not prohibited by any legal rules. Secondly, he claimed that the child's testimony at the trial was largely consistent with his statement.[49] This was a private admission with no legal value, since in the presence of the jury the barrister engaged in a monumental process of picking out tiny inconsistencies and blowing them up into major catastrophes on the child's part. He had ensured that the jury got the idea that the boy's evidence was simply "lies" that could not be taken seriously.

The judge reserved his decision and, while no ruling on this issue was available, the fact the prosecution reexamination ended with no reference to the child's police statement indicated the defense's argument was successful.

Other Prosecution Witnesses

The only other prosecution evidence was that given by the forensic medical practitioner who examined the child. In evidence-in-chief, his evidence was that the examination of the boy did not support or disconfirm the allegations of anal penetration. When asked about the possibility of injury to the anal tissue as a result of penetration, the practitioner stated that in his experience of children with anal injuries, the anus was capable of restoring itself to normal within a short period of time so that no obvious scarring or visible trauma could be found on examination (unless the injury was "horrendous"). Defense cross-examination was brief, highlighting only the evidence that the examination revealed no evidence of damage to the child's anus or of any healed injuries. The witness stated that was correct.[50]

Evidence of the Accused

The accused gave short and succinct evidence that revolved around denials of the allegations and promoting the defense narrative of revenge by the child, facilitated by his failed marriage to his stepchild's mother. In evidence-in-chief led by his defense counsel, he did not state his current address (no doubt the address of Her Majesty's prison would have severely damaged his credibility). Instead he was asked to give his former address and occupation. In cases where the accused has no prior convictions, this information is given loud and clear to the jury by the barrister. In this case, of course, no such statement was trotted out. As though to build the character of the accused, he was asked questions allowing him to talk about the family home he built with his former wife. When asked whether he had taken his stepson to the park at night, the accused said he never took the boy to the park alone; and, further, when asked if it was day or night that he took all the children to visit the park he said it was "midday" and only on weekends.[51] Given the minute details demanded from the child, it is a shame that the accused was never asked how he knew categorically that it was always "midday" when he took his children to the park and that it was always on a weekend.

In a series of unremarkable questions by his counsel, the accused denied ever sexually penetrating his son, denied threatening him with numchakus, and, when asked about threats to kill the child, responded, "No, I never threaten kids."[52] This was a rather strange comment, considering he was currently serving a hefty jail term for rape and threats toward an adult female—perhaps he meant that he only threatened women. Much of the evidence-in-chief of the accused covered places where he lived and worked, and technical points about what his work entailed. Not unexpectedly, he said he had never worked in Coburg and never took his child to worksites because of union rules.[53] A denial of working in a particular suburb, and stating that union rules prevented him from taking his child to a worksite, seem pallid evidence when compared to the compelling and detailed evidence of his stepson.

On the topic of his being overseas, the accused told the jury that his wife and children traveled overseas to where he was staying, uninvited. Further, he said that after his wife returned home from overseas, he telephoned her from where he was staying overseas to tell her their marriage was over, and she was very upset with him. Ensuring a neat fit with the defense narrative, he claimed this phone call occurred *before* his son made any disclosures.[54]

Cross-examination of the Accused

In cross-examination, the prosecutor showed the accused telephone records that showed a reverse-charge call to the home of his wife from the county in which he was staying in 1992, and that the call was made some time *after* the child had disclosed allegations of abuse and made his police statement. The accused denied it was he who made the call from that country. Since his wife knew no one else in that country, one feels the prosecutor should have challenged the accused to explain to the court just who the caller might have been. He said that he rang his wife to say their relationship was over and that she threatened to make him "pay" for ending the marriage.[55] This claim fitted perfectly the narrative of a revenge motive and, on a positive note, the prosecutor was on to this and suggested the accused was making up the time and contents of the phone call in order to attribute a "motive" to his stepchild.[56] The accused denied this, prompting the prosecutor to ask the accused about the character of his stepson when it came to lying:

PROSECUTOR: What do you say about that? [about attributing "motive" to child]

ACCUSED: It's not true.

PROSECUTOR: [Names child] is an honest boy, is he not?

ACCUSED: When he wants to be.

PROSECUTOR: When he wants to be?

ACCUSED: Yes.

PROSECUTOR: Have you ever known [names child] to make up lies before of the dimension that you're talking about now?

ACCUSED: I wasn't home long enough to notice.[57]

Perhaps the accused thought he could afford his flippant comment about not being at home long enough to notice any propensity in his stepson to lie, since his defense counsel had done such a good job of attacking the child's character through cross-examination. Without the evidence of the mother to counter the accused's evidence, and unable to link the absence of the accused from the country with his fleeing bail and later conviction on serious rape charges, the prosecutor's ability to counter the defense narrative was limited.

Some good attempts were made though. When asked in cross-examination about the companies and individuals he had done work for—with specific references to those connected with the allegations—the accused, reminiscent of evidence of so many accused, said he could not remember. In response, the prosecutor questioned the accused as to why he would not find it necessary to contact previous employers. The prosecutor asked this in order to, for example, establish the places (read suburbs) where the accused did and did not work. Such scrutiny at close quarters must have signaled danger as the defense counsel promptly objected to this line of enquiry, ensuring it ceased then and there. While the questions seemed very relevant, the ability to challenge and scrutinize the accused's evidence, in this and other cases, was frequently thwarted by the defense counsel by claiming all manner of unfairness and irrelevance. All too frequently, judges were seduced by such rhetoric, thus circumventing prosecution cross-examination.

On another score, the prosecutor did make a good attempt to reestablish the child's credibility on details connected with the first charged incident, in the following example:

PROSECUTOR: You see, [names child] [is] not making up this story about the four of you going to a plastering job is he?

ACCUSED: No, he's not.

PROSECUTOR: And he's not making it up about your driving there is he?

ACCUSED: Yes he is.

PROSECUTOR: The four of you went in a car, didn't you?

ACCUSED: Yes.

PROSECUTOR: In a vehicle?

ACCUSED: Yes.

PROSECUTOR: What sort of car was it?

ACCUSED: A Mitsubishi Trident.

PROSECUTOR: A four seater?

ACCUSED: Yes.

PROSECUTOR: Whose car is that?

ACCUSED: My father's.

PROSECUTOR: So [names child] [is] not wrong when he says your father came and picked you up?

ACCUSED: That's right.

PROSECUTOR: [Names child] [is] not wrong—he's telling the truth when he says that you worked, the four of you, on a house, isn't he?

ACCUSED: That's right.[58]

With limited resources and witnesses, the prosecutor sought to challenge the accused and restore the veracity of the child's claims.

Other Defense Witnesses

The only defense witness called was a former work colleague of the accused who proved a difficult witness by way of cynical responses to cross-examination. His evidence-in-chief for the defense was that the accused never took his son to worksites with him, that the colleague always worked with the accused on all jobs, and that a hired toilet was used at worksites, not the toilets on the premises.[59] When asked particular questions by the prosecutor, the witness responded by asking what it had to do with the case, was often casual and noncommittal in answers, and, when asked about any martial arts experience the accused had, joked that the accused had not been "practicing" on him.[60]

Outcome

The accused was acquitted of all charges and was returned to the state prison to serve the remainder of his jail term in relation to the abduction and rape for which he was previously convicted.

At the committal hearing, the child faced 863 questions, almost all of them from the defense barrister. At the trial, the child faced 211 questions from the prosecutor, 647 questions from the defense barrister, and six questions from the trial judge, totaling 864 questions. In all, the child faced 1,727 questions. The accused faced no questions at the committal hearing and at the trial faced 105 questions from his barrister and 183 questions from the prosecutor, totaling 288 questions.

Comment

In case study R v D, mother/child collusion around revenge was advanced with a defense stratagem that negatively constructed the mother by proxy. In my original research, this form of construction by proxy of mothers was used particularly in trials involving younger children, even when the mother gave evidence herself.[61] In this case, the mother's absence from the trial may well have worked against the credibility of the child.

In essence, the boy's evidence was consistent; even the barrister admitted as much, in the absence of the jury of course. The child was consistent in his evidence of circumstances leading up to each incident and consistent in describing the acts of penetration and threats about the consequences of disclosure. The inconsistencies in his evidence related to demands for peripheral details of the sequence of events and times and dates. All too often this stratagem is deployed with deadly accuracy, achieving remarkable success. The tactic may well bury the child's accurate recall of the alleged incident(s) under the weight of a long, drawn out litany of minor errors and inconsistencies. In this particular case, there was a delay of more than three years from the time he made his police statement to the trial. In that time, the boy had, as his mother stated clearly at the committal, told her at the time of disclosure that he wanted to "forget" what he alleged his stepfather did to him.

However, the consistent and unrelenting attacks on the child in cross-examination based on his recollection of peripheral details made the child, like so many other witnesses in these cases, easy pickings for an experienced barrister skilled in myriad ways to attack the credibility of rape complainants—especially children.

The advantages of making prior inconsistent statements a crucial defense narrative cannot be overstated; I analyze them in greater detail in chapter 7, "Forced Errors." These inconsistencies were woven into the narrative of mother/child collusion in the form of revenge for the father leaving the family home. In this case, the accused leaving the country was turned to the defense advantage through subterfuge.

This was a case with marked examples of a child being cross-examined in ways that often created confusion for the child and where no intervention was forthcoming.

Finally, it is interesting to note the turn of phrase used by the defense counsel concerning the child's legal relationship with the accused. Throughout the cross-examination of the child, the defense counsel referred to the accused by his first name; however, the defense counsel introduced the term "father," not stepfather (which was the lineal and legal relationship between the two) when attributing a motive of revenge to the child. This tactic seemed to be a deliberate attempt to weaken the parental relationship in the context of the alleged incidents of sexual penetration and threats around disclosure; but also to bring the relationship to a more intimate level when questioning the child about his desire to be like the accused, his "hatred" of the accused, and his anger that his "parents" were splitting up.

Notes

1. R v D (Victorian County Court, White, J. 1994), at 89.
2. See Glossary for explanation.
3. Taken from the policewoman's statement.
4. R v J (Victorian County Court, Barnett, J. 1993). For examples of threats to harm or kill the child and/or their mother (and even the child's pets), see, for example, trials from the original study alone: R v A (Victorian County Court, Davey, J. 1995); R v C (Victorian County Court, Spence, J. 1995); R v F (Victorian County Court, Wodak, J. 1995); R v M (Victorian County Court, Dixon, J. 1995).
5. R v D, committal hearing, at 5.
6. Ibid., at 10.
7. R v D, at 8–10.
8. Ibid., at 8–14.
9. Ibid., at 10–4.
10. Ibid., at 14.
11. Ibid., at 15.
12. It has elsewhere been noted that parental divorce or separation of some kind in which the offending parent is away from the family unit, can provide the opportunity for the child to feel able to disclose to the non-offending parent. See Goddard (1996).
13. Ibid., at 19.
14. Pentridge Prison, the well-known former state prison, is in Sydney Road, Coburg, an inner suburb of Melbourne.
15. R v D, at 21.
16. Ibid., at 22.
17. Ibid.
18. Ibid., at 21.
19. Ibid., at 25–7.
20. Ibid.
21. Ibid., at 27.
22. Ibid. See, for example, at 25.
23. Ibid., at 28.
24. I am interested in this concept since I have found other examples of children reporting similar conduct, a kind of special "look" they learn to understand and interpret. While they do not articulate it as a form of surveillance and emotional form of stalking, they are aware it makes them feel unsafe and under constant threat and surveillance by the offender. A number of victim/survivors have also reported another special "look" used by offenders to convey imminent abuse. Many child victims say they have learned to recognize this look and understand their father is informing them of his intention to sexually abuse them very soon, and that any resistance is futile. Some examples of this were found in my original research. See also the work of Salter (1988) who has commented on non-verbal cues used by sex offenders to monitor and control child victims.
25. R v D, at 28–30.
26. Ibid., at 26–8.
27. Ibid., at 37–8.
28. Ibid., at 40.

29. Ibid., at 34–6.
30. For example, six cases from my original research reveal children alleging having been sexually abused in the family vehicle after being driven somewhere by the offender.
31. R v D, at 47.
32. Ibid., at 45.
33. A female magistrate did the committal hearing and on a number of occasions she did intervene when long or complex questions and terminology were put to the child, to ask him if he understood the questions and/or terminology. The stark contrast between her positive interventions to ensure the child was not disadvantaged in cross-examination and the complete lack of any judicial or legal intervention here reveals differences in judicial sensitivity and awareness to the special needs of child witnesses.
34. R v D, at 38.
35. Ibid., at 48–9.
36. Ibid., at 40–1.
37. Ibid., at 49.
38. Ibid., at 41–2.
39. Ibid., at 52.
40. Ibid.
41. In R v A and R v C the child complainants were accused of being "coached" in their evidence when they gave an answer to a question that took the defense counsel by surprise. On both occasions, the children responded to questions that appeared deliberately misleading and gave evidence to clarify or challenge the defense's assertion.
42. R v D, at 56–8.
43. Ibid., at 56.
44. Ibid.
45. Ibid., at 58–61.
46. See Summit (1983); Summit (1988); Salter (1988); and Salter (1995).
47. R v D, at 60.
48. Ibid., at 84. This reexamination of the child occurred after the evidence given by the forensic medical examiner. The reason was that the judge reserved his ruling on the prosecution argument regarding presenting evidence to counter what he considered were defense accusations of recent invention by the child, until the following day.
49. Ibid., at 64–75.
50. Ibid., at 73–4.
51. Ibid., at 88.
52. Ibid., at 90.
53. Ibid., at 92–3.
54. Ibid., at 88–95.
55. Ibid., at 108
56. Ibid.
57. Ibid.
58. Ibid., at 105.
59. Ibid., at 111–4.
60. Ibid., at 115–6.
61. See, for example: R v A; R v B (Victorian County Court, Williams, J. 1995); R v C; R v D; R v E (Victorian County Court, Wodak, J. 1995); R v F; R v G (1996); R v L (Victorian County Court, Kelly, J. 1993); R v L (Victorian County Court, retrial, Lewis, J. 1996).

6 ▪ Case Study R v L

Allegations and Complainant Background

THIS PROTRACTED CASE involved an original trial, resulting in conviction on the majority of charges, with a successful appeal leading to a retrial. For reasons of clarity and space, the retrial forms the predominant basis of this case study, with reference to the first trial only where relevant for the purpose of highlighting contrasts and similarities.

The female complainant made allegations against her stepfather of long-term sexual abuse beginning when she was approximately nine years of age and continuing until just before her twenty-first birthday. The accused was charged with a number of counts, mostly involving penetration, including an act of penetration that led to a pregnancy and termination when the complainant was a young teenager.

The complainant's family life was difficult and complex. Her mother, a trained nurse, had remarried when the complainant was approximately eight years old, and the complainant alleges that her stepfather began sexually abusing her a short time later. The family lived in a provincial city, and soon after the mother's remarriage they moved to an acreage property in a small rural town. The complainant alleges the sexual abuse against her increased, and that her mother began to express concern at what she considered to be her husband's sexualized behavior toward her child. This resulted in a number of heated arguments between the complainant's mother and her husband, the accused.

A police statement and evidence from the mother at the first trial details severe domestic violence and this claim is supported by evidence from her children, including the complainant who had witnessed incidents of violence. With regards to her suspicions that her husband was sexually abusing her daughter, the mother contacted child protection services and local police on a number of occasions to report what she said was her husband's inappropriate sexual conduct toward her daughter. The daughter at this stage had not disclosed to anyone. Evidence of the complainant included that her stepfather became aware of a planned visit by police and protective workers, and ordered the children not to disclose anything about family violence or alleged abuse toward the daughter. A sibling of the complainant also corroborated this claim.

In her police statement, the mother claims that she continued to report her concerns and became increasingly distressed by the lack of response shown by police and protective workers. She also suggested that her husband was friendly with the local police and that this made it even more difficult for her to have her concerns properly addressed. She would later tell police investigating the alleged abuse that she experienced deep distress and depression as a result of her reported concerns being ignored. This distress culminated in a suicide attempt in the early to middle 1980s requiring medical intervention. As a consequence she was made an involuntary in-patient at a large mental hospital and was, in part, treated for her "paranoid" beliefs about her husband sexually abusing her daughter. She claims that she only secured her release as an involuntary patient when she retracted her claims about her husband's sexual conduct toward her daughter.

After being released from the hospital, she found herself unable to reconcile with her husband and children, and estranged from her local community. She says she was forced to leave the community, taking with her only a few belongings. Her daughter was approximately thirteen years old at this time.

After the stepfather gained custody of the children (the complainant and her three younger brothers), the family moved to a new home, and the complainant alleges that the abuse increased dramatically. She became pregnant as a result of the abuse, and the stepfather arranged for a termination. In the meantime, her mother and stepfather divorced, though he continued to have custody of the children and they in turn had very little if any contact with the mother for some years.

By her own admission, the complainant was estranged from her mother for some time, adopting the misguided (but understandable) belief that her mother had abandoned her and her siblings, leaving her to suffer horrendous abuse. Of course, this was not the situation, and after escaping the abuse years later, the complainant and her mother reconciled and became very close. At both trials, the mother provided full support to her daughter. One of her sons, a half-brother to the complainant, also reconciled with his mother and supported the complainant's charges. He made a police statement detailing, among other things, a particular incident of alleged sexual abuse he observed between the accused and the complainant.

The complainant reported she had few friends and never had any boyfriends. She completed most of her schooling but became increasingly distressed about the abuse, and just before her twenty-first birthday and with the help of a female friend, moved out of the family home.

A short time after this, she alleges she was harassed by her stepfather and that her younger siblings were upset and confused by her sudden departure from the family home, as they had come to view their older sister as a kind of surrogate mother. At the request of the stepfather, the complainant attended dyad counseling with him and, later on, group counseling with her siblings and the stepfather. All sessions were with the same counselor. This type of counseling caused specific problems for the complainant, as she recounted in her statement the awkward nature of the sessions. In one example, she says the secrecy surrounding her leaving the family home led to a particular counseling session in which her brothers vented their anger at her for leaving them, as they had come to see her as a mother figure. She felt angry and distressed since in dyad counseling her stepfather had openly acknowledged his sexual abuse of her. With little therapeutic support, and none from the accused, she tried to make her brothers understand that her departure was as a direct result of the sexual abuse she suffered by the stepfather.

Extensive records kept by the counselor after each session—and, indeed, a statement by the counselor—made clear that the stepfather fully admitted sexually violating his stepdaughter over a long period of time from childhood to adulthood. At first he had tried to deny it was "abuse," claiming his stepdaughter was, in his opinion, not harmed by his criminal conduct, and when the complainant was eventually able to leave home he attempted to make her return. The counselor's statement included information that the accused had contacted her prior to the trial and asked her not to pass on any of this information to police or courts, and, further, that his new de facto wife was fully aware of his previous sexual "relationship" with his stepdaughter.[1]

Later on, the youngest half-sibling of the complainant, still in his teens, made a statement to police. Aside from detailing an alleged incident of sexual abuse he says he observed as a young child, he also detailed a history of domestic violence perpetrated on his mother by his father. Moreover, he told police that since they became involved in investigating his half-sister's allegations of sexual abuse, his father had recently warned him not to tell the police about anything he had witnessed in the family home saying that he could well go to jail for such sexual conduct.[2] It was obvious that this teenager was deeply distressed by what had occurred in his family and by his father's demands for loyalty at the expense of truth.

At the first trial, the judge ruled the teenager's *voir dire*[3] evidence as inadmissible after a truly bizarre hearing in which the trial judge said he would subject the teenager to a test of his "connective memory."[4] After subjecting him to this form of judicial pop psychology, the boy's evidence was dismissed as the judge felt that the presence of social workers intervening on "family" life may well have influenced the boy's evidence about what he saw his father do and what his father told him. In fact, the judge suggested that the half-brother's evidence (witnessing an incident of sexual abuse through a bedroom window) was, according to the judge, more likely to have been "some *other* incident of *sexual play* and, therefore, not able to be linked to a specific charge [emphasis added]."[5]

The teenager continued to support his half-sister but remained troubled by what he regarded as his father's failure to take full responsibility for what had occurred, and worse, for causing so much additional grief by subjecting them all to a divisive trial. The family was splitting into two camps: those who supported the complainant, and those who supported the accused. After his father was convicted for the offenses, he wrote to him in prison expressing his distress and concerns. His father responded with a letter that greatly exacerbated the teenager's distress. Soon after being informed by the police that his stepfather had successfully appealed his conviction and a retrial would be held, this young man approached a counselor and stated that he could not come to terms with this information. Very soon after communicating his distress to the counselor, he was found dead from an overdose of drugs. Found on his body at the time was the letter his father had sent him from prison, rejecting him for making a police statement and for seeking to give evidence against him at the trial.[6]

The accused had worked in various unskilled and semi-skilled positions, including work at a popular tourist attraction, before undertaking a diploma course at a local TAFE institute, which led to him securing professional work.

The full-brother and half-sibling of the complainant supported their father and gave evidence against the complainant at both trials. I personally observed the 1996 retrial and analyzed the transcripts of that trial and the first trial in 1993.

Prosecution Evidence

The complainant aside, the evidence the prosecutor sought to include was the independent corroboration of the counselor. With regard to witnesses, the prosecutor would call evidence from the complainant's mother, the police informant, a former school teacher of the complainant, and a friend of the complainant from her secondary school years.

Evidence and Evidentiary Rulings

Naturally, a new judge presides over a retrial. A different prosecutor and defense counsel were also engaged for the retrial. For the purpose of clarification, it is necessary to briefly recount two major evidentiary rulings from the first trial since they were hotly contested at the retrial.

At the first trial, the prosecution sought to introduce the evidence of the counselor. This move was not without drama, however, since the counselor was hostile[7] toward the prosecution case and, only after being threatened with contempt of court charges, did the counselor present herself at court to give *voir dire* evidence for the prosecution. Defense counsel argued the counselor's evidence was inadmissible because it covered admissions about *generalized* abuse rather than specific acts for which the accused was charged. While this bone of contention frequently finds its way into defense arguments regarding evidence of alleged accused admissions,[8] the prosecutor was able to lead *voir dire* evidence from the counselor that could be explicitly linked to at least three of the charges on the presentment. After legal arguments from both sides, the counselor's evidence was ruled admissible, albeit in a modified and restricted form. Nonetheless, it was obviously a plus for the prosecution at the first trial to actually have compelling evidence of corroboration to support the evidence of the complainant, who was subjected to outrageous attacks on her character for the duration of that trial.

The first trial judge also allowed the complainant to give what is termed "relationship evidence"[9] in order to better contextualize her allegations. This included evidence about her delayed disclosure, and admittance to a psychiatric hospital for a short stay as a result of the trauma of her abuse. At the Court of Appeal, defense counsel successfully secured a retrial based on the wrongful admission of this latter evidence. Counsel claimed that the complainant's evidence regarding her reason for seeking admission to a psychiatric hospital should not have been accepted without supporting expert evidence being led from the psychiatrist who treated her. The Court of Appeal agreed, suggesting that her evidence was simply that of a *lay person* unsupported by expert evidence.

So while a complainant might reasonably be suspected to be in the best position to explain what led her to seek assistance from a mental health expert, the appeal judges disagreed. Moreover, the new judge presiding over the retrial specifically defended the rationale for dismissing this first trial evidence. The new judge pontificated over the appeal decision, explaining how such a decision was correct because the complainant's explanation was "an unsubstantiated opinion evidence from a lay person. Had there been evidence to support that opinion or her expression of an opinion, it would have been all right."[10] So it appears that expressing the impact of long-term rape on one's self can only be regarded as reliable evidence when given the imprimatur of an expert.

Obviously wishing to avoid such a pitfall again, the new prosecutor signaled to the judge his desire to call expert testimony. This expert testimony would serve to counter character attacks mounted by defense counsel regarding the complainant's delayed disclosure of her abuse and the fact that she remained in the family home until adulthood, despite suffering such abuse. This submission for expert testimony to explain victim/survivor behavior is very reasonable. Defense barristers routinely argue that if a child or young adult were *really* a victim of such alleged sexual abuse they would have made full, immediate and public objections and certainly would not have remained in the family home, especially into adulthood. The prosecutor also relied on the important legal principle enunciated by the Appellate Court in 1994 which agreed that in certain situations, expert testimony could be led by the prosecution to rebut defense attacks on complainants around delayed disclosure and behavior presented as "inconsistent" with the allegations.[11]

But from the beginning, the stance adopted by the new trial judge toward the possible introduction of expert testimony clearly indicated that he would not accede to such a submission. First he gave his own personal anecdotes about mental health professionals, and declared his belief that *his* comments "have more clout" when it comes to the complex area of human behavior.[12] By whose authority does his opinion have more clout? The self-accredited exercise of his own judicial discretion seems to be the only foundation upon which to rest such a claim.

Later, in his official ruling on the prosecution submission, the judge explicitly rejected the notion of "expert" testimony. What need was there for an expert? After all, the judge now contradictorily contended, surely the complainant was "quite capable of explaining the reasons for her (behavior)…her credibility is of course essentially a matter for the jury."[13] To be sure, in a world where traumatic responses from those who experience sexual abuse—particularly long-term intrafamilial abuse—no longer encounter the kind of prejudicial and ignorant interpretation that defense counsel so eagerly feed and capitalize on in a trial situation, such first-person lay testimony might very well be powerful enough to withstand strategic defense attacks.

Strengthening his view, the judge stated that "any reasonable jury" using "commonsense" would have "little difficulty" comprehending why a victim of long-term sexual abuse would choose to remain living in the family home for so long. Notwithstanding the received view that the public is generally now more aware of child sexual abuse and domestic violence, whether this awareness translates into a fuller understanding of the many complex issues surrounding long-term sexual violence and associated traumagenic effects is another question entirely. Some excellent research has shown that long-term violence endured by women and children is often viewed with skepticism (by the public, but even some professionals), and afforded less credibility than other types of abuse or violence.[14] Besides, the fact that defense barristers spend so much time and effort in their cross-examination highlighting delayed disclosure is indicative of how rewarding such a stratagem is, particularly when used in isolation. The judge himself further postulated that in his "opinion...sexual abuse accommodation syndromes" were "airy-fairy cuckooland stuff...and Alice in Wonderland" concepts.[15] The basis for such a substantive view is nothing more than personal opinion elevated to the status of judicial utterance and discretion. Comments such as these are again indicative of the judiciary pontificating an implicit worldview that is apparently impervious to challenge from professional disciplines outside their realm.

With the status of expert evidence settled, defense counsel moved to limit the prosecution case further by targeting specific charges on the presentment and possible corroborating evidence that might have otherwise been introduced. Defense counsel successfully petitioned for a large number of charges from the presentment to be dismissed on a clever technicality. His client, argued defense counsel, had divorced the complainant's mother prior to her turning sixteen years of age. Despite maintaining custody of the complainant and her younger siblings, defense counsel argued that any alleged incidents of sexual abuse *after* the girl turned sixteen were *not* criminal offenses since the accused was no longer *legally* her stepfather, hence there was no "incest." The judge agreed with this clever bit of technical spin-doctoring, which paved the way for a number of the charges—charges for which he was found guilty of at the first trial—to be nullified on the basis that:

> there was no improper relationship, *legally speaking*.... In terms of the fact that the *relationship* was no longer stepfather and daughter [*sic*], no longer incestuous from a *technical*, if you like, situation. [emphasis added][16]

The accused now faced only nine charges relating to indecent assault and full penetration of his stepdaughter, including penetration that caused a pregnancy (subsequently aborted). This clever and convenient technicality proved most useful in further eroding the prosecution case. Some of the obliterated charges were those explicitly linked to the counselor's evidence at the first trial and with these charges expunged, so too was the very powerful and damning evidence of the counselor.[17]

Despite divorcing her mother, the accused maintained custody of the complainant, and had been her stepfather since she was approximately eight years old. He was the only father figure she had ever known, and the fact that he maintained custody of her and her siblings after the divorce indicates the maintenance of the father-child relationship. Indeed, throughout the trial, the complainant always referred to the accused as her stepfather. To suddenly adopt a view that after the divorce, and after the girl reached sixteen, the accused suddenly ceased to be her stepfather is the kind of convenience-based mental gymnastics employed in the legal arena to remove evidence damaging to one's case.

Acceding to this tactic, the judge was now ready to preside over what one might call a kind of selective amnesia: the judge declared the trial to be one involving "an uncorroborated complaint, with old offenses." The prosecutor meekly[18] reminded the judge that originally the case *had* independent corroboration until the latter charges were all dropped. When the jury entered the courtroom for the first time, the judge apprised them of the salient points of the case and, with regard to the strength of the prosecution case, told them:

> from the accused man's side there is a flat denial that they [charged offenses] ever took place at all. There was just a blanket denial that any of those offenses took place, it is as stark as that.... Now it is a question of who you believe in a situation where it is as stark as that, where there is no other evidence except what she says and what he says.[19]

Further exemplifying the judicial amnesia that saturated this case, the judge later commented that it would be simply "terrible" if there was someone out there from the psychiatric hospital (where the complainant had sought help for her psychological distress) who was able to tell the court that the complainant's evidence of long-term sexual abuse was all a "psychotic" fantasy.[20] With the counselor's evidence expediently removed from the trial, the legal view was comfortably one of uncorroborated and old allegations making for "stark" evidence upon which to have a jury decide guilt or innocence.

With no evidence to rebuff the defense narrative, save for the evidence of the complainant herself, defense counsel was free to develop a narrative of the vengeful daughter. While defense counsel in the first case highlighted a narrative of emotional instability, especially with regard to her psychiatric treatment and soft drug use, defense counsel at the retrial avoided cross-examination of the previous mental health issues and soft drug use by the complainant. From reading the transcript, one may infer defense counsel was privately concerned that introducing such evidence may allow the prosecutor to admit the psychiatric files of the complainant which clearly reveal her reasons for seeking assistance and using soft drugs as a means to bury her emotional pain.

The sexual history of the complainant was a key factor in the first trial, as the complainant was at the time involved in a lesbian relationship. At the retrial, defense counsel chose to avoid cross-examination on several of the sexual matters raised at the first trial. I believe this was avoided for fear that the jury might adopt the interpretation that sexual abuse led this young woman toward lesbianism. The attitude that homosexuality may be linked to experiences of child sexual abuse is a reasonably popular belief among the public and some professionals. While defense barristers may very well generally appeal to social myths, stereotypes and prejudices, I am confident this was one social myth or stereotype they clearly wanted to avoid. I also believe that defense counsel may have been concerned that any reference to her same sex attraction might negate the stock-story defense narrative about a local unnamed schoolboy making her pregnant.

Complementing the stock-story narrative of the vengeful stepdaughter, defense counsel signaled an intention to make good use of transcripts: transcripts from the committal hearing, first trial (which actually involved two transcripts after the first trial was aborted, requiring her to give her evidence all over again in front of a new jury), transcripts from the *voir dire* at this 1996 trial; as well as her police statements.

After the successful appeal by the accused, the complainant made a new police statement to clarify what she described as "confusion" over several incidents she gave evidence about at the first trial. The crux of her new statement involved changing a specific date and a specific piece of evidence relating to cross-examination about the precise moment of losing her virginity.

She was cross-examined at length in a *voir dire* about this new statement and her evidence in support of her new statement was convincing. Her desire to clarify the date of an incident even caused the judge to wonder why she would bother to do this since her stepfather was originally found guilty of that particular incident:

> DEFENSE: Why did you change in your statement...the fourth statement, to say that it now occurred in January 1980?
>
> COMPLAINANT: Because when I was compiling [statement], I read the transcript of the [first] trial, put it away, thought about it, and thought, right, I'm going to have to re-write the truth, re-write it and make it clear enough—not copy what I'd said prior, but write the truth.
>
> DEFENSE: What, so previously what you had said wasn't the truth?

COMPLAINANT: To the best of my ability at a given time.

DEFENSE: It was the truth to the best of your ability at a given time. Is that what you're saying?

COMPLAINANT: Yes.

DEFENSE: So the truth obviously varies with you, depending on what you remember might be the truth at any given time?

COMPLAINANT: I think it indicates that I'm being honest, more so than indicating that I'm being inconsistent and lying. I had not referred to any police statements. I read—simply read the trial transcript, realized that I have to clarify this situation.

DEFENSE: Why? What was it about it that made you think you had to clarify it? It was perfectly clear?

COMPLAINANT: The fact that he'd been released from prison, for starters. I thought, well, something has to be done about this.

DEFENSE: You've got to change your story to get him, is that what you're saying?

COMPLAINANT: No, Sir.

JUDGE: The accused was convicted before Judge [names judge] of the [particular charge], wasn't he? That's what I don't understand. Why would you alter the date of the [particular charge] when you knew that your stepfather had been convicted of the offense relating to [particular charge]? Why would you alter the date when you knew he had been convicted of it?

COMPLAINANT: That wasn't a consideration for me.[21]

The above excerpt is a most telling piece of evidence. It shows a young woman concerned with clarifying her memory of a date, regardless of the possibility that it may harm her evidence when later used in front of a jury. Her concern was in the clarification of events she was forced to relive over and over in trials and in statements. In one sense she paid a price for this honesty as the jury acquitted him of this charge at this trial, but I believe that the complainant in this case would have regarded this to be an acceptable price since she was more concerned with establishing the facts around the events.[22] Victims of long-term rape do not generally keep a diary or calendar of events, and do not generally recall their abuse in linear detail, although the law responds as though the separation of multiple incidents of rape and assault over a period of time—especially a long period of time—should be automatically recalled as part of the proof process. A major impetus for the change in two incidents related to the complainant's better understanding of the technicality of virginity. The masculinist preconception with a broken hymen or other obvious physical signs being proof of rape pervades rape trials so that much cross-examination and forensic evidence is about locating evidence within this masculinist paradigm.[23] In cross-examination before the jury, this issue would be raised at some length.

The prosecutor highlighted that while the complainant's new statement involved the changing of two dates, her evidence about the actual incidents was precisely the same as that given at the first trial. The judge allowed amendments to the presentment to accommodate these new dates, and it was clear that defense counsel would use this altered evidence along with previous trial transcripts to both confuse the complainant and advance their narrative of fabrication. It soon became clear that the barrister further intended to use all previous transcripts and any amendments to also deliberately confuse the jury as part of his repertoire of "forensic skills" in defending his client. After indicating that he would be relying heavily on these previous transcripts and complainant statements, the judge acknowledged the possible impact of such a tactic on the jury's ability to clearly follow the case, saying:

> JUDGE: You're going to be cross-examining [complainant] on the basis of a prior inconsistent statement on a primary inconsistent statement and what she said at the prior, what she said at this, that and the other thing...defense by obfuscation rather than by anything else, it seems to me, the jury won't know what version they're dealing with.
>
> DEFENSE: Hopefully by the end of the day that's the view the jury will take...[24]

Conducting a trial by deliberate obfuscation of the facts and deliberate confusion, then, may be regarded as a legal virtue. From the very outset of this trial, the judge used proactive language to discuss the allegations against the accused. He frequently described the case as one about the complainant's "sexual relationship" with the accused, and, on one occasion described her police statements as a *Magnum Opus*.[25] Despite avoiding the issue of her sexual lifestyle, psychiatric treatment and previous use of soft drugs, defense counsel made such information known to the judge at the very beginning of the trial, prompting a mysterious comment by the judge that such information was something for "my little book."[26]

Despite not being involved in the first trial, the barrister was not shy in expressing his view that the complainant was a person with a "marked ability to run at the mouth," prompting the judge to ask the prosecutor a short time later whether he was able to "keep her under control."[27] Frequent examples can be found of defense counsel besmirching the character of a complainant prior to them entering the witness box. Such a strategy appears to be employed in the hope that projecting a negative image of the complainant might arouse a degree of personal judicial prejudice against the complainant even in their absence.[28]

Evidence-in-Chief of Complainant

In her evidence-in-chief, the complainant was led through each charge. The first incident of alleged sexual abuse occurred when she was nine years old. The complainant said her mother was in the hospital giving birth to her youngest sibling, and she recalls that she accidentally caused a small fire in the kitchen for which she received a belting from the accused and was sent to bed without any dinner. She alleges that, later on, her stepfather came to her room and cuddled her before lying on top of her and rubbing his erect penis against her leg. The prosecutor asked her if she wanted her stepfather to do this to her and she replied she did not.[29]

The second charge related to an incident when the complainant was twelve years old, and the family was now living on a small rural property. The complainant had taken part in a school walkathon and had somehow mislaid the money she raised. Her mother accused her of spending the money on lollies and cigarettes, which she denied, and told her she had to stay at home that morning until she found the money. In her evidence, she recalled searching her bedroom unsuccessfully for the money and, as a result, missed the school bus. With her mother left for work, and her siblings (other than her infant brother) left for school, she was home alone with her stepfather. She alleges her stepfather told her to make them both a hot drink and to come back to the parents' bedroom so he could have a talk to her about the missing money. There, she says, her stepfather said "that I was a pathetic liar and a thief and then he struck me on the side of the head with his fist and I was knocked to the floor and saw stars and got up. After a while he put his arms around me and pulled me closer to the bed."[30]

She gave evidence that he then proceeded to kiss her with his mouth open and pushed his tongue into her mouth before partially undressing her and indecently touching her. He then made her masturbate him:

> COMPLAINANT: And then he rolled on his back and asked me—well, got my hand and held it in a gripping position and put it on his penis.
>
> PROSECUTOR: What state was his penis in at this stage?
>
> COMPLAINANT: It was standing up.
>
> PROSECUTOR: Yes, and what happened, you say he has put your hand on his penis which is standing up; what happened then?
>
> COMPLAINANT: He moved it up and down about five times and then just—then said to me: "just keep doing it like that."
>
> PROSECUTOR: Did you do that?
>
> COMPLAINANT: Yes.[31]

In her evidence about what occurred immediately after this incident, she said her stepfather drove her to school, and on the way kept asking her about what he had done and whether she wanted him to do it again. She said she tried to ignore his questions, but he kept repeating it over and over, and when they finally reached her school he again asked her if she wanted "to do it again." Her evidence was that "I said 'yes,' when I should have said 'no.'"

> PROSECUTOR: Why did you say you wanted to do it again?
>
> COMPLAINANT: Because I wanted to get out of the car.[32]

Asking the complainant to explain her apparent permission for her stepfather to sexually assault her again was most likely designed to elicit basic information about the forms of acquiesce children make when faced with sexual abuse, but one cannot help but consider that such questions shame complainants—more particularly so given the legal predilection for decontextualizing such evidence.

The third charge related to the amended incident, involving an allegation of sexual penetration that occurred while on a horse ride. The complainant detailed an early morning horse ride arranged by her stepfather to a secluded area with some "smooth" ground for them to lie on. She said that the week before the ride, her stepfather had arranged for a condom, lubricant and handkerchief to be taken on that morning. After being told to undress, her stepfather removed his clothing and removed the condom and other things from his pocket. When asked what occurred, the complainant said that an incident of "incest" took place and at first seemed hesitant to describe the incident in detail. She described the penetration as having the penis enter her "body," and said that after her stepfather had finished "moving in and out" of her "he finished" and then wiped himself with the handkerchief. She says that upon wiping herself she saw "blood" around her vagina. Asked by the prosecutor how she was feeling at this time she replied, "Not very good."[33] She was thirteen years old at this time.

From a reading of the transcript I noticed that much of the complainant's evidence was given in a much more distant way than she had given previously, in that she sometimes spoke in the third person and used mechanical terms to describe certain incidents. For example, she described her father "indecently touching" her, and then says he went on to "unlawfully penetrate me," and on other occasions when describing penetration says that "incest" was committed.[34] It is possible this action was based on emotional survival.[35] At the start of the trial, in the absence of the jury, it was confirmed that the complainant was taking prescribed anti-depressants, and I noted at the trial that she rarely became visibly distressed or showed much emotion, and I attributed this to the effects of the anti-depressants. I recall wondering at the time whether it might have any adverse affect on how the jury might appraise her, given that they are invited—as they were in this trial—to assess the demeanor and body language of the witness.

The next allegation involved oral penetration in the lounge room of the family home. The complainant gave evidence that her stepfather asked to ejaculate in her mouth and she indicated "no," but that he did so anyway, and she pulled her head away. While it may seem an odd piece of evidence, the complainant was asked about any special "rules" imposed on the children in the house. She told the court her stepfather considered the lounge room to be the best room in the house, and so they needed his permission to enter the lounge room. However, the fourth charge also related to an incident in the lounge room, and the aforementioned evidence was no doubt elicited to support her claim that they were undisturbed by her younger siblings since they were banned from voluntarily entering the room without explicit permission.[36]

Charges five to nine all related to full penetration, including an act of penetration that resulted in the then teenage complainant becoming pregnant. One specific charge was said to have occurred when the family was moving. The complainant said that her youngest brother and mother stayed at the former family home while she and her other two younger brothers accompanied the accused to the new house they were moving into. In her evidence she told the jury that her stepfather claimed that it was best that the family split up overnight between the two houses to prevent any possible theft of property. Though they all slept in the lounge of the new house, the stepfather erected a furniture and blanket division in which her two siblings slept on one side with her stepfather and herself on the other. Her evidence was that during this night her father made her take part in vaginal intercourse. Soon after this particular incident, the mother left the family home permanently, resulting in what she described as her stepfather commencing frequent sexual abuse of her, without the use of any contraception. According to her evidence, he preferred to use the "withdrawal method" (withdrawing his penis from her vagina just before he ejaculated).[37]

Another allegation related to vaginal penetration soon after the accused arrived home from the hospital after undergoing some back surgery. In her evidence, the complainant said that her stepfather insisted on her adopting a different sexual position to accommodate his sore back.

During her evidence-in-chief, the prosecutor also used proactive language to describe the allegations, saying that the complainant "had sexual intercourse" with the accused. This proactive and passive language of father-daughter rape has been consistently identified across trials.[38] He also referred to the accused by name, with the title "Mr." rather than identifying the complainant's accuser as her stepfather. While these points might seem technical, the first point demonstrates the embedded language of mutuality when referring to sexual crimes in "incest" trials. The latter point shows that even the prosecutor had a blind spot when it came to linking the parental bond and, indeed, parental betrayal inherent in such a case. While this linguistic distancing could be expected from defense counsel as a deliberate ploy to create emotional distance between alleged victim and perpetrator, one might have hoped the prosecutor to be more conscientiously sensitive to such distortions.

When asked whether she had ever had sexual intercourse with anyone else aside from the accused, the complainant replied that she had not.[39] When giving evidence of the pregnancy and abortion, the complainant said that her stepfather originally wanted her to keep the child, saying they would move interstate and she could "pretend" to be his wife and raise her younger brothers as though they were her own children. She did not agree with this scenario, and told the jury that a discussion took place between herself and her stepfather in which they agreed that the official story to the local general practitioner and staff at the fertility clinic would be that a boy from school (who would remain unnamed) caused the pregnancy. It is interesting to note how many times this scenario of an unnamed boy from school that no one knows and the father-as-offender is not remotely interested in pursuing for making his often underage teenage daughter pregnant, is reported by complainants in such trials.[40]

Cross-examination of the Complainant

Defense cross-examination began with the usual technical demands for peripheral details. With regards to the incident connected with the walkathon money, the complainant was asked how she collected the money, how many acres they lived on, the fencing around the property, the size of the backyard, the distance of the road from the house, and a range of other questions. Building on the argument of denial of the charge, defense counsel canvassed in detail that the work records of the accused from that period indicate that he attended work consistently that week.

The complainant handled cross-examination on these points extremely well. When defense counsel put to her that the alleged incident could not have occurred on the basis that it would have been improper parenting for her mother or stepfather to leave a three-year-old infant unattended on a rural property, the complainant said such a question would be better put to her mother or stepfather, and not her. When the barrister labored the point about the work records for the accused showing that he attended work that day, the complainant said that the records did not prove that he was *actually* physically at his place of work on that particular day.[41]

After being asked to give a demonstration to the jury of how her stepfather allegedly struck her head that morning, defense counsel highlighted inconsistencies in her evidence: at a previous trial she had said she was struck with an open hand and now suggested it was a fist. Her response was that she could not recall if her stepfather used an open or closed hand, but remembers *where* she was struck. The pedantry increased as the walkathon incident was targeted. Defense counsel made much of the fact that in her original statement she said she had "lost" the money, but in her evidence at this trial said the money went "missing." In response to this, the complainant calmly replied that:

COMPLAINANT: I lost possession of it because it was no longer in my school bag.

DEFENSE: Well, why didn't you say that to police, that you lost possession of it?

COMPLAINANT: Because that's just how the truth was at the time. That's how...[cut off by defense].

DEFENSE: I see, that was the truth at the time was it?

COMPLAINANT: That's how—the best I could explain it.[42]

The above is reminiscent of Evan Whitton's point about the classic defense strategy of finding minute differences in *how* witnesses word their evidence about the same incident differently and using it to berate their credibility.[43]

It was not long before defense counsel moved on to the charge connected with the horse riding incident—one of the amended charges—and proceeded to produce excerpts from statements and previous transcripts, creating a mountain of paperwork that virtually concealed the bar table. As with all complainants in these kinds of cases, defense counsel reminded her almost incessantly that she "swore on oath": her evidence at the committal hearing, and then at the 1993 trial, and then in her statement, and then at this trial, and so on and so forth, was "truth" as sworn on the Bible. In fact in a very short space of time, making up only a couple of pages of transcript, defense counsel repeated the term "swore on oath" more than twenty times, as though trial by deliberate confusion and trial by repetition might be enough to convince jurors to acquit.[44] These repetitive phrases are designed to have a cumulative effect on the jury by reinforcing how the complainant "swore on oath" about things now shown to be incorrect—regardless of how minute the error—as well as hopefully and more importantly, unsettling the complainant. I suspect the barrister was not prepared for the complainant to answer so strongly to his continual attacks about which version was the "truth" given under a "sworn oath." The complainant continually reminded the barrister that she had made a "mistake," an "error" caused by a "difficulty locating (the incident) in a time frame" necessary for a charge to be linked to a specific date and was therefore "not a lie."[45] This ability to counter defense attacks with calm and cogent replies epitomized much of the evidence given by the complainant. Cross-examination on the topic of her loss of virginity brought to bear all the trappings of masculinist paradigms surrounding sex:

> DEFENSE: The occasion on which a young girl loses her virginity is an occasion that, generally speaking, is something that sticks fairly clearly in the mind of that young girl, correct.
>
> COMPLAINANT: Yes.
>
> DEFENSE: Is that the same for you? Is it something that's clear in your mind?
>
> COMPLAINANT: Yes.[46]

This trial is about the sexual abuse of girl child who had her virginity taken from her in an alleged act of rape by her own stepfather—not two teenagers on a date! The suggestion fits in with the Lolita-type syndrome, which places intrafamilial abuse as a kind of illicit but consensual affair, memorable for the girl rather than traumatic. The crucial element the defense wished to highlight is that the complainant had alleged at the first trial that she lost her virginity during a different incident but now wished to change her evidence that she actually lost her virginity at the horse riding incident because this is where she saw blood from her vagina. It is obvious from her evidence that the complainant has identified with the prominent and culturally embedded masculinist idea that a loss of virginity is signaled by the appearance of blood. This, of course, is not always the case, and the masculinist concept that a broken hymen must be present for proof that penetration occurred is also erroneous, though it is frequently uttered in judicial discourse to negate the evidence of child witnesses.[47] The complainant's response clearly demonstrated she held a technical understanding of losing one's virginity with the appearance of blood, and so believed that her original evidence about losing her virginity when fully penetrated on a previous occasion during the horse riding incident must be wrong, since that occasion did not reveal any blood.[48] This is not surprising because sexual discourse is saturated with the masculinist concept of a broken hymen—with blood as proof of its *breaking*—as evidence of lost virginity, rather than being associated with loss of virginity.

Loss of virginity is identified with evidence of part of a child or young woman's body being *broken*, rather than the sexual act that may or may not necessarily involve such "proof." However, defense chose to make much of this technical understanding, cynically suggesting how it is not possible to lose one's virginity twice, and repeatedly asking the complainant to explain how she could lose her virginity twice when in fact she was trying to indicate how *she* identified with her own recognition of losing her virginity.[49]

Again the barrister re-canvassed the issue of amendments to her statement, perhaps thinking that a second round would enable him to push her evidence into a corner where he could attack her more easily. He was in for a surprise. He put to her that her change of dates was proof that she was not telling the truth about her alleged abuse. In another solid exchange, the complainant responded by stating that it was in *her own* "interest that the truth be known," adding that her alterations to her original statements corrected errors in time only, and not content, and did not, therefore, indicate that she was lying.[50]

Perhaps aware of the tangible rebuffs to his rhetoric in front of the jury, the barrister switched topics, but not style, by attacking the credibility of the complainant's mother. Once again, the complainant proved a formidable opponent. When the barrister made an unflattering comment about her mother's difficulty recalling a specific time frame, the complainant replied, "I don't know. I don't read other people's minds or pretend to."[51] The unflattering comments about her mother increased as defense counsel sought to portray the mother as an unstable individual who posed a problem for the entire family. As the complainant moved to respond to this cruel portrayal, the barrister attempted to cut her off, but to no avail. In a calm and steady voice, the complainant looked toward the jury and stated that her stepfather sought to "undermine" her mother, "rejected" her, and treated her like "shit."[52] In what I perceived to be an attempt to douse a fire he unwittingly fuelled, the barrister told the complainant that he was not interested in *why* her mother had difficulties, only that she was *having* difficulties.[53]

No doubt the complainant's comments, despite interjections from the barrister, were a strong attempt to give what little context she could about her mother's home life, in an effort to disrupt the defense narrative of the "bad" and "mad" mother that was no doubt being deployed—even in embryonic form, as it was here. Suspecting the point may have hit home, and perhaps wanting to gather up his own thoughts about his next strategy, the barrister quickly called upon the judge to allow a break in proceedings.[54] I believe the complainant was alert to the defense construction of "bad" mothers after her experience at the first trial in 1993. The first trial barrister began to question the complainant concerning her mother's conduct within the family and her relationship with her, prompting the complainant to tell the barrister there had been no need for "collusion" between her and her mother.[55]

After a break in proceedings, defense cross-examination began with rapid-fire questions and statements, again interspersed with excerpts from various statements and previous trial transcripts that were as tedious as they were difficult to follow. Comments in the complainant's own statement about unflattering behavior by her mother were read aloud by the barrister and, isolated from any context, portrayed the mother in a cruel light. Questions about the alleged incident during the house move were canvassed. When the barrister asked the complainant, for example, why her father would want to partition off the lounge room when she had been sharing a room with her brothers anyway, the complainant rightly told the barrister that was a question he ought to be asking the accused and not her since it was he who did the partitioning.[56] On the latter issue, once again using proactive language, the barrister put to the complainant that she expected the court to believe that her father "indulged" in "intercourse" with her.[57] Once again, this proactive language, especially the "indulged" bit was a frequent linguistic turn used by defense counsel across a number of trials, as though the act of being raped by one's parent was an illegal but enjoyable act.

Moving on to other alleged incidents, previous transcripts were tediously reviewed before the barrister moved on to the subject of the complainant's pregnancy and termination. Defense counsel canvassed her evidence that her stepfather had originally suggested she go through with the pregnancy and they would begin a new life together as man and wife with her brothers being brought up as their children. Feigning indignation that his client could ever make such an outrageous suggestion prompted a change in facial expression from the complainant:

> DEFENSE: I mean, even you put a grin on your face then, didn't you, just now when I was asking you about this—there was a grin on your face when I was asking you about this, wasn't there?
>
> COMPLAINANT: I can't look at my face.
>
> DEFENSE: You are aware when you grin, aren't you?
>
> COMPLAINANT: A wry smile, maybe.
>
> DEFENSE: I mean the proposition is laughable isn't it?
>
> COMPLAINANT: It might be laughable for someone like you.[58]

As mentioned earlier, like other complainants who allege pregnancy as a result of intrafamilial abuse, they are well-advised by the perpetrator about the stock-story lie that a schoolboy, or other stranger to the family, made them pregnant. In dealing with the charge connected to her pregnancy and later termination, defense counsel put to the complainant that if her stepfather was indeed the perpetrator who made her pregnant then the truth is that she lied to staff at the fertility clinic and a teacher whom she told that it was an unidentified boy from school who was responsible. The complainant admitted that this was a lie.[59] A similar defense logic was put to complainants in other cases: that they "lied" when they told medical staff and others that it was an unnamed boy who got them pregnant and not their father, as though admission of such a lie about a charged incident, which the defense deny ever occurred anyway, should lead to the complainant being put in stocks since they are clearly admitting to having told a "lie."[60] And if they "lied" then, they could "lie" now.

Switching topics completely, defense counsel put to the complainant that she enjoyed an unusually close student/teacher relationship with one of her female teachers at secondary school.[61] The purpose of this evidence was to show that the complainant had ample opportunity to tell a trusted adult about supposed sexual abuse by her stepfather. It is a frequent tactic used in trials, to highlight people the complainant looked up to or enjoyed a close bond with and then pounce on the complainant for failing to tell this trusted friend about the alleged abuse. It may well be a useful tactic since there is a common belief that child and adolescent victims will disclose abuse to a trusted person. From my research and work, however, such disclosure represents a gamble for the complainant. Telling a trusted friend is dependent upon a myriad of other factors, including the types of threats used against children, their level of fear of the perpetrator, the victim/survivor's degree of self-esteem, and ability to trust as well as how they perceive the world outside of their complex world of pain and fear.

Just prior to a short adjournment, the judge must have sensed that the defense barrister was reaching the end of his cross-examination and asked him if he intended to "string it out" (the cross-examination) a bit longer, to which the barrister agreed he would.[62] The notion of stringing something out suggests a kind of game plan and even a deliberate form of inflicting unnecessary cross-examination against the complainant.

Perhaps as part of the plan to "string out" the cross-examination, after the break defense counsel resumed with a focus on the complainant's pregnancy termination—this time on the issue of her supposed freedom to choose to terminate her pregnancy. First the obligatory previous transcripts were used to highlight that the complainant had told a previous court that she had agreed with that defense barrister that she did not wish to keep the child that would have resulted from the pregnancy. Considering the circumstances in which a young teenager found herself pregnant, it is hardly surprising that

Case Study R v L

she did not want to continue the pregnancy. After securing agreement to this previous evidence, the barrister highlighted that she had also previously agreed that it was "ultimately" her "choice" to terminate the pregnancy.[63] The concept of "choice" would hardly seem a relevant description given the situation, but was used in this trial, as it has been used in others, to confer a sense of freedom, a sense of autonomy and agency for the girl/child-girl/victim to act without constraints.

Building on this dialogue around "freedom" and "choice," defense counsel highlighted that after leaving the family home (which she says she did to escape sexual abuse by her stepfather), she visited the family home to celebrate particular events and that she also visited her step-grandparents. These questions were designed to demonstrate "inconsistencies" on the part of the complainant. What seems inconsistent is, in fact, a common feature of sexual abuse, especially long-term sexual abuse where in public and social spaces, victims behave in a seemingly "normal" way toward their parent who is also their abuser. This form of image management is a survival tactic and very often one which victim/survivors learn to simulate as part of a trauma-induced adaptation to not only present an image of family normality to outsiders but, tragically, often to protect themselves; to reduce themselves from being targeted further by the offender. Their own fear of allowing themselves to consciously engage with their own feelings of distress and anger, and even hatred, which they have learned to suppress or turn inwards on themselves, motivates such a façade. Moreover, the well-oiled feelings of shame and guilt, of self-blame and fear of rejection if one disclosed, feelings of worthlessness and hopelessness, that feeling of entrapment as described by Summit[64] may also be major motivators. Roland Summit's work remains one of the most incisive studies of child sexual abuse and delayed disclosure, providing contextualization to the complex behaviors of victims of such abuse.

At the first trial, the complainant was allowed to give some evidence contextualizing her fear of her stepfather. At the retrial, she was denied any such opportunity. After establishing that she had visited the family home post-abuse, the barrister put to her:

DEFENSE: Now, your state of mind was, in 1987, one where, as a result of an incident, *the details of which are unimportant*, but your view was that you were, in fact, terrified of [stepfather]; is that right?

COMPLAINANT: I've been frightened of him for a long time. [emphasis added][65]

Deliberately de-contextualizing the complainant's fear, the barrister immediately juxtaposed her "fear" with evidence of her continued contact with the accused and his new de facto wife and her young daughter. Again, the purpose was to highlight inconsistent behavior in the complainant leaving home, giving evidence of being afraid of her stepfather, and yet visiting him and his new partner post-abuse. Promoting the good father image, defense counsel put to the complainant that there was no indication that her stepfather was sexually abusing his de facto young daughter, who (as he highlighted) was around the same age she was when she alleges the abuse began. As though such was logically contradictory with the complainant's allegations, a lack of overt sexualized conduct by the accused toward his new stepdaughter was used to undermine her own allegations. As expected, what followed next was the presentation of the often used, carefully manufactured family album, as the complainant was asked to identify photos. The barrister provided a running commentary alongside the photos, suggesting the complainant "certainly" did not look "terrified" when posing in that family photograph, and how "close" she was sitting to her stepfather in the next photo, and how if her allegations were true, then certainly she would have "reacted" differently to certain photographs, and so on.[66] The photos were tendered as exhibits for the jury.

Building to a crescendo of "inconsistent" behavior, family paraphernalia in the form of various greeting cards and a letter used at the previous trial were produced. As part of this ritual of humiliation, the complainant was made to read aloud what she had written in several Father's Day cards, which defense counsel asserted she had sent her stepfather post-abuse.[67] When it suits defense purposes, highlighting a parent/bond relationship formed part of the narrative, despite defense counsel arguing at the start of the trial that his client was technically no longer the complainant's stepfather after she turned sixteen years of age. In a similar tactic to case study R v D, defense counsel referred to the accused as "Mr." so and so until he wanted to promote the parent/child bond, and then clearly promoted the "stepfather" relationship in questions. Obviously the complainant only ever viewed the accused as her stepfather—pre-divorce and post-divorce, pre-abuse and post-abuse.

No doubt the complainant was fully acquainted with and prepared for this parade of supposed family endearments since they were made star attractions at the previous trial. At the previous trial, she, like other complainants in similar circumstances,[68] became deeply distressed at the use of these photos and cards, in particular being made to read them aloud. However, the next time around she showed no emotion whatsoever other than to state that she had spent years trying to pretend to herself that her abuse never happened.[69]

It appears certain the barrister must have felt short-changed by the lack of distress and/or anger that these narrative props aroused, since he promptly read aloud to the court the complainant's expression of distress and anger from the first trial:

DEFENSE: In fact when you were shown the first card [at the first trial in 1993] which has just been tendered, that is Exhibit Three, this was your reaction to that card wasn't it and you said this: "Drag this shit up, I hate your guts, I hate you so much, so much, don't wink at me." And then you said, "Fucking arse hole." That is what you said in court last time wasn't it...when that previous card was shown to you?

COMPLAINANT: Yes.[70]

One might reasonably contend that the barrister, feeling he was not getting a good enough bang for his dollar, engaged in a gratuitous exchange, as defense counsels across so many trials frequently engaged in.[71] But, on closer examination of the first trial, it is worth noting that in his charge to the jury, the judge commented negatively on the complainant's outburst, telling the jury that her own admission of "hate" toward the accused indicated an "intensity of emotion" that required him to "warn" the jury that when considering such an attitude they ought to "treat her evidence with care." According to the judge, greeting cards and letters indicated a "perfectly...normal and loving relationship of a father and daughter."[72] It is very possible that defense counsel hoped there might be a repeat performance on this point, and when it was not forthcoming, he believed that reading aloud this excerpt might be the trigger to another repeat display of anger and distress by the complainant and later judicial comment.

Not so. Still she remained calm and composed—almost as though trying to emotionally distance herself from the narrative onslaught being waged against her. As though desperate for an emotional outburst, defense counsel continued to hector around this issue forcing the complainant to identify the "hugs" and "kisses" she placed at the bottom of a greeting card. Before he could finish his no doubt well-rehearsed line, she asked the barrister "What's that got to do with the offenses that I have just outlined in the last two days?"[73] Ignoring her comment, he demanded she answer his question before moving on to produce yet another letter she wrote her stepfather and brothers upon leaving the family home for good.[74] The cards and letters were also tendered as exhibits for the jury.

The tactic of using photographs and greeting cards is well-recognized as an effective defense stratagem. Shortly after this parade of photos and cards, and in the absence of the jury, the judge commented that the complainant's explanation that she was fearful of the accused "pale in light of your [defense barrister] fusillade of exhibits." A short time later, the judge reiterated the power of this tactic, suggesting the complainant's behavior as linked to the exhibits went against any proposition she had been sexually abused by her stepfather.[75] Such "inconsistencies" were noted by a judge in another case.[76]

This narrative of "inconsistency" was juxtaposed to the defense narrative of *motive*, which in this case was connected with mother-daughter collusion and greed. First, defense counsel put to the complainant that she had applied for and received crimes compensation, before asking her to tell the jury just how much money she received. These questions were immediately followed by questions about her long-term unemployment and then linked back to her application for crimes compensation.[77]

With this evidence in front of the jury, defense counsel moved on, once again to the complainant's mother. While cross-examination on the mother-daughter relationship at the previous trial was quite intense, defense questions at this trial were very brief and seemed almost innocuous—or so it would seem:

> DEFENSE: You for many years had no contact, or very little contact between yourself and your mother, is that correct?
>
> COMPLAINANT: Yes.
>
> DEFENSE: However, in recent years you have tried to re-establish a relationship, correct?
>
> COMPLAINANT: Yes.
>
> DEFENSE: It would not be too harsh to say that your mother dislikes [accused] intensely, correct.
>
> COMPLAINANT: Yes.
>
> DEFENSE: I suggest to you [the sexual abuse] didn't occur—it didn't happen.
>
> COMPLAINANT: It did happen.[78]

In the above excerpt, the mother is constructed, albeit very briefly, by proxy through her daughter's evidence. The exchange introduces four concepts: estrangement, reconciliation, mother's dislike of former husband (and it goes without saying the complainant's dislike of her stepfather), and untrue allegations of abuse. On the surface these juxtapositions may seem unrelated, and the statement of the mother's dislike of the accused is never mentioned again in cross-examination; in fact, cross-examination of the complainant finished on this point.

However, consider what unfolded soon after, in the absence of the jury. The prosecutor asked the judge for permission to lead evidence from the complainant, in reexamination, as to why her mother disliked the accused so intensely. Before the barrister could rise to the occasion with the obligatory objection, the judge obliged on his behalf by rejecting such a request saying such evidence could only properly come from the mother, if such a question were even allowed to be put to the mother.[79] Yet, it was okay for defense counsel to garnish evidence of dislike from the complainant, but not okay to allow the complainant to tell the jury why she was aware of such knowledge. Scenarios like this unfolded across numerous trials where child complainants were asked, to my mind, inappropriate questions about parental discord and disharmony on the part of the mother, as part of a narrative of construction by proxy, but not allowed to contextualize why they might agree with such defense-led statements in reexamination.

Quite obviously the judge was only too aware of how the defense would use this isolated agreement to a loaded statement. Immediately upon blocking the prosecutor's wish to contextualize the complainant's agreement that her mother intensely disliked the accused, the judge made this comment to defense counsel:

> JUDGE: Are you going to suggest that the mother and daughter have got their heads together to fix him up or is that the *veiled inference* from that piece of evidence?
>
> DEFENSE: Your Honor, I will certainly be suggesting...the mother is now having an influence on her.
>
> JUDGE: On the daughter and she is going to really deliver the coup de grace?
>
> DEFENSE: Yes.
>
> JUDGE: As it stands at the moment, it would be an *inference* which the jury would be entitled to consider. [emphasis added][80]

So, while compelling corroborating counter-evidence is removed from the jurors' consideration, they are entitled to consider deliberately engineered innuendo. In an effort to ensure that this "inference" remained free from prosecution challenge, defense counsel assured they would never, ever, suggest mother collusion, or that she disliked her former husband when cross-examining her. Otherwise, the prosecutor might be able to introduce evidence from the mother of what he described was a:

> wealth of evidence in [mother's] statement which gives a long history of abuse, violence and things of that nature, visited upon her by the accused man which [has not been raised because of its "prejudicial aspect"]...[which includes] for example, nearly choking her to death and she says "that she tried to commit suicide twice because of her husband's behavior toward her.[81]

While defense counsel ensured they steered clear of inferring dislike or collusion when cross-examining the mother, damage to her character was accomplished through questions put to the complainant. Like so many other cases, the mother in case study R v L was portrayed as a colluder by proxy.

Still trying to have the boundaries of reexamination delineated by the judge, the prosecutor foreshadowed issues raised in cross-examination that he wished to clarify with the complainant in reexamination. One such issue had to do with questions about her crimes compensation application and its link to her being unemployed. The prosecutor wished to highlight the complainant's tertiary degree and her previous work history. "Fair enough," said the judge, "I mean as it stands, I can see what Mr. (defense barrister) has done. I mean it affords a *motive* for money grabbling...she had not worked and needed the money, and fired in the allegations [emphasis added]."[82] Certainly there are easier ways of obtaining money than putting oneself through a protracted father-daughter rape trial, but the logic of making false allegations in the hope of getting crimes compensation forms an intensive part of defense counsel repertoire.[83]

The second permission-seeking exercise was to have the complainant provide some context relating to a particular incident defense counsel asked her about in cross-examination. At the time, defense counsel described the circumstances around this particular 'incident' as "unimportant"—just prior to launching an attack by way of photo and card exhibits. Right on cue, defense counsel objected on the grounds that any introduction of evidence to contextualize the "unimportant" incident posed a "difficulty" for the defense case since it entailed evidence of a particularly "violent assault," which, he quickly added, was not the subject of any charges. The judge responded to this logic by suggesting defense counsel was "forensically" very eager for the complainant to agree that she was frightened of the accused. The judge felt he should allow the question as a matter for the jury to consider—though he added his own rider. Defense counsel had, he said, presented such weighty exhibits that the complainant's own explanation of her fear of her stepfather may well "pale" by comparison.[84]

The final ground for seeking permission to re-examine on a particular issue concerned an alleged telephone call the accused made to the complainant pleading with her not to talk to the police about the alleged abuse. The judge acceded to this request on the grounds that her behavior, as highlighted by the defense, was inconsistent with the allegations.

Paradoxically, despite these concessions, there were concerns all around that allowing the complainant to speak outside the legally scripted boundaries (decided in evidentiary rulings at the start of the trial) meant that she would be giving evidence outside of the silences imposed on her evidence. Both legal parties thought it best to have the complainant first give *voir dire* evidence away from juror ears, just to check "what her answer" would be to the questions. Certainly, agreed the judge, since it was not desirable to have her become "effusive." Certainly, agreed defense counsel, since there was the clear and present "danger" that she might come out with "something."[85] Perhaps this "something" was just too shocking to contemplate since the barrister never did finish the sentence about the "danger" of this "something." No time was wasted in recalling her for a *voir dire* (the second one she had undergone in this trial) to allow the judge to check that her evidence could be "contained" and if it could be "contained," she would be "advised" that when asked the same question in front of the jury, to ensure she gave the same answer as that given in the *voir dire*.[86] In this way, the legal script was minimally disrupted and there were no surprises to contend with. For reasons unknown, the final concession regarding the alleged phone call was not raised in the *voir dire* nor in reexamination in front of the jury.

Content with her "contained" answers, the complainant was free to present her *voir dire* answers to the jury. She provided evidence of her tertiary degree and told the jury she found difficulty obtaining long-term employment as a result of her problems with dealing with authority figures in the workforce. She denied making false allegations to obtain crimes compensation.[87] On the topic of the "unimportant" incident, which caused her to greatly fear her stepfather even more, her evidence was:

COMPLAINANT: On my twenty-first birthday, I went out [to family home] and I was assaulted.

PROSECUTOR: What happened?

COMPLAINANT: He put his hands around my throat and held me to the ground, and looked at me and then after a while got off, and was very threatening physically.

PROSECUTOR: So what happened?

COMPLAINANT: He stood in front of the door and said that I would not be getting out of the house alive...my main priority was to get out of the house alive.[88]

Asked why she continued to have contact with her stepfather and to send him greeting cards after leaving the family home, she gave a succinct and clear response that was poignant in its frankness:

PROSECUTOR: Why did you [send cards which expressed] feelings and send messages to him in a friendly way?

JUDGE: Terms of endearment.

PROSECUTOR: Why did you do that? Why did you couch those letters in those terms, in those cards in those terms? What caused you to do that?

COMPLAINANT: I'd learned certain ways to avoid being a target.

PROSECUTOR: Target from whom?

COMPLAINANT: From [stepfather].

PROSECUTOR: For what purpose?

COMPLAINANT: To avoid fear.

PROSECUTOR: You weren't living at home at this stage when these cards were sent and the letter was sent?

COMPLAINANT: Yes. What made me? Because I tried to forget it. I tried to pretend it didn't happen and that I was a normal adolescent or young adult.[89]

A narrative of *means* was not evident at the retrial, and it may well be that defense counsel felt the adult status of the complainant made it unnecessary to promote a narrative of means. However, at the first trial, defense counsel did mobilize a narrative of *means* around access to knowledge through literature. In that case, defense counsel subpoenaed her university academic transcript and cross-examined her about particular units in psychology and sociology she had undertaken. More specifically, she was asked about an essay she wrote on child abuse:

DEFENSE: And you were studying subjects such as psychology and sociology?

COMPLAINANT: Yes.

DEFENSE: And during the course of those studies you were in fact involved with some work to do with sexual abuse, weren't you?

COMPLAINANT: Yes.

DEFENSE: Was it the situation that you were, as part of your studies, that you were reading accounts by people that said that sexual abuse of one sort or another had taken place with regard to them. Wasn't that part of what you were reading and doing in terms of that work?

COMPLAINANT: Not specifically.

DEFENSE: Was that—whether specifically, were there accounts of what other people had said had taken place which were things that you read during that?

COMPLAINANT: I've read books like Jocelynne Scutt's book, and you know, I've read cases...

DEFENSE: Was that where you get [sic] the detail from to be able to describe these incidents concerning your stepfather?

COMPLAINANT: No.[90]

It was apparent from a reading of the transcript that defense counsel in the retrial utilized information and even some tactics from the original trial. Yet it is not unreasonable to suggest defense counsel in this trial may have avoided rehashing the above on the grounds that highlighting specific areas of her tertiary studies might be an area that builds her credibility rather than undermined it—especially given her excellent and consistent rebuttals to many of his questions and statements.

Her evidence finished, she was excused from the witness box.

THE MOTHER

While the mother faced harsh, and at times cruel, cross-examination at the first trial, she was able to provide some evidence of alleged serious domestic violence, corroborated by two of her children at that stage. At the retrial, defense counsel were extremely circumspect in their cross-examination of the mother after the prosecutor put them on notice, as noted earlier, that he would seek to introduce evidence of domestic violence should defense counsel suggest evidence of collusion or of her dislike of the accused.

The mother appeared nervous in the witness box and asked if she could be seated to give her evidence. The judge asked her if she had a physical disability, and when she said she did not, the judge refused her request to be able to sit down to give her evidence.[91] The judge's response seemed somewhat insensitive given the mother's alleged history of serious domestic violence (which the judge was aware of) which would have made it very difficult for her to be in the same room with her ex-husband, let alone support her daughter's allegations of long-term rape and sexual assault by the accused. No doubt contributing to her nervous state was the fact that her youngest son had died under tragic circumstances only several months prior to the trial. Her nervousness aside, in a display of personal integrity, she refused to enter the courtroom when first called as a witness by the court Tipstaff. Following her divorce she legally reverted to her maiden name, and when called to the court under her former married name she refused to respond. Legal counsel were miffed at what they probably considered a show of defiance. But when it became clear she would only enter the court when her correct name was used, she *was* called to the court by her maiden name, obliging the Tipstaff with an immediate response.[92] Her evidence-in-chief was brief and technical, consisting of evidence about the birth of her children and the places the family had lived, and descriptions of family homes and where the children had slept. She also confirmed her ex-husband often went horse riding alone with her daughter early in the morning on weekends.[93]

In cross-examination, defense counsel could be excused if he thought that he was back cross-examining the complainant, given the quick and lively—and no doubt at times unexpected answers he got from the mother. For example, when the barrister put to the mother that her own son would be coming to court to give evidence that a particular piece of evidence given by her daughter was wrong, the mother promptly responded by looking squarely at the jury and saying her son "will say anything his father—stepfather—tells him to say."[94] The remainder of cross-examination stayed close to technical details about the family's move to a new home, the order of furniture taken that day, who slept over at which house during the night, as well as evidence about a back operation the accused underwent, and how he discharged himself from hospital early.[95]

THE TEACHER

The teacher described as having a "close relationship" with the complainant gave very brief evidence consisting only of a confirmation that the complainant had told her she had become pregnant by an unnamed "boy," and that she once visited the complainant's family home while the mother and accused were still together.[96]

THE SCHOOL FRIEND

The school friend's evidence was extremely brief. She agreed she had been a friend of the complainant at school and had visited her home. She agreed with the defense claim that the complainant appeared to have a tense relationship with her mother and had a lot of domestic responsibility around the house, as her mother was often not there. She further agreed that the complainant never disclosed any sexual abuse to her and that she had spoken well of her stepfather.[97]

THE POLICE INFORMANT

The informant was called primarily to confirm the police record of interview (which undergoes editing prior to being played to the jury) and that the accused had no prior convictions.[98] The Crown case was closed with the evidence of the informant.

The Defense Case: The Accused

Evidence by the accused in this case was considerably longer than most other cases in this research. At the first trial, the accused gave no evidence, perhaps preferring to avoid being cross-examined about the counselor's damning evidence and his alleged domestic violence toward his wife. With any corroborating evidence removed, and the family life relatively sanitized as a result of judicial constraints placed on the prosecution case, defense counsel may have felt it safer for his client to give evidence.

His evidence-in-chief was fairly run of the mill, and seemed in part to be a deliberate tactic to perhaps try and normalize early family life, only to then introduce the narrative of a "bad" wife and "bad" mother to the jury. After giving the usual family history spiel (including places the family had lived and his own work history), his evidence moved chronologically through each charge.

With regard to the first incident, the accused denied disciplining his daughter, and denied indecently assaulting her. With regard to the second incident (in which he alleged he was home that morning and not at work), he told the court he had gone and looked up his old work records but the "clock-on cards" were no longer available. He did, however, confirm the dates he began and ceased employment with this particular firm.[99] I took note of this evidence, with more than a passing interest, on the basis that any evidence complainants had obtained access to historical documents or information (such as work, medical or other types of records) often led to defense accusations that such information was sought only to assist fabrication.

The allegation involving an early morning horse ride was denied. The accused stated that on that particular weekend his father and stepbrother were staying with them, and that "family activities" were the order of the weekend and not an early morning horse ride with his stepdaughter, as she alleges.[100]

Defense counsel led evidence from the accused regarding alleged penetration that occurred during a house move. The accused was said to have erected a barricade using boxes and furniture so that two of his sons were separated by a partition from him and his stepdaughter.

Continuing to use proactive language to discuss child sexual abuse, defense counsel referred to the incident as one alleging the accused "indulge[d]" in "intercourse" with his stepdaughter, which the accused denied.[101] On the charge of penetration soon after he had back surgery, the accused denied the allegation, adding that he was not capable of partaking in sexual acts at that time.

Pregnancy and termination were dealt with next and, in a familiar scenario for these trials, the accused spoke of feeling "angry" and "disappointed" with his stepdaughter and "confused" as to what he should do. He added that she told him it was an unnamed boy from school who got her pregnant, adding further that he did not want to know any of the details of the boy's identity since the pregnancy was to be terminated. When asked if he impregnated his stepdaughter, the accused gave the following responses:

DEFENSE: Did you father that child?

ACCUSED: Definitely not and I certainly wouldn't have wanted her to keep it if I had.[102]

This rather odd response to a standard question, reads—and sounded, I might add—almost like a Freudian slip, and I recall wondering if the jury read anything more into the response other than a denial. I noted also the evidential demeanor the accused was extremely calm. By that, I mean there were no emphatic denials as one might expect considering the type and content of the charges—a point I have noted in several other trials observed. So too, his response to answers seemed almost as though they had been rehearsed, coached through—a point I have also noticed in observed trials.

After making a flat denial of sexual penetration of his stepdaughter a couple of weeks after her pregnancy termination, his final evidence was to identify happy family snapshots—in particular, those that showed him with his new young stepdaughter, as though such photos axiomatically exonerated him from the charges.

Cross-examination of Accused

The prosecutor attacked the accused's denials by putting to him some of the context of the complainant's evidence around the first charge. For example, he put to the accused that he was angry with his stepdaughter for starting a small fire, smacked her and later on removed parts of her clothing prior to indecently assaulting her.[103] The accused denied all of this, and I feel certain the intention of the prosecutor was to compare his flat denials against detailed evidence by the complainant about the alleged incident. The prosecutor did this on a number of occasions, as though to force the accused away from flat denials in an effort to have him engage with the details provided by the complainant.

The prosecutor asserted that the accused was not happy with the rural property he purchased with his ex-wife, where a number of alleged incidents of sexual abuse occurred. The accused denied this, instead taking the opportunity to negatively portray his wife by telling the court they were forced to live in a "dump" and a "mess." He said he did not approve of his wife purchasing livestock, and that while he "tried very hard" to make the family home "better," his ex-wife's conduct caused the marriage to deteriorate.[104]

With regard to his stepdaughter's allegation that he was not at work on a particular morning (and when sexual abused is alleged to have occurred), the prosecutor brought to the accused's attention the fact that his former place of occupation sent around a notice to all employees warning them against the practice of clocking on for workmates in their absence. The prosecutor also put to the accused that his work involved some weekend work and it was routine for workers to then have a day off the following week, and that this would not show up on work records. Responses by the accused were that he could not recall such a notice being sent to all employees but there could have been one on the staff notice-board. He also maintained that he left work before his wife on the morning in question. He also denied that he struck his stepdaughter on that morning.[105]

As cross-examination proceeded, the prosecutor began to highlight inconsistencies in the evidence of the accused through his police record-of-interview. In cross-examination, he denied striking the complainant for losing her walkathon money. However, the prosecutor reminded the accused that in his record-of-interview with the police he said that he "may have" struck his stepdaughter. The accused's response was to adopt the answer that he never struck her.[106] Recall also that the complainant gave evidence of special "rules" laid down by the accused denying the children entry to the lounge room because it was considered the best room in the house. In his evidence-in-chief he told the court he had no rules about being allowed to enter the lounge room. But when the prosecutor rephrased the same assertion as that made by the complainant, the accused gave a different answer to his evidence-in-chief:

> PROSECUTOR: I suggest that the only time they were allowed to go in there [lounge room] was when they got permission from you?
>
> ACCUSED: Yes, that is correct.[107]

No doubt recognizing another instance of contradictory evidence, defense counsel was quick and lively to his feet to object to the question, but the judge allowed the question to stand. The prosecutor turned toward the incident alleged to have occurred while the family were moving house, and took the accused through very long and drawn out evidence, requesting detailed information about the mechanics of the move. The questions eventually led to the prosecutor asserting that the accused did in fact erect a barricade on that night in order to commit the act his stepdaughter alleged, an assertion the accused denied.

I feel the prosecutor missed an excellent opportunity to introduce doubt about parts of the accused's evidence with regards to the house move. For example, the truck was hired for two days and yet the accused apparently chose to use family vehicles to move furniture on the first day, rather than the hired truck. The prosecutor could have asserted that the accused formulated his evidence this way to fit with his narrative that there was no furniture available to make a barricade, as asserted by his stepdaughter. As it was, cross-examination on this issue read more like test of recall, as it lacked direction and any significant end point.[108]

Revisiting the pregnancy termination, the prosecutor asked the accused about his reason for taking his young teenage stepdaughter to an entirely different town to see a medical practitioner, prompting the prosecutor to suggest the following:

> PROSECUTOR: It wasn't in your mind at that stage that it would be better for her to see an out of town doctor, so that you wouldn't be involved or implicated in any way?
>
> ACCUSED: Not at all.[109]

The accused admitted he was aware the complainant used birth control soon after the pregnancy termination. In her statement, and at the first trial, the complainant alleged her stepfather urged her to go on the pill to avoid another pregnancy. When asked about the chores the complainant did and took on after the mother left the family unit, the accused maintained that his stepdaughter did no chores around the house. This stands in stark contrast to other witnesses who commented on the domestic responsibility of the complainant, though much of this never made its way into the trial.[110]

When asked about his stepdaughter having any boyfriends, I could not help but note the similarities between the accused's evidence and that of other fathers in trials on this nature. He told the court his stepdaughter did have boyfriends, but was forced to admit that he had never met or seen a boyfriend and did not know of her ever actually going out with a boy. He agreed also that she spent her spare time at home.[111] Cross-examination finished with the prosecutor asserting that every allegation detailed by the complainant was factual. The accused maintained his denial that they occurred.[112]

Reexamination

When reexamination commenced, defense counsel focused on the accused's evidence concerning the house move. Perhaps defense counsel picked up, as I did, the possible flaw in the accused's cross-examination evidence about having a truck for two days but only using it one day. Defense counsel asked the accused the reason for only using the truck one day. The accused said the truck blew a head gasket.[113] If the truck blew a head gasket on the Saturday, it seems hard to believe that such a serious mechanical failure was obviously fixed the same day given that it was apparently used the following day.

Defense counsel was obviously keen to re-establish the accused's credibility surrounding his dismal performance on the issue of an absence of any young males in the complainant's life (especially around the time of the pregnancy). To facilitate introduction of such evidence, he asked the accused to tell the court about his stepdaughter's "social life," and one could almost hear a gasp escape the barrister's lips when the accused told the court his stepdaughter had no social life he knew of. Tackling this glitch in the narrative of sexual activity with other males, defense counsel took a different tack, suggesting the complainant "would...have the opportunity to indulge in an act of intercourse" as a result of her attending secondary school in another town. The accused agreed, saying that she certainly would have had opportunities either at school or after school. No doubt thinking he was on a promising line of narrative development, the barrister seized the opportunity to capitalize on this point, but again it backfired dismally. After making it clear there was a two-hour time gap between the complainant finishing school at 3:30 p.m. and the accused finishing work at 5:30 p.m., the barrister asked about what she did in that timeframe. The accused said she either walked the fair distance to his work and waited for him to finish, or caught the school bus home. One could almost sense the barrister's apprehension given that these answers hardly substantiate the free two-hour period for the girl to "indulge" in sexual intercourse with other males. Instead, defense counsel suggested that there may well have been "occasions when she'd stay back at school for...activities?" Again, he was no doubt let down when the accused responded there were no such opportunities that he knew of, and reexamination finished on that point.[114]

THE STEPMOTHER

The first defense witness was the accused's stepmother who gave very brief evidence stating that she, her husband and the accused's stepbrothers visited the rural property from time to time. She agreed with the defense statement that she had never "observed" any behavior between the accused and his stepdaughter other than "normal" behavior one would expect between a "father and daughter."[115] The prosecutor did not cross-examine her.

THE SON

The second eldest son in the family gave evidence that he had never witnessed any inappropriate behavior between his father and half-sister. This kind of evidence is routinely given by siblings who support their parent. The question suggests that a lack of any observed inappropriate behavior is proof of no abuse, as though sexual assault occurs in public. In cross-examination by the prosecutor, his evidence was that no house contents at all were taken to the new house where an alleged incident of sexual penetration occurred.[116]

THE SISTER

The sister of the accused gave evidence that she cared for his children while the accused was in hospital undergoing back surgery. In what was beginning to sound like a veritable Gregorian chant, she also agreed with defense counsel's statement that she had never "observed" any unusual behavior between the accused and his stepdaughter.[117]

THE WORKMATE

A former work colleague and friend of the accused gave evidence that he loaned the accused his truck to move house (though no mention of a blown head gasket). He also said that workers were not allowed to clock on for other workers, and that the accused was "very prompt" and always on time.[118]

Up until this point, defense witnesses gave very brief evidence with little or no cross-examination. However, that changed as the next few witnesses gave more protracted evidence.

THE STEPSON

This witness was the full-brother of the complainant, and stepson of the accused, although he took his stepfather's surname and referred to him as "Dad,"—even though *legally* and *technically* he was no longer related to him and was older than sixteen years. In evidence-in-chief, he too agreed he had never "observed" any unusual behavior between his stepfather and sister, save for the normal father/daughter relationship. Moving through the various environments and incidents linked to the complainant's evidence, he told the court he knew of nothing unusual occurring on the night his stepsister alleged a serious physical assault by their stepfather.

He also gave evidence that he could not recall any incident in which his stepfather and sister went horse riding together early in the morning, or alone at any time. It is interesting that, on the one hand, all witnesses were keen to project an image of a normal "father-daughter" relationship but, on the other hand, project an image of the stepfather as never being alone with, or even having the opportunity to be alone with his stepdaughter—as though denying any and all opportunity for abuse to occur alleviates rather than creates suspicion. The artificial logic of "normal-but-never-alone" was frequently observed in a number of trials.[119]

Yet even this argument came unstuck during the stepson's cross-examination. The prosecutor reminded him that his evidence at the first trial was that his sister and father did, in fact, go for early morning horse rides alone and, further, that the accused had spent a lot of time alone with the complainant, his sister. Further, his evidence at the first trial was that the accused and complainant went horse riding to the specific area the complainant says she was taken by her stepfather where full penetration took place.[120]

Finally, in cross-examination the witness told the court he had not known his sister to have any boyfriends around the time period of the pregnancy, and, while it was a trite issue, the prosecutor briefly covered "chores" done by the complainant, and her brother agreed that she did quite a lot of domestic chores around the house.[121]

THE SURGEON

The surgeon who medically examined the accused some time after his operation (but did not perform it) was called to give evidence. Essentially, his evidence was to tell the jury about the type of operation the accused underwent and to support the defense claim that the offender would have been too medically unfit to have engaged in any sexual activities. While the surgeon was not prepared to make an unequivocal statement that a patient, after undergoing such surgery, would not engage in sexual intercourse at that stage, he did say it was "possible" but "undesirable," adding it was a "personal thing."[122] In cross-examination, the prosecutor asked the surgeon if he ever delved into the personal sexual activities of patients, and his reply was that he did not delve into this area "too deeply."[123]

THE STEPBROTHER

The accused's stepbrother gave particular evidence of a weekend visit he had at the accused's rural home. In verse and chapter, the defense led evidence from the witness that he, like those before him, had never observed any unusual behavior between the accused and complainant during his visits.

After establishing this, the witness went on to tell of the exact weekend he stayed at his stepbrother's property seventeen years ago. That weekend coincided with the charge of sexual penetration while on an early morning horse ride. This witness said it was simply "impossible" the accused and stepdaughter went for a ride that particular morning because he recalled they had not.[124]

The witness was a former member of the police force, and defense counsel wanted to lead evidence from the accused that being a former "trained" policeman meant he would have a "better ability to remember things than other people."[125] The frivolity of this point is amplified by the fact that the witness was only aged thirteen years or so at the time of the alleged offense; his police training came much later. Perhaps defense counsel wanted the jury to believe that his memory training skills worked retrospectively.

In general terms, the stepbrother's evidence was that the weekend was unremarkable. He observed no unusual behavior between the accused and stepdaughter as the family went about their normal activities. During cross-examination by the prosecutor, the witness said he never saw the accused ride any horse that particular weekend. In an almost comical repertoire that mimicked the accused's evidence around chores, this witness told the court since the accused had so many chores to do, he had no time to partake in rustic pleasures like horse-riding. The witness must have forgotten his own evidence of only five minutes ago, because then he told the court that everyone would be up "at the crack of dawn" with each of them doing particular chores around the property.[126] The witness was also at pains to press the point that at no time did the accused and his stepdaughter ever go horse riding together (as though he were watchful for this very activity). The witness stood vigilantly by this evidence and seemed despondent when the prosecutor suggested the accused and his stepdaughter could have gone for a horse ride very early in the morning before anyone was up. Since the witness had nowhere to go with this point, he found himself agreeing that it could be possible.[127]

If the weekend in question of his visit was so unremarkable because of its normalcy, one wonders why it remains so memorable seventeen years later. The complainant recalled this time frame, and with good reason, because she alleges that around this time, on a particular early morning ride to a specific area, she was fully sexually penetrated by her stepfather. What reason was there for the witness to remember an exact date of one of numerous weekend visits almost two decades ago when such a visit was uneventful?

No doubt the prosecutor was wondering this as well, since he asked the witness to tell the court of the other specific dates of later visits—dates which one would think would be easier to recall since they occurred marginally less than seventeen years ago. Not so. Aside from that specific weekend—the purpose of which was to provide an alibi for the accused—the witness could not recall the exact dates of any other later visits.

THE PAYMASTER

The former paymaster (who worked at the same employment as the accused when the second charge occurred) was called to give purely technical evidence to verify the pay records of the accused, and that no time-off had been recorded during that particular pay week. In cross-examination by the prosecutor, the paymaster did concede that some employees worked on weekends with no penalty or over-time rates, and took time off the following week without affecting pay records.[128]

This final piece of evidence closed the defense case.

Summing Up

Summing up by both legal counsels occurs at the close of the Crown (prosecution) and defense case and is not transcribed. As one judge observed, summing up gives legal counsel the opportunity to flavor their arguments and evidence with far more "theatrical license." Nevertheless, another judge in another case invited the defense barrister to spice up his opening address to the jury at the start of the trial so that it would "excite the interest of the jury."[129] It seems that, at either point, hyperbole and Machiavellian type speeches are often preferred to clear statements on facts and fact-finding.

I observed the summing up in this case and, while there is only room here really for comment, I did take copious notes about legal counsel's body language, voice intonation, gestures and comments. And, true to the above judicial comments, I found that some legal counsel regard the courtroom as a theatrical stage upon which they may strut their stuff.[130] Defense counsel in this case made light of some of the complainant's testimony as part of his dismissive approach to her evidence. For example, when discussing her evidence about her pregnancy and termination, the barrister made a vulgar joke about the possible outcome if the pregnancy had not been aborted.[131]

Judge's Charge to Jury

I was also present for the judge's charge and found myself again in the fortunate position of gaining access to the transcript of the charge, as these are not normally available with trial transcripts. Of interest, trial judges have the power to *edit* the trial transcript so the belief that trial transcripts reflect every word spoken is not entirely accurate.

Reminding the jury they are "judges of the facts," he told them they must decide the case according to the "evidence," before going on to tell them that this was a case with "very little direct evidence" so the "credibility" of the complainant and other witnesses was of "great importance."[132] It seems a contradiction to advise a jury of their special role as adjudicators of "facts" when highly relevant facts are deliberately removed from them.

The judge reminded the jury that the accused could have opted to exercise his legal right of silence but, instead, chose to give evidence and thus opened himself up for cross-examination.[133] True, but his "option" was surely a safe one, given the removal of evidence highly damning of his conduct and character. The judge went on at length about how the jury might use "inferences," "body language," and "demeanor" to inform their deliberations, while warning them to choose "reasonable" inference(s), as though such a concept can be neatly encapsulated and delineated in several easy steps to a group of individuals.[134]

The complainant's evidence was weighted with a "strong" corroboration warning to the jury, reminding them that the evidence of the complainant was "diametrically opposed" to the evidence of the accused, and noting that only two of them "know the truth of what happened."[135] This comment, of course, might have appeared meaningless if the evidence of the counselor had been admitted, as it was at the first trial. As part of the corroboration warning he told the jury:

> As a matter of logic, commonsense if you like, [in a] situation of one person's word against another there is a potential for error, and therefore it may be *dangerous* to convict without the presence of some other evidence that corroborates the [complainant's] evidence…. The reason for caution is a risk that where a person makes an allegation against another person making that allegation may be *motivated* by some hidden or mistaken reason to blacken the character of the other person by falsely accusing [another person]…therefore…it is *dangerous* for a jury trying such a case to convict the accused on the *uncorroborated* version of an accuser [complainant]. That does not mean you cannot convict in the absence of other evidence that corroborates the witness's version. It means that you can only do so after you have subjected that evidence to the most thorough and careful examination, and only after that examination when you are satisfied beyond reasonable doubt of the guilt of the accused [emphasis added].[136]

The corroboration warning makes implicit ulterior motives that may well be behind sexual abuse allegations, and alongside this jury warning was the legal warning about "delayed disclosure." In an almost circular statement, the judge made the usual confusing comment that, while a delay in disclosure—that is, a delay in making complaint—does not negate what the complainant alleges, since "the law confirms that complaints are not always made immediately after sexual assaults," it was nonetheless possible that a delay in disclosure might be understood as evidence that discredits the complainant.[137]

The possibility that a witness (read as complainant) may have been "inaccurate" about childhood memories as a result of "imagination" and "misinterpretation"[138] got a judicial guernsey, as though the complainant may have misunderstood her memory of repeated sexual penetration that the accused later admitted to in dyad counseling. Drawing again on the corroboration warning, the judge alerted the jury to the dangers of a delay in disclosure and thus the need to "scrutinize…with great care" the complainant's evidence.[139] It seems incredibly contentious for a judge to direct all manner of law and technicality at a jury and warn them almost incessantly about the dangers of the complainant's evidence, when the whole trial has been one of concealment, obfuscation and innuendo. A final point I want to raise is the strong and lingering focus around the complainant's recall as being unsafe and in need of close scrutiny. In his charge to the jury, the judge highlighted the young age of the complainant when the abuse allegedly began, and spoke in detail about problems of recollection and the need for a warning to caution the jury to take particular care scrutinizing this evidence. Yet he considered the evidence of the complainant's two siblings (aged only seven and ten at the time of the family moving house) as corroboration for the accused, and their evidence remained free of any weighting with a warning about recollection difficulties and the need for scrutiny.[140]

Recall that the complainant was asked about her mother's "intense dislike" of the accused, and that no such topic was canvassed with the mother, for all the reasons I outlined. At the time this defense question was put to the complainant, the judge recognized, even in embryonic form, the defense narrative of *collusion*. In his charge to the jury, the judge reiterated this part of defense counsel's cross-examination. Here I wish to demonstrate how agreement with a fairly innocuous question provides a platform from which to launch a powerful stock-story narrative about "bad" women. Remember that the complainant agreed with the defense proposition that her mother "intensely disliked" the accused. Now, while paraphrasing defense counsel's closing address in his judge's charge, the judge told the jury:

> Mr. [defense barrister] further suggests that [complainant] is what you might call a tainted *complainant*, having been *poisoned in her attitude* toward the accused by a *malevolent mother* estranged wife. They are matters raised by the defense and it is a matter for you to consider...certainly motive is a factor which you may consider...[emphasis added].[141]

The judge's comment demonstrates how inference and innuendo are central strategies used by defense counsel to promote a particular narrative construction. That the exposition of inferences can be postulated as evidence, whereupon they are equated with facts that may be adjudicated upon by a jury, identifies the predilection for cross-examining witnesses in a way that creates inferences and innuendo that can be later capitalized on. "Intensely disliked" become "malevolent" in the absence of any supporting evidence. Considering the judge advised the jury they could use "reasonable" inferences, one can see the central place of inference and innuendo in legal discourse. Having articulated possible grounds for collusion and motive around revenge, the judge went on to comment on the complainant's successful crimes compensation application, again paraphrasing the defense position that such evidence might suggest that a "possible motive for the invention or fabrication (of the allegations) is the quest for monetary compensation..."[142]

The jury were further reminded of the "dangers of convicting on the evidence of the complainant alone" without corroborating evidence.[143] This judicial rhetoric about the "stand alone" evidence of the complainant was of course compliments of cleverly applied legal technicalities that obliterated a most damning piece of evidence from the *scrutiny* of the jury. Only moments later, the judge again warned the jury about the "dangers" and "potential for error" with regard to the delay in disclosure, before adding that they may still convict if "careful scrutiny" of the complainant's evidence convinces them. The tensions within such judicial rhetoric warning juries about a delay in disclosure and uncorroborated evidence remains a feature of sexual-offense proceedings and its maintenance is fuelled by gender bias.[144]

The Verdict

Adjudicating for a little over a day, the jury acquitted the accused on the first seven counts, but convicted him on the eighth and ninth count, both of which were charges of "incest" and included the charge relating to penetration that caused the victim's pregnancy.

At trial, the victim/survivor faced a total of 1,732 questions: 472 from the prosecutor, 1,157 from defense counsel, and 103 from the judge. The accused faced a total of 606 questions: 359 from his legal counsel, 234 from the prosecutor, and thirteen from the judge. For interest, the complainant faced a total of 1,287 questions at the first trial (1993), with just about a thousand questions being from defense counsel. The accused faced no questions at the first trial.

Sentencing

Three witnesses were called to give "character" evidence for the accused, and defense counsel also relied on previous character evidence given for the accused at the previous trial. These witnesses gave all manner of evidence covering almost the entire life of the offender promoting a kind of *This Is Your Life*[145] narrative for offenders that knows no boundaries and is in stark contrast to the legal restraints placed on the victim of crime.

Legislation, introduced in Victoria in 1995, allowing victims of crime to present to the court what is known as a Victim Impact Statement[146] enabled the victim/survivor to present such a statement to the court, accompanied by a report from her current counselor. The purpose of the legislation was to enable victims of crime to present to the court, either through their own words and/or through advocates (such as a therapist or counselor or medical practitioner), the impact and consequences on their life of the crime(s) of which the accused was convicted. Incredibly the judge pondered just "how realistically would such a victim impact statement be of use,"[147] as though the idea of a victim of crime being able to tell of her terror and distress was such a novelty that the court was hard pressed to identify its place or value.

While this judge was prepared to accept a generous, positive view of the perpetrator at the sentencing plea, he was not receptive to evidence concerning the degree of suffering experienced by the victim/survivor. Defense counsel was keen for the judge to give little if any credence to the counselor's report, on the basis that the report was "highly inflammatory and clearly well beyond the context of (the two charges the offender was convicted of), and further, that the report was *couched* in terms that it can only be put as endeavouring to create a much worse picture [emphasis added]."[148] Here, defense counsel was able to make a value judgment as to the trauma of the victim/survivor based on nothing but his own bias as an advocate for the offender. One might also ask how much "worse" a case of intrafamilial rape needs to be, considering the offender was found guilty of impregnating his stepdaughter, which resulted in an abortion and then, soon after, vaginally penetrating her again. And so the counselor's report was excised from any further judicial consideration. A short time later, the judge made the flippant comment that the "victim impact statement makes no impact on me,"[149] as though the suffering of an individual had to somehow impress him or push an emotional button within him before it could be notionally acceptable.

Defense counsel presented what he believed were three mitigating factors that lessened the culpability of the offender. The first was the mother. Defense counsel suggested the mother's "behavior" created an environment for the abuse to occur, with the judge accepting the mother was part of the "equation" as a "mitigating" factor. Considering the constraints on her evidence, such a claim would seem a long bow to draw, but the role of inference and innuendo again played its part, in allowing the narrative of the "bad" mother to loom largely over the court. Two other mitigating factors in the repertoire of excusing the perpetrator from full responsibility for his actions included his *financial difficulties*—both at the time of his arrest and when the offenses on which he was convicted occurred—as well as his recurring *back problems*.[150] How a back injury and financial difficulties can become mitigating factors that extract responsibility from the offender for his criminal conduct toward his stepdaughter identify the kind of ludicrous and fallacious rationale that may be accepted by the judiciary. The ultimate insult to the suffering of the victim/survivor was defense counsel's sanctimonious appropriation of her educational achievements as an example of the good character of the offender, saying the offender was a man who:

has obviously put considerable effort and time into a young girl who, on any view of it, had a very difficult childhood with the break-up of two marriages, Your Honor, and despite that, with [offender's] presence, she was able to complete her high schooling and go on ultimately to complete tertiary education. What I am submitting to Your Honor is that there is a considerable body of material that indicates that over many years this man has been a decent, hardworking, caring and involved individual. *He has so far as the jury verdicts are concerned, transgressed on two occasions and they are occasions that are, on any view of it, a long time ago.*[151]

Since there was no legal exploration of the plethora of evidence pertaining to domestic violence endured by the mother or her eventual alienation, almost expulsion, from the family unit, the narrative of the bad mother and bad wife is uncritically accepted. The fact that the victim/survivor completed secondary schooling and obtained an undergraduate tertiary degree is a credit to the young woman's natural intellect, courage, and tenacity. In the defense narrative, however, the offender is credited for her educational accomplishments obtained both during the abuse and post-abuse. Moreover, defense counsel were so keen to push the technicality that the offender was no longer *legally* the victim/survivor's stepfather, and thus ought not face charges relating to intrafamilial abuse. However, as part of the new post-conviction narrative, the offender is made central to the achievements of the victim/survivor despite a legal emphasis on breaking any notion of a lineal bond.

Compiling a list of credits for the offender, and so far very little consideration for the victim, the barrister moved on to claim further credits via the jury verdicts, using the jury's verdict as a convenient forum to promote minimization of harm. The two isolated "transgressions" that occurred a "long time ago" prove useful in compressing the timeframe in which the abuse occurred thus allowing a legal claim of limited and isolated acts of abuse which, applying that logic, negated claims of the seriousness of the conduct. While the victim/survivor may only present evidence of traumatic impact of a crime that is specifically isolated to the charges upon which the perpetrator is convicted, defense counsel's presentation of the offender is not similarly constrained, nor subject to stringent arguments of relevance. The defense counsel, as in so many other cases, was free to present a long-winded narrative about the offender's pre- and post-offense life. Character witnesses, including a church minister and family members, told the court of their complete confidence in the offender.

Of more concern is the whittling away of any concept of harm to the victim/survivor *in virtue* of the jury's verdict. According to the defense barrister, the verdict indicates that the offender only *legally transgressed twice*. Had the evidence of the counselor been admitted, or even had the other charges not been excluded, the "legal" transgressions may well have been more.

The judge gave uncritical acceptance that the death of the offender's son was devastating for him and should be taken into account when sentencing. There was no such consideration for the victim/survivor. The fact that she lost a half-brother who stood firmly beside her in support and died tragically under circumstances (which even the defense agreed, were most likely connected to these legal proceedings) was not considered. Her pain and her loss were never factored in to the equation of her suffering.

Finally, prior to sentencing the judge wondered aloud if he ought to up the sentence "a couple of notches," since he was found guilty a second time around. However, defense counsel beseeched the judge to "actually give a lesser term"[152] since his client had already suffered so much. Perhaps still toying with the concept of actually increasing a previously light sentence for the same charge, the judge said he remained "troubled" by the fact that the judge at the first trial found a lack of remorse by the offender and wondered how such a finding was made by that judge and whether it still applied. Defense counsel quickly quashed this notion, saying perhaps the *counselor's* evidence had something to do with such a belief.[153] Since that evidence was removed at this trial—it may well be that, so too, was the consideration of no remorse. The judicial pondering over this matter never went any further.

In sentencing, the judge very briefly commented on the impact of the crimes on the stepdaughter, which you will recall included the charge of penetration which led to her pregnancy and abortion, saying:

> I find that as a result of the events she went through, the trauma of the abortion, [victim/survivor] has experienced feelings of loss and grief.... Other than the specific effects to which I have already referred, *I am not prepared, on the available evidence, to find that these offenses had any identifiable adverse consequences for the victim.* [emphasis added][154]

In *his* opinion, the young woman had suffered little. Her stepfather was found guilty of only two isolated charges, one of which resulted in the (then) teenager suffering a pregnancy and abortion. In an almost throwaway line, the judge conceded generalized feelings of loss and grief. But the private feelings of pain and anguish the victim/survivor made public—in order that a legal forum might better know her torment—were cheapened and cast aside.

One more final mitigating factor in favor of the offender was found. But it should have been cause for alarm rather than cause for verbal applause:

> I also accept that you have real prospects for rehabilitation which has already been demonstrated by the fact that...you managed to pursue a course ultimately enabling you to be employed by Community Services Victoria [as a Child Protection Worker]. I also accept the fact that you are unlikely to re-offend.[155]

The stark irony is that the offender gained employment as a Child Protection Worker is considered a virtue rather than causing any kind of reflective contemplation by the judge. One can only imagine what kind of comforting crystal ball he had to suggest that the offender was unlikely to ever re-offend.

The offender was sentenced to eighteen months jail, with a minimum period of twelve months to be served before he could be eligible for parole. In essence, he received six months jail for each charge of "incest," which carries a maximum sentence of twenty years.[156]

The Appeal

Once again, the offender lodged an appeal[157] against conviction and sentence arguing the jury convictions were unsafe and the sentence "excessive." The Director of Public Prosecutions[158] (DPP) also appealed against the leniency of the sentence.

While the Appeal Court judges demonstrated more depth of compassion for the suffering of the victim than that shown by the trial judge, they uncritically accepted the mitigating factors for the accused, agreeing the offenses were "old," which reduced their severity. The logic applied here appears to be that offenses perpetrated some time prior to their public and legal exposure should be seen as less abhorrent. It is a pity so many judges are blinded by the view that many sex offenses are "old," because the very nature of the crime is such that the modus operandi of the offender makes early disclosure and detection difficult if not impossible.

The Court of Appeal's decision was to uphold the DPP appeal and dismiss the offender's appeal. They increased the sentence from the original eighteen months to four years with a minimum of two years to be served before the offender would be eligible for parole.[159]

Comment

The defense narrative mobilized in this trial was around mother-daughter collusion as well as a motive of fabricating allegations for pecuniary gain. The latter narrative of greed is frequently mobilized in many trials from my original research. Given the exclusion of crucial prosecution evidence and constraints on the ability of the prosecution to fully contextualize the family environment in which the abuse occurred, a successful jury conviction (even if on a minority of charges) indicates some level of resistance to the defense narrative. It is my contention that much of this can be connected to the way the complainant presented herself at the trial and its possible effect on the jurors. I am not suggesting that a verdict of acquittal is the fault of the complainant—far from it, but I am suggesting that the presence of mind and obvious strength of character of the complainant continually outshone and out maneuvered defense counsel. Despite a very strong corroboration warning being given in this case, the jury did convict. Prominent and high ranking lawyers have noted the tensions in the giving of corroboration warnings. Such warnings are capable of virtually inviting juries to acquit when warned it is "dangerous" and "unsafe" to do so—even if the complainant is "thoroughly believable" and the jury convinced of the guilt of the accused.[160] Though it is not possible to know the internal dynamics that led to the jury conviction in R v L, I feel confident, from observing this trial and examining the transcript, that the complainant's personality was a contributing factor.

The focus on describing the victim/survivor as someone who did not undertake household chores was a feature point raised by the defense. It is very possible they feared it might lead the jury to consider that the stepdaughter began to play the role of wife and mother after her own mother left the family. Some masculinist literature on child sexual abuse promotes a view that a precursor for "incest" is the placement of the girl-child in a mother-wife role. There are also professional and public concerns about children taking on adult responsibilities. It might be that defense counsel was concerned that acknowledging the parental-like responsibilities of the victim/survivor could itself corroborate her stepfather's sexualization and sexual abuse of her.

A disturbing factor in this trial was the fact that the accused's de facto wife was allowed to sit through the entire proceedings. The same situation occurred in R v A, when the new wife of the accused sat through the entire proceedings. I am of the opinion that this is disrespectful to the complainant, especially as the new spouse is clearly in support of the accused and, no doubt, hostile to the complainant. This latter point clearly surfaced at this retrial of R v L, when a verbal and near physical altercation occurred as the complainant attempted to leave the courtroom area after giving her evidence.

Much of the legal narrative in this trial bore the hallmarks of classic family dysfunction theory. A pair of rose-colored judicial spectacles reversed alleged sexual abuse (proven at the first trial) after sixteen years of age to "consensual" sex on a technical understanding of "stepfather"—positioning the girl as some kind of Lolita. At the first trial, the mother was described as a "neurotic" and "useless" woman incapable of "running the home,"[161] and at the retrial, the mother was explicitly portrayed as a vengeful and colluding wife (so as to avoid prosecution evidence around domestic violence). At sentencing, the victim's suffering was minimized around an insulting dialogue, and the mother moved from colluder to common denominator in the offender's criminal conduct of raping his stepdaughter. In the first appeal decision, the judges commented on the accomplice warning, noting that the very act of alleging "incest" made the alleged victim "culpable."[162] This again demonstrates the hoary masculinist chestnut about victim culpability based on the lineal relationship of victim to offender, and a prejudicial mindset about sexual offenses against women and children.

Across legal discourse at all legal levels, an armory of excuses for the offender characterized the defense, while the character and suffering of the victim/survivor was minimized to the point of invisibility. An unholy alliance of daughter-blame, mother-blame and mother-daughter collusion is not far beneath the surface. These points aside, the jury verdict indicates that the victim/survivor was believed above the narrative of the colluding mother and daughter. Acquittal on most of the charges, however, is a sober sign of how successful the defense tactics of deliberate confusion and obfuscation can be.

Notes

1. R v L (Victorian County Court, Kelly, J. 1993), at 25–8, 287–93.
2. This evidence was given in the teenager's police statement as well as being given in a voir dire hearing at the first trial in 1993 at 270–7.
3. See Glossary for an explanation of this legal procedure.
4. R v L (1993), at 273–4.
5. Ibid., ruling.
6. All of this evidence relating to the sibling has come from several sources. I have read the police statement made by the sibling and read the entire transcript of the first trial. I have also read the letter the sibling received from his father while he was in jail following his conviction from the first trial in 1993. Evidence of the sibling's visit to a counselor detailing his distress at his father's successful appeal and the prospect of a retrial came from the police informant as well as member from the sibling's family. Details about the circumstances surrounding the sibling's death have come from the police informant, the mother of the sibling and the coroner's inquest, which listed the death as one resulting from "misadventure." Just before his death, the sibling tried to make contact with the police informant, whom he had come to trust. The detective was not available and the person who did speak with the sibling indicated that the boy was in a very distressed state.
7. Much of this hostility was considered to arise as a result of the personal friendship the counselor had once had with the accused outside of counseling. It further transpired that the counselor first met the accused when he was one of her mature-age students in a TAFE unit she was teaching and agreed to undertake dyad and family counseling with the accused.
8. For example, in R v E (Victorian County Court, Wodak, J. 1995); R v F (Victorian County Court, Wodak, J. 1995); R v J (Victorian County Court, Barnett, J. 1993); R v J (Victorian County Court, retrial, Campton, J. 1995); and R v M (Victorian County

Court, Dixon, J. 1995). Evidence of alleged admissions by the accused were rebutted with a series of defense arguments, among them, the claim that the alleged admissions were not confined to a specific charge (as though an offender would give an admission of long-term abuse that was accompanied by a virtual calendar of events covering every possible incident).

9. See Glossary for an explanation of this term.
10. R v L (Victorian County Court, retrial, Lewis, J. 1996), at 322.
11. The case in question is R v J (1993) 75 AcrimR 522. The judgment provided an in principle agreement that in cases of sexual abuse where the credibility and character of the complainant were attacked by defense counsel because of delayed disclosure and apparent inconsistent behavior (such as the giving of greeting cards or expressing familial affect to the accused) during the course of the alleged sexual abuse, the prosecution could call expert testimony. This expert testimony could be used to provide counter-evidence to rebut defense attacks on the character of the complainant. The judgment recognized that evidence contextualizing possible trauma-specific impacts associated with long-term abuse had a place in courtroom dialogue. I would hasten to add that care needs to be taken to avoid the way professionals and the law pathologize women's experiences of sexual violence.
12. R v L (retrial, 1996), at 119.
13. Ibid., at 217, ruling.
14. Research has documented the tendency for lay people as well as professionals to misunderstand the reasons why victims are unable to leave situations of long-term sexual abuse and domestic violence and remain in the family home. Delayed disclosure is another area that the public and professionals have difficulty in understanding. See, for example: Taft (1999), 64–9 and Feiner (1997), 1417. Feiner notes studies that concluded that the longer the duration of intrafamilial sexual abuse, the more jurors tended to attribute an element of blame to the victim/survivor. Howe (1997) highlights a number of community perspectives reported in the media about domestic violence and sexual abuse. Community polls and feedback indicate differing social attitudes toward victims of such violence, including public opinion polls reporting a lack of belief and empathy toward victims of violence. For a discussion about jurors' responses to child witnesses in sex abuse cases, see Schmidt & Brigham (1996). Other research has identified the degree of blameworthiness attributed to victims of sexual abuse among professional and lay people. See, for example: Gilmartin-Zena (1983) and Gilmartin-Zena (1988). Blaming victims for sexual abuse in a therapeutic setting has its foundational roots in family dysfunction theory. An example of attributing blame to a victim as part of therapeutic counseling can be found in Celano (1992).
15. R v L (retrial, 1996), at 218.
16. Ibid., at 235.
17. R v L (retrial, 1996), at 1–5.
18. Ibid., at 16. I directly observed this trial and I use the word "meekly" to describe the kind of quiet objection by the Prosecutor that quickly petered out. This is not a criticism of the prosecutor but rather a recognition that even he knew that such an observation would not serve his cause. His objection was, I thought, almost an involuntary action by someone who wanted to express a truth about a matter.
19. R v L (retrial, 1996), at 422.
20. Ibid., at 322–3
21. Ibid., at 208–9.

22. I feel confident in saying this since I had several discussions with this young woman after the trial when she initiated contact with me.
23. See Puren (1995).
24. R v L (retrial, 1996), at 23.
25. Ibid., at 4.
26. Ibid., at 3.
27. Ibid., at 3–6.
28. For example, in R v B (Victorian County Court, Williams, J. 1995) defense counsel suggested the complainant's mother should be in "parliament" because of what he described as her "speech" making. In other words, she refused to stick to the legal script. Accusing complainants or other witnesses who give answers other than a monosyllable of "yes" or "no" or "I don't know" as making "speeches" to the court occurred frequently. In R v J (retrial, 1995), the complainant's character was besmirched before she entered the witness box, and this became a main feature of the trial.
29. R v L (retrial, 1996), at 431–2.
30. Ibid., at 437.
31. Ibid.
32. Ibid., at 438–9.
33. Ibid., at 440–2.
34. Ibid. For example, see 441–50.
35. This young woman is a very intelligent and strong individual, and after the trial she requested to speak with me. She referred to her stepfather's conduct as rape and abuse, rather than the technical and mechanical details she gave at the trial. I have considered whether she had to switch off part of her emotional self in order to get through this ordeal and that part of this self-imposed strategy was to distance herself in the way she described the incidents. This is not uncommon as a number of survivors I have come into contact with have commented on how they often began by talking about their abuse in the third person—or, as often occurs, wrote about their own abuse in the third person as a safe way of describing their trauma.
36. R v L (retrial, 1996), at 443.
37. Ibid., 445–51.
38. I noted this in my original research as it occurred across nearly every trial.
39. R v L (retrial, 1996), at 450.
40. Three other trials from my research involved pregnancies, abortions and two births as a result of sexual abuse by biological fathers. In each case complainants were advised by the father to give a story about an unnamed, unidentified boy from school or in the latter case, an adult male, all of whom were unknown by the rest of the family but the supposed father of the child.
41. R v L (retrial, 1996), at 488, 498.
42. Ibid., 501.
43. See Whitton (1998), 101. See also chapter 2, "Telling Legal Tales" hereto which discusses this point.
44. R v L (retrial, 1996), at 505–8.
45. Ibid., at 506–7.
46. Ibid., at 512–13.
47. See, for example, Puren (1999).
48. R v L (retrial, 1996), at 513.
49. Ibid.

50. Ibid., at 523.
51. Ibid., at 527.
52. Ibid., at 528.
53. Ibid.
54. Ibid.
55. R v L (1993), at 144.
56. R v L (retrial, 1996), at 530–2.
57. Ibid., at 533.
58. Ibid., at 543.
59. Ibid., at 544.
60. Good examples can be found in R v M, R v H (Victorian County Court, Crossley, J. 1995) and R v J (1993, and retrial, 1995).
61. R v L (retrial, 1996), at 644–7.
62. Ibid., at 555.
63. R v L (retrial, 1996), at 556.
64. See Summit (1982) and Summit (1983).
65. R v L (retrial, 1996), at 558.
66. Ibid., at 558–60.
67. Ibid., at 561–2.
68. Family photos and greeting cards are frequent props used in defense cross-examination and a frequent tactic is to have the child or adult complainant read them out loud, most often causing them to exhibit deep distress. See, for example: R v J (1993, and retrial, 1995) and R v L (1993).
69. R v L (retrial, 1996), at 560.
70. Ibid., at 562.
71. A number of case studies in this book contain what I consider to be gratuitous comments and I found an abundance of them in my original research. In R v J (retrial, 1995) the judge at one point reprimanded the defense barrister for what the judge described as a gratuitous comment. Later the judge further commented that the barrister was continually making comments designed only to distress or anger the complainant.
72. R v L (1993), at 29a. Note that a judge's charge is not normally available but I was fortunate enough to obtain a copy.
73. R v L (retrial, 1996), at 562.
74. Ibid., at 563.
75. Ibid., at 576.
76. The case in question is R v J (retrial, 1995). I have noted elsewhere how many of the greeting cards and other paraphernalia which, despite often being old, some very old, are unusually well-cared for, in mint condition. It is as though these expressions of familial love are preserved should a child later disclose in years to come.
77. Ibid., at 563.
78. Ibid., at 563.
79. Ibid., at 573.
80. Ibid., at 574.
81. Ibid.
82. Ibid., at 572.
83. For example in R v A (Victorian County Court, Davey, J. 1995), the adolescent complainant faced almost identical questions when defense counsel in that trial highlighted her crimes compensation application with her current unemployment status. In R v K

(Victorian County Court, Lewis, J. 1994) the adolescent complainant was cross-examined about his application for crimes compensation and his desire to attend university and to purchase certain goods. In R v J (1993, and retrial, 1995) the complainant was cross-examined about the crimes compensation she received and this was linked to an explicit motive of "greed." In R v N (Victorian County Court, Stott, J. 1995) the complainant was cross-examined about her crimes compensation application, as were complainants in a number of other trials from the original research. On nearly all occasions the application for government funded crimes compensation was linked to a supposed motive.

84. R v L (retrial, 1996), at 571.
85. Ibid.
86. Ibid.
87. Ibid., at 581.
88. Ibid., at 577.
89. Ibid., at 579.
90. R v L (1993), at 180.
91. R v L (retrial, 1996), at 599.
92. I observed this incident and quietly felt proud at this show of dignity and integrity by the mother. I privately thought also, that her daughter no doubt inherited some of the strengths of character from her mother.
93. R v L (retrial, 1996), at 589.
94. Ibid., at 598.
95. Ibid., at 600–4.
96. Ibid., at 605–7.
97. Ibid., at 607–8.
98. Ibid., at 613.
99. Ibid., at 652–6.
100. Ibid., at 557–8.
101. Ibid., at 664.
102. Ibid., at 665.
103. Ibid., at 669.
104. Ibid., at 672.
105. Ibid., at 674–8.
106. Ibid., at 681.
107. Ibid., at 684.
108. Ibid., at 687–9.
109. Ibid., at 693.
110. Ibid., at 685–95.
111. Ibid., at 696.
112. Ibid., at 697.
113. Ibid.
114. Ibid., at 699.
115. Ibid., at 703.
116. Ibid., at 710.
117. Ibid., at 713.
118. Ibid., at 714.
119. See, for example: R v J (1993, and retrial, 1995); R v H; R v N; and R v M. In R v H, the mother's evidence bordered on the bizarre as she said she never left her daughter

alone with her husband at any time. Such a claim almost arouses suspicion as to why a mother would be so concerned that her daughter never be alone with the father while at the same time insisting upon a "normal" and loving father/daughter relationship.
120. R v L (retrial, 1996), at 727–34.
121. Ibid.
122. Ibid., at 745–50.
123. Ibid., at 450–1.
124. Ibid., at 759.
125. Ibid.
126. Ibid., at 754.
127. Ibid., at 758.
128. Ibid., at 769–73.
129. R v J (1993), at 1672–3, and R v J (retrial, 1995), at 2 (7/7/95), respectively.
130. Other researchers have commented how defense barristers in rape trials have used certain types of body language such as facial grimaces and tone of voice to convey disbelief, incredulity or contempt towards the evidence given by complainants in such trials. See, for example, Adler (1987) and Grix (1999).
131. Out of respect for the complainant I am loathe to repeat the comment because of the topic of the joke. Suffice it to say that the joke featured a crude hypothesis as to the possible outcome had the complainant's pregnancy been full term.
132. R v L (retrial, 1996), at 805.
133. Ibid., at 811–2.
134. Ibid., at 807–11.
135. Ibid., at 834.
136. Ibid., at 835–6.
137. Ibid., at 841.
138. Ibid., at 836–9.
139. Ibid., at 842.
140. Ibid., at 839.
141. Ibid., at 840.
142. Ibid., at 839.
143. Ibid., at 842.
144. For an excellent discussion on the legal problems around corroboration warnings in Australian law, see Davies (1999) and Heenan (2001).
145. A television show entitled *This Is Your Life* explores the lifetime biography of experiences and achievements of notable individuals.
146. See Glossary for explanation of this legislation.
147. R v L (retrial, 1996), at 866.
148. Ibid., at 876.
149. Ibid., at 877.
150. Ibid., at 882.
151. Ibid., at 897–8.
152. R v L (retrial, 1996), at 878.
153. Ibid., at 893–4.
154. Ibid., at 903.
155. Ibid., at 903.
156. Ibid., at 904.
157. See Glossary for an explanation of this legal procedure.

158. See Glossary for an explanation of this role.
159. R v L (retrial, 1996), appeal judgment.
160. See Davies (1999), 98.
161. R v L (1993), at 28a.
162. R v L (1994) 73 AcrimR 17, at 6.

7 • Forced Errors

Introduction

IN PREVIOUS CHAPTERS, I made reference to specious accuracy. This chapter builds specifically on specious accuracy with regards to cross-examination and the use of prior inconsistent statements to bolster the defense narrative. When cross-examining the complainant with regard to the charges of sexual abuse, the vast majority of defense questions target minute and peripheral details connected to specific charges. At times the defense will repeatedly ask the same questions, throughout cross-examination, sometimes slightly rephrasing the question, in the hope of obtaining an answer that varies, even slightly, to that given previously. Legally, these errors in evidence are referred to as "prior inconsistent statements," and legal counsel on both sides juxtapose these transcribed inconsistencies to present to the jury as exhibits "proving" the lack of credibility of the complainant or other witness.

In this chapter, I want to demonstrate the defense tactic of using prior inconsistent statements—which after considerable analysis I have termed "forced errors"—to identify how defense barristers plan their attacks on the credibility of the complainant's evidence through the narrow and highly selective use of minor errors in evidence.

In almost all sexual-offense proceedings, complainants are cross-examined first at a committal hearing in the Magistrates' Court. At such a hearing, the complainant is usually subjected to fairly rigorous cross-examination, as the defense gauges weaknesses and strengths in the complainant, and in the veracity of their evidence. Through a reading of committal hearings, one discovers that defense questions specifically target minor details, such as the clothing worn by the complainant at the time of the incident(s), the decor of the room, or other incidental factors relating to a specific incident, time frame, place and so on. The evidence given by the complainant at the committal is closely compared to the evidence in her statement prior to the commencement of the trial. At the trial which proceeds from the committal hearing, the defense barrister may therefore have already collated "prior inconsistent statements" taken from comparisons between the evidence in the complainant's statement and committal evidence. This means defense barristers have another layer of evidence, giving them at least three documents from which to construct inconsistencies: the complainant's statement, committal evidence and now, the trial evidence. If a jury has been discharged without verdict, either through a trial being aborted or a hung jury, the defense may have possibly four or five transcripts from which to attack the complainant's evidence on inconsistencies. In my doctoral research, I studied six such trials.[1]

Prosecution barristers do not have the same opportunity as defense counsel to collect the same level of prior inconsistent statements. For various reasons, witnesses for the defense are not required to make a police statement that can be examined prior to a committal and compared to their evidence at trial. This, then, limits the scope for the prosecutor to make comparisons between sets of evidence in contrast to the defense barrister. Moreover, the accused has considerable agency with regard to the evidence he may choose to give or not give within the court process. The defendant is not required to give evidence at the committal and is not compelled to give evidence at the trial since he may exercise his legal right to silence. As such, he is able to avoid—or at the very least limit—prior inconsistent statements. Moreover, prior to being presented to a jury as part of the defense "facts" of the case, the accused's record of interview (conducted by police, prior to being charged) is "edited" to ensure that questions or facts put to him by police and comments made during this record of interview (which defense counsel considers prejudicial to him and his case) are removed and cannot be used as evidence against him in the trial.

This practice limits the likelihood of inconsistent statements issuing from the accused and, if he chooses to give no evidence, he avoids entirely the possibility of a prior inconsistent statement. The bonus of this is that, should the accused *choose* to give evidence at the trial, the legal presentation of an accused's account will often have the appearance of internal consistency and smoothness as a result of clever legal editing, which limits prosecution cross-examination. There is no prior evidence for comparison, and specific barriers that protect the accused from the kinds of cross-examination leveled at complainants result very often in the evidence of the accused appearing more coherent and less fragmented. The accused's account is not marred with the kinds of silences and gaps so often found in the testimony of child and adult complainants as a result of evidentiary limitations that stifle and disrupt their stories. Often the accused's evidence can appear flawless: a blanket denial of all charges coupled with an assertion that the child's behavior is bizarre, or driven by ulterior motives, becomes easier. Such claims are less permeable and even protected from scrutiny.

Minor inconsistencies in evidence, or an inability to recall the exact detail given by complainants in evidence at a prior committal or trial—or perhaps even given in the evidence from the previous day—form a vanguard in defense cross-examination techniques. "Prior inconsistent statements" very often form the central tactic of defense cross-examination and are gainfully and skillfully employed. Limiting a complainant's evidence very often enhances a narrative of deception prior inconsistent statements are engineered to reveal.

"Prior inconsistent statements" are deliberately designed and sought after by barristers to lead the witness to a fault in their own evidence, hence my terminology in regarding them as *forced errors*. At the trial, the defense very often leads the evidence of the complainant into a predetermined fault; that is, the defense already has evidence of a prior inconsistent statement or, conversely, has a complainant's previous evidence in front of them and re-canvasses the issue in order to elicit any variation they can be immediately pounced upon as an "error" and becomes evidence of a "prior inconsistent statement."

Lawyers use the tactic of *forced errors* in an attempt to seriously discredit the evidence of a witness. This is a form of dual impression management, where the credibility of one witness is damaged and, as a consequence, the credibility of the adversary is enhanced. For the purpose of this chapter, an analysis of this concept focuses attention on forced errors used against the complainant or a supporting mother. I did not avoid analyzing forced errors used against the accused. There were few examples of *forced errors* used against the accused. When attempted, defense counsel was quick to claim unfairness due to irrelevancy, lack of context, or that the prosecutor was belaboring the point. In essence, a good deal less was made of prior inconsistent statements made by the accused—an interesting observation, no doubt, but one which does not provide material for a deeper analysis of their use for legal storytelling.

In essence, the use of forced errors allows defense barristers to put a question to the complainant knowing already that the question will eventually *force* the complainant into an admission that an earlier piece of evidence is inconsistent with her or his current evidence. Throughout the trial process, defense barristers collate these "prior inconsistent statements." They are then tendered as evidence to be given to the jury as supporting proof that the complainant has not told the truth.

Multiple Versions: Time and Topic Juxtapositions

While the tactic of some defense barristers is to deliberately confuse complainants, the effect of such maneuvers is often that the jury will also be confused. Case studies R v L (retrial) and R v G provide good examples of just how useful prior inconsistent statements were used as a mechanism in an effort to confuse a jury and complainant. Recall that in pre-trial arguments, defense counsel in R v L actually admitted he would be relying heavily on inconsistencies between the complainant's evidence taken from several transcripts to confuse the jury and complainant and obfuscate fact-finding. Aware of the impact that such a defense tactic would have on the jury and the complainant, the judge stated:

> JUDGE: You're going to be cross-examining on the basis of a prior inconsistent statement on a primary inconsistent statement and what she said at the prior, what she said at this, that and the other thing...defense by obfuscation rather than anything else, it seems to me, the jury won't know what version they're dealing with.
>
> DEFENSE: Hopefully by the end of the day that's the view the jury will take...[2]

In acknowledging the obvious defense advantages of such tactics, the judge in R v L conceded that the barrister "might score some big points...if you get the right information...you can discredit her on (date of specific charged incident)."[3] The judge further suggested that cross-examination on an inconsistent statement was a "common art" for lawyers, providing them with the opportunity to use "forensic skill and ability to make something of it."[4] Rather than seeking to elucidate trial evidence for the jury, the judge and defense barrister consider that the notion of defense by obfuscation and trial by confusion are just and worthy elements in judicial process.

Examples from other trials reveal a variety of techniques to create confusion: rapid juxtapositions between different transcripts, different times, contexts and topics. While prosecutors lead evidence from complainants and other witnesses in chronological order, that is, as the charged event(s) occurred, defense counsel most often use the strategy of putting questions to the complainant and other prosecution witnesses across a continuum of time and context. When, on occasions prosecutors and even members of the jury—not to mention complainant—complained of being confused by this process, judges justified such approaches as "testing the memory of the witness" to stop them from "fabricating."[5]

Putting a question to a complainant in cross-examination and then immediately following it up with a question on a different topic and a different time frame of perhaps three, five, ten or even twenty years and repeating this hectoring repertoire was found in abundance in many trials.[6] The purpose of this is clearly to confuse the complainant as well as the jury.

If defense tactics create such confusion among jurors and even prosecutors, the confusion created for complainants (child victim/witnesses, in particular) can have—and I would argue has had—significant implications for the quality of evidence given by complainants, as well as the degree of distress that such confusion may create.[7] The demand for complainants to give immediate answers to questions that jump from one specific date to years or possibly decades later is factually misleading and emotionally taxing.

It is important, also, to consider the removal of evidence through evidentiary rulings and the role this plays in confusing the complainant and the jury. Complainants are warned that there are certain topics they may not broach which results in deliberate gaps which defense barristers fill with their own narrative. These gaps are also dramatized to suggest a deliberate gap by the child. Staccato-type halts in the complainant's evidence artificially arise around questions and topics the barrister already knows cannot be answered properly because of evidentiary restrictions.[8] This leads to confusion—and, often, distress—for complainants, as the defense easily makes them appear to be prevaricators. Examples of this could be found in several trials that formed my original research.[9] Strong evidentiary restrictions on the complainant's evidence in R v J (retrial), coupled with defense questions on topics the barrister knew would be difficult to properly answer, led the complainant to make her own comment on the injustice of it all. The complainant responded, "As God is my witness, that is the truth, and the sick thing is you know it."[10] Judges, too, were aware of how their evidentiary restrictions imposed difficulties on the giving of evidence, especially by children, making them very susceptible to claims of errors in their evidence and, thus, prior inconsistent statements.

The Peripheral Becomes Central

While commonsense might dictate that it is impossible to recall every minute detail of one's life or of particular incidents, the mantra of defense cross-examination is that any and every detail, no matter how peripheral or minute, is central to the complainant's evidence. Further, such details can be demanded again and again in the hope that the slightest variation can be capitalized on by the defense to the utmost extent. Examples of this can be found in case studies R v L, R v G, and R v D. The judge in R v L commented on the opportunity for the defense to create advantages for themselves by creating an issue out of evidence that would otherwise be innocuous or irrelevant.[11]

Asking complainants about the clothing worn, such as what color skirt, underwear or pajamas they were wearing at the time of an incident; or asking about the interior of the car, its color, make and model; or what the child ate for dinner that night some five years ago are favored defense questions designed to push the complainant to provide exact details. Later on, the same questions, often slightly rephrased, are put with the specific aim of obtaining an answer that may vary, no matter how slight. Defense counsel is quick to exploit these variations, no matter how minor, and to claim that such discrepancies were "proof" that the complainant was a "liar" unable to tell the truth.

In the trial of R v C, the child complainant was questioned about her previous evidence regarding the family's visits to the home of a family friend. One of the charges in this case related to the evidence of the child that her father had vaginally penetrated her in the car, while taking her to visit a friend. The defense cross-examined the girl at length regarding the exact number of occasions she had visited her friend's house:

DEFENSE: You told the jury yesterday that you had gone to visit [friend]?

CHILD: Yes.

DEFENSE: Once, right?

CHILD: No, I went to visit her before with my family.

DEFENSE: But do you remember me asking you yesterday how many times you'd been to [friend's] house?

CHILD: Yes.

DEFENSE: And you said once to visit and once to spend the night?

CHILD: Yes.

DEFENSE: Do you want to change that now?

CHILD: We went a couple of times with my family.

DEFENSE: You remember giving evidence at the trial last week, under oath—I'll be referring to page forty-six beginning at line thirty-one, do you remember this question, "How many times approximately, have you been to [friend's] house?" Answer, "I've been to her house a couple of times." "More than once?" "Yes." "More than twice?" "Yes." "More than three times?" "Yes." "More than four times?" "I don't know." "So it could be four times or less, is that right?" "I think it was more than four times." "Would it have been more than five times?" Your answer, "Probably, I don't know." Do you remember those questions and answers?

CHILD: Yes.

DEFENSE: And then you come in and tell the jury at this trial, just been there twice, once to visit, once to spend the night. Now which is true?

CHILD: I've been to [friend's] house a couple of times to visit with my family.

DEFENSE: Which is true, two times or more than five? Which is true?

CHILD: More than five.

DEFENSE: More than five times is true?

CHILD: Yes.

DEFENSE: So when you told the jury, once to visit and once to spend the night, you were *lying*. You would agree with me, wouldn't you, that there's a big difference between two and more than five?

CHILD: *Yes*. [emphasis added][12]

A big issue was made of the child's inability to recall the precise number of times she ever visited her friend's home and leads to her being branded a "liar" for being confused about previous evidence in which she agreed to a numerical figure. The barrister also cross-examined the child in R v C at length about the color of the family car in which she alleged one of the incidents of sexual abuse had taken place. The father had owned several cars over a relatively short period of time and, understandably, the child gave responses at the trial that contradicted her statement and committal evidence regarding the color and interior design of the family car in relation to a specific incident on the presentment. The barrister highlighted these inconsistent statements in cross-examination of the child in a similar style to his questioning of the child about the number of visits to a friend's house. Similarly, complainants in other cases were cross-examined at length about minute details of the family car in which they alleged certain instances of sexual abuse occurred and were verbally harangued for the most minor inconsistencies.[13]

In R v D, the defense barrister relied almost entirely on comparing the evidence of the child between the committal and the current answers given at this trial, especially with regard to the alleged anal penetration of the child.

This kind of specious accuracy, demanding answers to questions around peripheral and miniscule detail provides barristers with an opportunity to glean variations in the child or adult's evidence and make them the central focus of cross-examination.

Often defense barristers purposely group multiple incidents of prior inconsistent statements together, often from several topics previously canvassed, so that the jury hears a monologue of previous transcript evidence from the defense barrister, accompanied by admissions of error in evidence by the complainant. Interspersed with the defense catalogue of minor errors in evidence are consistent reminders to complainants, especially child witnesses, by the defense barrister that they had given evidence "under oath" or had "sworn on the bible to tell the truth." Trials examined in this research were replete with examples of defense barristers highlighting inconsistencies, then feigning outrage and indignation at these evidentiary faults in the complainant's testimony. Moreover, barristers were not shy in reminding child witnesses, in particular, of the prison penalties for "perjuring" themselves, and how they "swore" an oath to God to tell the truth—and here they are telling lies to the court! These stylized performances juxtaposing errors with sworn oaths are entrenched defense strategies and are used to heighten the defense narrative, as well as intimidate and humiliate the child. On occasion, defense barristers put forward the prior inconsistent statements they have amassed on a topic or incident and "invite" the child to tell the jury which is the true version, thus further demoralizing and humiliating the child.[14]

In the trial R v K, the complainant was cross-examined about evidence he had given at the committal hearing which was almost a year prior to this trial. In his evidence-in-chief at the trial, the complainant was not sure about two peripheral details concerning an alleged incident of sexual abuse that occurred in 1987. The defense capitalized on this area in their cross-examination:

DEFENSE: You read through the [police] statement before you signed it in 1993?

COMPLAINANT: Yes.

DEFENSE: You even acknowledged that if you made a false statement, you might find yourself charged with perjury?

COMPLAINANT: That's right.

DEFENSE: You've said on an earlier occasion, haven't you, when you gave evidence in the Magistrates' Court, that you actually saw [sibling] on that day after you'd had a shower?

COMPLAINANT: I'm not sure.

DEFENSE: You can't remember what you said in the Magistrates' Court?

COMPLAINANT: That's right.

DEFENSE: I suggest you were being asked some questions about the presence of [sibling] in the house on this day, in the Magistrates' Court. Do you remember being asked some questions about that?

COMPLAINANT: Not about that specifically, no.

DEFENSE: I put to you that you were asked this question, page twenty-four "The rooms are all adjacent to one another with the doors open?" Do you remember being asked that question?

COMPLAINANT: No.

DEFENSE: Further at the same page you were asked, "Where did you see him?" in reference to [sibling], and you said, "In the lounge room when he was having his Easter egg." "That would be about half past eight?" "Yes, about eight, half past eight, something like that." "Eight or eight thirty on Easter Sunday 1987?" "Yes." "Specifically recall it?" "Yes, approximately that time." "You had a conversation with [sibling] at that stage?" "I can't remember, I think yes, I would have said hello and that." Now, do you remember being asked those questions and giving those answers.

COMPLAINANT: No.

DEFENSE: When you gave evidence in the Magistrates' Court, you'd taken an oath to tell the truth?

COMPLAINANT: That's right.

DEFENSE: So the truth as at 14 December 1994 was that you could specifically remember seeing [sibling] when you got out of the shower and he was in the lounge room having his Easter egg, and you had a conversation with him at that stage, about half past eight on Easter Sunday. That was the truth then?

COMPLAINANT: Yes.

DEFENSE: The event you described in your evidence-in-chief has occurred earlier than eight or eight thirty, is that right?

COMPLAINANT: Yes.[15]

During the trial in R v K, the adolescent complainant continually had his evidence from the committal used against him in prior inconsistent statements. In highlighting a prior inconsistent statement between the complainant's committal evidence and his current evidence at the trial, defense counsel put to the complainant, "so, the evidence today is...."[16] The comment suggests that the complainant's evidence changes under oath. The barrister in R v L similarly suggested the complainant's evidence was "flexible" under oath when highlighting discrepancies in her evidence.

It would seem that deliberately withholding factual evidence damning to the defense case merely highlights the "legal art" of obliterating facts, while minor inconsistencies in complainant evidence marks the individual as unable or unwilling to tell the truth. On one occasion, defense counsel in R v K charged that the young male complainant's evidence at the committal was inconsistent with evidence from the trial: at the committal, he believed his brother's bedroom door was open at the time of one of the alleged incidents; at the trial, he said he could not be sure if the other bedroom door was open or not. In response, the complainant said that the defense barrister was asking him questions in a way that led him a certain way so that his answers could only be "yes" or "no." The defense barrister responded to this suggestion by stating that there was no "trick" to his questions, and continued with his cross-examination questions still framed in a way that constrained the complainant to "yes" or "no" answers.[17] The net effect of this being to limit the complainant from partaking in any meaningful dialogue so that 'yes' or 'no' answers slide easily into direct agreement or disagreement on specific points.

Switching between time frames and context was a particular strategy mobilized in a number of trials, including R v G.[18] For example, in R v G, in a series of short questions, the barrister covered six separate topics over a period of approximately seven years.[19] It was clear from the transcript that the prosecutor and judge were having difficulty following the cross-examination because of these extreme switches between time frames and topics, leading the judge to ask just what time frame the barrister was talking about because he had clearly lost the judge.[20] As detailed in this case study, there was extensive focus on whether the complainant was hurt or not and the depth and duration of penile penetration, and slightest variations were used to both hector and humiliate the complainant. Recall that when the prosecutor attempted to re-build her credibility around this evidence, defense counsel opposed it on the grounds it was "unfair" to enable her to clarify not just the state she was in (when she gave her police statement), but the fact that she was up most of the night giving her statement to police. This point aside, the focus on depth and duration of penetration made the complainant's consistency in describing the actual incident invisible. Defense attacks on her evidence centered on miniscule details with which the legal fraternity has been obsessed for centuries when it comes to cases involving sexual penetration.

Evidentiary exclusions can aid and abet defense tactics in shifting the peripheral to the center, and R v B is a telling example. Repetitive incidents of alleged abuse, conducted in a ritual way, were distilled to only one charge in this case. The defense's isolation of one alleged incident (and evidentiary rulings which did not enable the child to contextualize her evidence around this isolated charge), created obvious difficulties for the child in giving her evidence, difficulties the judge was cognizant of. Under cross-examination, the child gave contradictory evidence concerning the sequence of undressing. In her police statement she had said that sometimes she was made to get undressed while on other occasions her father undressed her. From my reading of the transcript it was obvious that the conflicting evidence about who undressed whom arose from her difficulty isolating the exact sequence of events on that *one* particular, isolated incident. However, the jury was not privy to these constraints, so it was with ease defense counsel accumulated a plethora of prior inconsistent statements.

As the transcript extract reveals, these constraints caused distress for the child since she was only too aware herself that her confusion was the result of having given evidence of one isolated incident from an alleged litany of similar incidents:

> DEFENSE: And [accused] didn't take your clothes off?
>
> CHILD: No.
>
> DEFENSE: Each of you did it [got undressed] individually?
>
> CHILD: Yes.
>
> DEFENSE: Now, you could not be wrong about that?
>
> CHILD: No.
>
> DEFENSE: You have got that stuck in your memory?
>
> CHILD: Yes.
>
> DEFENSE: You never indicated that you would want to take your clothes of [*sic*] and not him take them off?
>
> CHILD: Excuse me, Your Honor but in my statement there's written down that it happened a couple of more times.[21] [Transcript records "witness distressed."]

A break in proceedings was called and the jury adjourned for the day. After the defense barrister complained that the outburst by the complainant prejudiced the accused, the judge made it clear that the jury would be told to ignore such outbursts.[22] Yet the trial judge in this case was well aware of the difficulties placed on the children as a result of his evidentiary rulings:

> I was told before we started that [complainant] had been advised not to volunteer [evidence of other incidents].... I appreciate it does create difficulties. It always does because it is really for the sake of the rules that are designed to favor the accused, it can lead to some confusion and some degree of unreality in evidence giving.... I feel that it's unrealistic to expect a trial to go through, especially with child witnesses, without some *slipping up of the plan* to avoid the reference. [emphasis added][23]

Evidentiary rulings are the prima facie basis for this "air of unreality." But of course it is precisely this "air of unreality" that defense counsel rely upon to discredit complainants. Indeed, a similar point about defense mechanisms designed to create an air of unreality in a complainant's evidence was mentioned in another trial.[24] When the child resumed giving evidence, defense counsel was again confronted with a child becoming distressed. Continually confronted with *errors* in testimony and instructed to only give "yes" or "no" answers in response to detailed questions understandably unnerved the child. As the difficulties continued and the child clearly became more distressed, the barrister was barely able to contain his annoyance, suggesting at one stage that the child was going for his "jugular" by her refusal to contain her evidence in accordance with judicial rulings.[25]

Defense counsel again complained of the difficulties the child was posing for him, prompting the judge to placate him again, saying:

> I can understand her position too because she—while an accurate answer to your [defense barrister] *carefully phrased question* does result in a question or not, nevertheless in the broad scheme of things, she wants to be able to explain...just because you say you phrased your question carefully, which I don't disagree with, does not overcome the problem that a *yes or no* answer may to her be *not telling the whole truth*, for argument's sake, which *she's taken an oath to do*. [emphasis added][26]

Here there is a clear recognition that having witnesses undertake an oath to tell the whole truth does not mean the whole truth will be revealed. But in the presence of the jury this fallacy is maintained as a sacrosanct feature of law. Leslie Feiner has demonstrated how the distillation of multiple charges of sexual abuse into a small number of charges (or even one charge) coupled with strict evidentiary rulings that accompany sex abuse cases, encourage "gaps in the story-line," gaps which defense barristers seize upon to discredit the child/adult complainant.[27]

Making peripheral evidence central might well be exacerbated through evidentiary rulings that whittle away prosecution evidence and decontextualize the allegations, making the amplification of minute details into a seamless monologue of *errors* in the complainant's testimony. The role of judicial discretion in deciding who can speak and what they can say— courtesy of evidentiary rulings—can well change the tenor of the trial and the narrative deployed in that particular case. In commenting on the obvious difficulties experienced by the child in R v B while giving her stultified evidence, the judge, while not prepared to allow any contextualization of her evidence, did wish the court to *bear* in "mind that with a different judge on a different day all this evidence might have been let in...."[28]

Such painfully frank self-acknowledgments of personal discretion to inform evidentiary rules makes explicit the problematic role judicial discretion has in shaping the development and deployment of legal narratives.

Peripheral and Minute Details

As stated earlier, defense barristers work very hard to obtain minute details from complainants from the committal as a means of piecing together minor inconsistencies that may then be used against the complainant at the trial through forced errors.

Throughout the sequence of defense cross-examination on peripheral and minute details, it is not unusual for barristers to continually compel complainants to provide an answer that could be juxtaposed to previous evidence, no matter how minute. This was a common occurrence in the majority of trials analyzed in the original research.

In case studies R v D, R v G and R v L, and in a host of other trials from the original research, complainants were asked detailed questions about clothing and décor, climatic conditions, sequences of removing clothing or sequences of other events connected with specific charges.[29] The following are excerpts from various cases to demonstrate this tactic and its usefulness in providing defense counsel with forced errors of prior inconsistent statements.

The first is R v N. The adult complainant was asked questions at the committal and trial about her age in relation to an incident that occurred more than sixteen years previously. At the trial she was asked similar questions about her age at the time of certain alleged incidents of abuse to bring any inconsistencies to the fore:

DEFENSE: When you first had occasion to make your statement, make your report to the police, you had to give quite some thought to this allegation, didn't you?

COMPLAINANT: Yes, we had to work back on ages.

DEFENSE: Because when you first made your allegation against your father, you were dealing with a time period, 1976, you say, when you were in form 1?

COMPLAINANT: That's correct.

DEFENSE: When I asked you a moment ago how old you were you said, eleven or twelve didn't you?

COMPLAINANT: Twelve, yes.

DEFENSE: I understood just a moment ago, and the jury no doubt heard you, that you said eleven or twelve?

COMPLAINANT: I said twelve first, the first time.

DEFENSE: Then you say eleven do you?

COMPLAINANT: Then I realized it was twelve.

DEFENSE: You were asked a similar question at the preliminary hearing, weren't you?

COMPLAINANT: Yes.

DEFENSE: I asked you, page 104, Your Honor, how old you say you were, in fact I will put the entire question, "At that stage, how old do you say you were?" Remember me asking you that?

COMPLAINANT: Yes.

DEFENSE: Do you remember your answer?

COMPLAINANT: No, I am sorry, I don't.

DEFENSE: The answer recorded in the transcript contains the following words: "Thirteen, fourteen, twelve, thirteen, fourteen. So at the beginning of this year when asked how old you were your response covered the ages thirteen, fourteen and twelve, is that right?

COMPLAINANT: Yes, I [defense interrupts].

DEFENSE: Is that right, is that what you said at the committal?

COMPLAINANT: I can't remember it but I agree with it.

DEFENSE: You can't remember giving that answer?

COMPLAINANT: No, I am sorry.[30]

This evidence was tendered, and was followed closely with questions about the color and model of the family car in which the complainant gave evidence of having been raped in by her father. The defense attacked the evidence of the complainant by reading excerpts from the committal where the complainant said the car might have been a dusty brown, and later said that it might have been an odd shade of blue. The defense finished their questions about the model of the car by complaining that the complainant could not even recall the evidence she gave at the committal as to the clothing she wore (albeit some seventeen years earlier).[31] Similarly, in case study R v C, the complainant was asked a detailed sequence of questions about the model, color and interior design of the family car, and—again—any variation in detail was tendered to the court as a prior inconsistent statement.[32]

Still on this case, the complainant was further cross-examined about the climatic conditions around the time of another incident which allegedly occurred more than twenty years previously. In evidence-in-chief, the complainant stated that her memories of the actual incidents of abuse were vivid in her memory because of its personal impact. As cross-examination in this case focused continually on peripheral details, such as the climatic conditions, an emphasis was taken away from any consideration of the contents of her allegations:

DEFENSE: Now on your evidence, given on the occasion [transcript records "indistinct" word] you say was somewhere in summer time when you believed you were on holidays?

COMPLAINANT: That's correct.

DEFENSE: Are you able to recall any other details about climatic conditions at that stage?

COMPLAINANT: It was warm.

DEFENSE: Just warm.

COMPLAINANT: Yes. It was warm. It was night time.

DEFENSE: Would you agree with the proposition, that your recollection of events that occurred, according to you, maybe twenty-six years ago, is somewhat hazy?

COMPLAINANT: Not of the incident, no.

DEFENSE: Just bear with me for the moment. You would agree that to think back as to what may or may not have happened over a quarter of a century ago is a difficult task?

COMPLAINANT: It's as if it happened yesterday.

DEFENSE: Is it? Right, as if it happened yesterday. Well, whilst you describe the events as if it happened yesterday, you can't even describe something as the weather with any degree of particularity beyond what you've said; is that right?

COMPLAINANT: That's right.[33]

In this example, the defense has no forced errors to use because the complainant's evidence at the committal and trial was that the weather was warm and that it was probably summer school holidays. Therefore, the defense barrister attacked the credibility of the complainant for not being able to recall the weather in more specific detail. One complainant actually challenged the defense barrister's questions demanding minute details on a topic not even related to the specific charge on the presentment. Seeing the trap of a no-win situation, she complained that if she were able to recall such details she would lose credibility for being able to "recall" such minute details, and conversely would jeopardize her credibility for not actually providing them in the court.[34]

In R v M, the defense counsel highlighted variations in the complainant's evidence concerning the sequence of a particular incident. Comparisons between her police statement, committal hearing evidence and now trial evidence were aligned to show variations involving the detailed sequence of being taken to a bedroom by her father, including the exact sequence of getting undressed and other minute details. The following excerpt is used to show the demand for detail. But while the actual incident was corroborated by at least two relatives of the complainant, defense cross-examination focused only upon minute details. This is a very lengthy excerpt, but necessarily so in order to reveal the forced machinations of prior inconsistencies alongside defense haranguing over peripheral matters:

DEFENSE: Your father did carry you into the bedroom, did he?

COMPLAINANT: Yes.

DEFENSE: When he carried you into the bedroom, I think you have said the light was not on?

COMPLAINANT: The light was off.

DEFENSE: There was a door to that bedroom?

COMPLAINANT: Yes.

DEFENSE: Did he close the door?

COMPLAINANT: Yes.

DEFENSE: When was that?

COMPLAINANT: When he carried me into the bedroom.

DEFENSE: How did he close the door? Did he close the door as he carried you into the bedroom or. . .

COMPLAINANT: As he carried me into the bedroom.

DEFENSE: How did he do that?

COMPLAINANT: It must've been with his foot.

DEFENSE: Do you say you can recollect after all this time the door closing as you were carried into the bedroom, carried in drunk?

COMPLAINANT: Yes, the door was shut.

DEFENSE: What happened after he put you on the bed?

COMPLAINANT: He got undressed.

DEFENSE: Where was he when he undressed?

COMPLAINANT: Next to the bed.

DEFENSE: He put you on the bed and then got undressed, is that right?

COMPLAINANT: Yes.

DEFENSE: Did he take all his clothes off?

COMPLAINANT: No.

DEFENSE: What clothing did he take off?

COMPLAINANT: His underwear.

DEFENSE: And his trousers presumably, did he?

COMPLAINANT: Yes.

DEFENSE: What did he do then?

COMPLAINANT: Pulled my underwear down.

DEFENSE: Did he hold you in any way whilst that was taking place?

COMPLAINANT: Well, after he pulled my underwear down he held my arms down. He pinned my arms down to the bed.

DEFENSE: After he removed your underwear?

COMPLAINANT: Yes.

DEFENSE: Had he touched you before he removed your underwear in any way?

COMPLAINANT: Touched me?

DEFENSE: Before removing your underwear, he hadn't touched you after putting you on the bed, is that so?

COMPLAINANT: Yes.

DEFENSE: Did you say anything to him before your underwear was removed?

COMPLAINANT: Yes.

DEFENSE: What did you say to him?

COMPLAINANT: I told him to stop.

DEFENSE: You just said "Stop," did you, "Stop this," when he was removing his trousers or something.

[Transcript records "No audible reply" from complainant.]

DEFENSE: When did you say "Stop," what was happening then?

COMPLAINANT: When he got on top of me.

DEFENSE: You have already said that he didn't get on top of you before your clothing was removed; that is correct, isn't it?

COMPLAINANT: Yes.

DEFENSE: You first spoke to police about these matters on 9 June last year; is that so?

COMPLAINANT: Yes, I think so.

DEFENSE: You made a statement to [names detective]?

COMPLAINANT: Yes.

DEFENSE: You have gone over that statement before giving evidence for the purpose of refreshing your memory; is that so?

COMPLAINANT: Yes.

DEFENSE: Did your father attempt to kiss you at any stage?

COMPLAINANT: Yes.

DEFENSE: When was that?

COMPLAINANT: When he was laying on top of me.

DEFENSE: Did you say to Detective [names detective] that your father laid on top of you and started to kiss you and took your underpants down after that; in other words, the *sequence* of events that you narrated to [detective] was that your father got on top of you and then took your underpants down; did you say that?

COMPLAINANT: I don't remember saying that.

DEFENSE: Would you have a look please at the second page of that statement; the bottom of that page. *You describe a different sequence of events in your statement, don't you?*

COMPLAINANT: Yes.

DEFENSE: Which is the correct version? Is it the version that you have given this court, or what I have put to you about what you have said to police?

COMPLAINANT: That's the correct version.

DEFENSE: In your statement, is it?

COMPLAINANT: Yes.

DEFENSE: So the sworn evidence you gave a short time ago is not in fact correct, is that right.

[Transcript records "No audible reply" from the complainant.]

DEFENSE: You appreciate the importance of telling the truth, don't you?

COMPLAINANT: Yes.

DEFENSE: You told a *lie* in that statement to police, didn't you?

COMPLAINANT: [Transcript records "No audible reply"]. [emphasis added][35]

The sequence of events regarding the removal of clothing not only provided a means by which to obtain and highlight prior inconsistent statements, but may also have the added impact of confusing a jury and distracting them from the substance of the charges on the presentment. A focus on matters peripheral to the incident promotes a particular kind of specious accuracy which defense barristers know would not be possible for the average person to recall, let alone a complainant recalling peripheral details of an alleged traumatic episode(s) within the artificial environment of a courtroom. Yet an inability to recall such details results in feigned indignation by barristers.

In R v C, minute details were consistently demanded from the child complainant, such as those detailed earlier, regarding how many times she visited the home of a family friend with her own family. Below is another example from the same case of defense questions put to the child about the child's overnight stay at a friend's house, in which the child gave evidence that the father had sexually abused her in the family car on the way over:

> DEFENSE: You say when you first arrived at [friend's] house you started playing a game with [friend] outside?
>
> CHILD: Yes.
>
> DEFENSE: So it was still daylight?
>
> CHILD: Yes.
>
> DEFENSE: Do you know how long it took to get dark that night from the time you first arrived? In other words, how long were you playing before you went inside?
>
> CHILD: Just for a couple of minutes.
>
> DEFENSE: So you played outside for two minutes?
>
> CHILD: Yes.
>
> DEFENSE: What else did you do at [friend's] house from the time you arrived? Let me ask you this. Do you remember eating dinner there?
>
> CHILD: Yes.
>
> DEFENSE: Where did you eat dinner?
>
> CHILD: In the kitchen.
>
> DEFENSE: At a dining table?
>
> CHILD: She had a table but we didn't sit at the table, we sat at where the taps were, she had this long bench.
>
> DEFENSE: Who made the food?
>
> CHILD: Her mum.
>
> DEFENSE: Do you remember how long it took to cook the dinner?
>
> CHILD: No.
>
> DEFENSE: Where was [friend's] father during the time you were eating dinner?
>
> CHILD: I think he was in the house.
>
> DEFENSE: Do you remember what time it was that you went to sleep at [friend's]?
>
> CHILD: It was in the night.
>
> DEFENSE: After you ate dinner, where would you have spent most of your time? In [friend's] room in the TV lounge? Where?
>
> CHILD: Me and [friend] were getting ready to go to bed.
>
> DEFENSE: Do you remember seeing [friend's] father there the night you say you slept over?

CHILD: I don't remember.

DEFENSE: I thought you said earlier he was there?

CHILD: I think he was there but I didn't see him while we were eating dinner.[36]

In this and the earlier example, defense counsel's urging of the child, at previous hearings, to declare a numerical figure of the times she had visited her friend's house and what occurred on one particular visit created precisely the conditions for prior inconsistent statements to be produced and highlighted. These forced errors were then used to attack the witness's credibility and accuse her of being a liar.

It seems obvious that the child would not have any real idea of how many times she has been to her friend's house and precisely who was there each time, but at the trial level it is made central to cross-examination and used to bolster defense claims that the child cannot help but tell lies.

The following is an example from a committal hearing that occurred in 1995 relating to sexual abuse by a man against his two very young stepdaughters. This case did not form part of the trials analyzed, as the offender plea-bargained for a guilty plea after the committal hearing, thus avoiding a trial. The following excerpt elucidates the importance that defense barristers place upon minute details from complainants in pre-trial hearings. The following passage refers to the evidence of one of the complainants from this committal hearing:

DEFENSE: Tell us what happened?

CHILD: Well, he just—I was awake and he called me into his room.

DEFENSE: Had you got up and gone to the toilet before that?

CHILD: Yes.

DEFENSE: Had you remembered to flush the toilet?

CHILD: Yes.

DEFENSE: You had. Are you sure about that?

CHILD: Yes.

DEFENSE: What happened then?

CHILD: He called me and I got out of bed and I went into his room, and he asked me to hop in bed, so I did. And then he started undoing my pajama buttons.

DEFENSE: Undoing your buttons?

CHILD: Yes.

DEFENSE: *How many buttons did you have on your pajamas?*

CHILD: Five or six.

DEFENSE: Did he undo each button?

CHILD: No, he only undid three, I think.

DEFENSE: So you say he undid three buttons; is that right?

CHILD: Yes.

[A short time later in cross-examination.]

DEFENSE: When he put his fingers inside you, did you make any comment?

CHILD: I'm not sure.

DEFENSE: This is the first time we're talking about isn't it?

CHILD: Yes.

DEFENSE: Had you felt anything inside your vagina before?

CHILD: Not that I know of.

DEFENSE: You'd never put anything in your vagina or put your own fingers in your vagina?

CHILD: No, I don't think so.

DEFENSE: So you're sure it actually went inside your vagina, or could you be mistaken about that?

CHILD: No, I'm not sure.

DEFENSE: Are you sure it was two fingers?

CHILD: Not the first time, I'm not sure it was two fingers.

DEFENSE: *How far in your vagina did you feel?* [Referring to accused's fingers penetrating her.]

CHILD: Sometimes it was all the way and sometimes it was *just half.*

DEFENSE: When you say all the way, to there, halfway, half of the fingers?

CHILD: Yes.

DEFENSE: So about two knuckles, is as deep as two knuckles?

CHILD: Yes.

DEFENSE: How many times do you think he would have got his two fingers in as deep as two knuckles?

CHILD: *I don't know.*

DEFENSE: *Can you try, because it's very important?* Would he have got his fingers in as deep as two knuckles once?

CHILD: About three times. [emphasis added][37]

Note, in this example, that the defense barrister was very keen for the complainant—who was only nine years old—to give specific details and to adopt them as her evidence. When the child said that she was not sure about a question, defense counsel encouraged her to give an answer in the positive. The uncritical and crude assumption is that a genuine victim would be able to tell the court just how many fingers and knuckles penetrated a small child's vagina—as though any child or woman should be able to give account of such evidence on demand.

Many of the examples reveal how children and adults, but especially children, often feel obliged in such situations to agree with a proposition that on the surface appears reasonable, or else to provide a detailed answer possibly out of fear that saying they cannot recall or do not know might make them appear less credible. At times, the ridiculousness of such information-seeking might seem obvious, but the fact that it is so aggressively sought from children in these trials suggests it is considered a valuable tactic, especially given the high rate of acquittal in sexual-offense proceedings.

Research on children's memory and recall has shown that children can order simple, familiar events but have difficulty ordering more complex and less familiar incidents. Also, in recalling events, children place more importance on recalling the simple order in which events occurred rather than "peripheral details."[38] Research has shown that children "may disorder the sequence of events but still correctly report that he or she was sexually assaulted."[39] In other words, they may accurately describe the incident but find it very difficult to provide the kinds of miniscule and peripheral details demanded by lawyers. After all children are not skilled in partaking in the kinds of technical and linguistic debates and verbal jousting that frequently occur in legal trials. Adult witnesses find this difficult enough. Lawyers are skilled in the craft of constructing questions to elicit and lead evidence a particular way and skilled in debating technicalities. Children simply do not possess these skills and are easy pickings for lawyers, as are many adult witnesses.

Researchers have also argued that children cannot be expected to remember exact dates of events, and that defense lawyers frequently capitalize on children's difficulty in recalling the sequence and dates of events in order to discredit the child's evidence.[40]

As Goodman and Helgeson point out, most adults would fail the memory recall expected of children, and that the purpose of such questioning was to "demoralize" children and to "wear them out and discredit them."[41] Other psychological research on children's credibility with regard to memory and recall has shown that "children are not in the habit of fantasizing about events that are likely to lead to court proceedings (for example sexual abuse) and may actually be more truthful than adults."[42] Another study argues that children, including very young children, are able to remember and retrieve information about past events, especially when such events are "personally experienced and highly meaningful."[43] Across the transcripts, adult and child complainants were cross-examined about minute and peripheral details. Their inability to recall details, coupled with a belief that not being able to recall or answer might make them appear to be lying about the abuse, their genuine desire to recall all facts and answer all questions itself ensnares them in the traps set by defense tactics. An inability to recall will result in them being berated for not being able to remember such peripheral details that the defense deems "important" facts. Should the complainants recall some of these details, they will be matched against the answer given to the same question at a previous hearing in order to berate them for any inconsistency. The same kinds of peripheral details demanded of children in cross-examination in the trials analyzed for this research have also been reported by Goodman and Helgeson. Questions about the room decor, what time they awoke, what they ate for lunch on the day of the assault, and other minute details are details that adults could not recall, let alone children.[44] This chapter, indeed this book, is replete with legal demands for such minute details.

To reiterate, Goodman and Helgeson cite research that found children as young as three years of age were able to recall correctly central information—that is, the actions performed—but had difficulty with peripheral details, as would most adults.[45] Psychological research indicates that stress and anxiety can affect the ability and willingness to retrieve or recall information and knowledge in people generally. It is only natural other stressful situations such as giving evidence in court can affect a witness.[46] It would hardly need emphasizing that complainants would feel far more stress and anxiety than most other witnesses, given the nature of the crimes they are to give evidence about, and the intimidating and verbally aggressive techniques used by defense barristers. Defense barristers are apparently well aware of this. The hyper-aggressive style of cross-examination exhibited by a number of the defense barristers in these cases is very effective in disrupting testimony, occluding relevant evidence, and undermining the credibility of complainants, both child and adult.

Conclusion

Evidentiary exclusions and constraints placed on complainant evidence, such as isolating one or only a handful of charges from a larger number of incidents, can create major difficulties for complainants in the presentation of their evidence. As demonstrated by the case studies discussed in this book, forced errors are a strategy that defense barristers use with ease as a way to create a negative impression against the complainant and promoting a strong, cohesive impression of the defense rebuttal of the complainant's evidence.

Prior inconsistent statements are a key tool to fill in imposed silences with stock stories of the lying, bad and ungrateful daughter or son. They are constructed with and serve to vindicate patriarchal edicts and theories such as Lord Hale and the need for a corroboration warning, Freud and his concept of the fantasizing child, and John Henry Wigmore and the lying and unstable child. Worse, forced errors and defense narratives imposed upon feelings of pain, injury and abuse open up the possibility of the ever-present seductive child as a "willing" partner to the abuse.

Some of the examples in this chapter highlight levels of unconscionable aggression in cross-examination of complainants and, as discussed in R v G, could be seen to contravene sections 39 and 40 of the *Evidence Act*. Exacerbating these defense tactics is the marked absence of judicial intervention in preventing aggressive and repetitive questioning.

In many examples, prior inconsistent statements were obtained by requiring simple answers and responses to complex and convoluted questions or statements. Complainants are required to agree or disagree with "yes" or "no," numerically commit themselves to specific figures, such as the number of times one visited a friend, the length of time one was penetrated, the time of day, or the specifics of clothing and weather. Long-winded questions and defense statements that read like speeches—with the demand for the shortest possible answer—not only conspire to force prior inconsistent statements, they also promote defense innuendo and inference. Alison Young identifies the defense tactic in which defense barristers ask complex questions of complainants and try to contain the complainant's answer to a simple monologue of "yes" or "no," only to later use these "yes" or "no" answers to support inferences and innuendo that form part of the defense narrative.[47] Conversely, when complainants respond with "I don't know" or "I don't remember" to minutely detailed questions, this too is used to support defense innuendo. In this way, the jury is presented with a deliberately orchestrated series of conversationally dysfunctional responses which can have a cumulative effect on the jury and impact on a subliminal level. The complainant's litany of *forced errors* is very often appositional to the confident evidence of the accused. Moreover, the jury is provided copies of these selected areas of inconsistent evidence so that they may consult them in their deliberations.

Forced errors are a tactic almost solely located among defense counsel, given the limited opportunity for prosecutors to mobilize this tactic. A noticeable difference in the cases where the accused gave evidence concerns not just the lack of questions from both legal counsel asking for specific or minute details, but the frequency with which many of the accused state that they could not remember even relevant details. The accused in case study R v G, for example, responded frequently that he could not remember specific details adding, reasonably, that it was "five years ago."[48] Such reasonableness is not afforded to complainants and their supporting mothers. Their failure to recall the most minute and peripheral detail is considered proof of lying and fabrication.

Concomitant to defense cross-examination using previous transcripts are the complainant responses of "I don't remember" or monosyllabic answers such as "yes" or "no." The jury hears a monologue from the complainant as opposed to a series of questions from the defense which are stated as "evidence" and as "proof." Such tactics can affect the jury unconsciously, as they hear the complainant admit to a litany of "errors" that often remain unqualified, in contrast to the confident questions of the defense that elicit a scripted response.

Prior inconsistent statements occupy a dominant place in the repartee of defense narrative constructions. Forced errors are an efficient conduit for the negative portrayal of complainants. Evidentiary limitations heighten the use of forced errors. A number of trials from the original research, including two of the case studies in this book (in which defense cross-examination drew heavily on prior inconsistent statements and questions demanding minute detail), resulted in acquittals.[49] Adopting the technique of cross-examination in order to demonstrate inconsistencies through *forced errors*, based on peripheral detail, is an effective tool skillfully deployed by barristers.

We have seen the construction of stock stories about daughters and mothers built around dominant stereotypes designed to negate their evidence that such sexual abuse occurred. The effective use of forced errors in constructing witness evidence as partial, confused or inaccurate can help to reinforce the defense narrative that the complainant is simply not credible.

One small measure that would help to reduce the role of forced errors are rules barring defense barristers from being able to cross-examine a complainant at a committal hearing. It is well known among the judiciary and lawyers that committals are used not only as "fishing expeditions" for future forced errors, they are also a legal forum for cajoling and bullying the complainant in the hope they will not proceed any further.[50] There exists some very good anecdotal material relating to complainants either choosing to withdraw from the process after their committal experience or, in the case of children, a parental decision to do so.

The purpose of a committal hearing is for the magistrate to decide on whether the accused person has a case to answer, and this is done through examining the various statements and evidence tendered to the court by the informant. There is no need for a complainant to undergo full cross-examination at this stage, since the magistrate ought to have enough evidence to make a judgment.

Notes

1. Note that such a situation occurred in cases R v A (Victorian County Court, Davey, J. 1995); R v C (Victorian County Court, Spence, J. 1995); R v G (Victorian County Court, Campton, J. 1995); R v J (Victorian County Court, retrial, Campton, J. 1995); R v K (Victorian County Court, Lewis, J. 1994); and R v L (Victorian County Court, Kelly, J. 1993).
2. R v L (Victorian County Court, retrial, Lewis, J. 1996), at 23.
3. Ibid., at 21.
4. Ibid., at 455–6. In several other trials, judges referred to defense lawyers as using a "forensic skill" in relation to identifying prior inconsistent errors and other cross-examination techniques.
5. For some good examples of this see, for example, R v J (retrial, 1995), at 350–8 and 399–407.
6. For example, cases R v J (Victorian County Court, Barnett, J. 1993); R v J (retrial, 1995); R v G (Victorian County Court, O'Shea, J. 1996); R v L (retrial, 1996); and R v N (Victorian County Court, Stott, J. 1995).
7. The time frame between the age of the child or young adult when a particular incident occurred along with the time span between their disclosure of the incident, and then formally making a police statement, and the time between disclosure, police statement and trial can create situations whereby the complainant may recall more details of an incident at the trial that were not in their police statement and vice versa. A reasonable explanation for this may well be that the complainant is forced to rethink and to relive incidents of sexual abuse and in doing so may recall more detail or even forget areas of detail previously noted in counseling files or a police statement. The child's age between alleged incidents of abuse and their disclosure and police statement, and so on, are also significant features that can result in a child not being able to recall some details retold over a period of time. Case R v D (Victorian County Court, White, J. 1995) is a good example. In this case, the child was attacked by the defense barrister in cross-examination for providing information about a specific incident that was not provided in the child's police statement or committal evidence. The child stated that since giving evidence at the committal he had begun to remember things about that specific incident. This response is most reasonable, but was seized upon by the defense to infer that the child was embellishing his evidence and that he was telling "lies." See R v D, trial transcript, 27–8, 49.
8. For example in R v J (retrial, 1995) defense counsel told the jury in his opening address that the complainant would create deliberate breaks in her evidence so that she could have extra time to fabricate her evidence. Considerable evidentiary restrictions in this trial were imposed on the prosecution case and complainant evidence causing the complainant considerable distress in giving her evidence. Similar distress was

Forced Errors 251

noted in other trials and has also been commented on in the Victorian Law Reform Commission, Sexual Offenses Interim Report (June 2003) See 4.21 at 153.

9. For example: R v J (retrial, 1995); R v B (Victorian County Court, Williams, J. 1995); R v C; R v D; and R v L (retrial, 1996).
10. R v J (retrial, 1995), at 325 (5/9/95). At the time of making this comment, the complainant had withstood close to eight days in the witness box. After her cross-examination finished nearly three days later, the jury was discharged and a new trial commenced.
11. R v L (retrial, 1996), at 455–6.
12. R v C, at 74–5.
13. Cases include R v J (retrial, 1995); R v C; R v D; and R v N.
14. See, for example, R v C, at 70–8.
15. R v K, at 186–92.
16. Ibid., at 189.
17. Ibid., at 194–6.
18. Other cases included R v D, R v L (retrial, 1996) and R v J (retrial, 1995).
19. R v G (1996), at 60–7.
20. Ibid., at 66.
21. R v B, at 26.
22. Ibid., at 31–2.
23. Ibid., at 40–1.
24. R v M (Victorian County Court, Dixon, J. 1995).
25. R v B, at 141.
26. R v B, at 47.
27. See Feiner (1997).
28. Ibid.
29. R v A; R v B; R v H (Victorian County Court, Crossley, J. 1995); R v J (1993, and retrial, 1995); R v K; and R v N.
30. R v N, at 40–1.
31. Ibid., at 44–8.
32. R v C, at 31–2.
33. R v N, at 27–8.
34. The complainant in R v J (retrial, 1995) was cross-examined at length about horse shows that she went to with her father over a period of nearly seven years. Defense demanded to know the dates of the shows, the time they arrived, what time the complainant had dinner, what she ate, what she wore, what time she went to bed, and what she wore to bed. Some of these horse shows occurred some eight years prior to the trial in 1995. Even more extraordinary, the complainant was asked in what order did she pack the horse tack into the horse truck for a show that occurred in 1987 and further, in what order did she wash her two horses and how she dried them. When the prosecutor objected to such harassment regarding the relevance of such questions, the trial judge responded that "it might be interesting to learn something" (about horse grooming). See R v J (retrial, 1995), at 182–96 (31/8/98). Note that the jury in this case was discharged and a fifth jury was empanelled before a retrial commenced, leading this time to completion of the case.
35. R v M, at 333–7.
36. R v C, at 34–5.
37. R v AJ (Melbourne Magistrates Court, committal hearing, 1995), at 8 and 15.

38. Goodman and Helgeson (1988), 117.
39. Ibid. See also Paciocco (1996).
40. See Goodman and Helgeson (1988) and also research by McNichol, Shute, & Tucker (1999). This research focused on children's testimony about repeated events, such as in chronic sexual abuse. The authors found that children who experience repeated events had increased recall for details but confused the timing of details across those events such as dates and places.
41. Ibid.
42. See Australian Law Reform Commission and Human Rights and Equal Opportunity Commission, Seen and Heard: Priority for Children in the Legal Process, ALRC 84 (Canberra: Human Rights and Equal Opportunity Commission, 1997), 305.
43. Ibid., 307.
44. See Goodman and Helgeson (1988). These authors highlight defense cross-examination questions that demand children to provide evidence of the decor of the room in which they allege abuse, the clothing they and/or the accused wore, what they ate for lunch or dinner on that particular day, even if the day in question goes back a number of years.
45. See Goodman and Helgeson (1988), 15.
46. Ibid., 118.
47. See Young (1998).
48. R v G (retrial, 1996), at 219.
49. R v A; R v B; R v D; R v G (1996); and R v N.
50. Schmitz (1988) and Blanchfield (1996).

8 ▪ Case Studies Analysis

Introduction

THIS CHAPTER BRIEFLY draws out the structural and thematic patterns found across the four case studies, as well as drawing upon other cases included in the original research to better demonstrate the breadth and depth of legal narratives. Following the introduction, the chapter is organized into twelve sections corresponding to these twelve thematic narratives.

As discussed in chapter 2, "Telling Legal Tales," defense narratives were governed by two broad aims: to present a story-line that inferred *motive* and *means*, with various sub-themes within these two frameworks. Narratives mobilizing a motive story-line are designed to explain why a child or stepchild of the accused would *invent* their allegations. To this end, revenge, collusion, mental instability and greed were introduced and tended to situate the complainant in the "bad" or "mad" daughter category. Occasionally complainants are situated across variations of both themes. Very often highly selective facts or incidents are taken from the complainant's life and used to bolster this motive narrative. Sometimes the behavior of the child—and possibly the trauma induced as a result of sexual abuse—was used against them.

Defense narratives of "motive" are most often complemented with a narrative of "means." In the presentation of their defense, counsel mobilized an "explanation" as to how the complainant, especially child and adolescent complainants, could have such an explicit knowledge and vocabulary with regards to the sexual violence alleged against their father or stepfather. These explanations centered on sex education, proximity to others who may possess certain sexual knowledge, influential mediums (such as literature, television and media) and, in some cases, a creative interest in writing poetry.[1]

These legal narratives are modeled on dominant hegemonies surrounding sexual violence—particularly the negative positioning of child and women victims of sexual violence—and afford a legal springboard at the pre-trial level from which to launch these narratives and eradicate any initial opposition.

These narratives continue to enjoy success because of the degree of sexism, prejudice and social myths surrounding intrafamilial sexual abuse mobilized among professional groups and still held within society. Very few reported sex offenses make it to court, and fewer result in a successful conviction. [2] If these defense narratives had no power to sway a jury they would not be so well developed and expertly deployed within a legal setting.

Section I
Judicial Discretion: Trial by Attrition

The crucial development of stock-story narratives begins at the pre-trial level where evidentiary boundaries are delineated. Constructing victims around stock stories of sexual violence could not be perpetuated in the courtroom without judicial complicity.[3] The degree of personal latitude implicit within the judiciary facilitates judicial discretion that has wide-ranging implications for the manner in which trials can be conducted.

The lack of judicial consistency in applying crucial legislation specifically designed to curb demeaning and unwarranted attacks on the sexual character of complainants is a significant factor across all the trials. So is the lack of consistency toward crucial collateral evidence supporting prosecution cases. Moreover, judges are well aware how their evidentiary parameters, especially the removal of evidence, encourage the promulgation of stock-story narratives and can create strong doubt in jurors merely by confusing them. An exemplary indication of this judicial awareness was provided by the judge in R v B who admitted that his evidentiary rulings had caused a child to become "confused." Without any apparent discomfort or sense of irony this same judge informed legal counsel that they should bear in mind "that with a different judge on a different day, all this evidence might have been let in…"[4]

Such self-acknowledgment of personal preference in the application of evidentiary rules negates the self-styled mantle of law as a process of neutrality and of fact-finding. Evan Whitton's concept of trial by voodoo springs to mind when considering the judicial discretion to position evidence within— or wholly exclude it from—a trial around the personal whims or prejudices of the judge.

The following deals with various structural patterns in evidentiary rulings found in the case studies as well as from the original research.

COLLATERAL EVIDENCE

A critical reading of the transcripts reveals a fairly well-orchestrated attempt to target prosecution evidence for either complete exclusion or strong modification. We saw the obliteration of DNA evidence in case study R v G, and how it advanced the defense narrative of fabrication by the complainant. Dismissing this kind of evidence was not an isolated event. In another case from the original research, DNA samples obtained from the accused, his daughter (who was the complainant in the case), and her three children revealed the accused to be the biological father of two of his grandchildren.[5] At trial this evidence was excluded, paving the way for defense counsel to accuse the complainant of promiscuous sex with other males who fathered her children.

Two case studies revealed prosecution evidence of alleged admissions of sexual abuse by the accused. Prosecution sought to use this as collateral evidence. In the original research, four additional cases also involved evidence of alleged admissions by the accused. They were either wholly excluded or modified prior to being presented to the jury.

In R v EF, the social worker's evidence was completely removed. In R v G, the results of DNA testing profiling the donor of the semen was excluded. In R v L, the counselor's evidence was removed by a clever legal sleight of hand, enabling the judge to tell the jury the trial was one without any corroborating evidence for the complainant.

SEXUAL INNUENDO AND SEXUAL HISTORY IN PLACE OF FACTS

Another pattern in evidentiary rulings pertained to the previous sexual history of the child or adult complainant. Despite the introduction of Victorian legislation (s.37a) designed to curb the legal preference for positioning child and women rape complainants as sexually promiscuous, the intended efficacy of this legislation has not been actualized.[6]

The appalling treatment of the complainant in case study R v G on the topic of her real and supposed previous sexual history is just one horrific indication of the very real propensity for legal trials to become legally sanctioned abuse. Three judges were appointed to this trial, and all three interpreted the legislation differently. This led to diametrically opposed rulings—the latter two of which had the ability to affect the tenor and focus of the trial.

In other cases, defense cross-examination of the complainant was met with scant objection by prosecutors. In a number of cases (where it was not obvious from the transcript that permission for such questioning had been granted), prosecutors seemed either oblivious to or did not recognize these breaches in evidentiary procedure. A similar finding has been found in recent research on rape trials in Victorian courts. British lawyer Jennifer Temkin also critically examines this area of evidence in contemporary sexual offense trials.[7]

One obvious feature characterizing evidential procedure was the judicial power to interpret the legislation consistent with the judge's own masculinist mindset about children and women alleging sexual violence. At times, defense barristers were able to introduce questions about the sexual history of the complainant through a "back-door entry."

In cases where alleged sexual abuse resulted in either an abortion or birth, the false stories their father/stepfather had primed them to tell mothers and medical authorities were then used to attack their credibility on two grounds. Firstly, complainant's admission that the original story was false was used to inflame a view of the complainant as adept at fabricating lies. Secondly, such admissions enabled the introduction of a narrative of casual sex with another or other unnamed male(s) who were actually responsible for the pregnancy. The complainant's alleged public story to protect herself and the offender is used against her at the trial in a doubly damning way.

This narrative scenario was played out in case study R v L, and in several other trials in the original research, causing considerable distress to the complainants. In one case, the complainant gave birth to children by her biological father and was duly attacked by defense counsel for "lying" on her single parent pension form by not recording who the father really was. To complete this humiliation, defense counsel had the complainant in this case legally *warned* her evidence could be used in order to have her indicted for criminal conduct with regards to her "lying" about the true paternity of her children.[8]

Society's double standards of the sexually active male as a "stud" and the sexually active female as a "slut" remain firmly entrenched in the social psyche. That it is trotted out with eloquent timing and disturbing efficiency in sex offense proceedings indicates its value as a weapon of destruction. Complainants, but also supporting mothers, were routinely portrayed as sexually loose women who *tainted* the minds and lives of their children and caused marital discord.

In those cases where the sexual history (or knowledge of sex) of the complainant and, where applicable, their supporting mother, was made central to cross-examination, the jury acquitted.[9] In cases where the canvassing of the sexual character of the complainant was allowed, the actual charges supposedly under investigation are either lost under the weight of interrogation and scrutiny of the child or adult complainant, or the interrogation itself negates the testimony *allowed* to be given by the complainant about the charges.

HEARING CHARGES IN A DE-CONTEXTUALIZED VACUUM

Another favored evidentiary limitation concerned de-contextualizing the environment in which the child or young adult complainant experienced the alleged abuse. This was especially apparent in cases of long-term sexual abuse, and the modus operandi of defense construction of the complainant in such cases has been well elucidated by Leslie Feiner.[10] Evidentiary rules that limit and exclude a complainant's evidence can have a devastating impact on the prosecution case, as Feiner has argued, by deliberately creating narrative gaps in the child's evidence. Such rules also affect the emotional well-being of complainants, causing them to give fragmented and disjointed evidence.[11]

Eroding and weakening prosecution evidence provides stock-story narratives with an artificial platform of power. Feiner paid particular attention to the legal practice of erosion and obfuscation in several cases involving allegations of long-term father-daughter rape.[12] These gaps are filled in with a type of narrative defense putty that ties them neatly to a stock-story narrative while fragmenting the evidence of the complainant.

This de-contextualization is particularly evident around delayed disclosure and behavior by complainants considered inconsistent with their allegations. An evidentiary inability to tell the court the reasons why the complainant was so fearful of the accused, and why they behaved as they did, enables an alternative defense narrative to easily overpower the legally vitiated evidence given by the child. This deliberate fragmentation of the complainant's evidence causes untold distress and frustration to those who come into contact with the legal system in sexual-offense proceedings.[13]

"Relationship evidence"—evidence involving the kind of relationship the complainant experienced with the accused—including evidence of threats, coercion, fear, exertion of control and surveillance over the child/adult leading to them not to disclose or flee from the abuse for some time is excluded. Explicit examples were found in my original research of judges dismissing prosecution attempts to include such evidence.

TRIAL BY OBFUSCATION

The subterfuge that often results from evidentiary rulings is not foreign to judges. In many instances, judges were often quick to articulate their recognition of the burgeoning narrative that was being developed within their judicial scope of evidentiary rulings. Worse, judges were obviously comfortable to sit and listen to defense narratives known to be misleading and, at times, manifestly inaccurate. As we saw in case study R v L, the judge was aware that much of the defense case would be on the basis of "trial by obfuscation," and informed the jury the charges under consideration had a marked absence of any corroborating evidence. In case study R v G, the complainant was interrogated about previous intrafamilial sexual abuse that legal counsel knew to be true, but the girl was frequently referred to as a liar about this information. She was further accused of unprotected sex with a male to explain the presence of semen at the time of the alleged offense by her father, while judge and legal counsel from both sides knew that the evidentiary absence of compelling DNA evidence gave life to this particular narrative.

At times, some judges even gave hints as to how the tactic might be better amplified, or made more effective, as discussed in case study R v L and in chapter 7, "Forced Errors."

CORROBORATION WARNINGS

Feminist legal scholars have examined how legal *warnings* concerning the untrustworthiness of a woman's or child's evidence in sexual offense trials was codified in eighteenth-century law, and continues to be a mainstay in contemporary legal proceedings. Jocelynne Scutt has detailed the relationship between psychiatry and law to promote the corroboration warning. This relationship is grounded in scientific claims about the female capacity to fabricate false allegations of rape and sexual assault.[14]

Across trials, judges provided jury "warnings" about the need for independent corroboration (as discussed fully in case study R v L). Attempts to reform corroboration warning legislation in view of its recognized gender discrimination have amounted to little more than tinkering at the edges, and even these have met with judicial resistance.[15] Of concern is the real danger some judges face when they choose *not* to give a corroboration warning in sex offense trials on the basis it is not merited, either in terms of precedent or legislation, only to have a successful conviction quashed on appeal for failing to provide such a warning. Conversely, a jury conviction can be quashed if a corroboration warning was not "worded" strongly enough. Examples of both instances were found in my original research. Of deeper concern is a recent Australian High Court Appeal claiming a *blanket warning* should be given in every sex offense trial, regardless of corroborating evidence.[16]

Section II
Psychoanalysis, Psychiatry, and Judicial Lore

Defense patterns in thematic structure and narrative design across the four case studies and other trials from the original research reveal the centrality of dominant psychosocial theories of intrafamilial child sexual abuse in legal discourse.[17] Dominant psychosocial theories translate into dominant social hegemonies, and are typified by stereotypes and social myths about "incest" and child sexual abuse. Using legal forums to tell and re-tell stock-story narratives, with scant regard for facts, allows the law, as a locus of social influence and control, to replicate and perpetuate the dominant order of the socially and culturally powerful. It further reaffirms gender dominance and gender stereotypes which are, on both fronts, detrimental to women and children, and discriminatory to their status as citizens of equal worth in society.

Freudian orthodoxy—with its belief that disclosures of "incest" are based on fantasy and a sexual desire by the child for sexual contact with the parent—has exerted considerable influence in professional and social discourses, and has been positively embedded in legal doctrine and discourse. Complementing Freudian psychoanalysis is family dysfunction theory. With its emphasis on "incest" as a product of dysfunctional families, it is self-blind to the all too often fact that "incest" occurs in families considered "normal" and "functional."

Like Freudian psychoanalysis, family dysfunction theory has influenced the legal response to intrafamilial sexual abuse.[18] Indeed in some respects, they are virtually the same "theory": both thematically position children and woman as fantasizers and sexual provocateurs. Family dysfunction theory makes it safe to *admit* "incest" occurred for the theory holds that children and their mothers are responsible for the abuse, while exculpating the offender from full responsibility.

Like a theoretical tag team, these two masculinist theoretical models are often mobilized in legal narratives in tandem. At the trial level, defense narratives promote fantasy and imagination by the complainant, alongside a narrative of revenge, collusion or greed. Trials resulting in a jury conviction lead to narrative of minimal harm, at times victim culpability, and the role of the mother as a causative agent.

Trials are liberally peppered with judicial banter both in the presence and absence of juries about colluding mothers and children's imaginations. In case study R v G, one judge commented that mothers and daughters work together as co-agents in all sorts of things. In R v L, R v A, R v B, R v C, and R v K explicit reference to mother-child collusion was a feature in cross-examination and judicial comments. In R v C, and the first trial of R v L, the judge commented on the role of "imagination" in possibly creating complainant's false belief of sexual abuse. In R v A, in the absence of the jury, the judge and defense barrister discussed the defense narrative that the child's allegations were "implanted" "in her mind" by the child's mother, and that the child's natural "imagination" enabled her to make a statement to the police of oral and vaginal penetration as well as aggravated sexual assaults.[19]

The patriarchal status quo of families was frequently regurgitated and reaffirmed across trials, as fathers were given a veritable library of excuses that contextually situated their criminal behavior as one induced by external stresses most often triggered by the conduct of wives. Harm to victims is minimized, and the victim is often circumscribed by legal edicts affirming them as culpable. In R v M, the judge considered the complainant as "equally guilty" for her father's long-term sexual abuse—insofar as the alleged "incest" really did occur. The prosecutor concurred with this "equally guilty" view of the complainant.[20] In fact, the Appellate Judges in the first Appeal Decision of R v L commented that "incest" was a charge "easily made," and one which immediately inculpates the child as a co-offender to the crime.[21]

Far from these stereotypes being mere vestigial cultural remnants, they continue to exert considerable legal influence. Scratch the surface of public opinion on child sexual abuse and stereotypes about sexual abuse, and victim-blaming comes to the fore.[22] Legal narratives continue to promote the fantasizing child, blame the victim, and minimize harm because of their propensity to appeal to jurors and judges alike. The stories appeal to deep-seated prejudices rather than fact, and conform to deeply entrenched beliefs reflecting the surface order of gender relationships and stereotypes.

I want to move on now to narratives mobilized by defense barristers structured around the two rubrics of "motive" and "means" and their subcategories.

Section III
Motive

THE BAD DAUGHTER NARRATIVE

The "bad" child narrative was mobilized in each of the four case studies, with the "bad" and "mad" daughter narrative operating alongside each other in case study R v G. In the first trial of case study R v L, a "bad/mad" narrative was also explicitly used. However, only the "bad" daughter narrative was concentrated on at the retrial.

REVENGE

Revenge against the father as a motive for complainants to make false allegations of sexual abuse was mobilized in case studies R v D, R v L, and R v G. It was also identified in seven other cases from the original study.[23] Most often the advertised motive was a child's dislike of her or his father/stepfather related to discipline, and vague claims of unresolved angst from childhood or adolescence. In a couple of cases involving adult complainants, the revenge narrative was alleged to have stemmed from a monetary or property dispute with parents, leading to false allegations. What should be noted is that, in nearly all of these cases, compelling collateral evidence supporting complainants was either completely obliterated from the trial or modified.

REVENGE AND COLLUSION

Seeking revenge against a father for perceived wrongs, especially where there was a marital breakdown of some kind, was a prominent theme. This was certainly the case in all four case studies, and could also be identified in five other cases from the original research.[24] A popular defense stratagem in promoting a narrative of collusion was to construct the mother and her marital relationship by proxy, through cross-examination of her child/children in particular. Capitalizing on the natural naivety of children, defense counsel portrayed the mother in damaging ways. Younger children appeared to be cross-examined much more about supposed marital disharmony than older children. Perhaps defense counsel felt that a younger child would be less guarded in talking about "fights" between their parents, and more pliable to defense assertions about mum not getting on with dad. This was especially the case in case studies R v D and R v EF, and was also put to use very aggressively through the cross-examination of children in two other cases.[25] In those cases, defense stereotypes of the greedy, vengeful and colluding mother were played out with stark antipathy.

Very often, the mother's positive relationship with her child was juxtaposed with marital discord. In doing so, the concept of collusion need not be explicitly highlighted in cross-examination. The implicit suggestion is that the mother's preference was to support her child over her husband as part of a plan of collusion.[26] Case R v L was an exemplary case of implied collusion becoming explicit in the defense narrative only at the closing stages of the trial. An initial admission by the complainant that her mother "disliked" the accused was later translated to a "malevolent" mother who had "influence" over her daughter and therefore might be considered a "motive" for the jury to consider.

Another example of this same tactic is found in R v C. The mother was cross-examined about marital disharmony and separation from her husband after her child's disclosures. Defense counsel was seeking to suggest that the allegations were fabricated so as to provide the mother—who was from a particularly strict religious background—with an excuse to leave her marriage. In cross-examination, two fairly innocuous questions are put to the mother:

DEFENSE: Your relationship with [husband/accused], you started having marital problems?

MOTHER: Yes, sir, we did.

DEFENSE: Your parents didn't like [husband/accused] very much?

MOTHER: No. My parents they loved my husband like a son....[27]

In this excerpt, the child's maternal grandparents come into the narrative frame, just as occurred in case study R v D (although here the questions are put to the mother, not the child).

While summarizing defense counsel's case in his charge to the jury, the judge noticed how the mother's marital problems with her husband formed a very large part of the defense narrative of revenge and mother/child collusion, but played no such role in the trial:

> Mr. (Defense) did not try to pull the wool over our eyes, or anything—he said we cannot point to a specific motive but, in a family setting and with a young girl, who can see into her mind, as he put it, as to what *motive* there may be to in some way *support her mother or perhaps get even with the father...because there is not a specific motive do not assume that there is not a motive.* [emphasis added][28]

The stereotype of a mother and child working together is often promoted in legal narratives and judicial comment. While the jury obviously rejected this assertion in R v L, recall that at sentencing the judge aligned the mother as a mitigating factor so the narrative enjoyed some success.

BADNESS AND GREED

Revenge was also linked to greed, and was activated mostly through a discourse surrounding applications for crimes compensation (as noted explicitly in case study R v L). In many cases, a careful juxtaposition of topics was used to strengthen and make clear links in the defense narrative. For example, highlighting the unemployment of complainants alongside their crimes compensation application occurred in case study R v L and one other case. Other cases linked monetary greed to plans by complainants to advance their education, or help their mother with home improvements. In several other cases, a futuristic desire of the child or unfulfilled wish was linked to a crimes compensation application. As shown in case study R v L, the judge was alert to the mobilization of this narrative in embryonic form and it was certainly present in other trials. Explicit use of crimes compensation applications to suggest or make outright accusations of a motive of fiscal gain occurred in eight cases.[29]

A defense narrative of greed as a motive may elicit support from a jury since there has become an increasing tendency in public discourse to associate allegations of sexual abuse with monetary gain.[30]

BADNESS AND THE SEXUALLY PROMISCUOUS

In case study R v G, the defense narrative clearly imputed sexual promiscuity to the complainant. Her homelessness, living on her "wits" on the street, and her frequent sex with her former boyfriend and other males were used to portray a teenage sexual provocateur. In several other cases from the original research, there was a strong focus on the sexual conduct of the complainants to portray them as irresponsible and unsavory in sexual character.

In 2002 I sat through a trial of child sexual abuse where the defense strategy was also one of projecting an image of young teenage sexual promiscuity. After cross-examination, defense counsel told a senior member of the police force they were "happy" to have successfully "portrayed the (complainant) for the little slut they [sic] are."[31]

In a recent case of intrafamilial sexual abuse, defense counsel successfully argued that the teenage complainant no longer be allowed to give her evidence via close circuit television on the basis that the girl had been seen outside of the court dressed in what he considered a "provocative" manner, and demanded, successfully, that the jury be exposed to her style of dress, among other things.[32]

Imputing sexual promiscuity and other negative features of a complainant's sexual character advances a defense narrative of a sexually experienced girl: an individual with not only the *means* to make explicit allegations but the unsavory character to make false accusations for all manner of reason, or even no identifiable reason at all.[33]

THE MAD DAUGHTER NARRATIVE

The "mad" daughter narrative was rarely used in isolation but either complemented the "bad" daughter narrative, or was the leading narrative with the "bad" daughter narrative playing a supporting role.

DOUBLE MADNESS

Case study R v G positioned the girl as sharing the same mental pathology with her mother, but at the same time inferred an individual madness—as though defense counsel were keen to hedge their narrative bets both ways. In the first trial of case study R v L, both mother and daughter were positioned as separately, but mentally unstable, as well as bad. In both cases the mothers were fully supportive of their daughter's allegations resulting in a relentless and extremely hostile cross-examination of both.

Case study R v G is probably the clearest example where supposed mental instability was used as a tool with almost no limitation on its application, despite lack of tangible evidence. Madness and badness were linked to two levels of collusion: deliberate collusion for revenge, and collusion facilitated by mental illness.

INDIVIDUAL MADNESS

In case study R v G, the first trial of case study R v L, and two other trials from the original research, complainants were portrayed as being mentally unstable, and this was used to justify a narrative of motive. No medical evidence was provided to support such claims, yet such narratives were advanced either by way of inference or explicit comments.

Sometimes these claims hung on highlighting certain behaviors by the complainant as symptoms of madness. Some of these behaviors were obviously trauma linked. It is distressing to see child and adult complainants emotionally bludgeoned for their "bizarre" behavior when their behavior is at least partially the *result* of such alleged abuse and cannot, then, be used to *undermine* allegations of abuse. But uncircumscribed by context, their behavior neatly fits the masculinist paradigm of mentally unstable children and young adults accusing their father of rape and abuse. On some occasions, even the most innocuous behaviors, such as having a palm reading or seeking help from a hypnotherapist, were woven into a defense narrative of mental instability.

Counseling received by complainants was also used to suggest an already unstable mind or, at the very least, grounds to argue that their counseling had *convinced* them of sexual abuse when no such thing had occurred. In one case the complainant was accused of actually adopting someone else's story of sexual abuse, given her own unstable mental condition.[34]

MADNESS AND THE VICTORIAN MADWOMAN

While not explicitly suggesting mental illness, several barristers imputed the susceptibility of child complainants to somehow create or adopt fantasized sexual encounters with their fathers. At times defense barristers put to children that they somehow *wrongly* came to *really believe in their own minds* they had been sexually abused when in fact they had not. Given the historical momentum of research detailing how susceptible children are to falsely believing they have been sexually abused, and the unreliability of children who allege sexual abuse, such a line of narrative development is hardly surprising.

Not unlike the Victorian Madwoman[35]—better known as the "hysteric"—many female complainants, especially young adult women, are situated as unstable hysterics, and their emotional distress is often used against them.[36]

As though to hedge their bets, it was not unusual for defense counsel to suggest multiple motives. In case study R v G, it was a confluence of mental illness and revenge against a father who divorced the complainant's mother. At the first trial of case study R v L, it was mental illness and mother-daughter collusion to exact revenge for a failed marriage. Similar confluence between mental instability and another form of motive were found in other trials from the original research.[37]

Section IV
Means

Across the case studies, children and adult complainants were portrayed as using both crude and ingenious methods of getting appropriate knowledge to "cobble together," as one barrister put it,[38] the classical tale of intrafamilial rape and sexual assault. Ranging across a continuum, recent exposure to a person or persons, media, film, or television were the favored "means" for accessing knowledge to help fabricate stories of explicit of sexual violence.

PROXIMITY

Proximity to others was a much-used stratagem to explain a child's knowledge of such sexual scenarios. Complainants knowing other children or adults who had also alleged sexual abuse was a prime defense tactic, and has been canvassed in some of the case studies reviewed in this book.[39] It was a frequent narrative scenario across trials. For example, in the case R v K, the defense barrister was explicit in suggesting that the adolescent had "acquired" knowledge about sexual abuse through his contact with a school friend who had also allegedly been sexually abused. Memorized details, not reality, gave rise to contrived allegations against his father.[40]

School playgrounds and social contact with other children seems to be a particularly interesting area for defense barristers to shore up their narrative of means, and appears to have judicial recognition. Often the preferred legal narrative of children obtaining explicit sexual details from social contact with other girls outweighs the lone voice of the child.[41] A dominant stock-story narrative is too strong against the voice of a child.

On occasions, the mother, according to defense counsel, was the culprit for providing her children with access to sexual knowledge, either through sex education or her own real or fantasized sexual life. Case study R v G is one example of a defense narrative situating the mother as partly responsible for her daughter's allegations; other trials revealed this even more strongly.[42]

Several children were asked about sex education or other human development studies received at home or at school—as though learning about human development and reproduction leads to false allegations of being raped and assaulted in a myriad of ways by one's father or stepfather.[43] Association with community groups who provide support for survivors of abuse was targeted, as detailed in case study R v G. Like a ready-made template, questions on the "means" of accessing sexual knowledge were replicated across trials.

CREATIVITY

Creativity was another popular explanation in the defense narrative stakes surrounding means. Indeed, it appears that prizes for creativity ought to go to some defense counsel given the imaginative ways they accused children of fabricating false allegations.

Creativity Type A: Literature, Television, and Media. Three complainants, including the complainant from case study R v L, were quizzed on ever having read any literature on child sexual abuse. Notably, feminist literature was targeted in two trials, with defense counsel explicitly arguing that complainants got their "knowledge" to fabricate allegations of child sexual abuse from such literature.[44] Even access to newspaper articles on child abuse, or television programs featuring child abuse, were raised as sources used by children to concoct explicit allegations of vaginal, oral and anal rape.[45] It seems even the possibility of watching a romantic movie containing sexualized scenarios of forbidden sex was material for defense counsel narratives of fabrication.[46] A preference for writing poetry was used on a couple of occasions to suggest that an interest in constructing prose and writing stories based on fantasy was directly related to an ability to construct stories of father-daughter rape. In such cases, defense counsel cross-examined child complainants about creative writing and linked it explicitly to the child complainants' allegations:

DEFENSE: Witness, as I understand it, you write some poetry?

CHILD: Yes, I do.

DEFENSE: When you are writing poetry, do you start off with an idea and then develop words around an idea?

CHILD: Yes, I'll pick a subject and then I'll write about it.

DEFENSE: And of course, some of those subjects would be fantasy?

CHILD: Fantasies?

DEFENSE: Yes, not reality.

CHILD: Yes, they would be yes.

DEFENSE: Do you draw them from just things that float through your mind?

CHILD: Whatever I'm thinking at the time I guess.

DEFENSE: I see. And then you get the idea, then you construct the story as it goes; is that the way you do it?

CHILD: Um, it's not really a story like a storybook, it's just a poem that rhymes.

DEFENSE: I see. Have you written stories of—I suppose you would have at school.

CHILD: Yes, in school, yes.

DEFENSE: And that's what you have done in relation to the event that you have alleged in this case, isn't it?

CHILD: No.

DEFENSE: Create a story.

CHILD: No.[47]

A similar accusation was put to the sibling of a complainant in another trial.[48] Standing legal commentary promoting an over-active "imagination" of children in these types of cases reveals why highlighting a child's creative skills can be advantageous to defense narratives. Recently, skills on the Internet were also alluded to as a possible "means" by which a child could access readily available child sex abuse information to help fabricate allegations.[49]

Creativity Type B: Professional Influence. Sometimes a person's profession, or interest in a profession or discipline, was enough to give complainants trouble if they dared allege sexual abuse. Several complainants were quizzed on their professional training and/or occupation, which was then used to suggest an avenue for the *means* to make false allegations.[50] Case studies revealed mothers as not immune to this strategy either; in R v G, the mother's nursing background was explicitly linked to her alleged mental disorder.[51]

Creativity Type C: Access to Therapeutic Counseling. Therapeutic intervention by way of counseling for alleged sexual abuse was another area from which to promulgate a defense narrative around means. This strategy was found in four cases from the original research, and is detailed in case study R v EF. Obtaining private counseling records to go on "fishing expeditions" is not only legally recognized, but routinely used in the hope of gleaning any information that may help barristers develop their master narrative to impose on the complainant. Examples of this were detailed in case studies R v G and

R v EF and other trials studied. Indeed, a plethora of research reveals the heavy reliance on using counseling files to discredit complainants in sexual-offense proceedings.[52] Despite the legal rhetoric, scant regard is often given to the emotional and psychological impact this can have on complainants.

A FUTURISTIC SCENARIO ON CREATIVITY?

Some years ago, a slight moral panic arose after it was revealed that some children had asked questions about a certain bear who appeared on a daily children's show, *Here's Humphrey*. Humphrey B. Bear has been on television screens in Australia for more than two decades wearing his usual colorful vest and tie. It seems some children had begun to ask why Humphrey was not wearing any trousers, and there was some consternation among media, parents and other interest groups as to whether Humphrey ought to be properly dressed, since children had noticed he wore a vest but no trousers. (No one apparently thought to respond to this whole affair by reminding the public that bears do not wear vests and ties, let alone trousers.)

While the story is good for raising a giggle and acknowledging a child's eye for detail, I could not help but wonder whether Humphrey might soon somehow find his way into a scenario of "means." Would a lawyer someday assert a child's allegation of a father without trousers was simply a "Humphrey B. Bear confusion"? Elsewhere, Australian television in the early part of the 1990s featured a show simply called *Sex*. Again, fearing I might be thought paranoid if I made my thoughts public, I wondered how long it would be before defense lawyers in child sexual abuse cases started cross-examining child witnesses on their exposure to this television show. I just hope these ditties do not give any ideas to defense lawyers who might be reading this book. If documentaries and television films can be woven into the narrative of *means*, no doubt Humphrey and his missing trousers and the provocative *Sex* show also can.

Section V
Constructing Mothers

MOTHERS WHO SUPPORTED THEIR CHILDREN

Across the four case studies, complainants were supported in their allegations by their mother. However, in case study R v D, the mother gave no evidence at the trial. The narrative of mother-child collusion was still deployed in each of these cases and was grounded in pre- and post-divorce discord. Supporting mothers were often portrayed through discriminatory stereotypes, either as colluders to their child/children's allegations, or as women of unsavory character. Either way, the narrative scenarios are designed to negate the credibility of the mother, and at the same time vitiate the credibility of her child's own evidence.

This narrative stance is replete in psychosocial literature on child sexual abuse and has made a natural progression into dominant legal discourse. Within an adversarial environment, the mother is regarded as colluding with her child/children against her (ex-)husband, especially where there is any evidence of marital disharmony, no less divorce or custody dispute. This form of collusion is also receiving growing support from the therapeutic environment.[53] Louise Armstrong has also noted the legal punishment meted out to mothers who support their child's/children's disclosure of alleged sexual abuse.[54] Lafree & Reskin conducted research on jurors' responses to victims in rape cases and found conservative jurors assigned little credibility to women whose behavior violated stereotypical notions of "proper" female behavior.[55]

Ultimately, in the narratives constructed by defense barristers, and most often supported by judges, women who believe and support their children against their husbands can expect to be attacked with impunity and punished for challenging the actions and authority of men. The audacity to believe their children above their husbands is a clear sign of their misguided defiance—a denigration and defilement of themselves as women, mothers and wives.

On the other hand, a noticed difference occurred in case study R v EF. It might be that the traditional role of the mother within her family and her traditional adherence to her culture actually bolstered her credibility against the defense narrative of mother-child collusion. Supplementing this point is another case that involved allegations by two girls of long-term sexual abuse by their biological father. They too came from a traditional non-English-speaking background and, like the mother in R v EF, the mother in this case adhered to traditional cultural edicts regarding her role in the family. When her children disclosed the alleged sexual abuse, she separated from her husband and gave evidence for her daughter (in this case, separate trials were also ordered) prompting defense counsel to infer mother-child collusion as a result of marital discord.[56]

While defense counsel promoted mother-child collusion in each case, the mother's character was free from the kinds of attacks found in other cases. From the jury's perspective, the mother's separation from her husband occurred only after disclosure, and it might be that her position in a non-Anglo ethnic group enhanced a view of her as a serious, sincere woman who had nothing personal to gain from giving evidence against her husband.

NON-SUPPORTING MOTHERS

Family dysfunction literature would have us believe that "incest" simply does not occur in families where the mother's presence is ubiquitous. In two of the trials from the original research, mothers who supported their husband against their daughter and gave evidence at the trial, were keenly portrayed by defense counsel as "homemakers," ever present in the home.[57] The logic governing these cases is that a mother's presence is equated with a kind of symbolic omniscience ensuring an ever-present mother would witness any alleged misconduct—a point suggested in family dysfunction literature. In one case during cross-examination of the complainant, defense highlighted how her mother "always" spent Sundays in the kitchen "baking for the family." Other evidence strongly promoted the mother as a dutiful housewife and homemaker. In another case, evidence led from the mother showed her as the ideal patriarchal model of a mother and wife. Her evidence portrayed her as a mother dedicated to domestic duties and childcare, arranging her days to allow her to *always* be at home before school, after school and in the evening.

These mothers contrast with the portrayal of supporting mothers who worked in the public sphere (unless it was to provide for a struggling family), who argued with and separated from their husbands, who took medication, who attended counseling, and most of all, who believed their children. Like Lafree & Reskin's research, mothers who supported their husband as opposed to their child were portrayed as women whose conduct respected "proper" female roles and behavior. While neither the supporting nor non-supporting mothers in these cases were primary victims, the comparison between these women and jurors' attitudes toward adult women in rape trials is worth highlighting. This is especially noteworthy given that those mothers who supported their husbands against their daughters were portrayed positively in terms of conservative and traditional stereotypes of the "good wife" and "good mother." Those who supported their children were portrayed in terms of the "bad" and "mad" narratives. Whether providing or denying support for their children, the construction, deconstruction or destruction of the mother's character is a critical narrative skill.

Section VI
Sentencing Patterns

CONSTRUCTION AFTER CONVICTION

A reading of trial transcripts reveals a change in tempo with regard to the legal construction of the complainant who can now be legally regarded a "victim" as a result of a jury conviction. Portrayal of the victim does not cease, but rather is transmuted to another narrative encompassing concepts of mitigation, intimation of harm, blame diffusion and, of course, the good father narrative. A jury conviction simply forces defense barristers to develop a post-conviction narrative—a narrative that once again lends itself to some of the dominant trends in masculinist literature on intrafamilial sexual abuse.

A jury conviction marks another beginning in the legal process and narrative construction, rather than an end to it. A jury acquittal, however, is never open to challenge. The complainant cannot plead their case in the hope that "a *different* judge on a *different* day" may well have led to a different outcome. For them, an acquittal is the end.

A characteristic of perpetrator convictions and appeals is a persistent narrative construction by defense barristers that mitigates victim suffering and apportions blame to wives, and other external factors. Research by Mitra, Edwards and Scutt is consistent with these observations.[58]

Very often, judges are able to impose their prejudice and ignorance onto the victim and even the supporting mother with incredible ease. With little critical media attention on these types of cases, judicial comments come under scant scrutiny. When the media does report outrageous comments by members of the judiciary regarding sexual offense trials, there is often a tendency to view such comments as merely "controversial" or showing one judge out of step with current thinking, and so on. Of real concern is that judges consider their comments representative of their judicial peers and the public when it comes to "incest" and other sexual offenses.

VICTIM IMPACT STATEMENTS

Victim Impact Statements were introduced in Victoria in 1995 and have been used in international jurisdictions for some time.[59] Their purpose is to provide the judge with the impact of the crime(s) on the victim so that their suffering and needs can be recognized and taken into account when deciding sentence. As discussed in case study R v L, the judge gave scant attention to the victim impact statement of the victim and, in fact, struck most of it out. A very similar course of action occurred in two other trials from the original study and has been reported elsewhere.[60] While Victim Impact Statements were designed to provide a legal mechanism for victim suffering—regardless of crime—to be presented formally to the courts for consideration at sentencing, evidence suggests it has not always translated into a recognition of suffering in sexual-offense proceedings.

This aside, a further complication with the legal framing of suffering in child sexual abuse trials concerns the need to identify only that suffering caused by the particular charge or charges of which the perpetrator was convicted. Legally, then, victim *trauma* relates only to those isolated charges that resulted in conviction. Their suffering is only real when the judge decides it is suffering. It is the *judge's* imprimatur that is needed for *their* suffering to become *real* suffering. Like the beads on an abacus, the trauma outlined in a victim impact statement is legally moved back and forth so as to measure how much pain will be afforded and how much will be negated.

Once again, the discretionary powers afforded the judiciary are at the forefront of this process. The pervasiveness of a legal mind-set that traditionally minimizes harm to rape and sexual abuse victims is unable to be surmounted through legal reforms such as Victim Impact Statements.

MITIGATING FACTORS: MINIMIZATION OF HARM

Abundant evidence demonstrates the legal effectiveness of minimizing harm to victims of sexual crimes. It was common to see and hear barristers invalidate the suffering of victims as detailed in their Victim Impact Statements for a range of reasons. Either the statement detailed forms of suffering deemed outside the scope of the *jury verdict* or supporting professional evidence was excluded or considered irrelevant. Or, quite simply, the barrister and presiding judge *decided* the victim suffered no harm. Mitra found evidence of appeal judges criticizing sentencing judges for *wrongly* taking into account the damaging impact of abuse on "incest" victims.

The social and emotional difficulties endured by victims as a result of the offender's conduct were either not taken into account, or treated as minor. In several cases, the rejection of victims by family members or other significant members of their community was never considered, despite being made apparent at sentencing. Abortions and pregnancies resulting in births were seldom singled out for special sanction at sentencing.

In case study R v EF, defense counsel attempted to minimize the seriousness of the offender's crimes against his young daughters, including an aggravated assault. In case study R v L, the impact of teenage pregnancy and abortion was minimized against a backdrop of an overwhelmingly positive appraisal of the offender.

Trials observed in 1999 and 2000 continued to involve judicial comments indicating a lack of harm to victims of sexual abuse, with Victim Impact Statements often being given scant attention.

The minimization of harm to victims of intrafamilial sexual abuse appears to be compounded by the widely held belief that the abuse of one's own child is somehow less horrific than the abuse of children not related to the offender. Since the child is the *property* of the father, the violation of his child's rights is considered less a crime than the violation of the "property" belonging to another man.[61] Echoing this point, Mitra cited a compelling example of a judge who, when sentencing a man for the repeated sexual abuse of his young daughter, told the offender: "If this girl had *not* been your daughter this would have been a *very serious* matter. [emphasis added]"[62]

MITIGATING FACTORS: MOTHER BLAME

Mother blame in intrafamilial child abuse has occupied a central place in family dysfunction theory and Freudian psychoanalytic literature, and has been absorbed into legal discourse to mitigate the conduct of offenders.[63] In case study R v L, the mother was singled out as a "mitigating" factor in the offender's criminal conduct due to what the defense barrister vaguely claimed was her "erratic" behavior leading to a marriage breakdown and subsequent divorce. A recent newspaper article reported the sexual assault of two adolescent girls was directly linked to the convicted offender's lack of sexual satisfaction from his wife.[64]

MITIGATING FACTORS: VICTIM CONSENT AND VICTIM-BLAMING

Another mitigating factor not present in the case studies presented in this book is victim blame. A solid body of literature locates sexually victimized children and young women as culpable agents in their own abuse.[65] Writing from a socio-legal perspective, Leroy Schultz considered child victims to range across a continuum from "accidental victimization" (just how children are *accidentally* raped and assaulted is not clarified) to full "seductive partner" and "initiator." He argued that physical and emotional trauma to children, including intrafamilial victims, have been "exaggerated" in the literature, and further suggested that some children found their violation "erotic."[66] Research on the legal response to intrafamilial sexual abuse has also found this factor well articulated in trials and sentencing pleas.[67]

In R v M, the victim was positioned as a partial co-agent to her own sexual abuse. Despite emphatic denials in her evidence that she ever consented to her father's continual rape, she was nonetheless situated as giving "reluctant consent" for her father to repeatedly abuse her over many years.[68] It seems that, very often, regardless of what victims tell the courts, in the end the legal point of view regarding the victim is impenetrable.

MITIGATING FACTORS: THE "GOOD" FATHER, "GOOD" CITIZEN

All the sentencing pleas examined in the original research revealed the incorporation of the defense narrative of the "good" father and "good" citizen.

Talk of "previous good character" and of "no prior convictions" was bandied about and judges were apt to lap up these idioms about public conduct, rather than recognize the private evil they obscure. In fact, charges of sexual abuse tend to be viewed as inconsistent with these character traits, especially where the abuse is alleged to have been long-term. Yet when an offender rapes or sexually assaults his child, particularly over a long period of time, this behavior must be seamlessly integrated into the life of the offender, if only to avoid detection, emotionally isolate the child, and secure the non-disclosure compliance of the child.

In fact, many offenders purposely groom their public persona so as to provide a credible counter-ballast to those outside of the home and, perhaps, even others within the home. As crimes of a sexual nature are considered covert crimes, it could well be argued that the "good" character of the offender may be a deceptive front connected to the commission, maintenance and degree of deception involved in these crimes. Cultivating the "good father" and "good citizen" image tends to prevent detection of the perpetrator's conduct while at the same time increasing the difficulty the victim faces in being able to disclose the offender's conduct, and then having her/his story believed. In all of the cases in this research, particularly those involving long-term abuse, the offender engaged in a premeditated pattern of behavior to commit and conceal his crimes. Upon disclosing the abuse, many of the victim/survivors were shunned either partially or completely from the family and denied their support. Many were rejected by relatives, neighbors and family friends who preferred to support the "good" father and "good" citizen over the "incest" victim.[69]

It might well be that a lack of prior convictions has more to do with good luck than good character, especially when you consider that some of the offenders were sentenced after being found guilty of sexual abuses occurring over a period of years. Research has shown that only a very small minority of sex offenders are convicted[70] and, even then, such a conviction only relates to the offense(s) for which they were convicted.

MITIGATION FACTORS: UNLIKELY TO RE-OFFEND

The claim that offenders were unlikely to ever re-offend is confidently asserted, as though the future conduct of the offender were assured. Often this uncritical assurance seemed guaranteed merely on the basis that the victim was so inexorably removed from the family that the offender simply would have no opportunity to recommit any abuse. No longer being part of the family unit, and no longer having contact with the father, actually worked to the offender's advantage.[71] The victim's forced exile from the family unit went without comment or censure except to mitigate the father's likelihood to re-offend. Clearly the post-abuse punishment meted out to victims of this type of crime should not be implicitly, no less explicitly, considered a positive factor in the sentencing or rehabilitation of offenders. In two cases, evidence that the mother would ensure her children had no further contact with the offender was worked into the defense narrative of "unlikely to re-offend."[72]

The other side of the "unlikely to re-offend" coin is promoting the fact that the offender sexually offended against his own children, and thus the community was safe from the prospect of recidivism. It seems the lineal relationship between victim and offender works not only to reduce notions of harm, but is also used to bolster the narrative that the offender poses no "real" threat to "the community" and thus less likely to re-offend.[73]

Section VII
Appeal Outcomes

Appeal decisions provide another form of attrition. In the original study, two cases (including R v L) were trials following successful convictions. Both resulted in re-convictions, and both resulted in further appeals against conviction and sentence. In R v L, an appeal against conviction and sentence was dismissed, while in the other case the conviction appeal was dismissed but the sentence appeal was allowed, resulting in a reduced sentence. In the original study, five first-time trials resulted in conviction, and three were successfully overturned on appeal.

Appeal decisions are highly technical, relying a great deal on wide interpretation and supposition on what a jury might have thought, could have thought, or even should have thought—a point examined in some detail by Australian barrister Lloyd Davies.[74] Retrial affords defense counsel the chance to reflect on possible gaps in the original narrative and, with the opportunity to have more evidence excluded at a retrial (as happened in R v L, R v J, and R v K), hope springs eternal for defense barristers in retrials. Yet defense counsel can also over-extend themselves. In R v K, a successful appeal resulted in a very new defense strategy—so new and dramatic it resulted in the retrial being aborted before it started, with no new proceedings beginning, ever.

Appeal decisions have different ramifications for victims and offenders. In one case, the offender plea-bargained, avoiding a retrial and securing conviction on only minor charges. In two cases, the prospect of a retrial issuing from a successful appeal led to a suicide attempt, leading the Director of Public Prosecution to direct a *nolle prosequi*.[75]

Section VIII
Coaching

In some cases, when children's evidence took defense counsel by surprise, claims of *coaching* were used in an effort to defuse and recover from such slip-ups. In several cases, child complainants were accused of being "coached" by an adult, usually their mother or some other unknown adult. This supposed "coaching" was generally woven into the narrative of means and occasionally put to use when a child's evidence thwarted a defense stratagem, such as occurred in case study R v D. In R v C, the child's honest rebuttal to defense assertions that she was a liar appeared to take the barrister by surprise, leading him to counter-respond with the charge of coaching:

> CHILD: They aren't [lies]. I wouldn't lie for something like this because I wouldn't want to break up my family and the only person to break up the family is my dad.
>
> DEFENSE: Someone told you to say that didn't they?
>
> CHILD: No.
>
> DEFENSE: You haven't spoken to anyone about when I cross-examine you, you say that particular thing, [you] say something like that?
>
> CHILD: No.
>
> DEFENSE: I put it to you that someone has been talking to you and *coaching* you on how to testify...It's true isn't it, someone has been *coaching* you how to testify?
>
> CHILD: No. [emphasis added][76]

In several other cases, the concept of coaching was not explicitly articulated but it was certainly hinted by references to the mother coaching her children in the evidence they would give against their father.[77]

Section IX
I Swear By Almighty God...

The law essentially forces children to lie under oath. It does so when it makes children swear an oath to God that the evidence they give to the court will be "the whole truth and nothing but the truth." Yet children are required by either prosecutor or judge, and sometimes by both, to suppress certain evidence and testimony. Sometimes they are effectively forced to give evidence that is clearly not the *whole* truth and sometimes actually false. In case study R v EF, the eldest sibling had to change her evidence regarding her sisters from plural to singular. In cases involving more than one complainant, children were made to restrict their evidence specifically so the jury would not be aware there was more than one child alleging similar—and, in some cases, the same—allegations. In R v J (retrial), evidentiary constraints caused considerable distress to the complainant prompting the judge at one stage to acknowledge that defense counsel seemed to be deliberately trying to upset the complainant by asking her questions he knew she was forbidden to answer.[78]

Section X
Language: Children of a Lesser Law

An important part of legal narratives around intrafamilial rape trials is the invocation of the term "incest" to denote parent/child rape. The pejorative meaning associated with the term *incest* not only embeds the term within a paradigm of stigma and ignorance, but the term is also infused with concepts of mutuality and consent. Elsewhere, I have argued strongly for the displacement of the word—as have other feminist writers—given that its characteristic definitions are grossly inadequate.[79]

The judicial predilection is to position "incest" victims as culpable co-agents to their own violation, and as individuals suffering minimal harm. The distortion of intrafamilial rape and sexual abuse under the shibboleth of "incest," and as occurring only in "sick" dysfunctional families—rather than a social problem associated with gender inequality—is further heightened by a published database of books in print throughout the world that lists the topic of "incest" under the subject heading of "crimes without victims."[80]

A feature of judicial discourse is the difference in language when discussing "incest" as opposed to the "rape" and "sexual assault" of children by non-family members. Judges are apt to use strong words of condemnation in cases of sexual abuse of children by strangers or those not related to the child/children.[81] Across trials, judges described fathers as having "lustful inclinations," of a sexual "relationship" between child and parent, of fathers showing a "guilty passion" toward their daughter, of "indulging" in an act of "intercourse," of "debauching" the child, "seducing" the child, and engaging in "sexualized behavior." This proactive language of mutuality promotes minimization of harm and attributes blame to the victim. Harm is minimized and, on occasion, a victim's testimony of suffering is ignored or treated with contempt. Even prosecutors commonly ask complainants about the intercourse they "had with" their father or stepfather, placing the act within a proactive paradigm that removes a sense of violation. At all legal levels, the language of the judiciary is one of victim participation in the crime. Yet these are crimes of intrafamilial rape and intrafamilial sexual assault. As Elizabeth

Ward—a proponent for the term rape as opposed to "incest"—argues, while "incest" may refer to the lineal relationship, rape denotes what is being done to the child.[82] This point is recognized by at least some of the judiciary who concede that "incest" ought to better be described as "father-daughter" rape.[83]

The terminology of "incest" does not delineate concepts of offender and victim. Rather it sets rape and sexual assault within a minimalist paradigm of sexual perversion in dysfunctional families, as opposed to a premeditated and calculated crime involving the worst acts of betrayal. Feiner has noted a similar linguistic displacement of victims in intrafamilial rape trials.[84]

Of course, this language complements dominant masculinist euphemisms that saturate theoretical literature on "incest," especially family dysfunction theory. Judith Herman showed similarities between the language and theoretical constructs in family dysfunction theory literature and the stories and language used in pornographic literature depicting father-daughter "incest." She considered how both forms of literature placed an emphasis on attributing blame to the mother for being frigid or unattractive, neglectful, unstable, or vengeful, while casting the girl child as a consenting and willing partner unharmed by her sexual abuse.[85] A similar template guides legal narratives and judicial discourse. Given the legal parlance sexualizing victims, attributing them blame rather than recognizing their pain, this institutionalized judicial discourse may be a third arena of discourse furthering Herman's point.

Section XI
Narrative Additions

Aside from narratives of "motive" and "means," there are several other structural and thematic patterns worthy of discussion: absence of an outcry; the master narrator as opposed to the monosyllabic witness; specious accuracy; and, its close relation, prior inconsistent statements.

ABSENCE OF AN OUTCRY

A centrally recurring point in the defense legal construction of complainants relates to delayed disclosure. Discussed in depth across various case studies, defense barristers argue that failure by complainants to make an immediate public protest about their sexual abuse is indicative of fabrication. Aside from linking delayed disclosure to evidence of fabrication, this tactic enables defense barristers to openly humiliate and denounce complainants' evidence. In every trial analyzed, barristers attacked complainants, sometimes in a most vitriolic manner, for failing to disclose the abuse immediately, for remaining silent after alleged repeated abuses, for "failing to stop" the conduct of their father or stepfather. Worse, very often specific evidentiary parameters set by the judge disabled complainants' ability to contextualize their behavior.

Despite the wide acceptance of delayed disclosure as a common traumagenic pattern in child and adult sexual abuse, the judiciary and some other professionals continue to assert a narrow perception of concepts such as delayed disclosure. In three case studies, children reported threats by the accused—should they tell their mother or anyone else about the abuse. In the original study, nearly all of the complainants reported threats and actual physical assaults related to both the commission of the crimes and the consequences should they disclose. Threats to injure them, their mother, or others they love—including pets—were frequent. Threats by the perpetrator to harm the entire family, commit suicide, kill the child, kill their mother or even their pets were also reported by complainants. Telling complainants that no one would believe them, that they and/or the offender would be locked up, that the family would be broken up, and that all these things would be *their fault* for *telling* were also frequently cited. Several older complainants faced another sinister layer of fear-induced silence: the perpetrator *reminded* them they were now (legally) adults, making it virtually impossible that anyone would believe them and, further, that they would be co-charged alongside the offender.[86] Clearly, concepts of consent and mutuality embedded in "incest" allow victims to be presented as co-offenders.

THE HAND THAT SIGNED...CRUEL INTENTIONS AND POIGNANT PAIN

As argued previously, a focus on delayed disclosure allows the defense to argue that such delays are inconsistent with claims of sexual abuse, especially long-term abuse. This stratagem was discussed in R v L and was also featured in another case of long-term abuse. In this latter case, the judge noted the excellent legal strategy of using family photographs and greeting cards to severely undermine claims by the complainant that they were abused by the accused, were afraid of him, and could not disclose for fear of retaliation.[87] As the victim/survivor in case study R v L surmised so eloquently, she wanted to believe she was a *normal* girl—not one subject to the shocking abuses inflicted upon her. As such, she forced herself to partake in normalized family activities and rituals, such as sending birthday cards, only to have them used against her later.

In the absence of normality and stability, children employ defense mechanisms to make themselves feel part of a loving, normal family with a loving, normal father or stepfather. Giving greeting cards and taking part in family activities is a critical part of this hurtful grasp to maintain emotional balance. Learning how to survive, how *not* to become a target, is a necessary part of appeasing the perpetrator on all levels. Also, the concept of putting on a public face is important and expected as part of our everyday presentation of the self, no less for children than adults.[88] Social desirability dictates how one is to behave in certain social settings. Children also learn that part of this public façade is playing the part of a normal, loving child. The learning involved is learning to survive and not be a target. The learning involved is how to put on a good front, of managing a particular family and personal image. It is learning the everyday presentation of self for everyday preservation.

These forces lead children to produce artifacts of false normality. And it is these same artifacts that so often work against the victim and give credit to the offender. Their very attempts to cope with abuse become the twisted insurance policy for the offender should the child ever disclose.

THE MASTER NARRATOR AND THE MONOSYLLABIC WITNESS

Readers may have noted how legal narratives often unfold with one dominant narrator voice. The complex irony within the trial is extraordinary. The accused is on trial for alleged crimes. Yet he may opt for total silence, letting his legal counsel do the talking for him. If the accused does decide to give evidence, he is protected from the kind of scrutiny about his life that his accuser experiences, regardless of age.

As argued previously, the rules of evidence create fractures and gaps in the spoken evidence of complainants. The complainant is the accuser and is attacked as though an enemy. She is the enemy because the system is adversarial and positions her, as a woman in a male enclave, as the enemy.

The person most vilified in the courtroom also says the least. The complainant's evidence-in-chief is proscribed prior to her entering the court through the distilling of charges. The result is a presentment of charges and evidentiary rulings that decide who can speak and what they can say. In most cross-examinations, complainants are reduced to conversationally dysfunctional answers or a simple monologue of "yes," "no," "correct," "I don't know," or "I can't remember" responses. The prosecutor, working on behalf of the state, is regarded as the Master Narrator since it is their lead that has brought about a trial. In fact, as this research has shown, the opposite occurs. Judges set evidentiary boundaries to advantage the accused so that the "facts" of the case support a defense narrative against which the prosecutor must surmount. The prosecutor attempts to rebut a stock-story narrative, but most often with limited resources by way of facts since they have either been disqualified or additional evidence cannot be led.

It is not always necessary for defense barristers to make explicit the narratives they develop in cross-examination. Seeking agreement to seemingly innocuous questions, or demanding a simple "yes" or "no" reply to complex questions or statements, provides the basis for barristers to embroider and embellish on these agreements in their closing address to the jury.

PRIOR INCONSISTENT STATEMENTS

As detailed in chapter 7, "Forced Errors," prior inconsistent statements predominantly revolve around the narrow and selective use of minor errors in evidence. These are used to build a narrative suggesting complainant fabrication. This was particularly evident in case studies R v D and R v G, and was a well-used tactic in trials involving children.

This bait and switch tactic of deliberately setting traps to hunt down inconsistencies (no matter how minor), and gathering them together in a neat package for the jury, often involves a process of putting long, complex and convoluted questions to complainants in an attempt to confuse them. Similarly, repetitive cross-examination and the ability to cross-examine complainants and other prosecution witnesses at committal hearings allows forced error answers to be dramatized in a subsequent trial or trials. A heavy reliance on this tactic complements the force and deployment of defense narratives.

SPECIOUS ACCURACY

"Forced Errors" also includes the related concept of specious accuracy, as it is closely linked to prior inconsistent statements. A feature of cross-examination is the often scant attention to the actual incidents being alleged by the complainant for which the accused has been charged. Much of this, of course, is due to the practice of attacking the character and credibility of the complainant and games of forced error "gotcha." Such defense tactics in child sexual abuse trials are so pervasive there is little need and less time to concentrate on the actual allegations as a whole.

As noted in chapter 7, "Forced Errors," children are able to accurately recall events—in these cases, events of serious sexual violation—but may well become confused about minor and peripheral details, including the sequence of details such as the order in which they got undressed, or who said what to whom and when, especially over time.

This confusion is not particular to complainants in sexual abuse trials, since any person would no doubt experience similar difficulties. But within these trials, reality is suspended, as child and adult complainants are taken to task repeatedly for not being able to recall minute details, often leading them to express distress and frustration. They are accused of being liars and fabricators.

Specious questions of accuracy often led to complainant evidence consisting of many "I don't know" or "I can't remember" answers. The trial transcripts where this tactic was gainfully employed show very long slabs of transcript in which defense counsel rolled out an endless list of questions on peripheral details—sometimes involving ten or more questions just on one specific detail—accompanied by a monologue of complainant responses of "I don't know" or "I can't remember."

This is a deliberate ploy designed to have a cumulative affect on the jury. They hear many "important" questions from the lawyer, but hear the child simply saying "I don't know." In a slightly different version of the same tactic, statements are put to the child rather than questions: "And you don't know whether the bedspread was on the bed, do you?" or "And the fact is you can't remember whether the car seats were brown or green, can you?" In this way, the jury hears a monotone of "No" answers which are used to portray the child as a liar and fabricator because a *truthful* complainant would be able to tell us all these facts.

As some of the cases studies in this book reveal, the preference for cross-examining complainants on peripheral and minute details is a ploy to make defense questions appear to dismantle the content of the child's evidence-in-chief, when, in truth, the questions are substantively vapid and rhetorically misleading. Other witnesses are also subjected to specious accuracy cross-examination, and, while a few prosecutors utilized this tactic, it remains one that is consistently identified with defense cross-examination. Any failure to satisfy these demands is paraded as evidence of false testimony.

Section XII
The Legal Authorization of the Narrative Template

In analyzing appeal decisions, I found a disturbing pattern across many of the reports. Very often the defense narrative is given precedence, regardless of its factual basis. The net effect of this process is that appeal judges tend to narrate a trial in the same factual vacuum originally designed by defense barristers. Appellate judges very often regurgitate and reaffirm the defense stock-story narrative uncritically, as though it were factual evidence. Excluded evidence from a trial most often remains excluded from any further legal examination or comment.

Appellate Court summary of the trial under review, then, tends to closely adhere to the legal narrative presented at the trial. Consequently, many appeal decisions read like propaganda documents, where stock-story narratives about vengeful and unstable children, and colluding and vengeful wives are reiterated. In this manner, legal storytelling within the courtroom gains momentum and credibility through uncritical propagation of appeal judgments. The template used by defense counsel and superimposed over trials—even those that lead to a successful jury conviction—are sanctioned at the Appeal level as they are uncritically regurgitated as the *facts* of the case under consideration.

While it may be argued that a jury conviction indicates that at least some of the defense narrative has been rejected, conviction does not change the fact that stock-story narratives have been elevated through the legal process. Even at this level, the voice of the victim is silenced, and the legal domination of a preferred narrative over fact is transmitted from trial to sentence and sentence to appeal. As many appeal decisions are reported and routinely placed on the Internet, it is no doubt further damaging to have the offender's version—with which they were threatened with for years to ensure compliance and delayed disclosure—regurgitated uncritically by judges as though the defense narrative was still true.

Many sentencing and appeal decisions read like patriarchal homilies, continuing to place women and children as culpable for the sexual violence that men inflict upon them. The judicial promulgation of dominant stock stories about women and children—more precisely, negative stereotypes of mothers and their children—not only negates their reality and experiences, but is legally reinforced through appeal decisions with the cyclical net effect of re-enforcing stock stories about intrafamilial rape.

Conclusion

Our case studies present a number of similarities in the dynamics of the abuse. The charges across each trial were serious, involving penetration. This is consistent with the original study and other research showing that the more serious forms of rape and sexual assault are common to intrafamilial sexual abuse.[89] Teenage pregnancy is also a frequent problem in intrafamilial rape, especially in long-term abuse.[90]

Three case studies involved delayed disclosure, and in the original study this was found in every case other than case study R v G. (The particulars of R v G, and possible reasons for this are reviewed in that case study.) There were also similarities in the alleged threats made to complainants as to the consequences of disclosure.

In each case study, as indeed in each case from the original study as might be expected, family structure and dynamics were different. However, a reading of police statements indicates a pattern of control and manipulation by the accused. In particular, police statements appear to show a man capable, in many instances, of presenting a public face different to that shown to his family or close friends. Several researchers have noted this point, by describing intrafamilial offenders as "perfect patriarchs," who are capable of projecting a very different public image in contrast to their treatment of their family.[91]

Despite similarities and differences in dynamics across each case, defense narratives molded mother and child around similar family scenarios involving marital friction, collusion and revenge. Counseling files and the child's social activities were often used as defense props to embroider the narrative. Yet the opportunity to contextualize their evidence of abuse was considerably narrower. In all of these cases, and others, the defense narrative would have been severely disrupted and possibly destroyed had judges not wholly excluded or modified evidence they happen to deem too prejudicial to the accused or "irrelevant."

The suppression of facts provides for the development of a specific genre of defense narrative dialogue that is sexist and discriminatory against women and children. The disrespect and open hostility metered out to many child and adult complainants in a trial setting, regardless of a conviction, remains palpable for many victim/survivors long after the trial. Trial by attrition—by way of evidentiary obliteration and modification—followed by a trial by ordeal—by way of character obliteration and distortion—ought not to be the features that flood our *justice* system.

A point I want to briefly comment on, but cannot explore in any depth, is that of *social death*. This is not the forum to undertake such an analysis, but I do want to alert the reader to the concept of *social death* as a long-term impact of sexual abuse. Erving Goffman used this term to refer to the kinds of stigma suffered by certain classes of individuals, such as those defined as mentally ill.[92] It is my contention that victim/survivors of sexual abuse suffer various and often multiple forms of social death as a consequence of the response to and treatment of their abuse by family, community, professionals and the legal system. In addition to suffering from sexual assault, the very essence of one's character and identity is abusively threatened at home only to be even more systematically stripped away in court. In its place stands an alien legal construction of themselves that they are often powerless to challenge, no less change.

While I am convinced that stock-story narratives would be deployed in trials even if all prosecution evidence were permitted, it is clear their power would be greatly diminished were complainants not silenced, their evidence not excluded, and their own experiences not distorted in accordance with a legal view of intrafamilial rape and sexual assault.

Notes

1. While all these sub-themes were not observed in all four case studies, my original research was able to bring out all of these sub-themes as repeated patterns across the fourteen trials analyzed. See Taylor (2001a).
2. See, for example: Victorian Law Reform Commission, "Reported Sexual Offenses and Prosecution Outcomes," in Sexual Offenses Interim Report (June 2003); Wightman (1995), 251–66; and Heenan (2001).
3. See Kaspiew (1995), 350–82, 379.
4. R v B (Victorian County Court, Williams, J. 1995), at 141.
5. The case being referred to is R v M (Victorian County Court, Dixon, J. 1995). In this case the DNA results indicated 99.3 percent and 97.5 percent accuracy that the accused was the father of the two children his daughter gave birth to. Detailed discussion about the legal arguments that led to this evidence being omitted from the trial can be found in chapter 6, "The Agency of Judges," of my 2001 Ph.D. thesis.
6. Victorian Law Reform Commission, Sexual Offenses Interim Report (June 2003) and Heenan (2001).
7. Heenan (2001), Temkin (2002), and Temkin (2003).
8. The case in question is R v M, and is detailed in my Ph.D. thesis.
9. I am referring to case studies R v A (Victorian County Court, Davey, J. 1995); R v B; R v G (Victorian County Court, O'Shea, J. 1996); and R v H (Victorian County Court, Crossley, J. 1995).
10. A discussion of her work can be found in chapter 2, "Telling Legal Tales."
11. Many victim/survivors have relayed to me their distress around this point and similar comments can be found in the Victorian Law Reform Commission, Sexual Offenses Interim Report (June 2003) 4.21 at 153.
12. Feiner (1997).
13. This same point about de-contextualizing evidence through evidentiary rulings and the adverse impact it has on victim/survivors who encounter such a process has been noted by the Victorian Law Reform Commission, Sexual Offenses Interim Report (June 2003), 153, at 4.20 and 4.21.
14. Scutt (1994b), 139–60.
15. See discussions around the corroboration warning in Heenan (2001), Davies (1999), and Young (1995).
16. Doggett v The Queen (2001), 208 CLR 343. See also the Victorian Law Reform Commission, Sexual Offenses Interim Report (June 2003) for a discussion of this case and its ramifications.
17. I elaborated this link in great detail in my original study. Susan Edwards (1996) has commented, similarly, how masculinist psychoanalytic theory has influenced medicine, politics, the public and law. Child sexual abuse allegations are viewed as stemming from children's fantasy or from sexual provocation.
18. I explored this link in depth in my original study. Charlotte Mitra also noted the influence of family dysfunction literature in informing and maintaining judicial bias against victims. See Mitra (1987).
19. R v A, at 224.
20. R v M, at 524, 527.

21. R v L, appeal decision (1994), 83 AcrimR 17, at 28.
22. This was apparent during the prolonged controversy over Australia's former Governor General Dr. Peter Hollingworth. Hollingworth eventually resigned over his appalling mishandling of proven and alleged child sexual abuse while he was Anglican Archbishop of Brisbane. Public opinion as reflected in opinion pages in the media showed a strong tendency to continue to blame victims and disbelieve them. See, for example, Taylor (2003) and Blaskett & Taylor (2002).
23. For example: R v A; R v H; R v J (Victorian County Court, Barnett, J. 1993 and Victorian County Court, retrial, Campton, J. 1995); R v K (Victorian County Court, Lewis, J. 1994); R v M; R v N (Victorian County Court, Stott, J. 1995); and R v O.
24. R v A; R v B; R v C (Victorian County Court, Spence, J. 1995); R v K (Victorian County Court, Lewis, J. 1994); and, to a lesser extent, R v O.
25. R v A and R v B.
26. Comparisons between the child's or siblings' good relationship with their mother—as opposed to their dislike of their father—was a feature in trials R v A; R v C; R v E (Victorian County Court, Wodak J. 1995); R v F (Victorian County Court, Wodak J. 1995); R v K; and R v L.
27. R v C, at 80–1.
28. Ibid., at 382.
29. R v A; R v B; R v J (retrial, 1995); R v K; R v L; R v M; R v H; and R v N (Victorian County Court, Stott, J. 1995).
30. See, for example, Bolt (2002) and Taylor (2002). In this article, I wrote about child sexual abuse within the Catholic Church, focusing in particular on recent media coverage and public comment, which included a suggestion that some individuals were motivated to make allegations of sexual abuse for financial reward.
31. I observed much of this trial, including the evidence of the complainant. The police informant in this case told me of these comments soon after they were made to him as he was upset that a child should be talked about in this way by any legal counsel.
32. Victorian Law Reform Commission, Sexual Offenses Interim Report (June 2003), 267.
33. The latter part of the sentence refers to a well-used legal verse based on the precedent in the case Henry and Maning (1969), 53 Cr App R 150, 153 where the judge warned the jury it was unsafe to convict on the lone evidence of a "woman or girl" given their propensity to lie for "all sorts of reasons...and sometimes for no reason at all."
34. R v J (retrial, 1995).
35. Much has been written about the specific historical period in medical discourse that promoted women as mentally unstable "hysterics," especially those who claimed rape, sexual assault and domestic violence. See Showalter (1987) and Ussher (1991).
36. See Taylor (2000).
37. In R v J (retrial, 1995), the narrative focused upon mental instability and fiscal gain. In R v N emotional stability was inferred against a backdrop of revenge against a father for perceived adolescent grudges. Interestingly, the motive of mental illness was mobilized in trials with female complainants.
38. See R v A; R v B, at 122–23.
39. R v A; R v EF (R v E and R v F); R v G; R v J (retrial, 1995), R v K; and R v L (Victorian County Court, Kelly, J. 1993).
40. R v K, at 231.
41. Prominent barrister and author Lloyd Davies reports on an Australian High Court Appeal involving father-daughter sexual abuse. The judges quashed the convictions

Case Studies Analysis

commenting, in part, that the child's "persuasive details" of sexual penetration could easily have "been learned from other girls." See Davies (1999).
42. These are cases R v A and R v B, in particular, and are detailed in my Ph.D. thesis.
43. Examples can be found in R v A; R v B; and R v L (1993). (Though sex education at school was raised in the absence of the jury, it was not raised in cross-examination.)
44. See R v L (1993) for an excellent example. In R v N, the complainant was quizzed about ever having read a particular feminist book on child abuse.
45. Examples are R v J (1993, and retrial, 1995); R v K; and R v N.
46. R v J (1993). The complainant was quizzed about whether she watched a particular and well-known movie detailing a forbidden type of sexual relationship.
47. R v A, at 249.
48. R v B, at 44.
49. This is a 2001 trial I observed as part of ongoing research.
50. See R v L (1993) and the complainant's welfare training. R v J (retrial, 1995), on both the occupation and psychology training undertaken by the complainant.
51. The other cases are R v A and R v B, as detailed in my 2001 Ph.D. thesis. I am also aware of two recent cases in which the welfare and nursing background of mothers was used very early in legal proceedings to suggest either that their training should have enabled them to identify "true" abuse or that their medical knowledge helped the child to fabricate abuse.
52. For contemporary literature and studies on this issue, see: Heenan (2001); Cossins & Pilkington (1996), 222–67; Bronitt & McSherry (1997), 259, 261; Victorian Law Reform Commission, Sexual Offenses Interim Report (June 2003); Olle (1999), 78–84.
53. See, for example: Thoennes (1998), 14–8; and Green (1986), 449–58. See also Armstrong (1994) as cited in this chapter.
54. See Armstrong (1994) and Armstrong (1990).
55. See Lafree & Reskin (1985).
56. The case in question is R v C, and forms part of the original research.
57. R v H and R v N.
58. See Mitra (1987), Edwards (1996), and Scutt (1990c).
59. Edwards (1996), 210–1.
60. R v M and R v J (retrial, 1995). See also Mitra (1987) and Wightman (1995).
61. I discuss in some detail this point and related matters in my 2001 Ph.D. thesis and also Taylor (2001b), 211–28.
62. Mitra (1987), 144.
63. I explicated this relationship in my 2001 Ph.D. thesis. Mitra (1987) and Scutt (1990c) provide an excellent critical appraisal of this fact. Wightman (1995) also provides a compelling example of the judiciary holding women accountable for their husband's raping of their daughter.
64. See Kelly (2002).
65. See, for example, Amir (1971). Amir's work was instructive in enshrining the concept of victim attributes that precipitated rape. See also Gilmartin-Zena (1983), MacKinnon (1983), and Scutt (1994b).
66. Schultz (1975), at 258.
67. See Mitra (1987), Edwards (1996), Scutt (1990c), and Taylor (2001b).
68. R v M, at 593.
69. This information has been gathered from a number of victims (not necessarily connected to the trials presented in this book), as well as from police informants. In a few

cases, victims of abuse were forced to take legal action to try and protect themselves from continued threats and harassment from the perpetrator, family members and even family friends acting as agents on behalf of the offender.

70. This claim is well known and accepted among researchers and professionals across a range of fields. But just to lend some credibility to the claim, refer to Cossins (1999).
71. This was made explicit in R v M, and was embedded within the sentencing narrative of R v J (retrial, 1995).
72. I am referring to R v EF and R v C.
73. While this concept was pushed in several cases, including R v EF, a report on intrafamilial sexual-abuse cases in the South African courts highlighted leniency in sentencing on the grounds that the lineal relationship in incest meant the crime did not threaten the general community. See Haller (2000).
74. Davies (1996a), Davies (1996b), and Davies (1999).
75. See Glossary for explanation of this legal procedure.
76. R v C, at 117–9.
77. This was clearly an inference in R v A and R v B.
78. R v J (retrial, 1995). See, for example: 158–9 (31/8/95); 309, 322 and 259–60 (5/9/95); and 256–9 (1/9/95).
79. See my 2001 Ph.D. thesis, Taylor (1997) and Taylor (2001b). See also Ward (1984).
80. *Books in Print* 1989–1990, vol. 1 (New York: Bowker), 1793.
81. I have noted this in my 2001 Ph.D. thesis and elsewhere. See, for example, Taylor (1997).
82. Ward (1984), 3.
83. Heath (1985).
84. Feiner (1997).
85. Herman (1981), 42–3.
86. The prospect of co-charging victims was raised in two cases from my research. I also know of two recent cases (2002 and 2003) involving complainants over the age of eighteen alleging long-term sexual abuse by their father where the issue of co-charging the complainant was discussed. Under the Victorian Crimes Act, "incest" allows for complainants aged eighteen years and over to be co-charged with the alleged offender.
87. The case is R v J (retrial, 1995), and explicit reference to this can be found at 409–11 (6/9/95).
88. The classic study and theoretical explication of this is Goffman (1969).
89. See, for example, Edwards (1996), 269.
90. Five pregnancies and three abortions were reported in my original study of fourteen cases.
91. See, for example, Herman (1981) and Maisch (1973).
92. See Goffman (1961).

9 ▪ Conclusion

THIS BOOK INTERROGATED the trial process as it unfolds and exposed all legal evidence for reader scrutiny. As transcripts become historical documents they can be selectively drawn from and referred to as precedent in future cases, and perhaps even as learning tools to assist other lawyers in the craft of legal narrative. In this way, legislation and the application of legal precedents merge to create over-arching legal realities that are biased and perpetuate the distortion of complainant evidence. Legal jurisprudence sanctions the abuse of children by silencing their experiences, eviscerating collateral evidence and reaffirming stock stories and gender-specific doctrinal narratives about children and sexual abuse within the family unit. The legal mistreatment of children and young adults alleging sexual abuse by a parent is tantamount to court licensed abuse. At times, active prejudice by the judiciary toward sexual abuse allegations creates a legal environment where legally sanctioned lying is considered a virtue and "forensic skills" are best put to use when they conceal or obscure known facts.

Most often, legal narratives are preordained templates presented to a jury as the "facts" of the case, for it is the law that decides who can speak and what can be said. Many of defense claims are built upon an absence of evidence, but more damningly, on an artificial legal vacuum created by the forced absence of complainant's voice and the complainant's experience.

Legal precedents and evidentiary rules operate as tools of legitimization to craft legal narratives. Stock-story narratives are developed, mobilized and sustained through these legal processes and sharpened on the prejudices that continue to inform a good deal of discourse around sexual violence. The application of legal precedents entangles the complainant in a legally pre-established identity. Children who have not yet disclosed, or who may still be abused in the future, have a ready-made legal identity awaiting them should they ever proceed to court. Their evidence has already been interpreted, a legal narrative already written—children are narrated prior to their courtroom appearance. A cloak of legal skepticism concerning their experiences awaits them. These courtroom prejudices have existed for centuries and have become stronger rather than weaker.

Questions of fact are twisted into technical interrogations applied with a masculinist legal gaze. Complainant experiences and voices are removed or modified on the basis they do not fit into a defense narrative, either historically or "factually." Through such extraneous filtration, an alternative defense narrative pervades the courtroom, parading as legal investigation. Most often, innuendos substitute for evidence. Without presenting evidence of proof, these innuendos and inferences often become the framework for the trial proceedings. Witnesses swear an oath to the truth—the *whole* truth, yet must stick to a legally constrained script of evidence.

Legal boundary-setting means that competing claims can be silenced or modified, ensuring the flow of information in controlled and predetermined ways. A theatrical performance ensues, as some judges and defense counsel were apt to notice. In this way, highly processed and stylized evidence is presented to a jury as the "whole" facts. Very often aware and affected by these constraints, complainants give their evidence as best they can, only to have their legally imposed gaps and silences used against them. Two contradictory pictures (that developed by the defense and that developed by the prosecution) coexist in the one trial, but those deciding the ultimate "truth" are never privy to the deliberate darkroom manufacture of these defense narratives.

Legal reasoning in sexual offense cases has been underpinned by the adoption of untested hypotheses concerning women and children and rape. The syllogism inherent in the legal narrative is composed of two major premises: women and girl children possess a dangerous sexuality, and their sexuality predisposes them to lie about sexual crimes committed upon them. Therefore, women and girls who allege rape are liars. When male victims allege sexual abuse, the logic of this reasoning forces them to be treated as pseudo-females subject to the same contempt. Like latter day witches, victims face a trial by ordeal and, most often, are damned—regardless of the trial outcome.

In legal discourse and psychosocial theory, the positioning of men as the authority figure in the family is consistently supported and promoted to the detriment of wives and children. The conceptual framework around "incest" consists of two diametrically opposed themes: allegations of intrafamilial abuse are dismissed as lies and fantasy while proven abuse is minimized and mitigating factors (often involving the victim and their mother rather than the convicted) are introduced. The lore of the "family father" remains intact. Legal discourse in the area of sexual violence has evolved in a way that mirrors dominant masculinist paradigms governing intrafamilial abuse. As a result, victims of sexual abuse face trial by proclamation rather than investigation.

The dialogue of disbelief, ritual humiliation of children and young adults, and feigned legal outrage is preferred over open investigation. Some lawyers are at pains to tell all who will listen that children are not cross-examined aggressively because any clever lawyer knows that to do so would be to lose the support of the jury. They fail, however, to point out that cross-examination, then, is best performed by stealth and deceit. Yet while it can be obvious to jurors, no less voluminously documented, that defense cross-examination fails to respect their own "non-aggressive" guidelines, legally sanctioned subterfuge is much more difficult for jurors to detect. Notwithstanding this point, it is quite obvious that what lawyers consider "aggressive" conduct in cross-examination (which they sometimes like to call "rigorous" cross-examination) differs vastly from those critical of this conduct. Besides, my research clearly showed in the majority of cases where aggressive tactics were used in cross-examination, the jury ultimately acquitted the accused. I am happy for the reader to decide if defense tactics detailed in the case studies in this book could be considered "aggressive."

Legal proceedings are often seen as the domain of the professionally initiated—as a science fully intelligible only to those specifically trained. Legally sanctioned courtroom machinations re-enforce this impression. The aim of this book has been to bring a sociological critique of legal principles and process into the public arena for scrutiny and debate. Law, as a state apparatus of justice, should not be regarded as an institution exempt from scrutiny or reasonable accountability. While I agree the judiciary system requires independence and freedom to apply discretion, it is not reasonable to assert that it ought to be completely free from governmental and public accountability. The government of the day appoints judges, and the public of the day appoints government.

Through the rigorous analysis of trials, legal claims of "neutrality" and "impartiality" cannot be sustained given the legal preference for narrative over fact. Consequently, sociologically naïve claims of judicial "fact-finding" and "objectivity" must be sociologically challenged. The judicial resistance to legislation designed to curb both the blatant and subtle sexist and prejudicial discrimination detailed in this book further strengthens claims that discretion is a tool used to obscure fact-finding rather than enhance it. I do not conclude, however, that judicial discretion must be eliminated. Discretion is an important—inevitable—part of the legal process. Unique case elements and dynamics must be understood and responded to. My concern is not that judges possess the freedom of discretion. My concern is with the exercise of that discretion.

While each victim/survivor has unique experiences of the acts of abuse perpetrated on them, including the emotional and often physical abuse that goes with such sexual violence, there exist significant patterns in intrafamilial abuse that cannot, and should not, be overlooked. Recognizing these patterns provides a deeper understanding of the traumagenic effects on victims, *modus operandi* of perpetrators, and responses of professionals.

A particular theme the law continually fails to appreciate is that of delayed disclosure and victim acquiescence to sexual abuse. Especially in long-term sexual-abuse cases, these responses occur as a consequence of the offender's conduct and trauma-induced suffering of the victim. Very often complex and perhaps counter-intuitive behaviors manifested by traumatized children are simply interpreted as evidence of the falsity of the alleged charge(s). Legal successes in isolating such behavior from any context prohibit these behaviors from being interpreted for what they are: emotionally complex coping strategies.

While evidence clearly suggests that at least some juries do not succumb to defense narratives built upon such misconceptions, these small beacons of hope do not negate the legal efficacy of such defense narration, nor does it negate the distress suffered by complainants subjected to these attacks— regardless of jury verdict. The judicial preference for de-contextualizing and fragmenting complainant evidence cyclically fuels a defense narrative focused upon delayed disclosure and perceived inconsistencies. Breaking this evidentiary-narrative, narrative-evidentiary cycle is extremely difficult.

In law, truth is not honored, nor does law seek to know truth more intimately. This is especially, painfully, so in sexual-abuse cases where the truth of children is neither sought, heard nor respected within our court system. Facts that support truth must remain outside the courtroom, legal orphans waiting in loneliness for someone to notice, for someone to care, for someone to let them speak and be heard.

Justice is not blind. All too clearly law approaches and responds to people of different color, gender and class differently. As a system, law privileges one group over another while purporting to hold all persons as equal. Our system of "justice" needs urgent rehabilitation so that the legal process may see and hear without prejudice.

When concepts of truth and fact are circumscribed by legal rules, our "justice"—that concept that we use to measure our democracy and refer to as a social barometer of our values—becomes a commodity distorted by those who possess and process it. As Evan Whitton reminds us, law defeats justice. One question the reader must keep in mind is: who determines these rules? Is it one particular gender or social class? And, secondly, who is advantaged by these rules?

The cases presented in this book and the analyses and arguments raised are by no means applicable only to Australian law. The work of feminist scholars from Britain, such as Susan Edwards, Carol Smart, Charlotte Mitra and Sheila Duncan; Canadian lawyer Alison Young and North American scholars Catharine MacKinnon, Leslie Feiner and Kim Lane Scheppele all reveal similar structural and attitudinal difficulties encountered by those courageous enough to confront the legal *system*.

This book reminds lawyers that they do not possess—and never have possessed—the mantle of clairvoyant "truth-seeking" or "objective" fact-finding. More importantly, they do not practice their profession in a "neutral" forum. Nor are they immune from holding and promulgating stereotypical and discriminatory attitudes toward women and children. But nor should they be permitted to use the law as a mechanism to so easily exploit these prejudices with frightening precision.

As mentioned in the introduction of this book, I have studied and observed trials up to and including 2003, and have found the same narrative patterns. Indeed, I have become so adept at predicting defense narratives, I can foretell the narrative script after reading the victim/survivor's statement, impressing police informants as they hear the narrative re-told for the "benefit" of the whole court. It is my hope that exposing these narratives leads to various reforms capable of subverting or at least mitigating their inimical influence. Judges—whether unaware, or as demonstrated, all too aware—of these narrative templates must consider the role they play in the legal perpetuation of these defense narratives.

My greatest fear, then, is not that this book will find its way smuggled into a defense narrative of "means"—the feminist, psychosocial literature responsible for children's explicitly detailed allegations. Rather, our legal system is in urgent need of significant reform. And it is much easier to write about judicial reform than enact major judicial reform. Evan Whitton, for instance, provides strong arguments for the removal of our adversarial system of law and replacing it with the European-styled inquisitorial system. Certainly our current legal system bears little if any resemblance to notions of investigating fact—unsettling they may be to widespread stereotypes and prejudices. But even an inquisitorial system is still subject to deeply embedded gender discrimination (and other forms of discrimination) among judges and lawyers. As such, a significant cultural shift in law and in society is required to really accommodate such reforms.

Our task, then, is to engage with our current system and agitate for change. Change requires each of us to be both amplifier and transformer. I would like this book to be used as a tool to diminish the power of stock-story narratives in one area of sexual violence, to disrupt the surface order of legal narratives, and to enable more rigorous, open debate about our system of justice: a system that consistently promotes legally constructed stories over factual evidence and the voices of witnesses. Agitation from across the social spectrum and legal sphere is required to break down these narratives and invalidate their mobilization in legal forums.

When investigations of truth and fact are governed more by rules than truth or fact, the rules have clearly come to undermine the judicial process. If rules are more important than truth, then truth-seeking and fact-finding are inevitable casualties. This must in turn prompt us to investigate these rules, to engage in what amounts to rule-seeking and rule-finding. How are these rules made? How do these rules work? And how do these rules advantage the defense and cripple the complainant? Can the law understand itself? Can the law understand that, when it debases children it, in turn, debases itself?

The list of recommendations below are not exhaustive, but present possibilities for reform and have been informed by my research and other work.

Strategies and Recommendations for Reform

RECOMMENDATION ONE

Critical consideration needs to be given to the role of expert testimony in cases involving long-term sexual abuse. Juries need to understand the possible traumagenic features of child abuse and child sexual abuse. This understanding, however, must be tempered by the recognition that many in psychiatry and psychology tend to pathologize victim suffering, as though their emotional distress and trauma is located intrinsically rather than caused by external factors—that is, the abuse.

The introduction of such expert evidence is one way of curbing defense attacks on complainants for delayed disclosure and other behavior considered inconsistent with their allegations. When confronted with familial paraphernalia such as photographs and greeting cards promoting a narrative of "inconsistent" behavior, prosecution is then positioned to lead rebuttal evidence by introducing "relationship evidence," "propensity evidence" and/or evidence of "uncharged acts," including expert testimony. At the very least, complainants would be able to contextualize their evidence to fill in the gaps and silences that so often punctuate their evidence.

While I acknowledge that there are cases where such prosecution evidence is allowed, it remains *ad hoc* and dependent upon the discretion of the presiding judge. Far more consistency is required to ensure fairness to the alleged victim, and to ensure a more complete understanding of delayed disclosure and other traumagenic behaviors associated with long term abuse.

RECOMMENDATION TWO

Complainants ought to be allowed their own legal representation to ensure that their rights as a witness are protected. Since the Crown brings the case against the accused, and the complainant is treated as a witness for the State, there are tensions as to the advocacy afforded them from the Prosecutor. Children, especially, ought to have their own legal representation in such trials, given their vulnerable status in society and law. As Australia is a signatory to the United Nations Rights of the Child supporting the right of children fair and just treatment, child complainants in sexual offenses should have legal representation for the purpose of protecting and advocating their rights, separate from the Crown Prosecutor.

RECOMMENDATION THREE

The United Nations Rights of the Child also states that no child will have their character impugned and, further, that, as far as possible, any hearing or process affecting them and their well-being make provision for them to be reasonably heard. While the UNRC has not been legislated in Australia, thus affecting its implementation, there are nonetheless grounds to agitate for child complainants to be protected from the kinds of emotional bludgeoning, hectoring, and demeaning cross-examination detailed in this book.

RECOMMENDATION FOUR

The State Government must work more closely with the Office of Public Prosecutions to ensure there is minimal time delay between the child's police complaint and the ensuing legal process. In a majority of cases detailed here (as well as original research), delays between the child's police statement and the eventual committal hearing and trial varied from eighteen months to more than five years. Given the propensity to argue the importance of memory and recall in these cases, it is appalling that such time delays occur so frequently.

RECOMMENDATION FIVE

Committal hearings in sexual offenses should be abolished on the grounds that they are used as exploitive fishing expeditions in order to harangue and intimidate witnesses prior to a trial. Magistrates are given a detailed police and prosecution brief of evidence, and this alone is enough to enable a Magistrate to decide the merit of the prosecution case. Committal hearings are not a forum for testing evidence as to guilt or innocence. Yet for far too long the committal hearing has been used as a launching pad for many defense barristers to start their campaign of hectoring and humiliating complainants.

RECOMMENDATION SIX

Immediate steps should be taken address the language and communication tactics directed at child witnesses by legal counsel. Judges should ensure that legal questions directed to child witnesses are suitably framed, taking into account the age and developmental aspects of the child as well as cultural differences. Evidence clearly suggests that judges and prosecutors do not intervene to ensure that children understand questions and statements put to them, even when it is patently clear the child is confused by the use of terminology or the complex structure of the question or statement. The disadvantages then for the child witness can be enormous and can affect the quality of their evidence and indeed the outcome of the trial.

RECOMMENDATION SEVEN

Police should consider the value of audio taping victim/survivor statements of sexual offenses where allegations involve multiple offenses; long term sexual abuse or historical offenses (offenses alleged to have occurred some years ago). Some jurisdictions currently audio-visual tape the statements of children for possible use at later legal proceedings. However this recommendation is not about using audio-visual or audio taped evidence for that purpose, but rather for the purpose of enhancing the initial police statement of a victim/survivor, especially in those cases where the victim/survivor is seeking to relay information about many incidents of sexual violation. Where allegations involve multiple charges, especially over time, victim/survivors very often do not recall the events in a lineal or chronological fashion but often relay them in a narrative fashion. As such, talking about one incident may prompt them to discuss or give thought to other related matters.

Victim/survivors often recount that being able to talk about their abuse as they recall it, especially abuse that occurred over time, means they are more likely to recall more incidents or details as the free expression lends itself to certain cues, prompts, and triggers that lead to other incidents and details that might otherwise be lost in a question and answer type interview or information-gathering exercise. A police officer sitting at a computer and asking formatted questions that require details as they unfold chronologically is not conducive to the way in which many victim/survivors recall their violation(s). Audio taping their statement may reduce their stress at having to stop and wait and think to answer points asked by the police. Instead it allows them to talk about their abuse as it unfolds in their memory. This was done very successfully in one case of long-term abuse from the original research and police and the prosecutor noted the value of this method because of the quality of the detail enabling a greater number of charges to be identified and assisted the prosecutor to be familiar with the details around each charge. The audio tape can be transcribed later and signed by the victim/survivor as their statement.

The Police should consider the value of audio taping victim/survivor statements of sexual offenses where allegations involve multiple offenses; long term sexual abuse or historical offenses (offenses alleged to have occurred some years ago). Some jurisdictions currently audio-visual tape the statements of children for possible use at later legal proceedings. However this recommendation is not about using audio-visual or audio taped evidence for that purpose, but rather for the purpose of enhancing the initial police statement of a victim/survivor, especially in those cases where the victim/survivor is seeking to relay information about many incidents of sexual violation. Where allegations involve multiple charges, especially over time, victim/survivors very often do not recall the events in a lineal or chronological fashion but often relay them in a narrative fashion. As such, talking about one incident may prompt them to discuss or give thought to other related matters.

Victim/survivors often recount that being able to talk about their abuse as they recall it, especially abuse that occurred over time, means they are more likely to recall more incidents or details as the free expression lends itself to certain cues, prompts, and triggers that lead to other incidents and details that might otherwise be lost in a question and answer type interview or information gathering exercise. A police officer sitting at a computer and asking formatted questions that require details as they unfold chronologically is not conducive to the way in which many victim/survivors recall their violation(s). Audiovisual taping or even audio taping of their statement may reduce their stress at having to stop and wait and think to answer points asked by the police. Instead it allows them to talk about their abuse as it unfolds in their memory. This was done very successfully in one case of long-term abuse from the original research and police and the prosecutor noted the value of this method because of the quality of the detail enabling a greater number of charges to be identified and assisted the prosecutor to be familiar with the details around each charge. The audio tape can be transcribed later and signed by the victim/survivor as their statement.

RECOMMENDATION EIGHT

The term "incest" is inadequate, inappropriate, and offensive as a term to describe the adult rape and sexual assault of children and young adults within the family unit. Aside from an anthropological framework that diminishes the term's accuracy, its saturation with pejorative connotations of consent, mutuality, minimal harm and victim enjoyment discriminate against complainants and victims at all trial levels. Victim/survivors should not have to use patriarchal language to describe crimes perpetrated against them. Any legal response to "incest" already strips them of their dignity. The terms "intrafamilial rape" and "intrafamilial sexual assault" better denote the crime.

RECOMMENDATION NINE

Victim Impact Statements should be given more weight in sentencing. Judges should be given a guide to assist them in sentencing to ensure they take proper account of patterns and features found in this type of crime—such as whether the victim has been physically or emotionally exiled from the family (or family members) as a result of disclosure; the role the offender may have played in precipitating and maintaining such estrangement; any aggravated consequences of the abuse, such as pregnancy, abortion, sexually transmitted infections, damage to area of the body penetrated (vagina or anus); consideration of the serious betrayal of trust involved in such abuse; consideration of adverse affects on the victim's relationship to their immediate community (as disclosure can alienate not only family but their community); indications of remorse by the offender and negative effects on family members supporting the victim/survivor. If no Victim Impact Statement is provided, judges should be advised to refer to a pre-compiled list to assist them with sentencing. Such a list would acquaint judges with some of the dynamics of intrafamilial abuse, since they are very often ignored or lost under the weight the offender's list of mitigating factors.

RECOMMENDATION TEN

Specialist training should be provided for judges and prosecutors who preside over and prosecute these cases. This may well involve the development of a specialist list, which has elsewhere been recommended by a number of other jurisdictions.

RECOMMENDATION ELEVEN

Specialist training should be provided for prosecutors to ensure they are better equipped to present cases of intrafamilial sexual abuse. Of great importance is the need for prosecutors to be aware of—and understand—the machinations of highly developed defense narratives and the nuances involved in these narratives. Such training enables prosecutors to recognize and be alert to the development and deployment of these defense narratives and stratagems and, importantly, ways to subvert and rebut them in court. Having a greater understanding of the dynamics of intrafamilial abuse, and indeed other forms of sexual violence, can assist prosecutors to better formulate questions, better advocate for the complainant, and, regardless of evidentiary limitations, look for those areas of evidence they can highlight that might otherwise have been overlooked.

RECOMMENDATION TWELVE

Judicial education of sexual violence. This suggestion is by no means new, but I want to reaffirm the importance of it. It is important that judicial education not be isolated to instruction and advice from within the judicial ranks or any particular profession. Just as the problem of child sexual abuse requires an inter-disciplinary response, so too judicial education should afford an inter-disciplinary approach, drawing on professionals and individuals from diverse fields and backgrounds.

RECOMMENDATION THIRTEEN

The appointment of an independent observer to monitor trials discreetly and report to an independent body on issues of concern. Aggressive legal mistreatment of child and adult complainants, or other conduct deemed to be a breach of ethical standards must be documented and reported.

RECOMMENDATION FOURTEEN

The above point leads to the recommendation that a Children's Commissioner be established to ensure the welfare of children across all social spheres, especially those involving contact with government-run and funded institutions, such as law.

Glossary

accomplice warning: This refers to the evidence of a witness legally regarded as a willing party to the criminal conduct charged. As such, their evidence ought to be regarded as unsafe without independent corroboration, although it can be accepted if a jury accepts it is truthful in a particular case. The "accomplice warning" is derived from case law precedent. A premise of the accomplice warning is that a particular witness, usually for prosecution, is considered an accomplice to the crime the accused is charged with and, as such, the witness may attempt to transfer sole blame onto the accused. The evidence of a witness deemed by the courts as an "accomplice" is considered to be "tainted," and an appropriate warning is given to the jury on accepting the evidence of a witness considered an accomplice. Accomplice warnings have been applied in cases involving "incest" on the basis that the victim/survivor is culpable to the commission of the crime committed against them, and thus their evidence is tainted relative to their complicity in the crime.

accused: A person charged with committing a crime, in this context, intrafamilial sexual abuse. The accused may also be referred to as the defendant.

appeal: After conviction and sentencing, the offender has twenty-one days in which to lodge an appeal against conviction, sentence, or both conviction and sentence. The appeal is then heard by the Appellate Court. Should the offender fail to have his appeal upheld he or she has the right to appeal to the High Court of Australia.

closed circuit television (CCTV): Under Section 37C of the Victorian *Evidence Act 1958*, in court proceedings involving sexual offenses the court can direct, or a complainant can apply to give their evidence from another room, outside of the court, via closed circuit television. This provision exists in other Australian and overseas jurisdictions for complainants in sexual offense proceedings, although there may be variations in who can apply to give evidence via CCTV. In Victoria, Australia, this legislation was enacted in 1991 as a response to levels of fear, intimidation, and stress victim/survivors of sexual abuse experience when having to confront the alleged offender in person, in the courtroom. To reduce the impact of these possible fears and stressors on such witnesses, closed circuit television was introduced. Observers have suggested that this option for giving evidence serves to reduce some of the fear and stress for vulnerable witnesses.

committal hearing: After the accused has been charged by the police, a committal hearing is held at the Magistrates' Court for the purpose of testing the evidence of the victim/survivor and other witnesses for the Prosecution. The Magistrate then decides if there is sufficient evidence to order that the accused be committed for trial in the higher court.

complainant/prosecutrix: An alleged victim who has made a complaint and statement to the police regarding a crime committed against them.

corroboration warning: The corroboration warning is based on a legal precedent first put into legal discourse by Lord Matthew Hale in the seventeenth century. Since 1989 the corroboration warning in Australia has been referred to predominantly as the Longman Ruling or Longman Direction, and was based on a case precedent involving intrafamilial sexual abuse in which the accused was the father of the victim/survivor. This warning or direction is given to juries in trials involving allegations of rape and sexual assault. The modern corroboration warning is premised upon the opinion that complaints made a great time after disputed events ought to be carefully scrutinized. The reasoning is that faulty memories and temporal delays may prejudice the accused's ability to demonstrate their innocence. For that reason courts should look for independent confirmation of the truthfulness of the complaint. The ruling cautions a jury about convicting on the evidence of the complainant alone, although a jury can convict on the complainant's evidence alone if they have carefully scrutinized the evidence. A judge may instruct a jury to carefully "scrutinize" the evidence of the complainant, and that they may convict on a charge only after applying such scrutiny. A judge may also invoke a stronger warning by telling a jury that it is "unsafe" and/or "dangerous" for them to convict on the evidence alone of the complainant, and that they must scrutinize the evidence of the complainant with extreme care and look for corroborating evidence. The stronger warning appears to have been given in the majority of trials in this research.

counsel: A barrister who appears in court on behalf of the defendant or on behalf of the Crown, the prosecution. Counsel for the defendant is most often referred to as the defense barrister, or defense counsel, and the barrister appearing for the Crown is most often referred to as the Prosecutor, Crown Prosecutor, or Prosecution barrister/counsel. In this research, the term defense counsel, barrister, and lawyer are used interchangeably.

count: An individual offense that has been charged (known as a "count" in the higher courts, and a "charge" in the Magistrates' Court).

County Court: One of the higher courts in Victoria, where serious offenses such as intrafamilial sexual abuse and other sex crimes are adjudicated.

cross-examination: After giving evidence-in-chief, the victim/survivor is cross-examined by the defense barrister. During the trial, the defense has the right to cross-examine all prosecution witnesses after they have given evidence for the prosecution. Likewise, the prosecution has the right to cross-examine any witness for the defense.

Crown: The Crown represents Parliament and the community. For the purposes of bringing a criminal prosecution against an accused person, the Office of Public Prosecutions (OPP) functions as the "Crown."

DPP (Director of Public Prosecutions): Also alternatively referred to as OPP: Office of Public Prosecutions.

editing of the record-of-interview: At the trial in the higher courts, the record-of-interview of the accused is edited prior to submission to the jury. This is done to remove any material the defense argues is prejudicial toward their client, or is deemed irrelevant by the defense and the trial judge.

evidence-in-chief: Evidence led by the Crown Prosecutor from the victim/survivor relating to the counts on the presentment.

judge's charge: Address given by the trial judge to the jury at the end of the prosecution and defense cases to explain the law and sum up the evidence prior to the jury entering deliberations. The "judge's charge" is also referred to as the "judge's direction."

Glossary 303

nolle prosequi: To discontinue a prosecution after the accused has been committed to stand trial. Such a direction is formally ratified by the Director of Public Prosecutions.

precedents: Some legal decisions that are upheld by higher courts, such as the Appeal Court and the High Court become what are referred to as legal precedents, and are often used by legal counsel to support their legal arguments and submissions before the presiding judge in a trial and before appeal court judges.

presentment: A document containing the offense(s) on which the accused has been committed to stand trial, or plead guilty, at the higher court.

prior inconsistent statement: In cross-examination of the victim/survivor or another witness for either the prosecution or the defense, legal counsel may refer to part of the original statement (or previous evidence given by the witness at the committal hearing or at a previous trial in the higher court) relating to the alleged abuse. Prior inconsistent statements are used to highlight contradictions in the evidence of the witness at separate hearings. Prior inconsistent statements are used predominantly against victim/survivors and their evidentiary contradictions are presented to the jury.

propensity evidence: Propensity evidence is very similar to relationship evidence and similar fact evidence. Prior to 1998 such evidence was allowed at the discretion of the trial judge. Propensity evidence is inadmissible at common law but now admissible by statute (R v Tektonapoulis, 1998, Aust. Crim. Rep.) to prove either relevant relationship evidence, or similar fact evidence, provided that it has sufficiently high probative value to be just to the accused to admit it.

record-of-interview: The audio-recorded statement of the accused taken by the police. The police are obliged to put the allegations to the accused, and ask him or her to respond to them. The accused does not have to answer any questions, and has the right to remain silent or to make "no comment" to the questions put to him or her by the interviewing police. At trial, the judge directs a jury that they are not entitled to draw any negative inferences concerning the accused's right to silence or "no comment" responses given in the record-of-interview as such is a legal right.

relationship evidence: Evidence of past acts between parties (accused and complainant) which establishes a relevant relationship for the purpose of explaining an apparent consent to activities, such as sexual activities, or to explain a failure by the complainant to complain about such activities. Relationship evidence allows the prosecution to provide some context to the evidence of the complainant, in that it allows the complainant to give evidence about such things as threats made to them by the accused. Similar fact evidence, like evidence of uncharged acts, was case law precedent until 1997 when the Crimes Amendment Act legislated relationship evidence as admissible in sex abuse trials. There are statutory bounds governing the application of similar fact evidence.

s.37a: Section 37A of the Victorian *Evidence Act 1958*. This section of legislation covers special rules of evidence in certain cases relating to rape, and includes rules of evidence surrounding the introduction of cross-examination of the complainant in order to canvas that complainant's prior sexual history.

sentencing plea: A hearing held after the conviction of the accused before the presiding trial judge. At this hearing, the defense argues for leniency in sentencing and presents mitigating factors. The prosecution answers such defense arguments.

similar fact evidence: Evidence of conduct on prior occasions led as possessing high probative value in demonstrating system or method, proof of identity, or negating allegations of accident or coincidence. Similar fact evidence refers to evidence indicating that on some other occasions the accused has acted in a similar way to that which is being alleged in court with regard to specific charges. This is similar to evidence of uncharged acts. Similar fact evidence comes from case law precedent and is allowed in trials, at a judge's discretion, to enable evidence by a complainant that the accused has acted toward her in a similar way, on occasions other than those detailed on the presentment.

submission: A process through which a dispute or question by either legal counsel is referred for arbitration by the presiding magistrate or judge. On most occasions, these legal arguments take place in the absence of the victim/survivor, and at the higher court in the absence of the victim/survivor and jury.

uncharged acts: At the time of this research, there was no specific legislation allowing evidence of "uncharged acts" to be given by a victim/survivor in evidence. Such evidence was admissible by judiciary discretion and was based on case law precedent. Evidence of uncharged acts is admissible either if they form particulars of a continuing offense, or part of the conduct under inquiry, and are sufficiently related in time and proximity to the disputed acts. "Uncharged Acts" allows for the prosecution to lead evidence from the victim/survivor about an alleged incident of abuse that is not a specific count on the presentment of charges presented by the OPP. Evidence of "uncharged acts" allows a complainant to give evidence of one or more alleged criminal acts of abuse by the accused for the purpose of providing context to their evidence. The evidence may be allowed in order to show an alleged propensity by the accused to behave in the manner alleged by the complainant. There are strict limitations in how a jury can use this evidence, and the trial judge directs the use of this evidence by the jury in his charge to the jury prior to commencing deliberations. The accused cannot be found guilty of an uncharged act, and evidence given by the complainant about an uncharged act cannot be used by the jury to infer guilt by the accused on other charges on the presentment. In 1997, the Victorian Attorney-General introduced legislation to allow evidence of uncharged acts in legal process, thereby removing it from legal precedent to legislation.

victim impact statement: In 1995, the Victorian Attorney-General introduced the use of impact statements as a means for victims of crime to inform the judge as to the impact that the crime and the offender has had on them. It is also permitted for an impact statement to be accompanied by reports from psychologists, counselors and medical practitioners supporting the victim of crime. Victim Impact Statements are not compulsory, and a victim may choose not to submit any statement or, alternatively, may choose to present a statement prepared by a psychologist, counselor, medical practitioner, or other person who may advocate on behalf of the victim.

victim/survivor: Where this term is used in the book, it denotes the victim of intrafamilial sexual abuse.

voir dire: A preliminary examination of a witness, in the absence of the jury, to determine whether the evidence given by him or her is admissible. In effect, *voir dire* functions as a "mini trial." The witness may be questioned by both counsel and judge.

Select Bibliography

Adler, Z. (1987). *Rape on Trial.* London: Routledge and Kegan.
Amir, M. (1971). *Forcible Rape.* Chicago: University of Chicago.
Anderson, B., & Zinsser, J. (1988). *A History of Their Own.* 2 vols. London: Penguin.
Armstrong, L. (1990). "Making an Issue of Incest." In D. Leidholdt & J. Raymond (Eds.), *The Sexual Liberal and the Attack on Feminism.* New York: Pergamon.
———. (1994). *Rocking the Cradle of Sexual Politics.* Reading, Mass.: Addison Wesley.
Ashe, M., & Cahn, C. (1994). "Child Abuse: A Problem for Feminist Theory." In M. Fineman (Ed.), *The Public Nature of Private Violence: The Discovery of Domestic Abuse.* New York: Routledge.
Australian Law Reform Commission and Human Rights and Equal Opportunity Commission, in *Seen and Heard: Priority for Children in the Legal Process,* (1997) Report No. 84.
Beaman-Hall, L. (1996). "Abused Women and Legal Discourse: The Exclusionary Power of Legal Method." *Canadian Journal of Law and Society* 11, 125–39.
Benedict, H. (1992). *Virgin or Vamp: How the Press Covers Sex Crimes.* New York: Oxford University Press.
Blanchfield, M. (1996). "Courtroom Warrior Goes to Battle for Accused." *The Lawyer's Weekly* 15, No. 35, 1–6.
Blaskett, B., & Taylor, S. C. (2002). "The Necessity for Additional Community Education to Counter Child Abuse." In *Proceedings of the Hawaii International Conference on Social Sciences, Honolulu, June 2002.*
Bolt, A. (2002). "Complain for Gain." *Herald-Sun* (Melbourne), 10 October 2002, 19.
Bronitt, S., & McSherry, B. (1997). "The Use and Abuse of Counselling Records in Sexual Assault Trials: Reconstructing the Rape Shield?" *Criminal Law Reform* 8, 259–291.
Brown, J., & Bohn, C. (Eds.). (1989). *Christianity, Patriarchy and Abuse: A Feminist Critique.* Cleveland: Pilgrim.
Celano, M. (1992). "A Developmental Model of Victims' Internal Attributions of Responsibility for Sexual Abuse." *Journal of Interpersonal Violence* 7, No. 1, 57–69.
Cossins, A. (1999). "A Reply to the NSW Royal Commission Inquiry into Paedophilia. Victim Report Studies and Child Sex Offender Profiles: A Bad Match?" *Australian and New Zealand Journal of Criminology* 32, 1, 42–60.
Cossins, A., & Pilkington, R. (1996). "Balancing the Scales: The Case for the Inadmissibility of Counselling Records in Sexual Assault Trials." *University of New South Wales Law Journal* 19, 2, 222–267.

Curtain, D. (1999). "A Child's Rights Can Survive Cross-examination." *The Age* (Melbourne), 8 March 1999, 15.

D'Arcy, M. (1999). *Speaking the Unspeakable*. Melbourne: CASA.

Davies, L. (1996a). "What Grandpa Did: Problems of Delayed Disclosure." *Brief* 23, No. 3, 10–2.

———. (1996b). "Rules of Evidence in Sexual Assault Prosecutions." In Balancing the Scales: Proceedings of the National Conference on Sexual Assault, Perth, June 1996.

———. (1999). "Protecting Paedophiles: Gender Bias in Child Abuse Prosecutions." *Australian Feminist Law Journal* 12, 95–110.

Davies, L., & Taylor, S. C. (1997). "Protecting Paedophiles in the Courtroom." Paper presented at the 15th Annual International Conference of the Australian Law and Society Association, La Trobe University, Melbourne, December 1997.

Delgado, R. (1989). "Storytelling for Oppositionists and Others: A Plea for Narrative." *Michigan Law Review* 87, 2411–41.

Duncan, S. (1994). "Disrupting the Surface Order and Innocence: Toward a Theory of Sexuality and the Law." *Feminist Legal Studies* 2, No. 1, 3–28.

Edwards, S. (1981). *Female Sexuality and the Law*. Oxford: Martin Robertson.

———. (1996). *Sex and Gender in the Legal Process*. London: Blackstone.

Ewick, P., & Silbey, S. (1995). "Subversive Stories and Hegemonic Tales: Toward a Sociology of Narrative." *Law & Society Review* 29, No. 2, 197–226.

Faludi, S. (1992). *Backlash: The Undeclared War against Women*. London: Chatto & Windus.

Feiner, L. (1997). "The Whole Truth: Restoring Reality to Children's Narrative in Long Term Incest Cases." *Journal of Criminal Law and Criminology* 87, No. 4, 1385–428.

Fife-Yeomans, J. (1997). "Legal Ethicist Blames Adversary for Image Problem." *The Australian*, 11 July 1997, 4.

Finkelhor, D. (1986). *A Sourcebook on Child Sexual Abuse*. Thousand Oaks, CA: Sage.

Geis, G. (1978). "Lord Hale, Witches and Rape." *British Journal of Law and Society* 5, 26–44.

———. (1986). "Revisiting Lord Hale: Misogyny, Witchcraft and Rape." *Criminal Law Journal* 10, 319–29.

Gewirtz, P. (1996). "Victims & Voyeurs: Two Narrative Problems at the Criminal Trial." In Brooks, P. & Gewirtz, P. (Eds.) *Law's Stories: Narratives and Rhetoric in Law*. New Haven, CT: Yale University Press.

Gilmartin-Zena, P. (1983). "Attribution Theory and Rape Victim Responsibility." *Deviant Behavior* 4, 357–74.

———. (1988). "Gender Differences in Students' Attitudes toward Rape." *Sociological Focus* 21, No. 4, 279–92.

Goddard, C. (1996). Child Abuse and Child Protection. Marrickville, Australia: Churchill Livingstone

Goffman, E. (1961). *Asylums*. Garden City, NY: Anchor.

———. (1969). *The Presentation of the Self in Everyday Life*. London: Penguin.

Goodman, G., & Helgeson, V. (1988). "Children as Witnesses: What Do They Remember?" In L. Walker (Ed.), *Handbook on Sexual Abuse of Children: Assessment and Treatment Issues*. New York: Springer.

Graycar, R., & Morgan, J. (1990). *The Hidden Gender of Law*. Sydney: Federation Press.

———. (1996). "Telling Tales: Legal Stories About Violence Against Women." *Australian Feminist Law Journal* 7, 79–93.

Green, A. (1986). "True and False Allegations of Sexual Abuse in Child Custody Disputes." *Journal of American Academy of Child Psychiatry* 25, No. 4, 449–58.

Select Bibliography 307

Grix, J. (1999). "Law's Truth and Other Lies: Women, Sexual Assault and the Criminal Justice System." *Australian Feminist Law Journal* 12, 83–93.

Grunseit, F. (1991). "Child Sexual Assault: Are There Alternatives?" In *Conference Proceedings of the Australian Institute of Criminology 1991*, 143–50.

Haller, V. (2000). "The Republic of Rape." *Sunday Herald Sun* (Melbourne), 2 Jan 2000, 46.

Heath, I. (1985). *Incest: A Crime Against Children*. Melbourne: Director of Public Prosecutions.

Heath, M., & Naffine, N. (1994). "Men's Needs and Women's Desires: Feminist Dilemmas About Rape Law Reform." *Australian Feminist Law Journal* 3, 30–52.

Hechler, D. (1988). *The Battle and the Backlash: The Child Sexual Abuse War*. Lexington, MA: Lexington Books.

Heenan, M. (2001). "Trial and Error: Rape, Law Reform and Feminism." Ph.D. thesis, Monash University, Melbourne.

Heenan, M., & McKelvie, H. (1997). *Rape Law Reform Evaluation Project*. Report No. 2. Melbourne: Department of Justice.

Henning, T. (1997). "Consent in Sexual Offenses Cases: The Continuing Construction." *Women Against Violence* 3, 4–14.

———. (2000–2001). "Beyond 'Beyond Reasonable Doubt': Wrong Decisions in Sexual Offenses Trials." *Australian Journal of Law and Society* 15, 1–41.

Herman, J. (1981). *Father Daughter Incest*. Cambridge, Mass: Harvard.

Howe, A. (1997). "Men's Violence in the News: The War Against Women." In S. Cook & J. Bessant (Eds.), *Women's Encounters With Violence: Australian Perspectives*. Thousand Oaks, CA: Sage.

Jackson, J. (1988). "Credibility, Morality and the Corroboration Warning." *Cambridge Law Journal* 47, No. 3, 428–54.

Kaspiew, R. (1995). "Rape Lore: Legal Narrative and Sexual Violence." *Melbourne University Law Review* 20, 350–82.

Kelly, J. (2002). "Jail for Sex Attacks on Girls." *Herald-Sun* (Melbourne), 4 May 2002, 12.

Kelton, G. (2003) "Rape Victims Hide Shame." *The Advertiser* (Adelaide), 26 November, 14.

King, M., & Piper, C. (1995). *How the Law Thinks About Children*. 2nd ed. Aldershot: Arena.

Lafree, G., & Reskin, B. (1985). "Jurors' Responses to Victims' Behaviour and Legal Issues in Sexual Assault Trials." *Social Problems* 32, No. 4, 389–407.

Leidholdt, D., & Raymond, J. (Eds.). (1990). *The Sexual Liberals and the Attack on Feminism*. New York: Pergamon.

MacKinnon, C. (1983). "Feminism, Marxism, Method and the State: Toward Feminist Jurisprudence." *Signs: Journal of Women in Culture and Society* 8, No. 4, 635–58.

———. (1989). *Feminism Unmodified*. Cambridge, MA: Harvard.

———. (1996). "Law's Stories as Reality and Politics." In P. Brooks & P. Gewirtz (Eds.), *Law's Stories: Narrative and Rhetoric in the Law*. New Haven: Yale University Press.

Maisch, H. (1973). *Incest*. London: Andre Deutsch.

Masson, J. (1984). *The Assault on Truth*. London: Penguin.

Mawson, M. (1999). "Whores, Witches and the Lore: Rape and Witchcraft, Legal and Literary Intersections." *Australian Feminist Law Journal* 12, 41–56.

McConaghy, N. (1995). *Sexual Behavior: Problems of Management*. New York: Plenum.

McNicol, S., Shute, R. & Tucker, A. (1999). "Children's Eyewitness Memory for a Repeated Event." *Child Abuse and Neglect* 23, No. 11, 1127–39.

Mertz, D. (1994). "A New Social Constructionism for Sociological Studies." *Law & Society Review* 28, No. 5, 1243–65.

Mitra, C. (1987). "Judicial Discourse in Father-Daughter Incest Appeal Cases." *International Journal of the Sociology of Law* 15, 121–49.

Mossman, M. (1986). "Feminism and Legal Method: The Difference It Makes." *Australian Journal of Law and Society* 3, 30–53.

Naffine, N. (1990). *Law and the Sexes: Explorations in Feminist Jurisprudence.* Sydney: Allen & Unwin.

Neame, A. & Heenan, M. (2003) "What Lies Behind the Hidden Figure of Sexual Assault? Issues of Prevalence and Disclosure." *Briefing* 1, 1–15.

Office of Crime Statistics and Research. (2002). *Crime and Justice in South Australia.*

Olle, L. (1999). "Protecting Confidential Counselling Files of Sexual Assault Complainants from Disclosure in Legal Proceedings." *Women Against Violence* 6, 78–84.

Paciocco, D. (1996). "The Evidence of Children: Testing the Rules Against What We Know." *Queen's Law Journal* 21, 345–93.

Porter, L. (2003). "How the System Abuses the Abused." *Sunday Age* (Melbourne), 15 June 2003.

Puren, N. (1995). "Hymeneal Acts: Interrogating the Hegemony of Rape and Romance." *Australian Feminist Law Journal* 5, 15–27.

———. (1999). "Lawyers' Court Shame." *The Age* (Melbourne), 1 March 1999, 13.

Rand, D. C. (1989). "Munchausen Syndrome by Proxy as a Possible Factor When Abuse Is Falsely Alleged." IPT Journal 1, Retrieved March 16, 2004. (http://www.ipt-forensics.com/journal/volume1/jl_4_4.htm).

———. (1990). "Munchausen Syndrome by Proxy: Integration of Classic and Contemporary Types." ITP Journal 2, Retrieved March 16, 2004. (http://www.ipt-forensics.com/hournal/volume2/j2_2_4.htm).

———. (1993). "Munchausen Syndrome by Proxy: A Complex Type of Emotional Abuse Responsible for Some False Allegations of Child Abuse in Divorce." *ITP Journal* 5, Retrieved March 16, 2004. (http//:www.ipt-forensics.com/journal/volume5/j5_3_1.htm).

Russell, D. (1983). "The Incidence and Prevalence of Intrafamilial and Extrafamilial Sexual Abuse of Female Children." *Child Abuse and Neglect* 7, 133–46.

Salter, A. (1988). *Treating Child Sex Offenders and Victims: A Practical Guide.* Thousand Oaks, CA: Sage.

———. (1995). *Transforming Trauma.* Thousand Oaks, CA: Sage.

Saradjan, J., & Hanks, H. (1996). *Women Who Sexually Abuse Children: From Research to Clinical Practice.* New York: John Wiley.

Scheppele, K. L. (1989). "Foreword: Telling Stories." *Michigan Law Review* 87, 2073–98.

———. (1990). "Facing Facts in Legal Interpretation." *Representations* 30, 42–77.

Schmidt, C. & Brigham, J. (1996). "Jurors' Perceptions of Child Victim-Witnesses in a Simulated Sexual Abuse Trial." *Law and Human Behaviour* 20, No. 6, 581–606.

Schmitz, C. (1988). "'Whack' Sex Assualt Complainant at Preliminary Hearing." *The Lawyer's Weekly* 8, No. 5, 22.

Schultz, L. (Ed.). (1975). *Rape Victimology.* Springfield: Charles Thomas.

Schultz, L. (1975) "The Child as a Sex Victim: Socio-Legal Perspectives." In Schultz, L. (Ed.), *Rape Victimology.* Springfield: Charles Thomas, 1975.

Scutt, J. (1986). "Sexual Assault and the Australian Criminal Justice System." In D. Chappell & P. Wilson (Eds.), *The Australian Criminal Justice System.* Melbourne: Butterworths.

———. (1990a). *Women and the Law.* Sydney: The Law Book Company.

———. (1990b). "Confronting Precedent and Prejudice: Child Sexual Abuse in the Courts." In K. Oates (Ed.), *Understanding and Managing Child Sexual Abuse.* Sydney: Harcourt.

———. (1990c). *Even in the Best of Homes*. 2nd ed. Melbourne: McCulloch.

———. (1991). "Law Reform and Child Sexual Abuse in Australia." In P. Hetherington (Ed.), *Incest and the Community: Australian Perspectives*. Perth: University Western Australia.

———. (1992). "The Incredible Woman: A Recurring Character in Criminal Law." *Women's Studies International Forum* 15, No. 4, 441–60.

———. (1994a). "Judicial Vision: Rape, Prostitution and the 'Chaste' Woman." *Women's Studies International Forum* 17, No. 4, 345–561.

———. (1994b). "Sexism and Psychology: An Analysis of the 'Scientific' Basis of the Corroboration Rule in Rape." In J. Scutt, *The Sexual Gerrymander*. Melbourne: Spinifex.

———. (1997). *The Incredible Woman: Power and Politics*. Vols. 1–2. Melbourne: Artemis.

Seddon, N. (1993). *Domestic Violence in Australia: The Legal Response*. Sydney: Federation.

Showalter, E. (1987). *The Female Malady*. New York: Virago.

Silverii, J. (2003). "The Trials of Sex Assault Victims." *Law Institute Journal* April, 2003, 18–23.

Smart, C. (1989). *Feminism and the Power of Law*. London: Routledge.

———. (1995). *Law, Crime and Sexuality*. London: Sage.

Summit, R. (1982). "Beyond Belief: The Reluctant Discovery of Incest." In M. Kirkpatrick (Ed.), *Women's Sexual Experiences: Explorations of the Dark Continent*. New York: Plenum.

———. (1983). "The Child Sexual Abuse Accommodation Syndrome." *Child Abuse & Neglect* 7, 177–93.

———. (1988). "Hidden Victims, Hidden Pain: Societal Avoidance of Child Sexual Abuse." In G. Wyatt & G. Powell (Eds.), *Lasting Effects of Child Sexual Abuse*. Thousand Oaks, CA: Sage.

Taft, A. (1999). "The Osland 'Family' Doctor: Contemporary Controversies in General Practice and Woman Abuse." *Women Against Violence* 6, 64–9.

Taylor, S. C. (1997). "Betrayal of the Innocents." *Journal of Violence Against Women* 3, 31–7.

———. (2000). "And Now Your Honour, For My Next Trick...Yet Another Defence Tactic to Construct the Mad, Bad and Colluding Mother and Daughter in Intrafamilial Sexual Assault Trials." *Australian Feminist Law Journal* 14, 121–31.

———. (2001a). "The Legal Construction of Victim/Survivors in Parent-Child Intrafamilial Sexual Abuse Trials in the Victorian County Court of Australia in 1995." Ph.D. thesis, University of Ballarat.

———. (2001b). "A Name By Any Other Word Does Not Necessarily Make It Merely Another Rose." In A. Mills & J. Smith (Eds.), *Utter Silence: Voicing the Unspeakable*. New York: Peter Lang.

———. (2002). "We Must Reprove the Wrong." *The Courier* (Ballarat), 2 July 2002, 9.

———. (2003). "The Past Should Not Be Forgotten." *The Courier* (Ballarat), 13 May 2003, 9.

Temkin, J. (1984). "Regulating Sexual History Evidence: The Limits of Discretionary Legislation." *Modern Law Review* 47, 625–50.

———. (1993). "Sexual History Evidence: The Ravishment of Section 2." *Criminal Law Review*, 3–20.

———. (2002). "Digging the Dirt: Disclosures of Records in Sexual Assault Cases." *Cambridge Law Journal* 61, 126–45.

———. (2003). "Sexual History Evidence: Beware the Backlash." *Criminal Law Review*, 217–43.

Thoennes, N. (1998). "Child Sexual Abuse: Whom Should a Judge Believe? What Should a Judge Believe?" *The Judges' Journal* 27, No. 3, 14–8.

Ussher, J. (1991). *Women's Madness: Misogyny or Mental Illness?* London: Harvester Wheatsheaf.

Victorian Law Reform Commission. "Reported Sexual Offenses and Prosecution Outcomes." In *Sexual Offenses Interim Report*, June 2003.

Waldron, G. (1995). "Criminal Justice Responses to Victims of Crime." In *Proceedings of Bringing It Together: A Victim Support Strategy, May 1995*.

Ward, E. (1984). *Father Daughter Rape*. London: The Woman's Press.

Weisberg, R. (1996). "Proclaiming Trials as Narratives: Premises and Pretenses." In Brooks, P. & Gewirtz, P. (Eds.), *Law's Stories: Narratives and Rhetoric in the Law*. New Haven, CT: Yale University Press.

Whitton, E. (1994). *Trial by Voodoo: Why the Law Defeats Justice and Democracy*. Sydney: Random House.

———. (1998). *The Cartel: Lawyers and Their Nine Magic Tricks*. Glebe, NSW: Herwick.

Wightman, M. (1995). "In Limbo: Young Women, Sexual Assault and the Rest." In *Proceedings of the National Conference on Sexual Assault and the Law, Melbourne, November 1995*.

Wigmore, J. H. (1970). *Evidence in Trials at Common Law*, 3A, reprint. Boston: Little Brown.

Young, A. (1992). "Child Sexual Abuse and the Law of Evidence: Some Current Canadian Issues." *Canadian Journal of Family Law* 11, 17.

———. (1998). "Insinuation and Implication: Some Defense Cross-examination Strategies." In *Who's On Trial?* Melbourne: CASA.

Young, M. (1995). "Guilty Verdicts of Juries in Childhood Sexual Assault Cases: Unsafe or Unsatisfactory?" In *Proceedings of the National Conference on Sexual Assault and the Law, Melbourne, November 1995*.

Index

accomplice warning, 217–8
adversarial system, 8, 10, 19, 23, 24, 26, 70, 268–9, 280, 293
appeal process, 76–7, 175, 216, 258, 271, 275,
Armstrong, Louise, 269
collusion, 38, 63, 69–70, 79, 87, 93, 103, 113, 118, 126, 137, 146, 167, 168, 189, 194–5, 199, 211, 216, 218, 253, 259, 261–5, 268–9, 284
constructing mothers, 268–70
Contemporary Munchausen's Syndrome by Proxy (CMSP). *See* Munchausen's Syndrome
corroboration warning, 26, 30, 31, 32, 210, 217, 248, 258, 285
deconstructing evidence, 257
delayed disclosure, 64–5, 67, 96, 99, 105, 278
and threats, 137–8, 152–3
Delgado, Richard, 21
Edwards, Susan, 7, 31, 271, 293
evidentiary boundaries, 2, 20, 37, 44, 48, 50, 92, 111, 124–5, 127, 128, 139, 196, 254, 280
evidentiary rulings, 44, 45–52, 85–104, 139, 175–181
fabrication, 23, 64, 67, 102, 105, 113, 114, 119, 126, 150, 163, 181, 201, 211, 249, 255, 266, 278, 281
family dysfunction theory, 29, 33, 217, 219, 259, 273, 278
Feiner, Leslie, 29, 30, 236, 257, 278, 293

forced errors, 225, 227, 236, 237, 239, 244, 248–9
forensic evidence, 50–2, 70–1, 122, 124, 163–4
Freud, Sigmund, 4, 5, 9, 130, 202, 248
Freudian, 4, 15, 41, 259, 273
Goffman, Irving, 284
Graycar, Regina, 26
greed, 38, 82, 194, 216, 222, 253, 259, 262, 263
Heenan, Melanie, 31
Herman, Judith, 278
incest, 4, 5, 9, 13, 14, 29, 32, 33, 35, 44, 54, 58, 77, 93, 100, 126, 129, 177, 183, 185, 212, 216, 217, 218, 259, 260, 270, 271, 272, 274, 277–8, 279, 288, 290, 297
and language, 218, 184–5, 187, 189, 201, 277
ingroups, 21
intrafamilial rape, 1, 2, 6, 7, 9, 10, 12, 29, 33, 36, 39, 129, 213, 265, 277, 278, 283, 284, 298
judicial discretion, 19, 31, 39, 86, 127, 176, 236, 254, 291
judicial resistance, 15, 50, 91, 258, 291
jurors' assessment of body language and demeanor, 34–6, 209
legal construction, 4, 8, 11, 21, 36, 37, 270, 278, 284
legal discourse, 2, 3, 4, 10, 13, 15, 18, 21, 22, 26, 27, 28, 29, 33, 37, 40, 42, 50, 129, 211, 218, 258, 269, 273, 290

legal narrative, 3, 6, 7, 8, 13, 19, 20, 21, 22, 23, 25, 26, 27, 28, 29, 32, 36, 37, 38, 39, 88, 94, 113, 122, 128, 217, 236, 253, 259, 260, 262, 265, 277, 278, 280, 282, 289, 290, 294
legal reform, 2, 5, 13, 15, 19
legal storytelling, 6, 8, 18, 19, 21, 26, 28, 34, 36, 37, 227, 283
legal template, 20
legally sanctioned lying, 39, 289
MacKinnon, Catharine, 8, 21, 27, 28, 293
marital discord, 37, 79, 158, 160, 256, 261, 269
master narrative, 20, 128, 267
master narrator, 20, 279, 280
mental instability, 38, 82, 86, 90, 113, 117, 125, 127, 130, 253, 264, 265, 286
minute details, 64, 66, 101, 104, 105, 106, 110, 123, 148–50, 151, 229, 236–247
mitigating factors
  and minimal harm to victims, 76, 213, 214, 260, 272
  for offenders, 76, 78, 213, 273, 275
Mitra, Charlotte, 29, 33, 76, 271, 272, 273, 293
mother-blame, 5, 218, 273
motive, 37, 103, 119, 146, 157, 161, 165, 168, 194, 196, 211, 216, 222, 253, 260, 261, 262, 263, 264, 265, 286
  and means, 6, 36, 37, 38, 39, 40, 79, 113, 198, 253, 260, 278
Munchausen's Syndrome
  Contemporary Munchausen's Syndrome by Proxy (CMSP), 88–94
  Munchausen's Syndrome by Proxy (MSP), 88–94
Naffine, Ngaire, 3, 17
outgroups, 21

precedents, 31, 40, 43, 258, 286, 289
prior inconsistent statements, 13, 33, 66, 168, 181, 225, 226, 227, 228, 229, 231, 232, 233, 234, 237, 238, 242, 244, 248, 249, 278, 281
psychiatry, 4, 5, 258
psychoanalysis, 4, 9, 41, 259
record-of-interview, 47, 75, 203
revenge, 28, 38, 63, 69, 70, 82, 88, 103, 114, 126, 127, 137, 146, 157, 160, 161, 164, 165, 167, 168, 211, 253, 259, 261, 262, 264, 265, 284, 286
Scheppele, Kim Lane, 8, 21, 27, 28, 293
Scutt, Jocelynne, 4, 27, 30, 198, 258, 271
sentencing, 32, 76, 77, 78, 213, 215, 217, 262, 271, 272, 273, 275, 283, 298
sexual abuse
  and offender use of non-verbal clues, 157, 276
sexual history evidence, 86, 87, 88, 90–3, 103–4, 114, 125, 127, 128–9, 179, 205, 255, 256
Smart, Carol, 7, 293
social death, 284
specious accuracy, 64, 225, 231, 242, 278, 281, 282
stock-story narratives, 30, 34, 55, 70, 79, 179, 211, 257, 265, 280, 282
Summit, Roland, 55, 191
Temkin, Jennifer, 130, 256
trial as theatre, 19
United Nations Rights of the Child, 295
victim blame, 260, 273
Victim Impact Statements, 212, 298
Whitton, Evan, 17, 19, 23, 24, 186, 254, 292, 293
Wigmore, John Henry, 248
Young, Alison, 248